Language in Social Worl

CW00595229

Language in Social Worlds

W. Peter Robinson

Blackwell
Publishing

© 2003 by W. Peter Robinson

First published 2003 by Blackwell Publishers Ltd, a Blackwell Publishing company

Editorial Offices:
108 Cowley Road, Oxford OX4 1JF, UK
  Tel: + 44 (0)1865 791100
350 Main Street, Malden, MA 02148–5018, USA
  Tel: + 1 781 388 8250

The right of W. Peter Robinson to be identified as the Author of this Work has been asserted in accordance with the UK Copyright, Designs and Patents Act 1988.

All rights reserved. No part of this publication may be reproduced, stored in a retrieval system, or transmitted, in any form or by any means, electronic, mechanical, photocopying, recording or otherwise, except as permitted by the UK Copyright, Designs and Patents Act 1988, without the prior permission of the publisher.

Library of Congress Cataloging-in-Publication Data has been applied for.

Robinson, W. P. (William Peter)
    Language in social worlds / W. Peter Robinson.
        p. cm.
Includes bibliographical references and index.
    ISBN 0–631–19335–9 — ISBN 0–631–19336–7 (pbk.)
  1. Language and languages. 2. Communication. 3. Sociolinguistics.
4. Human behavior. I. Title.
  P107 .R63 2003
  400—dc21

                                                                2002023052

A catalogue record for this title is available from the British Library.

Set in 10.5 on 12.5 Meridien
by Ace Filmsetting Ltd., Frome, Somerset
Printed and bound in Great Britain by TJ International, Padstow, Cornwall

For further information on
Blackwell Publishers, visit our website:
www.blackwellpublishers.co.uk

Contents

Figures

Tables

Preface

If an aspiring author is foolhardy enough to attempt to write about language in communication from a social psychological perspective, problems peculiar to that choice of topic have to be faced. The text itself will include references to what is involved in the achievement of effective communication. Questions will be raised about the extent to which speakers and writers take into account the current understanding of listeners and readers. Successful verbal communication might at some point be defined as:

> Not to let a word get in the way of a sentence,
> Not to let a sentence get in the way of its intention,
> But to send your mind out to meet the intention – as you would a guest –
> that is understanding. (Mencius)

Is the author sensitive to such issues in writing about language in communication? Is due heed paid to the implicit prescription? Are the messages conveyed and received accurately? To fail to communicate is like writing badly about how to write well. It is threateningly embarrassing, and any measure of failure comes too late for correction. A precautionary face-saving device is to point to the difference between knowing that something is so and knowing how to do it, but the awareness of the logical validity of this distinction does not necessarily serve to quieten the soul. What are the current states of knowledge and belief about language in communication held by students of any age majoring in psychology in Montana, Sao Paulo, Lagos and Singapore, assuming that their concerns have sufficient in common to render the question sensible and that they are fortunate enough to be reading this volume?

One can guess and trust that they will have acquainted themselves with the contents of one of the encyclopaedic American-style introductory psychology texts. Unfortunately this is unlikely to have mentioned the social psychology of language!

All readers will have much experience of language in use, but it will not be assumed that they have made a formal study of it at tertiary level. Hence the first three chapters are intended to serve as an introduction to the constituents of language, how they fit together, and how their articulation comes to render it a vehicle for communication.

What general knowledge and beliefs can be presupposed as common to all readers? What Mencius did not mention in the opening quotation was that successful communication depends on using what is shared as a basis for introducing the new. This is now very difficult. There is no global culture. There are no shared myths and legends. There is no shared literature. Historical examples are doubly dangerous in that they may be either unfamiliar or slanted misleadingly. Just as the new can be developed from what is shared, the abstract can sometimes be best exemplified through apt illustrations, but these too lack global familiarity. Where examples are used in the text, attempts have been made to render them comprehensible even if unfamiliar.

More generally, is one writing for skeptics or enthusiasts, optimists or pessimists? Are specific items to be learned for recall in grade-related multiple-choice tests or is there a concern to find out answers to questions about language and its functioning in communication? I shall assume that serious students have something in common; they are trying to find out which beliefs about topics are the most plausible constructions currently available. They will be neither too skeptical nor too enthusiastic; they will not persist intemperately with demands for evidence on matters psychological too greatly in excess of the demands they make for accepting the reasonableness of other beliefs they hold, but neither will they be too easily seduced by exciting ideas or persuasive gurus. They will exhibit patient respect for what authorities can give good reasons for believing, but will wish to probe the validity of such ideas against their own experience. Their eyes will be open and their ears will be alert outside the laboratory as well as within it. They will know how to evaluate the quality of evidence. They will not make a fetish of one technique or method to the general disparagement of others, but will see that methods are to be judged in relation to the kind of question being posed. They can accept and see that some explanations are better than others and why. Problem-centred and truth-seeking, they realise that while simplicity is to be preferred to complexity, reality is often complex and not immediately amenable to unmodified generalizations. Conceptual analysis is often a necessary preliminary exercise to be undertaken before academic or pragmatic progress can be made. On the other hand, while precision of definition is important, the discreteness and qualities of defined categories should not be pursued in excess of reality.

Most important of all perhaps, they will suspend judgment about the author and not categorise him as an "-ist" of any particular type. It seems to be a strange characteristic of social scientists that they have a propensity to classify each other with labels rather than ask what are the most sensible ways of investigating sensible questions. To save readers from coming to a false categorization, let me say that this particular volume is at risk of classification as being too eclectic. Some enthusiasts for "natural" data will find the citation of experimental findings anathema. From another perspective, hardline experimentalists may see some of the claims made as resting on uncritical interpretation of weak data, as too subjective and wishy-washy.

Ironically, social psychologists are the group of academics particularly concerned with the operation of *labels* and *stereotypes*, and the dangers of distortion and over-simplification that these can bring about. Forewarned, such readers will be careful to exercise restraint, focus on the best ways of conceptualizing relationships between what is written and what the writing is about, and reduce the significance of the personal and social identity of the authors to its proper irrelevance.

With such students in mind it becomes much easier to write. Such virtues of intellect are likely to be correlated with compassion and humor, so that their possessors will readily forgive mistakes and misjudgments! They will see irony as good-willed, humor as kindly, pomposity as simulated, and possible arrogance as modesty.

The structure of the text is orthodox, but the treatment does have peculiarities. First, the field is too large now for comprehensive coverage. The substantive topics selected are intended to exemplify the range and the different approaches available. There is an emphasis on the importance of being clear about conceptual foundations. Historically, too many social psychologists have been cavalier in their use of terms and prone to rush into the use of quickly administered and cheap measuring instruments, using readily available participants in premature experiments. The field has been too heavily driven by the cultural imperatives imposed on academics, and too little by the scientific issues. Hence, the emphasis here on the variety and eventual complementarity of approaches, methods, and techniques. It is not an oversight that the last chapter focuses on methodology. Neither is it an accident that some investigations are described and evaluated in considerable detail, whilst for others their results and interpretations are reported briefly. The variety of ways of finding out answers to questions has to be considered for all questions posed, and it is hoped that the detailed descriptions may help in this regard.

A final feature that may be seen as a personal bias is one that I see as a fundamental heuristic in any scientific endeavor. For any issue, data on the one hand and descriptions and explanations on the other, should be in dynamic dialectical relations with each other, with neither rushing too far ahead of the other. In a new field, this normally means starting out with natural observation and case studies, until it becomes feasible to describe the phenomena well enough to shift into systematic large-scale studies that may include surveys and experiments guided by hypotheses. Insofar as these are successful, it will be the "error variance" participants who are most interesting for further investigation. Why do they not act in accordance with the explanations being subjected to testing? The reasons may be trite, but they may also be important. These cyclical operations have stood other disciplines in good stead over the years, and it will be to the advantage of social psychology of language when we design studies fit for current purposes rather than because we have been socialized into a particular ideology.

Acknowledgments

The University of Bristol and its Department of Experimental Psychology have generously provided me with the material resources to bring this book to completion. I am pleased to thank Elizabeth Robinson and Brian Richards for their clear and straightforward comments on parts of the manuscript. I have not molested the ever active Howard Giles for his zippy insights on this occasion, but I am delighted to note our collaboration over the last thirty years in the promotion of the study of language and social psychology. Our hopes for the development of a Research Center for Language and Communication did not materialize, but it has been very satisfying organizing conferences and handbooks with Howard. If Britain itself has been slow to recognize that the social psychological perspective is central to the study of language in communication, at least some of her ex-colonies have taken up the challenge, with Howard as a lead pioneer.

CHAPTER 1

The Contextual Framework for a Social Psychology of Language in Communication: Aims and Issues

1.1 Introduction

Asleep we escape the pleasures and pains of interacting with other people. Waking, we face another day, and this brings with it the necessity of coordinating our behavior with that of other people. Unless we are hermits or members of societies where maximal silence is held to be a virtue, this coordination will require that we communicate with other human beings. Language may well invade our activities before breakfast, and we may not be able to guarantee safety from speech again until the last goodnight has been said. We can telephone around the globe from almost anywhere to almost anywhere. If we are to participate in our societies we need to be able to read and write. We can fax and e-mail, again on an international scale, if we so choose. And in the next few years we can look forward to visual as well as auditory internet connections, supplemented with conversions between speech and writing and simultaneous translations into a variety of languages. We converse. We know roughly how to interpret what others say, write, and do, more or less. We know how to speak and act, and they manage likewise. But what do we know? And how do we manage?

To answer these questions, persons with scientific pretensions will want to analyze what goes on in communication. They will find out what is already believed or known. They will observe what happens. They will try to construct descriptions and explanations of plausible kinds. They will take everyday activities apart, separating out the bits and pieces and exploring the relationships between them. They will look for regularities and patterns, all the time trying to make sense of what they observe and endeavoring to express this sense symbolically in terms that others can understand. They will try to classify. It is a hazardous business.

⌐ 1.2   The Nature of Verbal Communication

It is good to be able to record that studies of non-verbal communication in human beings and other creatures have flourished impressively over the last half century without the emergence of fundamental methodological and philosophical conflicts (Cappella & Palmer, 1990; Patterson, 2001; chapters 4 and 5). In contrast, the study of verbal communication has been and is suffering from pronounced disagreements, some of which can be viewed as unproductive and destructive. Others are simply irritating issues that are commonly present in young fields where key concepts still lack accepted definitions. Since much of the rest of the book reviews the substantial progress made in the theoretical and empirical study of topics at the intersect of language and social psychology, it is perhaps most useful to focus early on some of the issues of conflict in the frames of reference within which the study of language and social psychology is taking place, and to seek reconciliation among those in which the oppositions posed are unnecessary, false, or are in fact productive tensions within language and its usage. This will mean attending to some of the most elementary and fundamental issues, such as the very conceptualization of verbal communication, the nature and use of language, and the methodological issues associated with questions about the kinds of evidence which are to count as a basis for holding well-founded beliefs and within which kind of epistemological framework these are to be generated and evaluated (see chapters 11 and 15).

Successful communication between human beings incorporates encoding, production, transmission, reception and decoding within already shared frames of reference; for example, what is novel can be assimilated or accommodated to only when it becomes linked to what is already shared contextually. This apparently innocuous claim can of course be shown to cover many contestable issues. It is inherent in the nature of communication with speech or writing that its delivery and reception is sequential; it is impossible to say at once all that is intended. Hence, as already mentioned, it will be important for readers to avoid premature categorization of the writer of this text with any particular stereotype. To proceed, we shall need to analyze the components of communication and the relationships between them, and at this point I am caught on the horns of a dilemma. The strongest binary contrast in approaches to human communication is between starting with such technical problems as transmitting signals along a telegraph wire and gaining a purchase on the semiotic systems of whole cultures. Let me hasten to say that both of these will be addressed. However, I have found that while introductory semiotics is more commonly perceived as being full of exciting questions and insights, the advantages of these surprises are prone to dissipate as students become overwhelmed by the divergent possibilities of interesting questions. Once switched into the game, observant eyes, ears, noses, tongues or skins connected to active brains can proliferate an infinity of pertinent but uncoordinated questions. It becomes feasible and scientifically defensible to write a research monograph on the meanings and significance of the discernible details and their relationships of just one page of a newspaper, one TV news broadcast, one choir singing, five minutes of a psychiatric interview, a handshake, an almost anything. Generating questions to pose is easy; answering many of them and evaluating the value of the answers can be the work of more than a lifetime. How do we select what is worth doing from the array? How do we save our brains from being overwhelmed by what we find out? And how do we prevent our ideas from soaring into wild interpretations and implausible world-views?

The first question is unanswerable. One answer to the second is to start with the smaller and simpler. One answer to the third is to demand at least some empirical evidence to support claims made. Of course, we then have to agree on what will constitute adequate evidence, and we need to require that empirical evidence and descriptive/interpretive accounts of phenomena act as reciprocating constraints on each other. Data need to be evidence relevant to some issue. Ideas need to be anchored in plausible constructions of experience.

By such a route I am retreating to a justification for introducing communication as coded signals travelling as impulses along wires or through the atmosphere, before facing up to the cornucopia of semiotics. The initial model to be presented is skeletal and incomplete, emphasizing as it does a single message travelling in one direction only and focusing on the message rather than its origin and fate. This model can be and was expanded in due course to cope with multiple sequential exchanges occurring between real people through real time in real contexts.

Meanwhile, to begin at a beginning. Shannon and Weaver (1949) developed a model of information transmission that has become known as the *Conduit Theory of Communication*. It was not and is not a theory. It simply lists some of the components to be considered in any single communicative act. Referring to it as a conduit was intended to give the idea of a wire down which signals travel, relaying a message that emerges at the other end. Shannon and Weaver were primarily concerned with telecommunication and radio problems and the reduction in loss of information between source and destination. The model also presupposes that the en-

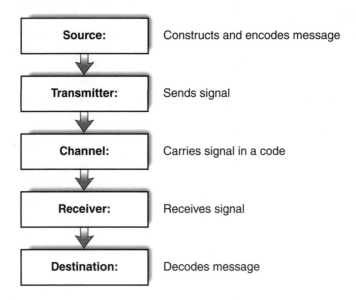

Figure 1.1   Shannon and Weaver's Model for Communication.

coder is intending to reduce uncertainty with the transmission, and knows how to reduce uncertainty, neither of which is necessarily the case in human communication. Here, the object is to introduce the basic model rather than report and evaluate its measures of success and its limitations across the whole range of its applications. One of the key concepts, *noise,* will not figure in this account, which is confined to the other five: *source, transmitter, channel, receiver,* and *destination,* along with the concepts of *signal, messages, medium* and *code.*

There is nothing contentious in selecting the nine features as components to be considered. If we wish, we can pursue any one of them into levels of greater complexity or specificity. We can apply the model from problems of the warning colors of wasps (black and yellow) through to human beings using private *ciphers* to mean the opposite of what they say. Before we ask more detailed questions about the code itself, we can ask the dangerously idealistic question about the true (real) meaning of any message. This has proved to be one of the great stumbling block to progress, and is one example of a false presupposition leading to a false opposition about the nature of both language and communication. Each candidate advanced as having the right to define the "real meaning" of a message can be shown to be unsatisfactory. If we claim that the *speaker's intentions* have the strongest claim, we may observe that the message itself may not be a culturally correct realization of the intentions, either in construction or delivery – or both. Wrong units (for example words) may be selected, either out of ignorance or anxiety. What is intended as a compliment may be delivered insultingly. How can we be sure of what the speaker's intentions were? We cannot be.

If we exclude intention, and suggest that the meanings of messages can be defined objectively, then it should be the case that there will be a cultural consensus as to the "real meanings" among proficient users of the language. Disagreements should not arise. If they do, one line of argument would be to invoke the defensible hypothesis of sub-cultural differences in meanings of the same patterns. But fruitful as such a defence can be initially, it will ultimately fail. The "real meaning" can only be in the text if the contextual presuppositions are shared fully. This entails of course that the meaning is *not* in the text, but in a cultural consensus. Involving abstractions such as the *generalized other* or the *typical member of the culture* will not salvage the situation, because their perceptions are necessarily not objective. The third possibility of defining the "real meaning" as the *interpretation of the reader* or hearer, shares comparable weaknesses to the other two possibilities. Interpreters have no special status as objective judges.

The rejection of all three of these possibilities might then be used to advance the idea that the true meanings are not the privilege of any one party, but are simply a matter of *negotiation* among the participants. If that is so, there is no true meaning. However this position of meaning as being negotiated has also been pushed to a *reductio ad absurdum* argument that the transmission model of communication should be abandoned in favor of fuzzy flexible perspectives, that will permit creative constructions by individuals who will be freed from the constraints heretofore imposed upon them. It could be argued that this position is self-destructive as well as self-contradictory. Since generally the use of shared conventions is the essence of the systems, particular changes have to be negotiated and cannot be asserted and demanded by individuals; otherwise Humpty Dumpty ends up talking to himself alone, or worse.

Since human beings seem to manage to communicate with language more or less successfully much of the time, perhaps those asking about true meanings have posed inappropriate questions. *Information Theory* was intended to provide ways of analyzing reductions (and increases) in uncertainty in transmission and not its elimination in its generation. Communication can reduce uncertainty, but it cannot eliminate it. Such a position copes with what may be defended as the most rational construction of reality without giving rise to a claim that there is an objective reality that could be discovered. In cases where some party claims that communication failure has occurred and where for some reason it is decided to allocate blame for the failure, there will be examples where it would be pragmatically silly not to blame one or other of the participants, but peculiar defences may well be made. In 1998 the President of the USA invoked a legal rather than a commonsense definition of "sexual relations" to justify the claim that he had not lied under oath: no communication failure and no lie. Later he changed his mind.

However, the focus on the transmission/reception components did lead to a relative neglect of the activities of the people, the encoder and decoder. The terms of *source, transmitter, receiver* and *destination* are still being attacked as implying passivity, an absence of agency, and a neglect of constructive/interpretive activities, even though it was as early as 1956 that Gerbner elaborated on and humanized these components. This should have precluded further adverse criticism of the model for being mechanical and passive.

In Gerbner's model, a human source actively selects and interprets from the external (or internal) environment what is to be encoded into a message, and the receiver is similarly an active interpreter of messages. Source and receiver can be interactive, and clearly are if conversing, and hence meanings and significance can both be negotiated. With his own special interest in media, Gerbner himself was more concerned with what the controllers of media select for transmission and what is made available to an audience, but his flow-chart could represent a conversation equally well.

1.3 Semiotics

The conduit model is not alone in having been misrepresented by subsequent critics for failing to achieve what it was not intended to achieve; it was indeed limited by its point of departure, but not as much as some antagonists pretend. Semiotics is the science of signs in all their realizations and given this scope, it is not surprising that semiotic approaches too have been a victim of the orientations of their progenitors. Semiotics has been further handicapped by its multi-discipline origins and continuing variety of practitioners. Peirce, the philosopher (1931–1935/1955) introduced an analysis of a relational approach between the signifier and signified, as the basis of the signification linkage to "meaning". The resultant triangle linked *sign, interprant,* and *object* to each other. Part philosophical, part literary critical, Ogden and Richards (1923) introduced a somewhat different triangle in which *reference* as thought was linked to a *referent* on the one hand and a *symbol* on the other, so that the symbol can *stand for* the reference. Both of these similar approaches were attempts to escape from the tangles and muddles that had engulfed philosophers such as Mill, Frege, Wittgenstein, and others who had difficulties in distinguishing between sense and reference (Mill, 1873), denotation and connotation (Frege, 1980), semantic and associative meaning, and the relationships between symbolic propositions and what they appear to be about (Wittgenstein, 1951; 1922/1961). The last continues to figure as a central concern (for example Davidson, 1984; 1986; Putnam, 1988; Rorty, 1991).

Independently, the linguist de Saussure (1925/59) had been developing his ideas on the distinctions between *langage, langue,* and *parole* (terms are defined in section 1.4), which also remain of crucial importance, but continue to be neglected by some monolingual English-speaking social scientists. Semioticians cite his observation that *signs* (symbols) gain their *significance* by virtue of contrasts with other signs in the *system*. In a sequence of signs, questions of both the sequence selected (*syntagmatic*) and the choices at each point in the sequence (*paradigmatic*) are important for meaning. (In non-linguistic systems more general questions of juxtaposition than sequence can arise, and in linguistic systems patterns of *collocation* [co-occurrence] are also important.)

From these three origins in particular, various systems for classifying signs have been developed, with comments being offered about the ways in which they function in a cultural context. Typically the materials used are referred to as *texts*, a term which can be extended to any cultural artefact(s). If, for example, a page of a newspaper is chosen, then a general question would ask which conventions of the culture are being used to convey what kinds of ideas. Questions can range from the size, shape and quality of the page, through the types of arrangement of language texts, photographs, and other graphics, to which items have been selected for reporting and how these have been framed. The Glasgow Media Group (1976) provide classic examples of such ideas in their analyzes of news broadcasts. It is not surprising that those who control the media should encourage particular perspectives through what they present and the way they present issues. It is the task of semioticians to find out how particular *readings* (interpretations) are encouraged by the devices available, and it could be their task to find out which readings are in fact adopted by which readers. This is certainly an activity for social psychologists to engage in. The citing of a verbal/visual example of presuppositions here should not be seen as excluding other domains; the issues are omnipresent in our everyday experience. Analysis of oil paintings through time and across cultures can be subjected to comparable treatment, as can clothes and ornaments worn, literature, or any other type of artefact.

Such activities have been very productive in generating ideas that have helped to raise explicit questions about matters previously treated as unproblematic or natural. They have been used to demonstrate how taken-for-granted "facts" should not be taken for granted. They have raised consciousness in particular about the moral qualities of our cultures and societies, including many of the false beliefs underpinning matters of procedural and distributive justice.

Unfortunately, the field has also generated its own difficulties. Where is the true meaning in an artefact or text? It is probably fair to say that opinions have been polarized between locating the true meaning as either in the text or in the *reader*, with the speaker or writer often conflated with the text. Either position can be criticized along identical lines to those used against the Conduit Model. We can never be sure what the intentions of the creator were. We can never be sure that the creator's product instantiates the intention. Which readers are to be credited with the right to decide which reading is correct? If a particular reading is "preferred" by experts, this does not transcend its subjectivity.

If the advocates of the expert approaches were to be criticized for just one characteristic, it would have to be for their predispositions to assume that their ingenious personal explanations of the richness of texts bear any correspondence either to the intentions of the creators or more importantly perhaps, to the interpretations of or influences upon ordinary readers. Such stories are often advanced and disseminated without any checks on their empirical validity; if they are not so evaluated, then they remain as plausible hypotheses awaiting testing. Not all experts make such unsupported claims.

In contrast, if the advocates were to be commended for just one strength, it might be their emphasis on the *multiplicity of meanings* available in texts (discourse or whatever material is being examined). Eco (1979) introduced a distinction between *closed* and *open* texts. A closed text is one where the reader has in theory only one plausible interpretation, the author having structured the meanings to minimize possibilities of other readings. An open text is not one where interpretations are impossible, but one with multiple possibilities, and in the light of the information provided, offer a bundle of options. His illustrations are literary rather than conversational. In narrative stories about crime detection or espionage, for example, the author typically leads the reader along a single track using a variety of literary devices to puzzle, excite, frustrate and otherwise retain the reader's attention on a predestined train of thought. This does not mean that there are no ambiguities or vagueness. It does not mean that the narrative has to follow a linear sequence of real time. The primary focus is on the eventual discovery of who has been deceiving who about what – an exposure of the constructed reality.

This kind of story contrasts with those depicted in the film *Rashomon* or Durrell's *Alexandria Quartet* novels; in each of these, the same events are played out from three different perspectives. As viewers or readers, we can appreciate this multiplicity of personal agendas. The use of repetition renders the multiplicity explicit. More commonly the uncertainties are left for individual characters (and readers) to interpret and act upon.

Insofar as many novels are narratives in which biographies of characters are woven together, they bear clear similarities to real life. Films and plays more so, since they add a visual channel. Soap operas go one step further in that their regular and long-term serialization add a continuity of years or even decades. The audiences they attract on a regular basis can extend to nearly half a country's population. Currently Britain has four indigenous TV soaps: two urban, with predominantly working class/lower middle class characters, one rural, and one suburban upwardly mobile. As Livingstone (1998) argues and demonstrates, these offer open texts whose characters have entered into the lives of their audiences as "real" people facing comparable difficulties and problems. The episodes provide ideas for ways of overcoming or resolving such difficulties, as well as setting up topics for conversation and characters for evaluation.

The study of ways in which these long-standing narratives mesh psychologically into the everyday lives of real people could help to re-anchor social psychology into the world it is expected to describe and explain. For the present, *narrative analysis* (see Sunwolf & Frey, 2001) in its various forms is not mainstream, but just as various forms of Conversational and Discourse Analysis have drawn attention to units and structures larger than that of the main clause and its coordinate and subordinate attachments, so narrative analysis may encourage an elaboration of those social–cognitive and attitudinal approaches which have adopted what is essentially a hypothetico–deductive model to single judgments in abstracted situations.

Whilst it is not strange that social psychologists would seek to generate theoretical models that can explain single judgments or actions in terms of general properties of the person in context, such judgments may be no more than task-specific reflective comments and in fact may bear little relation to the mechanisms that typically drive the scripts of the everyday talk and other actions of most people most of the time. Schank and Abelson (1977) are normally credited with the introduction of *Script Theory*, which was an attempt to describe behavior sequences in semi-ritualized contexts. Scripts for speech and writing, for monologues, dialogues, and polylogues can also be devised and tested for their descriptive generality. Combinations of narrative analysis and script theory have more than begun to have their status as explanatory models of behavior recognized (Abelson & Lalljee, 1988; Antaki, 1988; Cody & McClaughlin, 1990).

How these various approaches to verbal communication will come to be collated remains to be seen. There are clear kernels of importance, relevance, and validity in each. Their diversity in part reflects the frightening breadth of topics embraced by the concept of verbal communication. Some of the possible claims or emphases have already been explored to some limiting *reductio ad absurdu*m. Now their virtues need to be articulated.

1.4 Terms of Reference in the Study of Language in Communication

So far, a number of everyday words have been used in technical senses, and some novel words have also been introduced. At this stage it may be useful to specify how which words will be used in this text. Difficulties arise from several sources. One is that English may not make a binary contrast with two opposing words that cover the range, for example above/ below. While these mark two opposite vertical directions relative to an object, there is no single term for either above nor below, and "not above" means either at the same height or below! Another is that English may not make the distinctions needed, neither in its everyday usage or in its specially developed technical vocabularies. A third is that different academic disciplines, or even different persons within the same discipline, may use the same term with different meanings or different terms with the same meaning.

Even "communication" itself is not without its difficulties. For a display or action to be communicative, does its originator have to *intend* to communicate? Here no such requirements will be made. Those who wish to render intention integral to communication have difficulties referring to animal displays and much human behavior.

French makes useful distinctions with *langage* as the superordinate term embracing both *langue* and *parole*, with langue being used to refer to the language system and parole to its use. English has three phrases for coping with the phenomena of parole: speech and writing, verbal behavior, and language use (or more rarely language behavior). Do each of these three include the vocalic/graphical? My guess is that while almost all linguists would include vocalic/graphical features within linguistics, most social psychologists would treat them as components of non-verbal behavior, probably on the grounds that the meanings are not being carried by the phonemics, lexico–grammar, and semantics of the language system. Fortunately, these are issues of labelling at a super ordinate level only. The area of vocalic features with its three sub-areas is distinctive, and graphology has been a recognized legitimate area of study for years, even if to date the inferences drawn about character and personality on the basis of handwriting have not stood up to systematic empirical testing. Social psychologists have been disposed to link the vocalic with the non-verbal for two main reasons. One is that those interested in non-verbal communication (NVC) have invariably asked about NVC in animals, many of which have vocal but not verbal capacities, and one question typically posed here, and discussed in chapter 4, relates to how much can be communicated without involving language. The other reason is connected with the first in that the functions of the vocalic and the other non-verbals are prone to be treated as comparable to each other and contrastive with those of language.

One danger of separating the vocalic from the verbal, even for analytic purposes, will be apparent through most of this text. Transcriptions of speech are frequently reduced to be similar to this text, i.e. no vocalic indicators are recorded. If the Stanislavsky method school of acting required its students to be able to say "hello" in more than 50 ways, these presumably had over 50 distinguishable sub-purposes beyond the common one of greeting. As is illustrated in chapter 11, "the cat is on the mat" may be semantically equivalent regardless of which word is stressed, but where the stress falls is determined by which of six different questions it is an answer to.

Conversational and discourse analysts (Potter and Wetherell, 1987; Turnbull, 1992) have developed transcription rules that go beyond ordinary prose in certain respects, but these do not include all the variations in pitch, volume, duration, and timbre that an expert in prosodics might require, and they are both comparatively light on paralinguistic and extralinguistic information. In polite English society, no one would ask whether John tells lies, but if the question were posed, then the answer should be the equivalent of "Oh no," with the delay in the reply determining whether this actually meant "Yes."

Even with the selection of terms met so far, the issue of different terms with the same meaning, and the same terms with different meanings remains unresolved. Barthes (1968) uses *denotation* for the object referred to by a word and *connotation* for the individual person's total set of experiential associations of the object. This contrasts with the consensus among philosophers who agree on denotation as reference, but treat connotation as comprising the criterial or prototypical features of the concept as a semantic unit; it provides the comparative and contrastive qualities mentioned by de Saussure. Psychologists are as careful as philosophers in distinguishing between *semantic* (connotative) and *associative* meaning, but 'associative' is used for the same purpose as Barthes uses "connotation." No discipline has developed the minimally differentiating three terms to cope with denotation, connotation in the philosophers' sense, and associative meaning used by psychologists. Here *denotation* will be used for reference. *Connotation* and *semantic sense* will be treated as synonymous, and used to refer to the sets of criterial or prototypical characteristics that define or capture the concept, i.e. their sense. Ideally this specification would include all the similarities to and differences from cognate and hence confusable concepts. If one follows Wittgenstein's proposal that the meaning of a word is its use, then this is its semantic sense, provided that there is a consensus among competent users. "Associative" meaning will be used to refer to the personal experience of the words and their referents.

It is to be regretted that terms central to the whole enterprise remain sources of discord and muddle, and there is no way that suggestions offered here are likely to do more than evoke feelings of further regret that we cannot arrange for an *Academie de Communication* to recommend to all relevant journals and publishers and the invisible college of scholars as to which term is to be used to mean what. We lag way behind biologists, chemists, geologists, and physicists in agreeing terms. Some colleagues are simply carefree and careless in not including definitions of terms in the text or in glossaries and inventing their own usage unnecessarily. It is to be hoped that this section will help to carry the reader through the text.

1.5   Summary and Implications

The chapter has referred to mundane conversational exchanges, the reflective thinkings of scientists, and the wider contexts of the studies of communication. Any culture is embedded geographically and historically, with a selection of its natural and humanly created objects and events being accorded symbolic significance. While social psychologists have been inclined to focus on the two-person face-to-face (FtF) conversational dyad as having some special significance as the prototypical interactive set of processes, we have to acknowledge the relevance of the givens of climates and cathedrals, TVs and mobile phones, rituals and uniforms, museums and theme-parks, flora and fauna. The semioticians are entirely right to draw attention to the plethora of possible and actual extra-linguistic vehicles of meanings influencing our lives. Language may be used to refer to and exploit these, but it is easy to see that they also have non-verbal power. Someone desecrating a war memorial might be lynched without words being spoken. A person wearing an invented uniform may derive authority from it. It is no accident that the price of red roses rises for St. Valentine's Day. A setting sun on a Mediterranean verandah can create an ambience that is difficult to achieve in an Arctic blizzard. We shall meet these considerations again in chapter 2 and Table 2.3, where the point will be stressed that all language use occurs in particular contexts that will be relevant to its likely meanings and significance.

That our routine daily contexts are typically treated as shared givens is liable to cause us to ignore how much they presuppose and lead us into the temptation to dash straight into the structures and processes of the conversations which make up the commonest form of language use by individuals in our kind of society, but we must delay. So what is this language system whose use is so liable to be taken for granted?

CHAPTER 2

Language in and out of Context: Structure and Substance

2.1 Language

According to Morris (1946) language is composed of

1 A plurality of arbitrary signs, which have
2 A common significance to a group of organisms,
3 A significance independent of the immediate situation, and
4 That are produced as well as received by the users;
5 It is a system in which signs are articulated by certain rules of combination.

   In an extended treatment of such a definition we would need to define and defend the choices of *arbitrary, sign, significance, independent of the immediate situation, system, articulated* and *rules of combination*, but as it stands, the recommendation helps to set the scene.

   The signs of a language may be made up of units of sound that can be represented in the International Phonetic Alphabet by symbols like [p], [i] and [n] (see Crystal, 1998). They may be made up of visible marks like *pin*. Many languages have both systems, with variable and varying degrees of isomorphism between them. Very few languages rely on fewer than 25 of either. The phrase "group of organisms" does not exclude non-human beings, but arguments about the competence of other species are probably trivial in the sense that the answers arrived at depend upon the definitions chosen; we can continue to investigate the natural and human-initiated capacities of other creatures (and machines) without prejudice as to whether we label the systems they come to master as *languages*. The signs are not to be combined in haphazard fashion. To have meaning and significance only certain combinations are acceptable among adults, and those combinations are associated with particular meanings and significance. Acts of speech and writing can transcend the here-and-now, escaping the immediate limits of time and space; they can refer to the past or future as well as the present, to the *there* as well as the *here*.

Other definitions mention additional characteristics such as a facility for constructing novel sentences and a reliance upon cultural rather than genetic means for intergenerational transmission (Hockett, 1958: see table 2.1). For Chomsky (1957) the essence of language resides in its facility for pairing patterns of sound with patterns of meaning. Since patterns (structures) are constructed from units combined in accordance with specifiable rules, this comment is consistent with Morris's definition and serves to highlight a feature left obscure by him.

Morris did not mention *meaning*, which will be treated here as different from *significance*. One can ask what significance for action the meaning of a pattern has. In the European Union the meaning of a road sign with a bent shape upon it is that there is a bend in the road just ahead; the significance for action is that any driver travelling too fast to negotiate that bend should prepare to reduce speed. Morris half-appears to jump over meaning (*semantics*) to arrive directly at significance (*pragmatics*). In contrast Chomsky does not proceed to the point of asking what people are likely to do or can be expected to do when they receive messages. It is not however surprising that Chomsky did not proceed to the extra-linguistic; in elaborating his concern to find rules that could generate grammatically acceptable surface structures of sentences from their deep structure constituents, it was inevitable that preservation of the elegance of the rules could be bought only at the price of postulated *ideal speakers* and of relegating the behavior of real speakers beyond the boundary of interest. To study structure in that manner, without attention to behavioral functions, not only resulted in ignoring substantial components of the study of language in communication, it thereby also missed solutions to some of the issues he himself tackled. It also deprived Chomsky of any source of evidence against which to check the truth–value of his hypotheses. The persistent inability or unwillingness of apologists for Transformational Grammar (TG) to state conditions for refuting the truth–value of any claim they were making should have been challenged earlier as being a symptom of mysticism replacing science; science must have checkable hypotheses. While Chomsky's ideas were being heralded as revolutionary for linguistics, a less time-bound observer might have viewed the move as one kind of structuralist replacing another (Bloomfield, 1935); neither approach seemingly being aware of more comprehensive views of language which were capable of posing different questions about language and its workings. The Prague school

Table 2.1   Hockett's (1958) Design Features of Human Spoken Language

---

1. Vocal-auditory channel
   (communication occurs by the producer speaking and the receiver hearing)
2. Broadcast transmission and directional reception
   (a signal travels out in all directions from the speaker but can be localised in space by the hearer)
3. Rapid fading
   (once spoken, the signal rapidly disappears and is no longer available for inspection)
4. Interchangeability
   (adults can be both receivers and transmitters)
5. Complete feedback
   (speakers can access everything about their productions)
6. Specialization
   (the amount of energy in the signal is unimportant; a word means the same whether it is whispered or shouted)
7. Semanticity
   (signals mean something: they relate to the features of the world)
8. Arbitrariness
   (these symbols are abstract; except with a few onomatopoeic exceptions, they do not resemble what they stand for)
9. Discreteness
   (the vocabulary is made out of discrete units)
10. Displacement
    (the communication system can be used to refer to things remote in time and space)
11. Openness
    (the ability to invent new messages)
12. Tradition
    (the language can be taught and learned)
13. Duality of patterning
    (only combinations of otherwise meaningless units are meaningful – this can be seen as applying both at the level of sounds and words, and words and sentences)
14. Prevarication
    (language provides us with the ability to lie and deceive)
15. Reflectiveness
    (we can communicate about the communication system itself, just as this book is doing)
16. Learnability
    (the speaker of one language can learn another)

(see Vachek, 1966 for a review) of linguists and the anthropologists/linguists deriving from Malinowski (1949) through Firth (1951) were not being trapped by a perspective that saw language only as a system.

Preferring the word "rule" to "system," Halliday (1978) traced a history of differential emphasis upon *language as rule* versus *language as resource* back into the mists of antiquity. In that framework, both Bloomfield (1935) and Chomsky (1957, 1965) became the heirs of Plato, classifying, abstracting, and generalizing from selected examples against ideals culled from some vision of what a classically-trained mind might wish language to be like. Meanwhile, politicians, lawyers, and advertising agents perpetuate the practical and degraded rhetorical tradition of the later Sophists. Earlier Sophists such as Protagoras were concerned with how language worked as a vehicle for persuasion and communication, just as the Prague school, Firth, and more recently Halliday (1978) have been concerned simultaneously with language as resource and language as rule.

2.2   Language as System and Language as Resource

Halliday (1978) opposed *rule* and *resource*. Somewhat diffidently, my current preference is to contrast *system* with *resource*. If we contrast the opposition of views of *language as system* with *language as resource*, and ask what other contrasts correlate with this, we find that the pair can be associated with a series of parallel oppositions that are not all entirely linguistic – neither are they quite parallel. However, if one were to ask whether the listing of any pair would be more sensible if it were reversed, the answer would be "no."

Part of the purpose of this book is to explore some of the reasons why there are associations between the sociological and psychological on the one hand and the linguistic on the other. In the meantime, let us note the absurdity of an exclusive emphasis on *either* language as system *or* language as resource. Language only developed and continues to develop as a system because it is a resource; the developments extend its utility. Language is only viable as a resource because it is a system whose particular units, rules and conventions are known, understood, accepted, and generally followed by a sufficient number of communicating people. This would seem to be obvious, and if it is, why is there so much disagreement and fuss?

The reasons are many, and differ from group to group and from individual to individual. For a few their beliefs may be simply an expression of their personality; some people find it difficult to submit to order, and oth-

Table 2.2 Language as System and Resource

LANGUAGE
as

SYSTEM	RESOURCE
Structure	Function
Unity	Diversity
Rule Observation	Flexibility
Prescription	Description
Correctness	Effectiveness
Propriety	
"Pure"	"Degenerate"
Knowing "that"	Knowing "how to"
Idealism	Realism
Nominalism	Pragmatism
Stability	Change
Conservative	Progressive
	Anarchic
Educated	Uneducated
Cultivated	Earthy
Elite	Ordinary

ers cannot cope with any threat to order. For others, the emphasis on one side rather than the other may be based on a judgment that the forces of the other side are becoming too strong at a particular point in time, and citing school curricula as their concern. If we ask questions about whether or not linguists are trying to describe or prescribe, the answer is that they are trying to describe. However, if we ask whether or not their products, such as grammar books and dictionaries, are descriptive or prescriptive, the mistake is to choose either answer. The correct answer is to ask about functions rather than the purposes, and then the answer is "Both." For example, at its inception, a dictionary may well describe how the diction-ary-maker thinks some usually undefined but nevertheless highly literate sample of persons in a language community do use or have used the words listed; what meanings these words were given and have acquired and to what uses they have been put. While prescriptive elements could easily enter into these processes, in theory the venture is a descriptive one. But once the dictionary is published, the meanings and uses listed will have prescriptive force. People will consult dictionaries to learn how to use words in accordance with what appear to be the conventions of the society. This will be especially true if the society has a formalized educational system whose authorities recommend and support the use of dictionaries. To deny that any grammar or dictionary has *de facto* prescriptive power is to ignore the realities of social processes. How are people to learn the conventions appropriate to the language use in their communities within which they communicate without prescription? One cannot use a system based on conventions unless one follows those conventions. Much learning, or even all of it, could be oral, but it will still be prescriptive, and once linguists intervene to describe and codify, the community members are likely to use the descriptions as the rules. Given that there is variability in the culture, any description is likely in itself to be an abstraction of norms. In any case, the speech of sub-cultures will change: sounds will shift, new words and structures will be constructed, and old ones will be given new meanings. If a change is accepted by certain groups then the norms of these groups will operate to encourage would-be members to use these forms. At present in the Western world, we can see these forces working vividly among teenagers and other special groupings such as drug-takers and geeks. The speech helps to identify a group member, just as the clothes or other actions help to identify one. One of the interesting features that might be claimed for the speech of such groups is its rate of change; this has the effect of isolating both outsiders and those whose membership is either half-hearted or lapsing. (Oddly enough, the facts of these matters have yet to be systematically documented.) While then linguists are correct in claiming that they can study rule systems without subscribing to those systems themselves, and while they may well believe that they are disinterested observers, the systems they are describing are socially prescriptive and necessarily so.

Of potentially equal interest to a social psychologist is the nature of the relationships between those who emphasize language as system and those who emphasize it as resource. While no one has studied this matter empirically, it would seem that extremists on the resource side (linguistic anarchists and extreme progressives) do not presently constitute a strong force in either the academic or the educational world. At the other pole, conservative extremists are a force in the land, and the conflict seems to be mainly between those who are defending a view of language as system and those who insist on its dual character. The defenders seem to despise and fear the dualists. They argue for the preservation of proper pronunciation, correct grammar, for words having "real" meanings; it is wrong to sometimes split infinitives. The extreme position simply ignores the historical character of language. Most of those who argue the case for viewing language as resource endorse the validity of the positive case of those who assert the importance of language as system, but are themselves treated as though they are anarchists or creative eccentrics. This is a good example of the bible's assertion "Those who are not with us are against us" and its social psychological update as the assimilation/contrast hypothesis (Sherif & Hovland, 1961).

One way of beginning to answer some broader questions about the conflict is to ask why the attitudes are not reversed. A quick answer to that question might be that although one could conceive of a language in a state of total ossification, it is impossible to conceive of one in a state of perpetual anarchic change. The idea that individuals should shift the meanings of their phonological, lexico–grammatical, semantic and pragmatic rules continuously is both logically impossible and practically absurd. If the language system serves to send negotiable messages from one head to another, there must be some consensus about the meanings and significance of the constituents of the code. That perpetual substantial change is indefensible might explain why there are no extremists on the resource side. Maintenance of the status quo is a defensible if unpragmatic position to adopt and allows extremists on the language as system side to have a case.

Anarchists and progressives were linked in the diagram, and it is in part the failure of the conservatives to see the difference between the two that leads to the clash. With the measure of stability and consensus that English has achieved, it could be judged there are still very severe problems of individual and sub-cultural negotiations about meanings without encouraging excessive moves towards uniqueness of meanings. Although in one sense users of English individually have unique (associative) meanings for both the units and structures we use because we have unique biographies, in a more important sense our command of English cannot be a command of an individualized language – in this sense a "private language" is a self-contradictory concept. Barzun (1959) must be right when he points to the nonsense of a student defending a totally illegible handwriting on the grounds that at least it was his own; handwriting that is not legible even to its writer has ceased to be handwriting. Noises decodable to oneself only are not a language. While on the one hand we can argue against the dangers of solipsism, we must not confuse this with a wish to exploit the power of the language to express original thoughts that can be understood or responded to in some enlightening way. No innovation, no progress. Change is not progress, but the distinction between the two is sometimes possible only in hindsight.

It may be expected then that language as system will have conservative defenders to preserve it and to protect its transmission from generation to generation. In France the Academie française is a live historical relic of such a conservatism, even if its prescriptions have little influence on everyday talk. A language has to be conservative to be a language, and it is sensible and efficient for its conservers to preserve commonality and uniformity. Only if those conditions are met can language be used as a resource. However it is also true that it is only by breaking rules and introducing new units and structures that we can change rules and extend the expressive and communicative power of the system. For so long as human beings keep trying to extend their knowledge, to enhance their powers of expression, and to construct new identities, languages must change. For this, old words must then be given new meanings, old structures used to serve new purposes. New words and even new structures must be invented.

For example, people who did not (or even do) appreciate the niceties of the difference between what some males claimed were no more than marked and unmarked linguistic terms may eventually try to introduce new pronouns. Will it be "hes" for he/she, "hir" for her/him, or what? The American Psychological Association Manual was early to discourage the use of "male" pronouns, and authors now currently have to struggle to use plurals to minimize the incidence of the offensive words in many public documents. Why can there not be single gender non-specific human pronouns? One is tempted to argue that the sooner the Americans take official action for neutral pronouns the better. Only individuals can initiate change, but institutional endorsement would be necessary to achieve that particular shift, and the United States is the only country that would have the sense, audacity, and power to authorize the new genderless words and perhaps maintain the pressure for their diffusion and acceptance. But it seems that even they do not dare to try to save us all from this irritating and accidental deficiency of English.

This then is part of a dilemma. Language as culturally transmitted system and resource traps its users at the same time as it offers them opportunities for development. The tension is inescapable, and an appreciation of this can help us to see which changes in a language are likely to be more or less difficult to institute. When television was invented and it became a part of the furniture of most homes in most societies, the word "television" was diffused and abbreviated quickly. It has been followed more recently with the host of acronyms now associated with Information Communication Technology (ICT), which have been also been diffused with great rapidity. However, when the Soviet government attempted to abolish the tu/vous distinction as a discriminator of social relations, the task proved to beyond their power and they gave up. To de-sex pronouns or disambiguate particles such as "or" or "if" in non-totalitarian and even totalitarian states could take a hundred years or so to achieve some minimal criterion of adoption in a speech community. In Europe only English lost "thou," "thee" and "ye," Re-negotiating meanings with a hundred million people is qualitatively as well as quantitatively more difficult than negotiating or re-negotiating them within small groups. For oneself, one can privatize, change, and abbreviate the language as much as one likes for intra-individual communication. Within a dyad that involves frequent encounters, people can likewise privatize and abbreviate. With small groups, negotiation and re-negotiation are possible, but become more difficult. With very large groups certain kinds of change may be virtually impossible to achieve, even after civil wars or revolutions. Language as system enjoys the inertia of its history, and even language as resource enjoys the inertia of those who have learned to use it as it has become!

Ideally we would instantiate these ideas through a comprehensive sociocultural history of a language (see Baugh & Cable, 1987; Wardhaugh, 1998). This exercise would help us to see how much and how little we have achieved by way of understanding how language works. We would come to see for example that some of the great linguistic efforts of earlier centuries have dealt with only very limited aspects of the total range of problems and puzzles. Bloomfield's (1935) contribution to phonetics and phonology edged forward understanding of language as a sound system. Chomsky helped to re-conceptualize syntax. The study of language as resource has hardly begun to germinate. Halliday (1985) has persistently argued the case for adopting an integrated approach to the two perspectives. Austin (1962) and Searle (1969, 1975) have initiated ideas of language as enabling doing through saying. Garfinkel (1967) and Sacks (1971) have asked pertinent questions about language in use, and yet other early approaches to the analysis of discourse (Brazil, 1975; Coulthard, 1977) were perhaps symptomatic of a swing in orientation that will eventually oblige us to reconceptualize our descriptions of language.

These new wines have burst old bottles, but we can still pour out the old wine first and taste its flavour – before becoming concerned about its potability. We must also remind ourselves that any claims about the character of language are prone to be too strong, if one is trying to generate claims about the international variation in the ways in which sounds and marks are linked to meanings via lexico–grammatical units and structures. With readers of English in mind and sufficient empirical work in social psychology having been conducted using English, it is appropriate here to focus mainly on the workings of English. (This restriction should not be interpreted as being attitudinal.)

⌐ 2.3 How the English Language Works

An excellent introduction to English and its workings is offered by Crystal (1988). A more forbidding volume of 1779 pages sets out the perceived state of its grammar (Quirk, Greenbaum, Leech and Svartvik, 1985). Halliday's (1985) own introduction to his functionally based grammar of English takes up 387 pages. The advanced state of its phonetics and phonology is displayed by Gimson (1994). The beginnings of its semantics are exemplified by Lyons (1977, 1995) and of its pragmatics by Leech (1983) and Levinson (1983). Reducing this encyclopaedic achievement to a few pages is not possible, but a sketch can be made (see Table 2.3).

In any particular dialect of English some forty five sounds (including a brief silence as a unit) have what is called phonemic significance. It is the difference between these sounds that can make a difference to any message we transmit: [pil] is different from [dil], which is different from [vil]. *Phonemes* can be sub-classified, with a few anomalies, into vowels and consonants. These are combined in short sequences to form *morphemes,* which are often referred to as the elementary units of meaning. [pil] is a lexical morpheme. To which the grammatical morpheme [s] can be added. Of the three combinations cited, two are morphemes of English, whereas the third has not so far been used in any indigenous forms of the language. English has in fact only used a small sample of the phoneme sequences that it might have used to create its morphemes, and yet the language already comprises well over 100,000 morphemes, without having recourse to many long sequences. In their turn, one or more morphemes are used to make up a *word.*

English currently boasts over a million words, of which almost half are technical terms. The same word form may have many distinguishable linguistic meanings associated with it. *The Shorter Oxford English Dictionary* lists thirteen meanings of "about" and twenty three for "table". Estimates of the size of a person's vocabulary are rough and ready affairs, partly because what is to count as a word still lacks consensus, partly because of

Table 2.3   Language Structure and Content

System		and	Resource	
Phonology	**Lexico-grammar**		**Semantics** (Meaning: denotation, connotation)	**Pragmatics** (Significance for action)
Phonemics	**Morphology**			**Categories of Relevance**
phonemes (45+)	morphemes [gram?] [lex, 1000K]	⇕	classes: markers of plurality gender, comparison, case, tense	Setting: where
syllables [1K+] feet	words [gram, 150] [lex, 500K + ordy] [lex, 500K + tech]	⇕	classes? thesauri (a) elemental features? (b) fields e.g. color?	Participants: who Ends: purposes; functions Art characteristics
Intonation	**Syntax**			Key: how
tone group [5?]	group [3+]	↕	nominal, verbal, adverbial	Instrumentality (1) channels (2) code
	clause [16+]	↕	free, subordinate, relative etc.	Norms
	sentence [4] (declarative, interrogative, imperative, exclamatory)		statement, question, command, exclamation	Genre

Phonetics

phones
(air flow)
(shape)
(stop)

(pitch)
(pitch change)

(volume)
(duration)

speech act [6+ or α]

propositional content → illocutionary force → perlocutionary force

Units: One or more units at one level are *combined* sequentially to form a structure which functions as a unit at the next level up (down)

the multiplicity of senses for many individual words, and partly because there are differences between what we can recognize with contextual support and what we can produce when left to our own devices. Even as early as six years of age an average child may well use 2,000 words and understand some meanings of over 10,000. Wagner's (1985) estimate of 20,000 tokens in 12 hours from a two-year-old gives an idea of how much talking can be done.

Words can be classified in various ways, semantically as in a thesaurus, or grammatically in terms of the ways they can enter into more complex structures. As an example of the latter we can cite Fries (1952), who separated them into two main sets of classes (grammatical and lexical). Many of those in his lexical classes 1, 2, 3 and 4 would be called nouns, verbs, adjectives, and adverbs respectively, although the "sentence frame location" criteria of Fries render such correspondence less than perfect. In a sample of 1000 words of conversation, Fries found these made up all but 93 percent of the different words, but only 66 percent of the total number. One third of the speech consisted of the 154 *function* words, that Fries classified into 15 other groups, corresponding roughly to such labels as determiners, auxiliaries, emphatics, negatives, conjunctions, interrogatives, etc. Sometimes these 154 are referred to as *grammatical* words: suffice it to say that when one of them is to be used, any grammatically acceptable choice is from a much smaller set than when the selection is made from one of the other four classes.

We have already mentioned that many words have more than one meaning and that is so in two senses. A distinction has been made between *linguistic* meaning, which represents some abstraction of what members of a speech community might agree about the connotation of the term, and *associative* meaning which is the psychological significance that word has for a particular individual – an accumulation of the particular psychological associations the word evokes for that person as a result of his/her past experience with both the word and its referents. "Dog" may be a quadruped with certain other criterial or prototypical attributes for the speech community generally; for James its mere mention may cause him to tremble at the memory of the savaging he once experienced from a Rottweiler. Cutting across these we have also begun to appreciate that single words may not only refer to items that have no identifiable characteristics in common (Wittgenstein, 1951) and that the categories which they connote are not homogeneous – they have internal structure: games do not have criterial attributes, only family resemblances. In a fascinating series of experiments and analyses, Rosch (see for example 1973, 1978) discriminated between degrees of category membership. Lakoff (1979) cited sixty or so devices in English for qualifying category membership: *par excellence, typical, run-of-the-mill, technically speaking*. Whereas a robin is a typical bird, a penguin is only a bird technically speaking. A robin is not just "technically" a bird, a robin is a real no-nonsense bird, a bird par excellence as well as a typical one. Emus are more bird-like than penguins. Is archeopteryx a bird? Rosch develops the idea of *prototypical* members of categories, noting that although "natural" categories lack homogeneity and have fuzzy boundaries, some of them may have non-arbitrary foci; cross-language studies of colour words provide one candidate for the latter category (Berlin & Kay, 1969), in that the most frequently distinguished color hues rank similarly across other languages.

The attribute of fuzziness allows innovation. The meanings of words can be extended in various ways, one of which is to push out the boundaries. Extension by metaphor is another means. Not only will many individual words have several linguistic meanings, each of which may have prototypical realizations and indeterminate edges, for any particular person an individual word will have a unique associative set of meanings unshared by other speakers of the language.

This brief digression into meanings of words is not simply indicative of an inability to control divergent thinking. An appreciation of the points made helps us defend ourselves against the posing of silly questions. "When do children understand "why?" can be seen to be ill-conceived if it is the case that there are several meanings of "why," each with fuzzy boundaries, and each of which can be interpreted at more than one level of analysis. One can ask whether the first signs of comprehension and/or production of "why" by children are limited to a particular sense of the word, and if so, which and why. There are many other questions that might be asked, but to be sensible they must not make false presuppositions, for example that there is a single meaning of "why." Baby's utterance of a "first word" is a construction for parental pleasure and not a landmark in language mastery.

Words are combined into *groups* (phrases), groups into *clauses* and clauses into *sentences*. The rules which govern the permitted combinations of these sequences constitute the *grammar* of the language. Linguistics usually treats English as though there are three types of group (nominal, verbal and adverbial). The number of clause types suggested is variable, but is usually greater than ten and less than twenty. *Free clauses* are distinguished from *bound clauses*, that cannot stand alone. Bound clauses can be coordinate (linked with such conjunctions as "and" and "but") or subordinate (linked with "because," "if," "wh-" words etc.). While these higher order structures are few in number, the large number of morphemes and words, in combination with the many varieties of structures operating within each of these levels allows an infinite number of sentences to be constructed. Four types of *sentence* are distinguished (*declarative, interrogative, imperative,* and *exclamatory*), and these are treated as the smallest self-standing structures for utterances, although many utterances are more abbreviated. In terms of default transparency, declaratives are used for making *statements* (propositions), interrogatives for asking *questions,* imperatives for issuing *commands,* and exclamatories for *exclaiming*!

Its free-standing quality does not mean that the sentence is the most important unit. No one unit is more important than another. A symbolic system could be a language with only *two* levels of lexico–grammatical units, but no known language relies on this minimum. Neither is the word the basic building block either in its role as a grammatical unit or in its capacity as a lexical item. In English the word has properties that make it psychologically and pedagogically more important than the morpheme or the syllable, but linguistically it is as dependent on other levels as they are on it. Clearly the wider the functional vocabulary that a person can deploy, the greater the possibilities for the efficient transmission of meanings, but in itself a rich vocabulary gives potential not performance. It is true that the words of a language like English stand out, especially after we have made lists of them in dictionaries and after we have instituted teaching procedures that emphasize them – and left gaps between them in written texts. Nevertheless, the point bears repetition that knowing one meaning of a word is not the same as being able to include the relevant idea in one's head readily and effectively in communicative acts – as many learners of foreign languages can confirm.

While linguists have written coherently and constructively about phonetics, phonology, and grammar, have compiled magnificent dictionaries, and offered guidance about "Received" and other kinds of pronunciation and proper usage, so far they have been less successful with *semantics* and *pragmatics.* Semantics has led a varied life (Lyons, 1995). Traditionally, philosophers have been chronically worried about the relationship between words and sentences on the one hand and what they "stand for," if anything, on the other. Are words names for essences of objects and actions that exist in ideal form? Are sentences pictures or facts? What is 'this' the name of? While one can see why many of the philosophical questions have been raised and can appreciate the arguments around the topics, perhaps the answers to be found are not nearly as tortuous and complicated as we might imagine. Part of the problem derives from trying to verbalize matters that require more than patterns of words to understand. Wordings and experience are integrally related, and neither can be reduced to or entirely separated from the other. Both concepts and propositions can disappear into an infinite regress of words, but they are saved from doing so when they link to shared experience. (Where did the idea originate that presentation and communication of knowledge is better if it can be expressed verbally rather than through demonstrations, diagrams, or formulae in other symbolic systems?) That point is taken up with considerable acumen under the improbable title of *Zen and the Art of Motorcycle Maintenance* (Pirsig, 1976). Neither Piaget (1970) nor Popper (1963, 1972) seem to have suffered from many of the problems that have afflicted most post-Platonic philosophers. I can do no better than recommend a reading of those authors, preferably in reverse alphabetical order, for a defense of the view that the correspondences between propositions and what they are proposing is neither mystical nor extraordinarily difficult to grasp. When we make statements about the world, we are talking about our constructions of reality. We can never be certain that what we are saying is true, and it can always be treated as incomplete. Such statements are not personal inventions – in Piaget's terms they are forced inventions – and neither are they pure discoveries. This idea of reality acting as a check upon the possible falsity of our attempts to construct a language that corresponds to it is not too distant from what Everyperson could be persuaded to agree with, if they decided to think the problem through.

That kind of epistemological semantic problem is clearly distinguishable from those to which linguists and psychologists have paid attention. Linguists have asked themselves about the meanings of all the units and patterns in the language system: aspects, moods, and tenses of verbs; gender identification; the plural morpheme; and so on through the many other features. In this tradition, semantics has been concerned with similarities and differences in meanings at all levels of linguistic analysis. Within that framework it makes sense to ask what phonological contrasts have what grammatical and lexical functions with what semantic significance. Subsequently TG grammar began to be concerned that semantic features might be coded in the deep structure, and semantics re-emerged as exciting level of analysis. Lyons (1995) has recently tried to organize the state of the art, relying heavily upon psychological as well as linguistic contributions. The approach known as *componential analysis* that breaks meanings of words into defining attributes strung out as a conjunctive list is treated extensively. For example, words about family members can be classified in terms of gender, generation, closeness of kinship etc. Some evidence is beginning to appear that casts doubt upon the psychological reality of these classifications of meaning. This approach has focused mainly on words, but other higher level linguistic structures are now included in the up-surge of interest.

But, as we realized many years ago, semantics is not the end of the affair. All language functions in a context. Sentences are used. They are used to make statements, to ask questions, to give orders and exclaim. Different utterances may serve a common end: "It's cold today" and "May I borrow your coat please?" are both utterances that might be used to obtain a coat (Soskin & John, 1963). Conversely, the same formal utterance could have a different significance in different contexts. A recital of "Baa Baa Black Sheep" would be interpreted differently if heard by a two-year-old child, a prodigal son returning, or a learned committee of discussants. *Pragmatics* focuses on the way in which variations in contextual variables and linguistic features interact to change the significance of the speech for the actions and reactions of listeners and speakers.

The distinction between semantics and pragmatics is not always easy to hold in the face of difficult examples, and some academics doubt that it can be sustained. We have cited the difference between the meaning of a road sign and its pragmatic significance for drivers. We can find examples of phrases whose semantics have at first sight faded into insignificance in comparison with their pragmatic import, for example "God be with you" becoming "goodbye" or "bye," and it was not until the English penny reverted to a decimal status that the abbreviation of *d* for the Latin *denari* was dropped. But this is perhaps misleading. The semantic contrast between one form of leave-taking and other acts such as greeting remains.

Discussions of the meanings of declarative sentences used to make statements whose truth–values are checkable at least in principle can cite a claimed correspondence between the wordings and the reality represented as the meaning. The utterance of "the canary is singing" will, if true, mean that a canary is actually singing. With "It's cold today" or "That coat of yours looks warm," we could say that the meanings (in terms of semantics) are transparent, but their pragmatic significance is opaque. Only for "Lend me your coat?" and "May I borrow your coat?" is the pragmatic significance transparently interpretable from a knowledge of the meanings of the words and structures. As already mentioned, imperative and interrogative forms are "prototypical" vehicles for commanding and requesting, whereas declarative forms are prototypically vehicles for making statements. It is perhaps tempting to think of forms for which the semantics and pragmatics are in their most obviously decipherable relations as corresponding to the idea of unmarked forms in grammar and lexis. What can be taken for granted is made as transparent as possible and what is new is likewise made evident. In such utterances for example a declarative sentence means both what it says and that its producer is making a statement. What the pragmatic significance is will require an analysis of the context of situation to diagnose. It may be to inform the listener of something they did not know, to remind them of something they would prefer to forget, to warn them, to humiliate them. Some developments have not found it necessary to refer to a distinction between semantics and pragmatics. Searle's (1969, 1975) concept of *speech act* seems to be mainly pragmatic, but not entirely so – likewise Grice's maxims (1975/1989) for the maintenance of conversation or rules for turn-taking (Sacks, Schegloff and Jefferson, 1974) in conversation. Halliday distinguished between what is *said* and what is *done by saying*, viewing the latter as being outside language as such, but simultaneously stating that he would prefer not to press for rigid separations (1978, pp. 54–56).

Early discourse analysts (for example Sinclair & Coulthard, 1975; Coulthard, 1977) were concerned to create units of analysis beyond the sentence in two respects. First, they argued that linguists need to cope with units larger than the sentence because language as used in real life (for example in conversations, monologues, letters and books) has structural relations superordinate to the sentence. Second, they argued that the units have to be of a kind other than lexico–grammatical; the labels for their categories take on a more psychological and functional character – *act, move, exchange, transaction*. At first sight these seem to be more pragmatic than semantic, but that may not really be so in the final analysis. One strand of the Birmingham work on discourse (Brazil, 1975) was potentially revolutionary for the model of language so far presented. The linear sequence used here, which began with phonemes proceeding through lexico–grammar to semantics and pragmatics, could have been reversed. We might have begun by asking what people do with language. But if *either* sequence is assumed to have significance for the way individuals manage to speak or children learn language we could be in trouble. To presume that children learn phonemes first, then morphemes, *et seq.* until eventually they learn to do things with the language can easily be discredited. The reverse idea that they do things and develop language skills to cope with these problems may be slightly more plausible, but this too is misleading. It is probably least inaccurate if one adopts a position that asserts that children eventually and generally develop competence with and skills in all aspects together – pragmatics, semantics, lexico–grammar and phonology. To conceive of this fourfold componential development is not easy, but the four questions can be asked about any new unit that is integrated into the child's repertoire. Children have to be able to recognize its phonological identity, to know how it can be fitted into or used as sentences, to have some idea of its meaning, and some idea of its occasions of use. Of course any of us coping with a new word, for example, may initially only have very limited knowledge of fewer than all four features, but if we are to succeed in using it appropriately, all four must eventually be mastered in some measure.

But does the portrait of language so far drawn miss any crucial ingredients? Certainly speech act theory, discourse analysis, and conversational analysis have expanded horizons, and have added substantially to the achievements in phonetics, phonology, lexico–grammar, and semantics, and the second also re-opened the previously neglected topic of *intonation* that may cause us eventually to re-conceptualize language as system more generally. Brazil (1975) developed Halliday's analysis of the five *tone groups* in English, a tonic segment being the segment of an utterance marked by pitch/stress.

The central set of contrasts is marked by reference to two systems: *tone* which attends to the pitch *change* characterizing the stressed syllable in the tonic segment of a tone group and *key* which is partly referable to the pitch *level* of the tone group as a whole. Brazil contrasts the following utterances:

1   // when I've finished Middlemarch // I shall read Adam Bede //

2   // when I've finished Middlemarch // I shall read Adam Bede //

In 1. the speaker is addressing someone who already knows that he, the speaker, is reading *Middlemarch*, and is stating his future intention as the item of news. In 2 this intention has already arisen in some way and what the speaker is announcing is *when* he will be realizing it. Brazil suggests that the *fall-rise* tone marks the knowledge that is already shared by speaker and listener, while the *falling tone* marks what is new. He suggests that the former function may usefully be called *referring* (r) and the latter *proclaiming* (p). Utterance 1 above can then be written:

1   // r when I've finished *Midd*lemarch // p I shall read Adam *Bede* //

English additionally has two tone selections referred to as *intensified* alternatives of *r* and *p*: a *rise-fall* (r+) for intensified r and a *rise* (p+) for intensified p. Hence //p+ "when I've finished Middlemarch" implies "and not a moment before." Finally a *low-rising* tone ( ) realizes a neutral option whereby the speaker avoids either proclaiming or referring, signalling but a minimal involvement.

The second aspect of tone contrast is *key*. Brazil recognizes that the pho-netic features of this are variable and none is invariably present, but chooses prior *pitch level* as defining and suggests that English makes use of three levels: High, Middle and Low, where these are defined in relation to the previous tone group. A mid-key selection leaves proclaiming and refer-ring acts as stated, but the choice of high or low shows the speaker takes for granted the existence of a *closed* set of options in an already negotiated frame of reference. The use of high key with referring tone assumes that a potential contrast has already been established, whereas with proclaiming tone its use exploits a contrast not yet attested to by either party. Contrast in this context implies carefulness of selection of a particular feature to draw particular attention to it. Selection of low key may signal redun-dancy //mid p "we gave it to our neighbours" //low p "the Robinsons" // meaning that of course you know that already. It can also imply causal or consequential relations between statements //mid p "the lecture was can-celled" //low p "the speaker was ill" //. The connection between the two can be seen very easily.

This abbreviated account of Brazil's (1975) analysis only begins to intro-duce the complexities of the intonational system, but suffices to make the point: *intonation is crucial to the (intended) function of an utterance*. Until we know the *stress* and *pitch* patterns, we cannot tell what is already taken for granted between speaker and listener and what is now being added. We do not know what the array of possible messages was from which the particular one has been selected. In an important sense we have no idea why the person was saying what was being said. Once we have the into-nation, we know to what the speaker is drawing attention. If the cat is still sitting on the proverbial mat we can construct a range of utterances utiliz-ing the same lexico–grammatical form and the same phonemes, but vary-ing what is presumed to be new for the listener. Whether we wish to say that meaning remains constant, but pragmatic significance changes or that both change I do not know. What is clear is that this kind of analysis links language as system to speakers transmitting messages to each. Linguistics becomes linked to psychology, language to communication.

The implications for much work on language are profound and radical. Intonation will need to be included in analyses not simply as an additional layer but as an integral component. Historically, too much speech has been transcribed and stripped of significant features during the process. Coders and theoreticians are left puzzled by uncertainties and ambiguities that a text with intonation would resolve. Chomsky's ambiguous sentences like "The shooting of the hunters took place at dawn" would have been disambiguated if recorded as genuine utterances rather than strings of written words. What is being done with speech can begin to be seen if what has been said has not been denuded of how it was said. (The very distinction between the what and the how is potentially misleading if one assumes that the pragmatic significance is linked only to the former).

A too-heavy reliance on written text has doubtless led many linguists and others to a delusion that the meaning is in the text. In their imaginative comparison between the perceived status of written and oral presentations Olson, Torrance, and Hildyard (1985) argue for the premier status of writing as a vehicle of truth. But if this is so, then a writer has to try to compensate in some way for what is necessarily lost by not speaking and that is quite a different matter from taking speech delivered as speech, writing down the words and assuming that the meaning is in the text. To decide that prosodic features were paralinguistic or extra-linguistic and then ignore them is extraordinary, and yet account after account of the development of language mastery in children has been presented without intonation marked (or studied). Halliday (1985) and Wells, Montgomery, and MacLure (1979) are exceptions to this tendency. To have analyzed speech without cognisance of context was odd, to have stripped the speech of a major component of its significance was doubly odd. Both were in fact extraordinary traps into which to fall.

As it happens, social psychological studies have been less affected by this blinkered view than linguistic ones, mainly because the coding frames of social psychologists have not depended on syntactic analysis to the same extent as those of developmental psycholinguists. In the future this may not be so, and social psychologists may have to ask themselves to what extent they see speech in written form without prosodics rather than hear it with them – and come to realize that this is a handicap. Perhaps only very few social psychologists can hear the variations in stress and pitch as such, and it certainly seems to require guided experience to begin to identify and recognize the relevant contrasts. I suspect that many who continue to work on social behavior and speech will find it necessary in the future to attend courses on intonation to sharpen perception and to extend their personal knowledge of how it functions to give significance to speech. Certainly students of conversation will need to transcribe stress, pitch movements and change. The neat demonstrations of Sacks (1971) of the infinite regress that results from trying to replace wordings with verbal explications of their significance might have been saved from this regression had they incorporated Brazil's indicators of "what can be taken for granted" and "what is new." Such ideas were implicit in the older Hellenic distinction between *theme* and *rheme*, but recent linguistics intent on language as system has been ignoring that strand of its lineage.

At the pragmatic level we have yet to be presented with a development of or substitute for Hymes' (1967) list of factors relevant to choices open to a speaker. Hymes suggested that the word SPEAKING can itself serve as a comprehensive mnemonic to remind any user or investigator of the components associated with variations in speaking or writing. These are:

(S)   Setting the Scene
(P)   Participants or Personnel
(E)   Ends as (1) Objectives, (2) Outcomes
(A)   Art Characteristics
(K)   Key
(I)   Instrumentalities: (1) Channel, (2) Code
(N)   Norms of Interaction and Interpretation
(G)   Genre

Not surprisingly the English language is not so accommodating to Hymes' ingenuity that he can select labels whose meanings are self-evident. Further, the categories chosen hide some factors that might be considered important, and bring others into a prominence that they do not merit. This feeling of unease cannot however be translated into reasons that can be justified. *Setting* and *participants* are clear in their meanings. Places of worship and sports grounds, parliaments and patios, factory floors and beaches, predispose respectively towards different kinds of discourse. If we have a topic and function in mind, we would choose one setting rather than others. We would not raise certain topics in certain settings. While we know the general fact and we probably do not make many mistakes in our everyday lives, we might have some difficulty in expressing this "know when" verbally and systematically. How we are to classify settings is more problematic (see chapter 10.5). What one talks about and how one does so shifts from person to person. Young children are not addressed as though they are teenagers. Men do not speak to women with the same vocabulary that they use to other men in all settings. Degrees of friendship and differential power affect the speech in predictable ways (see chapter 8). It is important to distinguish between ends as objectives and ends as outcomes; the more common everyday words for these terms would be *purpose* and *function*. The purpose may be to bring two parties into agreement, but the interaction may lead to an intensification of the disagreement. The intention might be to initiate a friendship between a potential husband and a best friend: the outcome might be playing bridesmaid. Hymes does not make the further necessary distinction between avowed or apparent purposes on the one hand and real or actual purposes on the other. The same distinction can be made for functions. Sociologists have traditionally used the terms "manifest" and "latent" to refer to the difference. The avowed purpose might be to clarify a problem, the real purpose to humiliate a rival. The apparent purpose of an advertisement may be to avail you of this opportunity to buy this wonderful product, the actual purpose simply to persuade you to buy. The innocence of the populace in its failure to distinguish between what appears to be happening and what is really happening is a constant cause of anguish for those of us who have been paid to learn to be critical thinkers. That "function" is accorded the same status as the other SPEAKING variables is one of the misleading aspects of Hymes' classification. *Function* has a prior importance in the study of language in use that needs to be emphasized, as much of the rest of this book will argue (see chapter 3 especially).

Art characteristics is an unfortunate umbrella opened to cover *form of message* and *topic*. *Form* appears to distinguish between prose and poetry, between narration and explanation. *Topic* refers to the manifest content of the speech, and at first sight, one might say that this is too important a source of variation to relegate to a sub-heading, but there is no obvious explanation that can be used to support that feeling of unease. *Key* distinguishes the tone, manner or spirit in which an utterance is made and received; in reporting the key we often use adverbs like "solemnly," "graciously," or "humorously" to indicate our perception. *Instrumentalities* refers both to the channel of transmission and to the code. The channel distinguishes between speech and writing, and also between media, for example telephone and face-to-face conversations. *Code* refers both to language in the sense of Chinese rather than English, and to lower levels of the same division by sub-code, dialect, or variety for example American English, Australian English, BBC English. (It needs to be noted that encrypting messages to preserve secrets relies on "ciphers" and not "codes," this is an example of an unfortunate decision against everyday usage.) By *norms of interaction* Hymes intends those specific rules that we must follow if a conversation is to take place, rules like speaking with appropriate volume and not interrupting. (As far as I can see, he does not mean norms of interpretation in the sense of being able to decode the significance of an utterance in terms of the Gricean implicatures of chapter 8.6). *Genre* classifies the type of speech act as a prayer, a lecture, or a sales talk, for example.

This scheme does not appear to have been elaborated, modified, or checked since it was first proposed as a framework for sociolinguistic work. However, even in this original form, it suffices to illustrate the extent of the problems facing the person wishing to learn to use a language: knowing what units and patterns are appropriate to convey which meanings involves a correct knowledge of how to handle this whole range of variables as well as being able to string together the units using the correct grammatical rules of combination, and having the phonological or graphical skills to realize both.

2.4   Implications for the Study of Language in Communiciation

The implications of the contents of the last few pages are both reassuring and frightening for the further pursuit of the study of the relationships between language and social behavior from a social psychological perspective. They are re-assuring because so much of the detailed knowledge needed for progress is already to hand; it is already within our experience as speaking and writing human beings surviving in our societies. We have to reflect upon the activities of ourselves and others to render this potential knowledge conscious – and then check it empirically and systematically to see if it is valid. (Note that this process is not one of introspection, and neither is it one of intuition; it is one of thinking about what we can remember). When we combine the products of these activities with our current observations, we can begin to use our imaginations to generate hypotheses about what is going on, and then use further observations to probe our interpretations of results. We can begin to organize the ideas developed, and to create a meta-language (a terminology to talk about language) to describe and explain the fruits of these activities. Being able to operate the system successfully is not the same as knowing how to talk sensibly about language and how we use it. It is this latter I have to try to achieve here. Medicine did not stop its enquiries when it discovered that the body already had a *tacit knowledge* of digestion, respiration, sensory motor coordination and the million other processes involved in the system maintaining itself.

We can also be re-assured, and daunted, by how much has already been accomplished by way of description and explanation within linguistics, psychology, sociology, and anthropology. Linguistics has long since mastered many of its problems at both concrete and abstract levels of analysis, as an inspection of the works on the shelves of any university library should reveal. There is a tendency to underestimate what has been accomplished, and it is well to remind ourselves of the knowledge already achieved. For example, the construction of the International Phonetic Alphabet (IPA) marked a very important stage in the study of speech. Its systematization of so many elemental sounds and its facility for transcribing these from audible features to visible marks have provided a framework for describing very many linguistically significant sounds in very many languages. Some languages employ features outside the range covered, only the simplest sounds are included, prosodic features of critical significance are not incorporated, and some linguists believe that the *phone* and the *phoneme* will not survive indefinitely as useful concepts. Notwithstanding these points, the IPA can be used to capture a very large amount of variation between and within the several thousand languages spoken by human beings. Any replacement for it and its underlying concepts will have to add to as well as include its achievements. The phonetics of speech and hearing are well-developed, and descriptions of the place and manner of articulation of speech sounds, the processes of speech perception, and the systems used to encode and decode sounds are well documented (see Gimson, 1994).

Consider too the number and size of dictionaries that have been accumulated and published for language and dialects of languages! It is a salutary experience to reflect upon the labor involved in compiling and collating the knowledge enshrined in such tomes as the full *Oxford English Dictionary*.

The state of knowledge about grammar is not nearly as parlous as pessimists would have us believe. While it is true that contemporary linguists are currently in a state of conflict about exactly what theories of grammar should be achieving and how they should set about the task, such debates do not negate the value of past work, and they are usually seen as necessary aspects of progress. An examination of Jespersen's (1922) much maligned "traditional grammar" will begin to show just how much of a constructive nature could be said about English even in the dark ages; Quirk et al. (1985) much more so.

Two oppositions pinpoint much of the current squabbling, the first bearing some relation to the already mentioned opposition between language as system and language as resource; structuralism versus functionalism; descriptive versus generative grammars. The approaches of Bloomfield (1935) and Chomsky (1957, 1965) both subordinated function to structure.

Seeing that language is a construction of the human species, it would be strange if function were not prior to structure. Any piece of technology is created, survives, and develops because of the functions it can be made to serve. But as well as providing affordances, the structure of an instrument sets limits to what is and what might be done with it, and similarly the structure of language defines one set of parameters limiting its use. This being so, it is difficult to see how anyone could adopt anything other than a functional/structural (or a structural /functional) approach if they are interested in how language works as it is used by people. To study structure without paying attention to function is as absurd as to study function without paying attention to structure. What is important is to study the articulation of the two, a view propounded in Prague in the 1930s and probably due to be heard again soon (see Vachek, 1966).

The generative versus descriptive controversy within grammar is likewise a false opposition. Again it is not a matter of "either . . . or," but "both . . . and." If the assertion of either emphasis is used as grounds for the denigration of the study of the other, dogmatism is triumphing over rationality. Any generative grammar must be able to refer to the categories upon which the generative rules operate: it therefore presupposes the existence of a good description. A descriptive grammar that took no account of how sentences can be or are constructed from their constituents would be losing one critical basis against which the sense of its categories might be justified. If one wishes to understand the human body, it is necessary to study both anatomy and physiology; parts without processes is as absurd as processes without parts. Language involves processes as well as parts. The developments of the TG type of grammar (Ouhalla, 1994) is complementary to and is complemented by the descriptive kinds of analysis prosecuted by Fries (1952).

It has already been suggested that linguistics has not advanced strongly in semantics and pragmatics. While we, the users, have little difficulty in handling the specifics and the particulars of both, Quillian (1966) found that writing out the semantic network of even a small number of words involved hundreds of thousands of entries. One source of complication is theoretically that any word derives its meaning as a contrast with all other words in the system; hence its meaning is describable in terms of its similarity to and difference from all the other words in the language. If one takes a common word like "man" or "get" and begins to write out what one knows about its meanings in terms of the rules governing its proper use, pages fill up with surprising rapidity. Perhaps it is because we do not indulge in such activities that we underestimate both our knowledge and that of others.

Pragmatics too is frightening because of the very large amount of knowledge involved. Reference has already been made to Stanislavsky's alleged demands for fifty different "Hellos," and of course this can be done, each variant shading and changing the pragmatic significance of this single unit. I once saw a theatrical sketch in which the line "I am the Duke of Buckingham's servant" was declaimed in a succession of re-enactments of a single scene over a period of some ten minutes. The idea had begun to pall before the script had been completed, but the variations were continuing to be different, and could have been sustained for longer. As already claimed, the elimination of the SPEAKING variables and their prosodic realizations from utterances so that one can study "the sentence" is liable to lull the analyst into forgetting that utterances achieve significance only in use. Imagine a study of music that divorced itself from an interest in performances of any kind, so that it could study the composition of pure music!

My suspicion, and it can be no more, is that much of the apparent complication surrounding the study of semantics and pragmatics inheres not in the conceptual difficulty or complexity of the subjects, but rather in the threat of the vast amount of detailed knowledge we already have available to be organized. The writing out of the specifics of large quantities of low-level knowledge as a prelude to theorizing does not have great appeal to academics hoping to catch a grand law almost by accident; Robinson's Law is a consummation devoutly to be desired, far beyond beyond any dust-gathering coding frame. We probably need to examine the significantly different ways of saying "Hello" (different defined by an appropriate panel of listeners) and map the underlying semantic structure. We could do the same for the Duke of Buckingham's servant and examine the differences and overlap between the two. Such work would quickly begin to tell us something about the *keys* of SPEAKING. This leaves social psychologists in the position of having access to a large amount of detailed *knowing that* in addition to the *knowing how*, that for the present we are unable to organize economically. My guess is that when this organizing work begins to get under way, it will be successful only if it adopts a functional/structural approach: the behavior of people using the language must become the anchoring and checking standard for analysis. This approach should meet linguists coming from structural/functional perspectives. This does not deny the value of studying language as an idealized system; it warns that the results of these desirable enterprises must be checked against an empirical reality if the resultant theories are to remain sensible.

Table 2.3 provides a sketch of what has been referred to in chapter 2, with some approximate estimates of the number of distinctive units typically listed for some of the categories. There is no advantage in denying the grandeur and complexity of the system and the infinite etics of its value as a resource. This diagram has not included the written variants of the categories. The structural characteristics probably apply to most of the European family of languages, but how far it would apply to the other 5,000 or so languages extant at present, I cannot say. What is omitted from Table 2.3 is the issue of how to classify and diagnose the communicative functions served by language.

CHAPTER 3

Functions of Language

3.1 Introduction

Any mature account of the functioning of language in communication will relate forms (phonology and grammar) and content (lexis and semantics) of language to functions in experience and behavior. There is nothing odd about starting with a linguistic unit in phonology or lexico–grammar and asking questions about its role both within the language system and beyond it. Post-vocalic /r/ was of interest to Labov (1966); quantitative variations in alternative ways of pronouncing it were correlated with variations in situation of utterance and social categories of speakers – in New York City. As Coulthard (1977) illustrated, the sentence forms (free clause) of declarative, interrogative, and imperative can each serve for making statements, asking questions or issuing commands. Horn (1989) has written a massive text on the single operation of negation – in English. Whole texts can be written on single units at any level. It is feasible to begin with a unit or structure and find out how it functions in talk and writing, but that would be a strange point of departure for a social psychologist. An alternative approach is to begin with functions and ask how units and structure serve these. Whichever point of departure is adopted, any later successful constructive description and explanation will link the two sets of components. How do these units and structure function both in the language system and as a resource for human users?

Historically and appropriately, linguists have begun their enquiries with language, and social psychologists have begun with people. Linguists have always been in danger of focusing on units and structures within the language system to the exclusion of their use. Social psychologists have always been in danger of asking how bits of language behavior fitted into social psychological theories – or ignoring language altogether. The divergences and tensions remain (see chapter 15 for some of the oppositions within social psychology itself).

And I am a victim too, caught as a current saying has it, between a rock and a hard place. One conclusion from chapter 3 will be that utterances are etically multi-functional. In context participants and observers may choose to focus on one or more function to the exclusion of others, but those others will be available. If this is so, then how can much of this text be organized under the headings of *Functions* when it is recognized that any attempts at specifications of units and structures serving these may simultaneously be available for serving other functions as well? At the worst it would be possible to devise a single exchange in which all functions are being served by a pair of utterances. After all Labov and Fanshel (1977) were able to use a single exchange as the basis for a whole text of plausible functional interpretations. The short answer is that the preference for a functional/structural approach is a way of ordering the field from a social psychological perspective and that as a heuristic it may prove to be the most fruitful empirically and theoretically.

With human tools it is always reasonable to ask what were or are they for – at least as a point of departure. Language is a human creation and began its existence as a tool. Its current realizations reflect the inventiveness and activity of our ancestors. They created its possibilities as a vehicle for communication, and in turn they became partial victims of their technological achievements – as we all are, constrained and freed, simultaneously and inevitably. We should then at least feel free to ask functional questions about this tool of language, across the whole range of its phenomena, from the specific, concrete, and particular utterances of individuals on specific, concrete and particular occasions through to "What is language for?." When we begin to try to answer such questions we may decide to drop them, but we would be foolish not to pose them.

And what questions might we ask about a single utterance? Sidestepping the non-verbal components of the act pro tem, and taking on board some (unspecified) taken-for-granted assumptions, some questions that might be posed about a greeting of "Hello Charles" could include the following:

1   What kind of utterance is this? What are its possible functions in human behavior?
2   Given that we decide that in the particular context it is a *greeting*, why was this act performed rather than any other?
3   Why were the phonological realizations of the sounds involved as they were?

Each of these questions is asking about what the linguists call paradigmatic and syntagmatic options. A social psychologist might not use these particular terms and would prefer to ask why this member of the set rather than any other and why this sequence rather than some other sequence, but that is a matter of terminology only. The general intention of the exercise would be to account for the options actually taken up from those that might have been taken up. We can also ask more general questions about the *etic* possibilities.

4   What are the characteristics of the behavioral options of each of the sets from which selections were made? What are the alternatives for: 1 greeting (speech act); 2 Hello, Charles, etc. (lexical choices); 3 intonation (stress, tone, key); rates and types of pausing (paralinguistic features); 4 variants of vowels, consonants and elisions and voice quality (the former might be constructed into superordinate concepts such as *accent*).

5   How and why did the speaker come to learn the characteristics of each of the many systems from which the particular options were selected?

6   What does the speaker believe to be the relations between the forms and content and their pragmatic significance?

7   How much control and of what kind can/does the speaker exercise over his/her "know-how" about greetings? What are the determinants of variation in this control?

The first seven questions are heavily sociolinguistic in primary orientation. Psycholinguistic questions might also be posed.

8   How is the relevant linguistic/sociolinguistic knowledge stored?

9   How does the relevant hard (soft)ware make the selections, and how are these transformed into the utterance emitted?

10   What were/are the internal forms and representations of the learning processes?

All these questions could be posed at the level of the individual differences (differential or personality psychology) and social groups, as well as for members of the human species generally. Assuming the species level of analysis has a measure of validity, we can ask how much of the variation between people is superficial to underlying universals. What variation is attributable to membership of socially-defined categories, including sub-cultures and cultures? Some of the answers to these questions might well feed back into grander questions as to why the relations between forms, meanings and behavioral significance have the characteristics which they exhibit. Why do particular languages afford whatever choices they do permit at particular points in time? By that time however social psychology has been left behind.

Before such questions explode into an infinite array across all possible acts of speech, we had better look to the modes of answer that might be considered acceptable for those questions that impinge most obviously upon the activities of social psychologists, noting whether appeals to function might have a defensible role to play.

Each of the first four would in everyday life frequently find itself being explained via an appeal to function. To label the function would require an appreciation of the context of situation of utterance, including an account of the history and present state of the relations between speaker and listener. A mild loosening of the imagination can quickly generate a host of uncommon contexts in which to locate the remark. It is dangerously misleading to confine contexts to the presumed most frequently occurring, i.e. two speakers of English who are already acquainted and meet at least fairly frequently – the addressee being male. The last time I heard "Hello Charles," it was addressed to a distinctly female hamster. Others have no doubt heard it said to unknown burglars, and even non-existent fellow survivors on a life raft. What precisely is being done with the remark cannot even be guessed at without an appreciation of the context of utterance; quite literally the possibilities are infinite and always will be.

If however we were to conduct a sample survey of naturally occurring instances and checked its reasons for occurring, we would presumably find it commonly used as a greeting and its actual occurrence frequently explained by reference to normative expectations. Within a certain sub-culture and given certain social parameters, it would be customary to offer a greeting either *en passant* or as a prelude to further interaction, and which alternative is selected would be in part or wholly signalled by the embedding non-verbal actions. The utterance of a greeting would serve to signal an absence of abnormality. We could add that from what we know of late-twentieth century American and English middle-class sub-cultures (see chapters 6 and 8) that the use of this particular form is presumptively indicative of a role relationship between the interactants of some degree of solidariness and relatively equal power (or superior power for the speaker in a situation where institutionalized norms do not prescribe titular or other forms of address) (see chapter 8.3 and 8.4). The functions served by the choices are the claiming or the marking of a particular kind of role relation within a specifiable range of settings. The prosodic features in fact may mark nothing out of the ordinary, but they might have indicated surprise, pleasure or other emotional states, either genuinely expressive of the state and disposition of the speaker and/or manipulative of the state/disposition of the listener. The phonological realizations of the sounds might serve the same function, but could also mark the personal and social identity of the speaker, revealing, according to the particular facts of the matter, such features as sex, age, socio-economic status, ethnicity, region of origin and habitat, etc.

For each of the specific or general forms of the first four questions functional explanations would appear to have a major potential role to play; indeed it is difficult to avoid the conclusion that they are essential in all cases and sufficient in themselves for some. We could, as we can always, ask supplementary "why" questions that could lead to causal or purposive explanations. For example, particular emotional states might be treated as causal determinants of the prosodic and paralinguistic character of the utterance. We have already suggested how the use of a particular set of vowel and consonant pronunciations might be integrated into the notion of accent, the use of which might be explained by recourse to a citation of social determinants whose biographical dominance has never been brought into the awareness of the speaker and to that extent never become a matter of apparent choice. On the other hand, the accent used could be a deliberate attempt to masquerade or re-define a social identity.

The successful description of the systems from which the selections are made will be achieved in part by observing and matching forms to functions in their natural range of occurrence. This cannot be done without some initial hypotheses as to which constitute significant variations in forms, and initial guesses about the parameters of context of situation; and it is likely that the anvil of function will be integral to the forging of the linkage between the two. We can begin with putative lists of forms or functions, but how they are in fact associated with experience and behavior will eventually determine which phonologically or logically separate forms have categorical functional significance. We have to involve ourselves in a guess-and-test operation to evaluate the fruits of our inventions and apparent discoveries. Suggested functions will have entered into the inquiries both as heuristically useful guides and eventually as explanatory templates to account for the forms used.

It is of course just as impossible to study function without regard to structure (form and/or content) as it is the reverse; in this sense, functionless structures are as hypothetical as structureless functions. Hopefully "Charles" has enabled us to see that function has a crucial role to play both as a heuristic challenge and as a significant basis of explanation for variations in speech we can observe. How then are functions to be classified?

3.2   A Framework of Functions

The value of any taxonomy is relative not absolute. There is no *the* taxonomy for any universe of discourse. How objects, events, or activities are best classified will relate to the scientific or practical purposes for which the classification is to be used. With plants, classifications systematizing human nutritional properties will not correspond to those for arranging pharmaceutical properties. Each of these will differ, if the focus is shifted from human to other creatures. Classifications locating plants in eco-systems or climatic preferences will differ again. A very wide variety of functional/structural relations can be used as a basis for sorting. The question which has been posed for biological phenomena is whether or not the structural/evolutionary system has some superior status to others. It could be that this is the most useful all-purpose list, the most fruitful default base from which to examine possible re-classifications for specific purposes. That is an empirical question, moderated by some ultimately unprovable judgments as to what is or is not important. Other sciences present the same issues, as do the human sciences, and as do speech functions. The value of any pretentious taxonomy will have to be assessed in the light of the quality of descriptions and explanations that can be associated with it. Unfortunately we have yet to reach a stage of development with social psychology of language in communication where informed debate can be held. Classifications have been made, but few have been subjected to any empirical evaluation, and none have been cross-checked against alternative systems embedded in competing theoretical frameworks.

Halliday posed the problem of classifying functions from an educational and developmental point of view, proposing that:

> We shall try to identify the models of language with which the normal child is endowed by the time he comes to school at the age of five, the assumption being that if the teacher's own "received" conception of language is in some way less rich or less diversified, it will be irrelevant to the educational task. (1969, p. 28)

He then examined six models of language that might be imputed to or inferred from the behavior of a five-year-old child: instrumental, regulatory, interactional, personal, heuristic and imaginative. While this analysis was not subject to empirically-based evaluation, Halliday (1975) subsequently organized his description of the early language development of his son by charting the growth of options within these functions, the above list being supplemented by the informative (representational) function. At the earliest stages Halliday could map forms onto functions, but argued that with the emergence of the boy's initial mastery of the lexico–grammatical system, both functional possibilities and the variety of their formal realizations of functions became so great and diverse that his taxonomy would cease to be valuable for studies of later development.

Wells, Montgomery, and MacLure (1979) reported great difficulty in separating and scoring functions with texts of children of comparable age. Eventually they differentiated seven main functions: control, expressive, representational, social, tutorial, procedural, and egocentric speech for self. Each has potential for finer classification. Control, for example, was sub-divided into twenty seven types, for example want, suggest, threat, promise, refuse, query, intention, etc. Such delicacy set within a framework of analysis that includes mood, categories of surface structure, topic and presupposition, intonation and context, had great potential for checking Halliday's pessimism; the pudding has yet to be cooked however. In this case the scoring manual offered prototypical examples of each, recognized that an utterance can be multi-functional and confronted but did not solve the issue of which perspective to adopt in assigning functions – speaker's intention, hearer's interpretation, or generalized other's judgment (see chapter 1). Coder's best guess in the light of all the evidence available also appears to be the case with Halliday.

Early discourse analysts (Sinclair and Coulthard, 1975) relied on similar criteria. In their analysis of classroom interaction Sinclair and Coulthard isolated twenty two kinds of discourse *acts* (for example marker, starter, directive, nomination, evaluate, conclusion) which were seen as combining to constitute *moves* of framing, focusing, opening, answering and follow up, that in turn combine to form *exchanges*, that make up *transactions*, that make up *lessons*. This hierarchical system also allowed only one function per act, and the names given to acts had a linguistic as opposed to psychological flavour – as befitted the perspective adopted and given that such a level of analysis can be defended. As we have already mentioned, however, function-in-discourse is not function-in-behavior, and social psychologists have to attend to both and the relationships between them.

What then is to be done here? It would be very odd to ignore the contributions of discourse analysts, sociolinguists, and philosophers. Eventually we might hope to see articulation, convertibility, and transposition across disciplines, but it is too early to expect to find such hopes realized as yet. At present it is perhaps most desirable that social psychologists develop classifications that fit their purposes, while being watchful for opportunities for articulation with those of other disciplines.

A comparison of the lists mentioned does have implications for some requirements that taxonomies of functions of language should meet:

1   They should cover all uses of language. That the system should be potentially hierarchical as well as categorical is apparent. How many levels and how fine the sub-categories should be can only emerge in specific contexts. In this text marking is divided into four sub-categories and regulation five, but the boundaries have no peculiar status. In this respect, resultant taxonomies have some similarity with classificatory systems in botany, zoology or chemistry – or even grammar.

2   As an insurance policy against a possible failure to be exhaustive, and because social psychologists would also be interested in them, any classification of functions ought to include paralinguistic and extra-linguistic features of utterances, and non-verbal behavior more generally. That these might also be treated separately is true, but in the early stages of an attempt to be comprehensive it is better to make the frame of reference too wide rather than too narrow.

3   Such categories as are used should be as clearly definable as possible:

i)   For Aristotle, a good definition of a term in a system was one that specified its relationship to *all* other terms in that system with which it might be confused, with especial attention being given to *similarities* and *differences*.

ii)   Verbal definition is essential, but needs to be supplemented by indications of how exemplars of the category are to be reliably recognized when they occur. In principle at least, any category must be capable of operational definition, wherever possible in terms of the linguistic forms unique to or possible within that function. (A weakness of this text is the absence of recordings of examples.) When this cannot be achieved, contextual information relevant to identification should be given. The greater the extent to which these definitions can be linked to concepts already available in linguistics, psychology, and other behavioral sciences, the better.

iii)   Given what is already obvious about language many many units and structures are unlikely to be clearly demarcated from contiguous categories; ambiguity and overlap are likely to be more common than discreteness.

We must recognize that the pursuit of clarification and refinements within the verbal domain alone leads to infinite regression – to appreciate the meaning and significance of concepts and their hypothesized relations requires an assessment of the realities which they are intended to describe and explain.

4   It should additionally be realized that any taxonomy will be inadequate. The inadequacy will stem partly from the nature of language itself, and partly from human behavior. Both have possibilities for change and re-organization within and beyond present imaginings. The inevitable inadequacy also stems from the degree of generality attempted. To have any generality entails missing some contrasts that could be made. For particular and limited objectives, more detailed analyses of the situations under consideration will be required, but it is to be hoped that a general framework can keep investigators sensitive to functions over and above those hopefully contained within their immediate perspective.

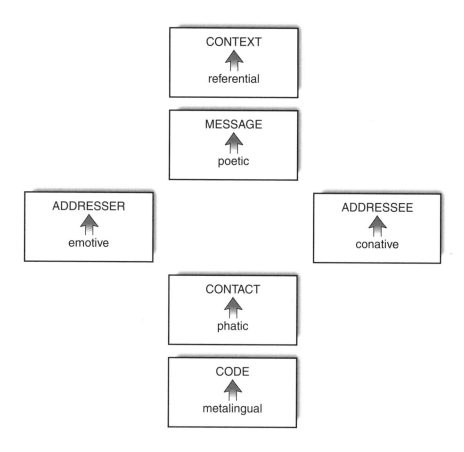

Figure 3.1   Functions of Language Distinguished by Focus of Attention. Capital letters are used to denote the object of focus, lower case for functions. After Jakobson, (1960)

With these desiderata in mind, I am obliged to reject the classifications of functions so far offered and to prefer an elaboration of Jakobson's logically derived taxonomy. In a concluding statement at a symposium, "Style in Language" Jakobson (1960) (see Figure 3.1) offered an artistically presented classification linking functions with different possible prime foci of an utterance. He took six components of the speech event – addresser, addressee, context, message, contact and code – and associated a focus on each of these with functions labelled respectively: emotive (expressional), conative, referential, poetic, phatic, and metalingual. Illustrating each with examples, Jakobson achieved a measure of systematization in that we can see how by shifting the point of interest, we change the sorts of question that we can pose about an utterance. Neat as this was, it has remained relatively undeveloped and incomplete, except with respect to the poetic function, which was after all Jakobson's immediate interest. An elaboration of Jakobson's model is set out in Table 3.1.

A number of categories are taken from taxonomies already referred to, while others have been invented. The scheme is by no means complete, and probably not exhaustive. The list also makes a compromise between feasibility and delicacy. The categories are particularly differentiated for the social aspects of behavior. They are not all at the same level of analysis, for example certain types of social relationship are marked by differential rights to control others. Particular utterances are most likely to be categorized as serving several functions at once, but that is a fact of life that coding systems ignore to their own detriment. This multi-functionality applies to the etics and emics of utterances. While the prime focus of each category is clear (see Table 3.1), *the different bases for evaluation* are, in my view, an important distinctive feature not cited as a testing device in other lists of functions. The links between function and form are variable. The reason has to be that this is in fact true of the relationship between the two aspects.

The use of the word "transparent" carries some risk of being misunderstood. So would "essential" or "primitive." There is no implication that the transparent form is the best form. While it may be true that the transparent forms were historically prior, that is neither relevant nor examinable. Certainly the order of development in children is likely to turn out to involve the same form being used for different functions at a number of points in the child's growth, so that "transparent" cannot be defined by ontogenetic priority. The transparent form could be the one that foreigners learning the language find most easy to understand, but that is not necessary. The claim that is being made is that if we wish to associate function and structure in the speech of a mature speaker, then the 'transparent' linkage is the one that makes more immediately apprehended sense

Table 3.1 Functions and Forms of Language

Functions	F1 Encounter Regulation	F2 Regulation of self (a) states (b) behavior	F3 Regulation of others (a) states (b) behavior	F4 Marking and regulation of social relationships
Everyday name of activity or products	Greeting, Turn-taking, Leave-taking	Talking to oneself	Jokes, jibes, commands, requests, threats	–
Prime focus of verbal act	Participant interaction	Encoder	Decoder	Relationship encoder/ decoder
Transparent linguistic forms: Description	Finite sets of special words, pauses, questions	Abbreviated imperatives?	Forms of humor imperatives, questions, modal verbs, etc. A finite set of semantically associated verbs and phrases	Rights and duties to use of socially prescribed forms of address, and utterance
Transparent linguistic forms: Examples	Hi! Jane! What do you think? Ciao!	Now, one teaspoon of mustard. Pull yourself together.	Joke 42 Now, baldy. . . . Jump! Will you . . .? You must . . .	Sir! Sweetie! Let us pray
Basis of evaluation	Attention contracted? Contact made? Flow maintained? Ending satisfactory?	Is action facilitated by talking? Is affective state affected?	Made to laugh? Humiliated? Obedience obtained? Dissuaded?	Choice and sequence Right for accepted ways of defining roles?

Functions	F5a Expression of states	F5b Marking of encoder states, personality, social identity	F6 Performatives	F7 Representation of non-linguistic world involving: discrimination, organization, storage, and transmission, in spheres of knowledge: 1. logics 2. aesthetics 3. ethics 4. facts: everyday 5. facts: sciences 6. facts: metaphysics
Everyday name of activity or products	Exclamations Swearing	–	Promising, betting etc.	Many: stating, arguing, reporting, remembering, thinking (?). Problem-solving: defining, analyzing, processing, synthesizing, evaluating
Prime focus of verbal act	Encoder	Encoder	Non-verbal accomplishments	Correspondence of verbal act to non-verbal world
Transparent linguistic forms: Description	Vocatives, swear words, terms of endearment	Para- and extralinguistic features, overt statements. Phonology (accent), grammatical, lexical, choices etc.	A finite set of semantically associated verbs used in normatively and legally prescribed forms	Declarative sentence forms

Transparent linguistic forms: Examples	Oh my love! xxxx!	I, I, I think . . . I'm scared 'otel; 'ain't no . . . lavatory	I name this ship the Bubbly Bosun	The cat is on the mat. If A, then B! Doggie will bite! All gone, Daddy
Basis of evaluation	Feel better?	Correct diagnosis made or impression conveyed?	Intended act performed successfully?	True or false with premises of universe of discourse? Is argument valid? Are rules of game followed?

Functions	F7a Instruction	F7b Inquiry	F8 Meta-language functions
Everyday name of activity or products	Teaching	Questioning	Linguistics, psycho-linguistics, sociolinguistics, philosophy, English language courses
Prime focus of verbal act	Mastery by decoder	Acquisition of knowledge for encoder	Language and speech
Transparent linguistic forms: Description	Various	Interrogatives	Various
Transparent linguistic forms: Examples	–	–	–
Basis of evaluation	Did pupil learn?	Are gaps in knowledge filled?	Knowledge of how language works increased?

than any other. For free clauses it would be silly not to link statement to declarative, command to imperative, and question or request to interrogative. There would have been no point in having three different forms if there were not different activities that merited the distinctions. The functions can only be served if there is formal discrimination; that is essential to any useful system. That human beings have elaborated and will continue to elaborate upon and complicate this simplicity is to be expected and has to be accepted.

The direct association of "The cat is on the mat" and the event so represented requires only one level of cultural knowledge to apprehend its meaning and, in context, interpret its pragmatic significance (see chapter 11). A second-order cultural sophistication, which utilizes other forms in order to convey the same facts politely, cleverly or deferentially, must be viewed as derivative rather than essential. The avoidance of rudeness in asking direct questions in the interrogative form in Japan is associated with other questioning forms developing as secondary features. Similarly, the giving and receiving of appropriate insults in a certain section of male Australian society is a mark of acceptance and friendship that the polite middle class migrants can misunderstand as rudeness and hostility respectively – because they take the remarks at face value or literally, and do not realize that being called a "rat-faced Pommie bastard" can signal acceptance in the group.

Cultural values of politeness, irony, or humour, and assertions of status and power, are persistent forces acting for the introduction of derivations from and developments in the language system. A leader of fashion in speech and clothes must break the rules to retain leadership. The form this breaking takes may be accepted as the new rule, which in turn must be broken once universally followed. Successful fashion leaders repeatedly undermine their own success. And so it is with speech. At first, Eliza Doolittle's injection of "bloody" into her utterances horrifies her new aristocratic friends, but once her interjections are defined as the new "smart talk," they can be used freely to punctuate the conversation. The action of these forces is presumably one of the major reasons why the dissociation of form and function in English has achieved the complexity it has. More static, feudal, or caste societies are likely to have preserved simpler and more direct links between form and function. However, the English situation is not one of hopeless complexity, because most of its users still manage to be effective communicators! Reference has already been made to a variety of verbal forms each indicative of a hope for a coat, but these will not be identical in their pragmatic significance. Soskin and John (1963) listed six forms:

1 It's cold today (structone)
2 Lend me your coat (regnone)
3 I'm cold (signone)
4 That looks like a warm coat you have (metrone)
5 Brrh (expressive)
6 I wonder if I brought a coat (excogitative)

The regnone is the unambiguous and "transparent" form in this instance, but one can quickly imagine circumstances where its utterance would be considered rude. It demands a straight "Yes" or "No" in reply. Its utterance does not offer the possibility of the listener pretending not to understand. Face can be lost, offense can be given or taken. Anything other than a quick "Yes, you're welcome" would cause problems. Which indirect form one would employ as a first move in the negotiations is likely to depend on the values of a number of contextual variables. "I'm cold" might be an odd statement to make if one had been sitting by the other person's fireside for the previous hour and a half. To find out what is acceptable and normative, one would have to observe relevant interactions or ask people, and preferably both (see chapter 8).

Eventually it will be necessary to explore the nature and extent of the linkage between functions and structures in detail. The ultimate detailed possibilities for investigation are limitless if one begins to choose combinations of SPEAKING (see chapter 2) variables that are unlikely to occur; some combinations would have no appropriate form and content because the situations contrived, while empirically possible, have not been integrated into the culture. Which proverbs should a South African miner exchange with a Burmese lawyer on the Indian Pacific railway as a means of discussing their attitudes to euthanasia, without offending each other? There are no established rules or conventions for the very unlikely, or even the undesirable. What words are to be used about lavatorial activities among adults? To hear UK nursing staff complain that recent arrivals from overseas do not understand "bowel motions" or "stools," but do know 'disgraceful' words, highlights the dilemmas occasioned by having no affectively neutral words for a number of bodily bits and functions that need to be mentioned in certain medical contexts.

The collection of relevant data and the writing out of functional/structural linkages will involve a natural history that may ultimately rival the labors of the dictionary makers and grammar writers in its scope; immensely tedious in detail, but very exciting at the points of discovering the rules and principles underlying them. It would be doing for pragmatics and semantics (and more), what dictionaries have done for words. It would in fact be doing more, because dictionaries only hint at usage with such appellatives as "colloquial," "familiar," "illiterate," and "vulgar;" currently they do not indicate any more about propriety, fashion, and other factors regulating the significance of particular lexical choices. The dictionary don't say which words is posh and which unposh. If you want to be posh, you will will need to find out whether a mirror should be a glass, and that while dessert may be the kind of fruit you eat with port, it is not a pudding! We are a long way from collecting, collating, and explaining these kinds of information. The eight functions listed in Table 3.1 are more useful than the original six of Jakobson's because they retain his logic, but extend the range in psychologically and socially useful ways.

If my guess is correct, it is rational to secure the behavioral side of our categories: to treat function as prior. And "function" here means function in behavior, not function in language as system – to repeat a point already made. Nouns may function as subjects or objects within the grammatical system, and they may function as names of objects semantically. Nouns have no function in behavior, however. Only utterances can have pragmatic significance. The relative strength on the social side is one reason why this list is to be preferred to others which might have been mentioned. Another is that the functions are identifiable operationally in terms of the criterial *questions for evaluation*. The relevance or otherwise of those questions to utterances indicate which functions the structures were serving. The lack of clarity and precision in the definitions of individual functions and the absence of exhaustive contrastive analyses between functions is in part compensated for by the inclusion of those questions. Any utterance can be placed in one or more category, and in practice always more than one etically and normally more than one emically. For utterances to be pragmatically successful, they may well require appropriate contiguous non-verbal behavior.

The main reason for accepting the classification pro tem relates to the current state of the social psychology of language. If we look to fields within social psychology the foci of interest correspond to the foci in Table 3.1. Studies of encounter regulation, the regulation of self, the regulation of the states and behavior of others, the marking of identity and social relations are core areas of social psychology. Representation and its cognate functions severally form clusters of problems, often construed in terms of communicative efficiency. For example, studies of encounter regulation (chapter 7) do not typically include asking how the identities of the participants are marked, but they could do. This is not to say that cross-functional studies could not be conducted. They could and should, but for the most part, they have not been.

3.3   A List of Functions – with Illustrative Introductory Comments

Function 1: Encounter Regulation (see chapters 5 and 6)

Everyday Names – examples: Greetings, turn-taking, leave-taking
Prime Focus: Participant interaction
   Transparent Linguistic Forms: Description – A finite set of specifiable noises, lexical items, phrases, and clauses constitute the greeting and leave-taking sequences. In face-to-face (FtF) encounters, speech roles are exchanged using non-verbal as well as verbal devices; these latter include direct and indirect questions, pausing, trailing, and unfinished utterances. Examples: Hi! How are you? What do you think? Ciaou!
   Basis of Evaluation: Is contact made? Is the flow of conversation maintained smoothly? Is termination achieved without unnecessary protraction and misunderstanding?

Commentary

At least this activity is one that is now reasonably well understood, and often there are direct associations between structures and function. There is a need to conduct an ethnography and to plot the range of terms, phrases, and devices used by each sub-culture. Which variations in meanings are associated with what choices? Only 35 years ago we were very ill-informed about role exchanging in conversations, but this aspect of behavior is now much better documented. Hints about the subtleties of maintaining 'good' conversation can be found in advisory texts, but these matters remain relatively uninvestigated and unevaluated, and are beyond the scope of this text.

Function 2: Regulation of self (states and behavior) (chapter 7)

   Everyday Names – examples: Talking to oneself, soliloquizing
   Prime Focus: Speaker
   Transparent Linguistic Forms: Description – As yet unknown, but this speech may be shown to consist mainly of abbreviated imperatives with self-reference and other obvious references left implicit. Examples: For tying laces – Left over right and right over left. For pulling oneself together – Right, that's enough of that nonsense.
   Basis of Evaluation: Is the affective state or performance modified by talking? Is the emotion relieved at all?

Commentary

Interestingly enough we have no idea as to the effectiveness of these utterances. There is some evidence that young children are more likely to
speak to themselves when tasks become more difficult, but whether this
speech is regulatory or merely accompanying we do not know.

Function 3: Regulation of Others (states and behavior) (chapter 7)

Everyday Names – examples: Jokes, jibes, commands, requests, threats
Prime Focus: Receiver
Transparent Linguistic Forms: Description – While these forms are heterogeneous it is likely that particular types of attempts to control others
are describable. Requests may have a basic formal description in terms of
closed questions requiring something other than a reply for realization.
The imperative sentence form is the transparent form for commands, although modal verbs can serve similar functions. Words like "unless" and
"if," along with other features, help to define threats.

Humor is broader than jokes, and although the possibilities are limitless
there are set forms for jokes, and there are rules about necessary conditions of "funniness." Examples: Jump! You must . . . Unless you . . . Puns,
sick jokes.

Basis of Evaluation: Smiles evoked? Obedience obtained?

Function 4a: Regulation of Social Relationships (chapter 8)

Everyday Name: No colloquial general names, but many of the relevant
activities have phrasal names, for example Keeping the peace
Prime Focus: Qualities of the Relationship
Transparent Linguistic Forms: Description – Charles was greeted with
an "Hello!" in chapter 3.1.1, and the idea of there being two general dimensions of power and solidariness in relationships was mentioned there.
This set of ideas is developed in chapter 8, but it may be helpful to anticipate the essence of that account here. Brown (1965) isolated these two as
being the basic underlying dimensions of all social relationships. Asymmetry of terms of address and reference implies a difference of power in
the two roles, although symmetry in itself *cannot* be used to infer equality.
"Solidariness" is used to refer to variations in inter-dependence or cohesiveness, a relationship that may depend upon different grounds in different cultures: kinship, friendship, intimacy, or group membership. Cultures

mark increases in solidariness by changing the speech forms deemed proper within conversational exchanges. Particular types of role relationships are likely to have clear markers. These can be used in attempts to regulate as well as to mark, but there are special verbal processes involved in changing and maintaining particular role relationships that emphasize regulation rather than marking. These can have general labels such as "accounting," "antagonizing," and "negotiating," or more specific labels such as "courting." Examples: My excuse is . . . Can't we compromise . . . ? Shall I compare thee to a summer's day?

Basis of Evaluation: Are excuses and justifications accepted and relationships restored? Is agreement reached? Is a partnership secured?

Function 4b: *Marking of Social Relationships* (chapter 8)

Everyday Name – n/a
Prime Focus: Relationship between emitter and receiver
Transparent Linguistic Forms: Description – The obligation or right to use specified forms in certain role relationships may require a speaker to shift language or sociolect. Terms of address and reference are one sign of the nature of the role relationship, but they are only one small feature of what are normally complicated but well-defined systems. Reference has been made to changes in use being attempts to regulate relationships (Function 4a). Examples: Yes, Sir! Daddy. Sweetie! Let us pray.

Basis of Evaluation: Are the choices and sequences appropriate for the roles?

Commentary

The speech appropriate to role relationships of various kinds may be written formally into books of protocol and etiquette. It may rest upon conventions transmitted by word of mouth and observation.

Function 5a: *Expression of States* (chapter 9)

Everyday Name – examples: involuntary exclaiming or swearing
Prime Focus: Speaker
Transparent Linguistic Forms: Description – expressive vocatives such as terms of endearment and swear words. Examples: Darling! xxxx!

Basis of Evaluation: By definition pure expression has no function beyond itself.

Function 5b: Marking Characteristics of Emitter (Emotional State: Personality: Social Identity) and Setting (chapter 10)

Everyday Name – n/a

Prime Focus: Emitter

Transparent Linguistic Forms: Description – The vocal features that are most commonly alleged to mark emotional states are aspects of voice quality, paralinguistic, and extralinguistic features, but there can be overt statements about feelings. The marking of personality has not been studied extensively, but *what* is said is likely to be informative as well as *how* it is said. Social identity is also marked by voice quality, but more particularly by phonological, grammatical, lexical, semantic and pragmatic features. Examples: I, I, I, think . . . I'm scared. 'otel; lavatory; pudding.

Basis of Evaluation: From the receiver's point of view the question is one of correct identification. Are the inferences valid? From the speaker's point of view, the problem is one of conveying the intended impression or leaking an unwanted one.

Function 6:   Performative Utterances

Everyday Name – examples: Bet, promise, reply

Prime Focus: A non-verbal achievement

Transparent Linguistic Forms: Description – Austin (1962) provided a list of varieties and examples of verbs in English which *do* something by saying. Searle (1975) refined and tidied Austin's analysis. Acts such as promising, apologizing, naming ships, or baptizing children are examples of performative speech acts. The use of the appropriate verb is not normally sufficient in and of itself to guarantee that the act has been accomplished. Particular norms, rules, and forms will prescribe which other linguistic and non-verbal features must be present or absent for the putative act to be successful. Fingers crossed behind one's back will not save a slow payer from a bookmaker's wrath. On the other hand, not anyone can call together twelve just persons and true to pronounce someone guilty – due process of law is a necessary condition of verdicts and sentences having legal force.

Basis of Evaluation: Has the act that has apparently been performed actually been performed? Is the bet or promise binding? Is the contract valid? Were the contextual prerequisites in place?

Commentary

Although performatives are a significant feature of living, they are not discussed further in this volume. Whether the performative function merits a category of its own is debatable. They are separated because of their unique causal properties; they are directly effective in a way which no other wordings are. Orders can be disobeyed, requests ignored. The agency of a listener is not overcome by mere words. It may be a case of shoot or be shot, but that is a choice. A promise is a promise. "I promise you I will come tomorrow" commits S (the speaker) to coming. To be successful, such an utterance does not have to use the first person, the "you" does not have to be explicit, and the active indicative present is not obligatory. However, all such performatives can be re-structured to that form.

Of Austin's five classes of performative, only three survive Searle's (1975) re-appraisal:

(i)   *Commissives* are acts whose point is to commit S to some future course of action. The direction of fit is world to words, and the sincerity condition is intention (for example promise, covenant, contract, guarantee, swear, warning).

(ii) *Expressives* register the psychological state specified in the sincerity condition (for example apologize, congratulate, thank). There is no direction of fit; their statement is the act.

(iii) *Declarations* by properly constituted persons in properly constituted circumstances bring about the correspondence between the words and the wording (for example declaring war, resigning, appointing, marrying, naming); the utterance brings about the match between words and world, and sincerity issues do not arise.

The total set of these verbs is not large, but they are both informally and institutionally important. Guilty in law gives the judiciary the right to punish offenders. Lying in court after swearing to tell the truth can attract a charge of perjury. Contracts and guarantees likewise have the force of law behind them. Pardons granted by authorized persons are pardons. Such matters may not arise as issues for the everyday lives of many people, but they constitute the structural core of the social structure of their societies.

Function 7:   Representation (chapters 11, 12, and 13)

Everyday Name – examples: Statements, arguments, reports, memories, ideas, problem-solving, analysis, synthesis.

Prime Focus: Correspondence between verbal product and non-verbal world.

Transparent Linguistic Forms: Description – Declarative sentences – arguments, theories, descriptions, explanations, narratives, etc. Examples: The cat is on the mat. All gone, daddy.

Basis of Evaluation: Are statements true or false, within the appropriate premises of the relevant universe of discourse? Are arguments consistent?

Commentary

In the past, representation of absent events has occasionally been held to be *the* function of language, and certainly one can still find books where other functions are totally ignored. In fact there are still no estimates of the extent to which this function invades the everyday lives of everyday people. It does, however, occupy a prominent role in formal and informal education. This use of language is the foundation of all verbally mediated aspects of the "knowing that" integral to mathematics, languages, literature, fine arts, history, physical sciences, biological sciences, human sciences, and technology. Much of this knowledge is stored in verbal form outside people's heads, on tapes, in books, and in other manuscripts. Much is retrievable in verbal form from inside people's heads. It is communicated with a reliance on verbal form. It is extended and refined through a use of language. It is isolated by Searle (1975) as one of his set of speech acts. As he points out, it is the condition of the world which is meant to determine the words used; the evidence about the state of the world is the standard against which *representatives* are evaluated. His analysis notes that it is expected that S sincerely believes what he or she says, but that they can be in error.

Both instruction (F7a) and enquiry (F7b) are associated with representation, and all three may involve communication with the self as well as communication with others. Imaginative dialogue with one's self may well be an important means of helping to resolve mental conflicts experienced and hence a way of increasing knowledge on the basis of what one already has. Mathematics is nothing but the products of logical deductions made from sets of axioms of various kinds.

Skill with this function can have consequences for intellectual development that increased knowledge and skill in other functions would not. For example, learning the speech appropriate to more roles and how to use it extends the number of roles under control, and learning the characteristics of geographical dialects increases the number of correct identifications that can be made. In neither case is there a change in the *quality* of the knowledge. If theorists such as Bruner, Olver and Greenfield (1966) are correct, confrontations expressed in verbally formulated contradictions are necessary but not sufficient conditions for the development of fundamental changes in the organization and nature of knowledge. There are grounds for according this function a special significance in the study of language and behavior (see chapter 11).

Function 7a: Instruction (chapter 11)

Everyday Name: Teaching
Prime Focus: Mastery of knowledge and skills
Transparent Linguistic Forms: Description – While the units and structures will exhibit considerable variety, a time may come when we are able to specify some features commonly present in such discourse. Certainly scripts for instructional purposes have particular specifiable characteristics for direct and indirect teaching.
Basis of Evaluation: Did the verbal means employed facilitate the learning intended?

Function 7b: Inquiry (chapter 11)

Everyday Name: Questioning
Prime Focus: Acquisition of knowledge by poser
Transparent Linguistic Forms: Description – Interrogatives. Examples: What is he on about?
Basis of Evaluation: Do the interrogatives serve to fill the appropriate gaps in the knowledge of the asker?

Function 8:   Meta-language Functions (chapter 11)

Everyday Name: Linguistics, psycholinguistics, sociolinguistics, philosophy, language courses
Prime Focus: Language and speech
Transparent Linguistic Forms: – None.
Basis of Evaluation: Do statements made reflect what language and speech are and how they work?

⌐ 3.4 Commentary

While the functions listed will form the initial basis for structuring the remaining chapters, two possibly obfuscating topics need to be added, along with a mention of one much-to-be-regretted omission. Questions about functions 1 to 8 can be asked about individual utterances and exchanges, but many events will be at grander levels, for example genre. It could be silly to ask about the primary function of a conversation, or an evening of reading and to expect and answer highlighting one of the eight. Reading a chemistry text might be satisfying curiosity (F7a), and listening to a radio programme might be aimed at having a laugh (F2) but either could be serving more general functions.

In addition to the seven functions which will be treated further, it is perhaps worth noting that in twenty-first-century Britain there are at least three very general reasons for verbal behavior which appear to be operative: phatic communion, escapism and avoidance, and conformity to cultural norms.

Phatic communion

Malinowski (1949) suggested that in societies he was studying, people would sit around and talk in a manner that suggested to him the idea that the effect was one of, "Here we are together, sitting around, having a chat. Isn't it nice?" An amiable ambience of friends and/or kin relaxing, punctuated by occasional remarks. In England this would be most stereotypically represented by small numbers of regular male customers gathering in a village pub of an evening. The conversation might be desultory and slow moving, with a topic bias of grumbling about the government, especially in relationship to countryside matters. Ingroup solidarity would be registered occasionally. Families and friends likewise, especially on festive occasions. In Greece and Italy the café substitutes for the English pub. Whether such personal observations are more than stereotypical has yet to be investigated. These activities might be viewed as reciprocating regulation of states of others, but separation into such components detracts from the whole.

Escapism and avoidance

Speaking, listening, writing, and reading can also help us to escape from the undesirable, the unfaceable, the insoluble, and the unsolved. Traditional belief would have it that "escapist" watching or reading normally involves "poor quality" materials, but there is no reason why apparently "high quality" treatises or *conversazione* might not serve the same function. The tradition may be a rumor maintained by an elite to justify its own indulgences!

The issue can be complicated by noting that there is a distinction to be made between a chronic commitment to escaping as a salvation from facing up to what has to be confronted eventually and the occasional reading of a novel at the weekend after a particularly tough week at the factory. Such materials can enable the mind to be cleared. They can be relaxing – they can be indirectly regulating the states and behavior of self (F2). Further, excursions into fantasy may lead to the arrival of solutions to problems; this may be particularly common where problems are intellectual puzzles of some kind, and the fantasy material facilitates some lateral thinking.

Such a dustbin category may be empirically useful for referring much of the behavior of people in urbanized industrialized and post-industrial societies. Where engagement with speech and writing are providing either enough stimulation to keep one on a bridge between boredom and facing up to problems or as a releaser and re-vitalizer, its characteristics are likely to be relatively unpredictable. One might expect utterances serving this function to contain a high incidence of well-rehearsed phrases of a ritualistic kind, but these can also occur in other contexts for other reasons. One might expect books read generally to be "light," romantic or amusing, but this might conflict with the norms of what is and is not allowed for the persons concerned.

Since the actual content and form may be impossible to predict and almost anything might be serving this function, this means that any inferences from structure to function will only be very weak. Furthermore, structures more typically associated with other functions may be serving this function and thereby reduce the strength of inferences elsewhere in the system.

Unfortunately, the preferred methodologies of the human sciences in use at present do not lead to descriptions of how people actually spend their days, so that we do not know who exploits language to these ends, how often and in what ways. All we can do for the moment is to note that it happens. This kind of activity may take on the appearance of the phatic communion just referred to.

Conformity to norms

There are also times to speak and times to keep silent. When speaking, the volume must be neither too low nor too high for the occasion. When listening the eyes should perhaps observe but not stare at the speaker. It is unusual to read during church sermons. It is unusual to write letters at strike meetings. Our sub-cultures and cultures have conventions about the occasions when verbal behavior is inappropriate and when it is required. Newspapers seldom contain blank columns because nothing newsworthy was available to print. Radio stations receive phone calls if transmission is not continuous. Students hand in pieces of prose that look like essays, but where the truth value of the statements made may have been accorded a lower priority than the institutional imperative to write so many words by a deadline. Lecturers have to keep lecturing. Norms exert demands that require the appearance if not the substance of certain kinds of speech and writing.

As with verbal behavior that achieves escape from reality, this use of language will not be confined to the use of particular units or structures. Once settings and participants are given specifications however, the range of permissible forms and contents will be circumscribed, but not too prescriptively. One of the difficulties newcomers to groups and societies experience is that of finding out what they have to say or should not say in order to be acceptable and not to give offense. Joining groups often involves informal as well as formal induction and passing testing devices that require appropriate verbal behavior. Groups can use failures of members to conform as a basis of exclusion, and conformity as the price of membership.

Both avoidance of dispreferred activities and conformity to norms are reasons for listening and talking, reading and writing that may render questions about the constituent details relevant only to those who seek unconscious determinants for all behavior. They are mentioned only to illustrate the point that one of the weaknesses of the classification offered here is that, although it may be relatively easy to organize and locate subordinate sets of units and structures from Table 2.3 to insert in Table 3.1, the superordinate realms are being left unspecified.

Writing

More embarrassing personally is the neglect of writing. Shortage of permitted space alone dictates this. There is much less research on writing than there is on speech, but the omission is to be regretted. The assertion that there is much more speech around than writing carries no implication that there should be more research into it. The assertion that speech is historically and developmentally prior to writing, and that therefore writing is parasitic on speech carries no entailments about the value of research into writing. The assertion that speech is natural and writing is not is both irrelevant and misleading.

All of the functions mentioned for speech have counterparts for writing and merit attention. The relative advantages and disadvantages of speech or writing have clear relevance to the psychology of influence, as evidenced in written agreements and contracts. Most dramatic and of greatest import are the arguments that the development of literacy enabled our species to transform its technological and cultural possibilities. Among others, Jaynes (1976) has argued that the literacy of the elites of Ancient Greek cities was necessary for the explosion of knowledge and ideas that were generated then and that a parallel transformation was initiated in Western Europe by the Renaissance and diffused following the invention of printing. Of the few psychologists interested in the psychology of literacy, Olson et al. (1985) have generated a range of ideas about the added power of literacy.

Even before the ICT revolution with its immediate and infinite access to those who have the facility, people with appropriate library tickets in the UK might have direct access to 50,000 books and indirect access to 500,000. We can engage in dialogue with Plato and Aristotle, Shakespeare and Thomas Aquinas, Newton and Darwin. We could note the differences between the psychology of early heroes such as the illiterate Achilles and later ones such as the too-literate Hamlet, and perhaps consider which higher cerebral functions depend on literacy. To proceed beyond reflection to experimentation may risk accusations of potential political incorrectness, but eventually such work will have to be done. As was noted earlier in this chapter, whilst the achievements of the human species are realized in the artefacts around us, the knowing-that underpinning these lies in the texts of libraries and museums. Written records enabled the species to reduce the limitations imposed by distance and time, and they enabled individuals to transcend their orally limited environments.

Although this is not the place to expand on the theme that the exploitation of writing has enabled human beings to re-organize and transform their mental capacities, it is clear that such a case can be made out. If that case is eventually made out and sustained, then there ought to be outcries and outrage at the implications for the status of illiterate people. If societies are to be as inclusive as possible for their members as their rhetoric asserts, then effortless competence with reading and writing are necessary conditions for such participation in the twenty-first-century. As with studies of writing, the analysis of relevant views extends beyond the current frame of reference.

Elsewhere (Robinson, 1978, 2001b and in chapter 12 here), I have tried to argue that rationing literacy has been one of the weapons utilized by elites to enhance or maintain their power, wealth and status. From Ancient China and Egypt forward to the present day this has been true of monarchies and dictatorships, along with priesthoods and aristocracies. In the quasi-democracies of today, the least literate of the lower social classes suffer the additional indignity of being blamed for not taking advantage of school systems that are structured to cause them to spend some 15,000 hours during which so many of them can be reminded repeatedly how "backward" they are relative to their age group peers. If the functional illiteracy (and innumeracy?) rates of the UK and USA are between 15 and 20 percent, how is it that the Japanese have achieved almost virtually zero illiteracy with their educational system? The last great opportunities to reduce illiteracy rates in the UK and USA in the 1960s were sabotaged by "liberal progressive" governments in both countries, aided in part by the activities of academics (Robinson, 2001b).

In the interests of brevity, initials will be used in the main text with S standing for speaker and L for listener, and it is left to the reader to consider when SW (speaker or writer) or LR (listener or reader) would be more appropriate. Such analyses extend beyond the current remit. Here the concern is with more general issues than socially-based differences in communicative effectiveness overall.

However, given what has been implied about non-verbal communication, it would be improper and foolhardy not to locate verbal communication within communication that includes the non-verbal, and it would be unwise not to begin with non-verbal communication in non-human animals.

CHAPTER

4

Non-Verbal Communication (NVC) in Non-Human Creatures

4.1   Introduction

It may be possible to contrive examples of language-based communication among human beings that are encodable, transmissible, and decodable independently of non-verbal information, but this is certainly not the case for most relevant speech activities. In these, the non-verbal components are very often essential for interpreting the pragmatic significance – and sometimes the semantics of the verbal acts – in both face-to-face and technologically mediated communication. Hence, they need to be considered before we plunge into descriptions and explanations of the roles of language in communication.

Furthermore, whatever the current state of play in the definitional arguments about whether the concept of "language" should be extended to endow bonobos or chimpanzees with the capacity to use it, animals a long way down any evolutionary chains engage in non-verbal communication (NVC). This means that successful identification of the functions served by NVC in animals gives some indication of what can be achieved without language, and the identification of the units and structures involved may aid and complement investigations of human NVC. This will apply particularly to questions about biology versus culture, and it will suggest limits to what studies of language can fail to reveal if NVC components are not incorporated into analyses.

Here, there is no need to climb the evolutionary tree of NVC and its branches. Apt illustrations will suffice to show which of the functions of language discussed in chapter 3 are *not* realized in the NVC of the non-human animal kingdom, and to take just one more preliminary step back before going forward, it will be useful to set NVC itself in the basic world of living organisms and the two fundamental functions of survival and reproduction. Survival involves more than feeding, but obtaining such food is a necessary condition of survival. This has its linked requirement to avoid becoming the food supply of some other creature. Each of these may be associated with gaining and holding territory, which may also be linked to reproduction. If the reproduction is sexual, then the males and females have to meet and select mates, engage in the mating, and, in many species, bring up their young to self-sufficiency. Where group living occurs, there may be distinctive social positions of hierarchy or specialized functions, and NVC will be needed to recognize and identify these. Among vertebrates, for example, there is great variety in the extent to which species flock or herd together, and this is relevant to their requirements for efficient communication. Likewise, quality of habitat will be relevant: communicating in forests requires different modes from open plains. To anticipate what is to follow, the functions served by NVC in the animal kingdom will be mapped on to the appropriate sub-set of the human language functions set down in chapter 3, but will also include a heavier emphasis on the biological: feeding, fleeing, fighting and mating.

4.2 Avoiding Starvation and Predation

As already noted, vegetarian animals and those at the lower rungs of carnivore ladders have to eat and drink enough without becoming food for someone else. Foraging may be a necessary activity, but it is a dangerous one. The variety of devices for attack and protection is infinitely open-ended, as many people will have seen on the popular and ubiquitous wildlife TV programmes. What many of us have not experienced directly in our urban habitats has been mediated to us by those who make such films and videos. Camouflage is one device that serves to hide both predators and potential victims. Color schemes of stripes and spots hide both large cats hunting and zebras feeding or resting. Stick insects are well named, and some butterflies have leaf-colored and leaf-shaped wings. Plaice and other flatfish change their color as they disappear into the surfaces on or in which they rest. Evolutionary mutations can act within a few generations to convert brown tree trunk resting moths to blacker forms more suited to the sooted chimney stacks of England's nineteenth century industrial revolution. Such forms of camouflage extend throughout the animal kingdom, from the simplest to the most complex species. Just remaining still can be a remarkably successful device for both potential predators and their victims.

A variant of the reverse principle also operates. Show yourself, but appear to be more dangerous or unpalatable than you really are. The so-called warning colors of red and/or yellow combined with black may deceive predators, as can the massive horns of stag beetles and claws of fiddler crabs. (In males the two latter also serve for intra-species fighting in mate selection.) To give just one example of nature's complexity. The Death's Head Hawk Moth lays its eggs in bee nests. Typically, bees sting small invaders to death, but this moth has black and yellow rings and a passable replica of a bee's face on its thorax. The caterpillar is comparably striped, excretes pheromones, and emits squeaks similar to those of a queen bee. Not only are the phases of the moth's life cycle rendered safe from bees and protected by them, but they receive regal treatment as well. Appearances do not have to be static. They can be dynamic. Baring teeth, snarling and barking at threatening attackers serves to protect dogs. Crest reddening, feather raising, hissing, pecking and clawing can help to protect birds.

These characteristics are relevant to individual creatures surviving, and many operate at family or group level. Some ground-nesting birds have displays that can lead would-be predators away from their young. Lapwings run away from their nest, simultaneously issuing a distress call and dragging what looks like an injured wing, which typically makes a speedy recovery when the predator has been distracted sufficiently. Alarm calls are common among birds that flock. In some animal groups, such as meerkats and marmots, there are special sentries posted to watch out and call out when predators threaten. Geese flying in squadrons make repeated calls, which I have inferred serve to locate the group for stragglers, especially in fog and snowstorms. In forests, the howling of wolves and the chattering of monkeys reduce the chances of members of the group getting or remaining lost.

These kinds of stories can be repeated over and over again, throughout the animal kingdom. Some of the displays are genuine warnings to predators, others are not. The displays that are efficient are not random: they signal potential injury to an attacker. Real and apparent weapons threaten; claws, pincers, and teeth. So do actual or exaggerated size, noise and threatening movements. Alarm calls sound like alarm calls to human beings. Such then are some of the signalling (or camouflaging) displays that may facilitate predation and avoidance of predation. Actually being able to flee faster than the predator can chase does not require displays for its effectiveness!

If the diet includes other animals, then these capacities need to be reversed; chasing faster and being an effective killer are necessary. Over and above these realities, as already mentioned, camouflage and other means of remaining undetected prior to our attack will be important. Cat carnivores need to stay down wind of prey if they are not to be smelled. Their colors need to blend with the savannah. Their stalking movements need to be slow and silent enough to be undetectable to their prey.

4.3   Achieving Reproduction

Sexual reproduction requires a male and a female to mate. It is not uncommon in the animal kingdom for males to propose and females to dispose. Hence, many species have flamboyant males who display exotic colors or magnificent appendages or sing splendid songs to entice females. Magnificence in itself may not be useful beyond its capacity to attract, and more homely considerations may be relevant. For some fish and reptiles and for many birds and mammals, the male needs to have control over sufficient territory and build a suitable home for offspring. Male birds of paradise and weaverbirds create elaborate nests for would-be partners to inspect and evaluate. Male robins and seals set out defended boundaries to their territory for females to enter, mate, and breed. Male sticklebacks do both.

4.3.1   Mateship

Human beings occasionally combine comments about how civilized they are with the observation that they are great killers of their conspecifics, an uncommon feature of non-human behavior. It does occur between individuals or groups that mark out territory and within groups to mark status, for example pack hunters such as wolves. Among some seals males may mark out their territory, whilst females in a harem establish their status. Many birds are territorial when nesting, even those that crowd into enormous colonies on rocky cliffs or islands.

However when disputes have been resolved and the boundaries or statuses negotiated, ingroup members display greeting rituals of mutual recognition that mark them off from outsiders. Within mating pairs of sea birds such as kittiwakes and guillemonts, head bobbing and beak clicking result in cooperative rather than aggressive behavior. Lions returning to prides rub heads. Some of these male/female relationships extend well beyond a single mating. Some extend until the male is displaced by a "fitter" successor, others last a life-time. When reproduction is associated with relationships extended beyond the sexual act there are likely to be non-verbal ways in which the bonding is secured.

⌐ 4.4   Criteria of Competitive Advantage

At this stage it can be noted that for both survival and reproduction the marking criteria divide into two rough categories with a fuzzy border between them: The functional and the symbolic – and the mixed. Being stronger and faster is clearly advantageous for foraging and fighting, and both can be similarly beneficial to the chances of offspring surviving to maturity. Strength may well be correlated with size generally, and with the power of attack weaponry particularly. In such cases size is iconic in that its connection with substantive power is indexical rather than conventional or arbitrary. In contrast, bright colors and simulations of weaponry are not. In so far as they serve as signals to other members of the species then they may be "functional," but there may be no direct linkages to pragmatically beneficial characteristics. Too much splendour in the tail of the male peacock can be a handicap in terms of survival, and being fortunate enough to find some old bits of plastic may impress a female bird of paradise, but is otherwise an irrelevant happenstance.

⌐ 4.5   Animal NVC in Relation to Functions of Language

The biological imperatives of efficient survival and reproduction clearly offer a fundamental frame of reference for thinking about NVC in animals, which in turn serve to mark power and solidariness, but if the level of analysis is shifted to the list of language functions drawn up in chapter 3, how many of these can be seen to have equivalents in the non-human animal kingdom? For most of the following, two illustrations will be employed, one from non-primates and one from chimpanzees. Chadwick-Jones (1998) offers a recent review of the latter.

F1: Encounter regulation

Many mammals and birds use setting, posture, gestures, gaze, touch, and smell to negotiate the kind of encounter that may emerge from an initial mutual attention. Will this encounter lead to a contest for territory or dominance? Will it lead to mating? Smith (1977) describes in detail how various movements and calls of birds reduce the initial uncertainties towards a "negotiated" specific type of interaction. Van Lawick-Goodall (1971) provides similar analyses for chimpanzees. Specification will determine likely forms and contexts of the substantive interaction. Many mammals and birds that have developed relationships with each other or are set on developing them exchange greetings. Beak clacking in some seabirds has its complement in head rubbing in lions. Courting Great Crested Grebes have a ritual *pas de deux* worthy of human ballet dancers, a dance first described by Huxley (1930).

F2: Regulation of self

It has not been possible to suggest examples of F2 that do not rely on speech.

F3: Regulation of others

The regulation of others is linked to the type of the social relationships between participants in any interaction. In species where one male services many females, outsider males challenge incumbent supremos. Which male stag is to mate with a herd of does is stereotypically defined through winning a possibly bloody and serious fight, and it is true that fighting is a typical mode of deciding the issue in many species. However, the fighting may be more symbolic than injurious. Any debilitating injuries sustained reduce the survival chances and fitness of both of the contestants, and for many creatures there are clear signs of submission that bring the fight to an end before such injuries are sustained. A male wolf accepting defeat lies on his back and renders himself vulnerable to a deadly biting of his throat. Such a position triggers a cessation of the fight, and the loser does conform to stereotype and "slinks" off with a bowed head and lowered tail. Mate selection rituals in many fishes, amphibians, reptiles, birds, and mammals generally seem to involve males displaying and proposing and females doing the disposing, as already mentioned. What counts as an attractive display varies enormously from species to species, but normally size, speed, agility, brightness, home-building, and fighting prowess are factors predictive of success. Similar indicators of fighting strength are likely to be relevant to be relevant for achieving higher positions in any status hierarchy that a species has. Among hens one can observe what is literally a pecking order, with the engagements to challenge the pecking order resulting in lesser losses of feathers from the upper parts of the body for the victors. Note that commonly the wings are not attacked. Chimpanzees signal opportunities for others to groom them. Mother chimpanzees allow their young to be cuddled as and when the babies make the demands. This can facilitate the reduction of fear.

F4: Regulation and marking of social relationships

Regulation would be concerned particularly with changes to role relationships. Rights to feed first or to mate with females are typically changed by pretentious males attempting to mate with females, for example. Typically such efforts are challenged by any dominant male, symbolically or agonistically, and either the old pattern is maintained or a new one instituted. Lion cubs are likely to be killed by their fathers, if they do not learn quickly from his non-verbals that he feeds first, even though it is usually the lionesses who have made the kill.

Animals other than humans also need to establish, maintain, and terminate role relationships with con-specifics. Particularly those that live in groups are likely to have status hierarchies, mating patterns, and rules for moving, feeding, defence and other activities. Investigators of primates (Van Lawick-Goodall, 1971; Chadwick-Jones 1998) have not found it difficult to identify the cues of distance, orientation, posture, gesture, facial movements, actions, vocalizations each with particular functions, and, with the exception of the significance of particular vocalizations, these map neatly on to their human equivalents.

F5a: Expression of states

Whilst human beings may be the only creatures that cry and laugh, chimpanzees and dogs display what looks like sadness, happiness, anger, and fear, and they do so in ways which human beings can readily identify from their postures, gestures, movements, facial expressions, and vocalizations.

F5b: Marking states and identity

These functions are particular realisations of the general functions already mentioned and refer to the expressions and perception of emotions, motivation, traits, and roles. Those with protracted experience of domestic dogs may indulge in excessive anthropomorphizing, but are unlikely to make mistakes about apparent happiness, sadness, fear, and anger. States of hunger and/or thirst are signalled, as are sexual arousal and moods. Varieties of dogs differ clearly in their traits, as do individuals within a variety. Their predilections for the mutual anal sniffing that can cause their owners repeated embarrassment on walks appear to index status, along with the occasional bristling, barking and biting. More generally it can be said that dogs mark dogginess.

Not surprisingly, human beings are particularly impressed by the efficiency with which sea-bird parents and offspring identify each other in vast colonies or flocks of look-alikes. Unique colors on beaks or harmonic squawks serve such functions. In sheep the bleating so uniform to the undiscriminating human ear helps to ensure mother ewe–lamb pairings. Monkey and ape species differ in the number of facial expressions and vocalizations available to mark status and identity, and the chimpanzee's repertoire is estimated to be approaching twenty, with both specific face and vocalization being paired for almost all states. It has been suggested that their facial arrays are richer than those of human beings.

F6: Performatives: F8: Metalinguistic

By definition neither can be conducted non-verbally, and hence cannot occur non-verbally.

F7:   Representations of non-linguistic world

Any temptation to dismiss the idea of animals achieving representation must itself be dismissed immediately. The classic work of Von Frisch (1967) exposed how the dance of the honey bees returning to the hive could signal to fellow workers the direction, distance, and effort required to reach a food supply and the amount of nectar available in it. Birds and primates have specialized calls for when they locate food supplies, and can vary sound alarms when predators appear, with frequency and intensity signalling immanence. Among meerkats, marmots, and baboons, sentries are posted to keep watch on behalf or their groups.

At this point it may be noted that these representations are not indicating belief, but are action imperatives and are highly specialized, with iconic qualities of importance or urgency typically being represented by increased frequency or intensity of behavior. These last derive presumably from heightened physiological arousal. The messages are reminiscent of Wittgenstein's (1951) games of "Slab here", but being "Food there," "Food here," "Predator in vicinity," their emission being designed to regulate the behavior of others and self, here and now. In short, although it is evident that non-primates can generate information about the location of food and signal danger, these are more properly located under Function 4: Regulation of others. This is also true of some chimpanzee and bonobo interactional activities. What to say about the token combinations achieved by Washoe and Sara (Gardner & Gardner, 1978) or the bonobos of Savage-Rumbaugh and Lewin (1994) is more difficult to decide. Suffice it to note that human NVC shows the same limitations for the representational function.

F7a: Instruction, F7b: Enquiry

These functions of language were separated out in this text because of their special significance in human development and activity; some of us seem to spend our whole lives learning, aided by instruction from ourselves or others. Instruction is most likely to take the form of modelling appropriate behavior, but without direct guidance or manipulation. Parents of birds may model flying and food gathering until their offspring became competent. Chimpanzees may model the use of sticks for termite extraction for the young. For neither function however is it helpful to seek equivalence of communication between non-humans and humans. Non-humans do appear to act tentatively when exploring. They do appear to be curious, and certainly with our nearest ape relatives, their faces look to be registering interest, puzzlement, and irritation. However, typically these are solitary activities and are not inquiries of other con-specifics.

4.6   F1 to F9: Vocalization in the Eastern Phoebe: Ambiguities and their resolution

Ambiguities and their resolution are given a special section because it is easy to forget that for negotiation a sequence of exchanges is necessary, with choice points at which negotiations may lapse or change direction. Analyses of the songs of the Eastern Phoebe (Smith, 1977) exemplify the principle. A brief /tp/, makes available the information that either attack or escape behavior has become anything from just slightly more likely to highly probable, while the bird is likely to be indecisive about either selection (Smith, 1977, p. 61). Ambiguity had three facets: what the bird would do, the probability that it would do it, and that the bird was not decided. The options in terms of the very many possible behaviors in its repertoire are considerably narrowed by the /tp/, but no final selection has been made.

Smith's efforts to pin down the messages of calls involved considerable detective work: when does the call occur (time of year, time of day; in flight, just before flight), where (near nesting site, or tree tops); in the presence of whom (alone, mate, predators); in what activity (foraging, copulating, attacking, escaping)? The category system for coding had to capture the actual displays and their functions, and for the Eastern Phoebe fourteen displays were provisionally associated with nine functions. No single display was linked with one function only. Vocalization signalled either attack or escape, whereas ascending flight displays signalled any one of six. "Seeking to act" as a function was associated with only two displays, whereas indecisive behavior was associated with twelve of the fourteen displays.

It is perhaps risky to argue for too direct a correspondence between human non-verbals or speech acts and bird displays, but one can be struck by at least two common characteristics: One is that specific acts narrow the range of possibilities – the options are reduced; the second is that the options still afford more than one possibility. To pursue the possible similarities and differences further could be most rewarding. Suffice it to assert at this point that we may be making inappropriately specific demands of coding frames and theories if these are designed to link acts and functions in more than disjunctive terms.

What is our underlying model of speaking *Homo sapiens*? At one extreme our idealization may represent the creature as an omnipotent and omniscient agent, fully aware of intentions and able to realize these through the use of appropriate speech and other behavior. At another extreme our model may be of a fully determined victim whose speech is determined by circumstances. Perhaps there are situations where either one of these models is in fact realized, but there are others which are much more messy. Berger and Bradac (1982) have argued for the importance of the reduction of uncertainty in initial encounters between persons finding themselves talking in relatively open situations in our kind of society, and they must be right in the sense that we have acted in some way, and acts have form and content. Negotiating is a narrowing of the options of each participant is a necessary condition of proceeding beyond the first "Hello!", but at the same time as we are narrowing, we may well be keeping possibilities open. Ambiguity of messages is a helpful device both for testing out the feasibility of interaction developing in some directions rather than others and for allowing retrospective reinterpretation if this proves desirable or necessary. This applies particularly in competitive situations.

4.7   Features Common to Animals and Human Beings

In both the biological and psychological literatures, the innate/learned distinction and its biological/cultural variant have been driven into strange, simplistic, wrong-headed oppositions and contrasts. Here it will be asserted quite simply that there must be innate origins which are physically represented for *all* non-human and human experience and behavior. On the other hand, the demonstration of the where and how of the representation of acts such as "promising" in the brain will not, when it is achieved, shed light on the nature and meaning of "promising" or its operation in social contexts. This speech act is an example of a cultural invention and convention. What is innate may or may not be modifiable by experience. If we take the example of bird songs, some are pre-programmed to the extent that the young need never hear an adult to generate its song, for example cuckoos. Others, such as starlings have innate and learned components. Chaffinch populations in Europe exhibit variations by geographical area such that their "accents" can be mapped like isoglosses. The parrots and mynah birds that are trained to speak are obvious examples of modifiability.

If these observations are taken as a background to considerations of similarities and differences between animal and human non-verbal communication, the following generalizations might be made:

1   There are many species-specific formulae which may have functional equivalents in human beings, but whose signalling is based on quite different indicators. Human babies do not use spots on mothers' beaks to identify them. We do not dance to show con-specifics where food is. Vocalizations in bird-song do not have sensible equivalents in humans. Much animal communication relies on sensory discriminations beyond the limits of our unaided capacities, particularly smellings and soundings.

2   In contrast, many of the NV indicators that are operating in the animal world have been easily identified by human students of animal behavior. It has been very fruitful to assume as working hypotheses that certain aspects of distance, body movements, postures, gestures, facial expressions, and some vocalizations are operating like ours, and typically, subsequent observational checkings have supported the hypothesis. This has been particularly true in respect of ape behavior. This is not surprising. If our apish ancestors developed displays for anger and aggression, fear and submission, contentment and excitement, why should the lines of descent to us and apes diverge in respect of such displays? And it will be similar too for those indicators of arousal released in higher intensity or rate of activity. If they are good enough for apes, then they are likely to be good enough for us. For those indicators that display animal/human continuity, we would expect that in our species these would be similarly registered across cultures, emerge in similar forms early in childhood, perhaps even in children whose senses are reduced in some measure, for example in hearing or vision.

3   A variant on the combined surface and deeper similarity relationships for some NVC between us and other animals is to have superficial

differences, but deeper similarities. So, for example, greetings on meeting members of an ingroup are likely to involve mutual exposure combined with attacks which do not eventuate, head rubbing in lions, mutual grooming in chimpanzees, and shaking hands or testicle pulling in human beings. Attempts to join a group will be typically involve tentative and deferential approaches, with submissive postures and gestures, be this among wolves or human teenagers. Superficial structural differences are likely to have deeper functional similarities.

4   That geographically-separated groups of human beings develop different indicators from each other should not be surprising, since this is already widespread in the animal kingdom. It is possible to chart isoglosses for the songs of some birds, the River Rhine serving as one boundary for the songs of the chaffinch. Troops of baboons and chimpanzees have NV identifiers within the group that distinguish them from other groups. Human cultures have amplified the range and number of such distinctions.

4.8   Discussion

Whether readers are more impressed by the similarities or the differences between NVC in animals and human beings is a matter for subjective judgements, if anyone feels the need to make such an evaluation. Why bother? The similarities are clearly considerable. For many of us, what is important is the details and the principles of how the members of many species communicate with each other and with other species, and what they communicate about. Both the similarities and the differences with and between species are fascinating – at least to those of us who enjoy that kind of sense of wonder.

For some of us, there is a special interest in how human beings differ from the rest of the animal kingdom. For others of us, differences and similarities are of equal interest. For those of us with a research interest in this area, we have to be members of the second group, because we need to understand why both the similarities and the differences have come to exist – and to specify how and when they operate to what effect. This text will argue that the development of language as system and resource has extended human prowess beyond our nearest primate relatives, both quantitatively and qualitatively. However, the spirit of that argument is in scientific terms rather than that of ingroup distinctiveness and superiority. Certainly there are both continuities and discontinuities in NVC between human beings and other animals, in particular the higher apes.

CHAPTER

5

Human Non-Verbal Communication

5.1 Introduction

Not every social psychologist would recommend *"Man-watching"* by Morris (1978) as the best introduction to the centrality and diversity of non-verbal features in human communication, but no one else has yet collated a more impressive pictorial array of NVC, and this topic cries out for modes of presentation that correspond to the mode of the feature, with verbal commentaries as supplements. Perhaps too many of the photographs he selects display physical attractiveness and intimate details of beautiful young people for scholars to believe that precedence for publication was assigned to the academic over the commercial, but a counter-argument would quickly observe the ubiquitous concern of modern societies with the same matters. Certainly too, the 70 headings he uses for his sections lack the orderliness preferred in scientific taxonomies, but those he selects make human sense and provide wide coverage of the field. The great strengths are the pictorial representations of the visual and visible-tactile. The vocal and olfactory are necessarily harder to communicate without benefit of auditory and olfactory materials. Advances with multimedia are such now that it is possible to look forward to dynamic as well as static presentations and auditory and olfactory displays to add to the visual in museum or archive collections of NVC. Morris also provides a bibliography covering the extensive literature on NVC topics. Argyle (1988) offers far fewer photos, but much more empirical evidence about the status of cues, and moves more systematically towards synthesizing interpretations.

In this text, NVC is not the primary concern, and as with non-human NVC, coverage and commentary will be no more than illustrative, but the point must be reiterated that it is absurd to consider language on its own in relation to communication. The non-verbals are omnipresent in oral communicative acts. The categorization of non-verbal features adopted will follow the precedent of Argyle (1988), but it will be noted that social psychology has yet to expand its world to encompass the multitude of encounters beyond the Face-to-Face (FtF) interaction of two persons who are usually presumed to be engaged at an interpersonal rather than an intergroup level. Much of the work has been with western student participants. This imposes cultural limitations on the generalizations that can be made, and it also means that most of the variability arising from the very array of social positions in the matrix of power, wealth, and status is missing. The variability across the divisions of labor and leisure relevant to the horizontal and vertical segregations in societies are underestimated. Social stratification in western societies is such that where people live, what they live in, what they wear, and what they do is heavily, if not obscenely, differentiated. Very few people spend significant amounts of time engaging in a variety of lifestyles. Very few readers of this text will have lived in Mayfair or a South African township, or in the shanty towns of Manila or Sao Paolo. Very few will have visited run-down council estates of the larger British cities or the tougher areas of New York or Washington. For different reasons, very few will have spent short seasons on the Cannes–Colorado–Davos–Henley–Ascot circuit or one of its variants. Are any readers carrying around the 1,000 page etiquette rules for NVC that used to reside on the shelves of British diplomats? Encounters across the deeper cleavages in societies are usually intergroup not interpersonal; we meet across these divides only when enacting roles associated with our social positions. Those larger worlds have yet to be charted by social psychologists, and almost no studies of NVC have been conducted among members of those groups which would be expected either to deny access to social psychologists or of those which academics would be fearful of approaching, for example the yakusa. One consequence is that investigations have neglected the factors which define social identities prior to encounters. Here these will be at least mentioned, and the list of features therefore follows.

5.2 Features of NVC

1 Background resources
2 Clothing and adornments
3 Setting and arrangements within setting
4 Space, distance, and contact
5 Posture and movement, including gestures
6 Facial expression

7   Gaze
8   Vocalization
9   Smell

Treatment of each category is limited to noting its existence with a limited number of illustrations and references. In chapter 4 the primary concern was with which functions could be served by NVC in non-human animals. In chapter 5 the matrix is reversed to ask which cues can serve which functions. Where appropriate further mention of particular cues is offered in the language-focused chapters which follow.

5.2.1   Background and Resources

Most people cannot trace their ancestry back to the tenth or eleventh centuries, but some can, and in the UK at least a few still own the land occupied by their ancestors at the beginning of the first millennium. The amount and quality of land and property owned or otherwise controlled are still a major marker of wealth and status in long-established capitalist and feudal societies, although, following the industrial and now commercial revolutions, fortunes made and their material accompaniments may not have been translated yet into commensurate properties. The several-million-dollar-a-year payments now received by chief executives, opera singers, world sports' champions, stars of small and large screens, and high stake criminals have also still to be transmuted into dynastic accoutrements.

It is important to remember that speech markers are no more than symbolic indicators, and that the proximal NVC displayed by those with vast power, wealth, or status are initially a dispensable part of their profiles, given sufficient substantive realities. Bill Gates can wear what he likes, drive what he likes, and speak how he wants. He can afford to be free of many of the norms constraining members of various Establishments. But, once drawn into the network and social activity timetable of the very rich and aristocratic, their contemporary normative frameworks will exact a curtailment of individual freedom, and within limits, that will include what one says, how one says it, and how one conducts oneself non-verbally. In reverse manner, the symbols alone are insufficient grounds for acceptance by a group. Whilst Professor Higgins' views on speech classifying status may be valid, knowing the speech and the NVC will not in themselves enable people to pass as members of social groups, high, medium, or low. Particular life-styles and matching sets of resources are also necessary. Veblen (1912/1925) wrote an insightful portrait of the leisured class that still has echoes in present-day societies. Census data and commentaries on these provide indications of the parameters of differentiation within societies. Argyle (1994) summarized his interpretation of British data.

Background and resources set limits to what can be communicated non-verbally. Whilst rich people do not have to live in castles or drive Porsches, poorer people cannot do either. Addresses and material possessions are clear markers of social identity (F5b), and within the category of the same social identity, markers of personality (F5b). They are likely to regulate the states and behavior of others (F3), at least by affecting the probability of any encounters and interactions taking place. One of the interesting features of complex societies is the ways in which members of social groups do *not* encounter each other, except for specific task-related interactions. The encounters of each of us are likely to be limited to others demographically like ourselves. This is true of age, religion, ethnicity, gender, and social class. In the UK it is not just residential area and jobs that are linked to social class. Leisure activities, for participants or observers, are class-linked. So are shopping and transport. Consumption of food and drink are class-linked in terms of what, when, and where. It is difficult to cite an analogy that captures this idea of members of groups moving around the same country, but for the most part only encountering the members of their own group, except for instrumental transactions. Nettworks of informal encounters are mainly of others of the same or contiguous social classes of origin or destination.

5.2.2 Clothing and Adornments

If one reflects seriously about the topic, the multi-billion dollar industries devoted to these aspects of NVC are quite frightening. It is easy to see how the selection of dress and adornments act as markers of power, wealth, and status. To be trite, one can observe that the leaders of the various institutional pyramids typically appear to be larger than they are. Their crowns or mitres exaggerate their height. Their epaulettes and decorations enlarge their shoulders and chests. Thcy are permitted to carry symbols of their offices which would be classified as dangerous weapons among the ordinary citizenry. As with fur-raising and noise among chimpanzees, the symbols exude dominance and superiority (F4, F5a, F5b). In a more ironic manner that chimpanzees can not exploit, some dictators play a meta-game, at least in public, and dress very plainly, as one of the ordinariest of people.

Below the structured elites, what can be afforded remains a symbol, and this permeates most groupings within societies, each with its own frame of reference. Within each grouping however, clothing is also a marker of individual differences in personality. The same person in six different outfits will encourage the drawing of six different sets of inferences about their personality; clothes are of course a major vehicle of impression management. Gibbons (1969) set out a neat platform of hypotheses about the workings of fashion, that has not been followed through, but then neither has the study of clothing more generally. Argyle (1988) provides a summary, while Kaiser (1985) and Roach and Eicher (1965) offer broader coverage.

5.2.3 Setting and Arrangements within Setting

For anyone who initially discounts the selection of setting as relevant to the conduct of human affairs, the difficulties that countries have in choosing places to negotiate the endings of wars can serve as a warning. The seventeenth century thirty years' war in Europe was to be settled at negotiations in Hanover. After two years of continuing argument amongst the six or so states as to who would stay where, the peace treaty was signed by other delegations elsewhere. The early 1950s war between North and South Korea ceased about 50 years ago, but no peace treaty has been signed in the house especially built half in each of the warring countries borders across Latitude 38N at Panmunjong; an ingenious solution to an inability to agree on a neutral place for discussions. The USA would not issue a visa for Yasser Arafat to address UNO in New York, and so the UN members flew to Geneva for the speech. The beginnings of a resolution of the Palestinian/Jewish conflict appears to have been brokered in Oslo. At a less serious level, it might be asked why football teams find it so much easier to win on their home grounds? The pitches are supposed to be uniform in size and texture, and supporters can travel.

Just as settings are relevant to the feasibility of holding intergroup encounters as well as their probable outcomes, so they are relevant to the interpersonal equivalents. In meetings with potential or actual friends or partners, different settings afford different possibilities and probabilities of the qualities and outcomes of interaction. Cinemas and cricket matches differ. So do sands with sunshine and sangria differ from hot chocolate drinking in cemeteries at the mid-winter solstice. Fitness for purposes, given the understandings of the participants, is what is important in the selection of setting (F2, F3, F4).

Who owns the room? What kind of furniture is to be used? To end the war in Europe in 1945 there were arguments about how many Germans should be present and where they would sit at the Potsdam Conference. It has already been noted that at Panmunjong a building was constructed so that delegates from North Korea and its major ally China could sit in North Korea with the South Korean and the UN/US delegates in South Korea. When the Southern delegation accidentally introduced a slightly taller flag than the Northern on its table one day, a competition developed until both flagpoles touched the ceiling. Then the South backed down, and its flag is still slightly shorter than the northern one. Who sits in the largest and probably most comfortable chair at formal and informal meetings and is on the dais, if one is available? Who sits behind the desk with the gavel and red telephones?

In the 1950s there was considerable interest and research into behavior in small groups and the effects of restricting communication channels on efficiency and satisfaction (see Cartwright & Zander, 1960). Other things being equal, a spoked wheel arrangement was more efficient than a Y which was more efficient than a circle. If the most central person was incompetent however, the order was reversed. For average personal satisfaction, the circle gave more than the wheel, which gave more than the Y. Artificial as these manipulations were, they permitted modelling of restricted communication channels in organizations.

Arrangements of seating affect preferences for conversational purposes and perceived competitive and cooperative dispositions, with cross-cultural variations. Given two people sitting and interacting at a rectangular table, four possibilities were compared: 1. Opposite – along the length; 2. Opposite – across the breadth; 3. side by side along the length; and 4. orthogonal. For conversational purposes, the preferences were 4(44 percent), 2 (38 percent), 3(11.5 percent) and 1(4.5 percent). For co-operative activity, the preferred order was 3, 4, 2, 1 for both American and British participants, but for a competitive activity, the US first preference was 2 (41 percent), but the British was 1 (51.5 percent) (Cook, 1970).

Why then do candle-lit dining tables in restaurants claiming an ambience of intimacy sit couples opposite each other? The hypothesis would have to be that co-operativeness can be taken for granted and eye-contact with prolonged gazing takes precedence – and facilitates interpretation of feedback in reaction to what is said (see Section 5.2.7 on gaze).

5.2.4   Space, Distance, and Contact

The classic work on preferred distances for interaction was done by Hall (1959, 1966), who adopted a cross-cultural perspective. For so-called Anglo-

Saxons standing, there were four zones; 1½–4 feet was preferred for personal dyads, moving to ½–1½ feet for intimate interaction, and distancing to 4–12 feet for social activities and to 12 feet plus for public talks. For personal dyads, Latins preferred a separation of 2 feet, and Arabs less still. Collett (1971) reported that English undergraduates trained to stand close were preferred by Arabs, even though they were clumsy in their efforts to adopt Arab norms. In their 1977 review of studies in the area, Altman and Vinsel concluded with some elaborations to Hall's model. Sitting rather than standing and formality of occasion were each associated with greater distance, as was not liking the other.

Sommer (1969) posed questions about distance in terms of personal space, a concept generalizable to animals as well as people. As is common, people differ as a function of situation, personality, and social group membership, but each person has notional boundaries around them to cross which gives rise to discomfort or more active reactions. Whilst Hall and Altman and Vinsel were focussed on everyday interaction, Sommer's range extended to the territoriality of streets, neighborhoods, and countries.

Here it will need to suffice to note the continuing relevance of differentials of solidariness and power (see chapter 8), which will be moderated by the practical considerations of ease of communication – and its qualities of cooperation versus competition.

Bodily contact is an equally massive topic involving wide-ranging issues of comforting and fighting, courtship and mating, greeting and departing, feeding and playing. What is required, permitted, and taboo varies with situational and social factors. Which bit of Person A is touching which bit of Person B and the different kinds of touch (Jones and Yarborough, 1985) all add to the complexities of the meaning and significance.

5.2.5   Posture and Movements, especially Gestures.

As long ago as 1957, Hewes could record over 1,000 studies of posture, and the photographs of Morris (1978) point to the richness of gestural information. Birdwhistell's (1970) analysis of kinesics is a classic. Mehrabian (1969) provided an early review, Argyle (1988) a more recent one. First, it may be noted that there is cross-cultural variability in the postures deemed appropriate for marking particular states and attitudes. Second, within any culture there will be institutionalized norms for postures to be adopted by persons performing particular offices appropriate to their social positions (for example priests, judges) or activities (for example dressage, pillion riding, standing on trains). Third, respondents asked to judge states, attitudes, and relationships can make reliable judgments on the basis of stick-people, drawings, photos and videos. These judgments are generally valid, even without contextual support. Whilst it is possible to find differences in solidariness and power underlying these variations, the specification can go beyond this into such states as being curious, angry, reflective, or smug.

Gestures have been equally well-explored and defined (Ekman, Sorenson & Friesen, 1969; Kendon, 1981). Data collected by Johnson, Ekman and Friesen (1975) yielded 76 hand-movements whose functions could be described in their own right by respondents. These *emblems* fell into commands and requests (F6), marking own state (F5b), encounter regulation (F1), insults, replies and "unclassified." Sign languages depend heavily on gestures. A second class of gestures were labelled *illustrators* and are coordinated with speech. Often these have iconic or metaphoric correspondence to the content of what is being said for example grand movements for important points. These two do not exhaust the kinds of movements that can be made. People play with their hair, face, and elsewhere. Their movements can be fast or slow, expansive or slight. They can fidget. Just for this last, Mehrabian and Friedman (1986) found that fidgeting correlated with frequency of drinking, eating, and smoking, and having music and television on.

5.2.6   Facial Expression

Given three recent texts with "face" in the title, their contents must be treated as more impressive sources than these few hundred words (Ekman, 1982; Fridlund, 1994; Russell & Fernandez-Dols, 1997). All three concentrate on the links between expressions and states, for the most part emotions rather than motivation. What faces can manage is highly differentiated, and both static and dynamic variants are associated with a range of functions. While the texts pay due attention to its value for expression of states (F5a), marking of emotions (F5b), and marking of social relations (F4), it can be involved in encounter regulation (F1), it has potential for marking both personal and social identity, and is seriously implicated in such activities as deception and either masking or feigning of states.

As elaborated in chapter 9, with psychologists still failing to achieve consensus on a taxonomy of emotions, the distinctions between emotions and other states, and the extent, if any, of universality across cultures, the field has not yet stabilized its frame of reference. That said, at the level of everyday talk psychologists are able to report many studies linking particular expressions to particular states, and have been able to do so for over half a century (Schlosberg, 1954; Woodworth & Schlosberg, 1954). Since human beings rely heavily on vision and since the face is such an informative feature, it is not surprising that it is a major source of reliable and valid information about others, especially in cooperative situations.

5.2.7   Gaze

The saying that "A cat may look at a king" is supposed to derive from times when subjects were not permitted to do so. "Staring out" until the other looks down or away has been a standard children's game, perhaps serving as a precursor to more serious exercises of dominance in adult life (Strongman & Champness, 1968). However, as well as this role, mutual gazing has been an indicator of intimacy between equals. As will be shown in chapter 7, the gaining and losing of eye-contact is an important component in floor-apportionment for speakers. Gaze is not just gaze. Establishing eye-contact is a precursor to being served in restaurants or being given a chance to speak by a committee chair (F1). If made with an adjacent passenger on the London underground, it increases the chances of that stranger correcting false information proffered by a confederate (Sissons, 1971). In FtF, in coordination with the qualities of utterances, increases in the percentage of mutual gaze precede exchanges of speaking turns (Kendon, 1967). Simultaneously, with listening to what is being said L's eyes are scanning S's face for additional information (F7b) (Yarbus, 1967). Whilst Mehrabian (1969) found that interviewees thought an interviewer liked the looked-at more participant more, Thayer (1969) showed that people "stared" at in a library became uneasy (F3), and too many of us may know the risks of evoking "Who do you think you're looking at?" in drinking venues. Some of these results are well-known to survivors of urban life, but some are not. The range of functions performed by eye-contact, including looking away, blinking and pupil-dilation are taken up in their respective function chapters.

5.2.8   Vocalics

Of all the non-verbal features, how things are said is the most integral to the interpretation of any utterance. The individual categories of vocalics are not in dispute, but their grouping and labelling differ across authors. Closest to the verbals in that they are unavoidable are pitch, pitch change, volume, duration, and timbre. The first four have simple correspondences between physical properties and psychological experience, the last is more complicated and refers to the tones through which the other four are realized, for example breathy, creaky, etc. (The linguists' transmodal term of "color" does not convey what is intended as well as samples on a tape recorder.) Along with pauses both filled and unfilled, these features are prime indicators of Hymes' variable of key. They indicate what is presumed to be already shared and what is new (topic versus comment). They can disambiguate the ambiguous and can render the unambiguous ambiguous. Is the intended meaning the transparent one or its opposite? Is the remark sarcastic, ironic, facetious? Is it serious or joking? Is the aggressiveness real or game-playing? One of the most serious omissions in written texts is that of the notations for these features. Just to write the sequence of words so often omits the pragmatic significance, and even the semantic qualities and grammatical structure of utterances. Minds/brains socialised into and attuned to these features do not suffer from any ambiguity if the shooting of the hunters takes place at dawn (see chapters 2 & 3).

Frequently these features are viewed as paralinguistic and contrasted with extra-linguistic features which label can be used to refer to all the other categories from 5.2.1 to 5.2.7 – and especially to noises such as sighs, grunts, screams, and other utterable sounds. Sometimes pauses, stutterings and stammerings are treated as extra-linguistic, sometimes as paralinguistic. These features are neglected both in social psychology of language in communication and in second language learning. Those of us who have been privileged to undergo serious second language learning were taught how to grunt, laugh, and cheer appropriately in foreign. The extra-linguistic vocalics and the paralinguistic features are involved in all but the metalinguistic functions. It may be safe to suggest that they are least important for straightforward exchanges of representational information, but that they are crucial ingredients of successful communication in all the explicitly social functions. How this comes to be so is exemplified in the relevant chapters.

In the past psychologists seemed to be uncertain as to whether to categorize the vocal with the non-verbal or the verbal. Whilst there are grunts, growls, and trills which have no connections with language, much of human vocalization is an integral component of speech. As spelt out in chapter 2, there is a whole range of extra-linguistic and paralinguistic signals associated with the utterance of speech extending into the pronunciation of the phonemes themselves. Fortunately the question of where to draw the line between the non-verbal and verbal ceases to have analytic significance if we focus the enquiry at the finer operational level of classes of features, for example gestures, pitch, phonemics, and treat the binary split as no more than a crude device with some limited value.

5.2.9 Smell

Smell is to be mentioned mainly as a contrast to its value to non-human NVC. Stale sweat, bad breath, and cosmetics are main variables for humans, all relevant to close encounters, and particularly to sexual activities and their associated leisure or otherwise (F3, F4). Each can serve as an involuntary or voluntary marker of emotional states, personality, and/or attitudes to and expectations of another (F5a, F5b). However, compared to the role of smells in much of the rest of the animal kingdom, smell is much diminished in human NVC. As many people experience, the life of the domestic dog appears to revolve heavily around smells as markers of territory, indicators of sexual status, and for wild dogs availability of prey. It can also serve as a defense against predation. Vision, sound, and smell are all significant for dogs. For those who are tempted to view human beings as the apex of all evolutionary ladders, our reduced NVC with olfaction is a corrective. From rats to dogfish, there are many many examples of creatures for whom smell is the primary sense for all activities.

⌐ 5.3 NVC in Relation to Functions of Language

A full summary of the classes of NV factors relevant to communication might implicate every set of factors in every function, but the oversimplified one adopted here still points to the massive value of the non-verbals to communication. A broad distinction might be made between F1 to F6 and F7 and F8, with the non-verbals having more importance for the former and the verbal for the latter.

Is this too strongly contrastive? For F8 verbal communication is both necessary and sufficient. For many written communications, the representational function (F7) is both necessary and sufficient; the truth of any statement is independent of the non-verbals of the authors. The states and identities of the authors of the literary heritage are irrelevant to the use living people can make of the texts. Likewise, the semantic truth–values of oral statements are not contingent upon the non-verbals of S, L, or context. The pragmatics will rely heavily on Hymes' SPEAKING factors. It may also be noted that Sign Language, considered as a special case of a system of gestures, facial expressions, etc., can serve the representational function and that in everyday FtF conversation, the non-verbal features will form an integrative component of communicative acts.

Likewise and more so with inquiry and instruction. Inquiries can be made with raised eyebrows and puzzled looks, but most of the time verbal realizations will be necessary for a precise specification of the gaps in knowledge and belief to be filled. The efficacy of non-verbal and verbal channels for instructional purposes will depend heavily on what is to be learned. Logics can come to rely solely on symbolic interaction, sensori-motor skills cannot, and classical and operant conditioning are functioning before and after any verbal competence is achieved. For F6 both appropriate verbal and non-verbal acts are necessary and sufficient for successful accomplishment.

As was seen in chapter 4, for non-human animals NVC is and has to be sufficient for the exercise of F1 – F6, and each class of factors has been shown to impact on each function. Hearing a recent radio broadcast about the history of Shaw's *Pygmalion* serves as a reminder that it is easy to overestimate the role that command of non-verbal skills plays in the possibility of misleading others. Eliza Doolittle did *not* become a member of the aristocracy or the upper middle class. Acceptance by social categories requires credentials beyond a knowledge of etiquette and a command of appropriate vocalizations and verbalizations. In her case she needed the cash and the connections. Social groups are by definition exclusive and have norms relevant to acceptance as full members. Appropriate vocalizations are only one set of criteria of evaluation, but as will be argued in chapter 9, it is the orchestration of the total presentation that is important for both marking and regulation. The metaphor of an orchestra is a very helpful one in that while synchronized performances differ in quality, listeners are particularly susceptible to the notes of instruments that are out of tune with the rest. It must also be remembered (see chapter 9) that this idea of orchestration does not exhaust the roles of NV features. Especially in the case of vocalizations, the pragmatic significance of utterances can be reversed, lightened, and otherwise changed by changing prosodic features. Sentences in declarative forms can become questions or commands. Sarcasm and irony can both be achieved by prosodic means.

5.4 Organizing NVC

To begin to bring order into the manifold of human NVC it may be helpful to think of the factors in terms of qualities of operation, the degree of discretion available to the displayer, and related to this second, a distinction between self-expression and "attempt to pass as."

5.4.1   Qualities of Operation

Some cues are relatively static and permanent, others dynamic and ephemeral. Some cues are discrete and categorical, others are continuous in variation. Anyone arriving at a meeting will be dressed in clothes that cannot be changed; jeans and wind-jacket cannot be transformed into a dark grey suit. Clothes are discrete and categorical. Seating arrangements are set and categorical, although modifiable subsequently. To stray into language, written contracts and taped-recordings have a degree of permanence (and hence accountability) that unrecorded oral agreements and conversations do not.

The *relatively static, permanent, and discrete features* are appropriately valuable as markers of *relatively stable* identities (F5b) and social relationships (F4). These relationships can be construed in terms of the two dimensions of power and solidariness, or in terms of particular pairings of a biological–social (for example mother–son) or social interpersonal (for example friends) or a social positional nature (for example general–sergeant, doctor–patient).

In contrast, the *dynamic, ephemeral, and continuous* variables offer resources both for signalling *variability* in the salience of certain aspects of a social relationship and for negotiating change in a relationship. Given the situations where Goffman's face-concerns are paramount, then any move towards change is face-threatening. In mate-selection pairings-off, normative in early adulthood, moves towards greater intimacy simultaneously risk rebuff from the other and impose upon the other. Hence the value of the *ambiguities* in reducing spatial distance. Any reduction by X can be reciprocated by Y, accepted by Y, or rejected by Y moving further away. Likewise with smiling, touching, or amiable mutual gazing. What is true of the solidariness dimension is also applicable to attempts to increase or decrease power differentials. In both cases to be direct is a high risk strategy. There are no routine face-saving replies to "Will you marry me?" or its non-verbal equivalent of presenting an engagement ring over a candle-lit dinner.

Ambiguity of initial signalling was referred to in chapter 4 as existing between non-human con-specifics. In species where male birds build nests, potential female partners entering the territory may be permitted to remain or be driven away, but subsequently the females who are allowed to inspect the nest and its builder may reject the offer and fly off. Courtship in some fishes, many birds, and many mammals can be marked by progressive reductions in ambiguity and narrowings of uncertainty about mutual acceptability in ways not unlike human courtship. Ambiguities of language are also available to human beings. The idea that language is used to reduce uncertainty is too strong a generalization; both cooperative and competitive negotiations can invoke careful manoeuverings with sustained ambiguities.

5.4.2   Constraints on the Personal Use of NVC

The human species is limited in what can be achieved with biological characteristics. A person can jump for joy, but not to impossible heights. Over time, human technological wizardry has extended sensory-motor and information-processing powers, but human beings cannot kiss and cuddle a partner one kilometre away. Neither can we be attracted by their scent at such a distance, unlike Emperor Moths. Each of us has limited material resources. What we live in, what we drive (if anything) and what we wear are limited by both our resources and our values. Our knowledge and skills set limits to our displays of NVC. In Western societies what children learn about NVC is mainly happenstance. Few people practise and hone their social skills and fewer still receive instruction in such matters. Somewhat absurdly we can be encouraged to spend many many hours learning and practising skills for sporting activities, but not so for self-presentation. Worse still, cultural norms of politeness may well act against us discovering and remedying mistakes once we become adults. The conduct of other people also sets limits. Anyone with the material resources can acquire tickets to fashionable venues and first-class accommodation in hotels, planes, and trains. However, if fellow-guests or passengers do not treat such persons as ingroup, then they remain outgroup. Immaculate NVC (and VC) is no insurance against being ignored or cut. Finally, it would be odd not to include Machiavelli's "fortuna" as a factor. Thinking particularly of cross-cultural encounters, in which misinterpretations can be spectacular, whether a person survives initial encounters can be a matter of luck. Westerners serving overseas with the Peace Corps or Voluntary Service Overseas used to be particularly at risk for insulting or otherwise offending those they went to help. Who would expect a smile and an extended hand to be interpreted as an aggressive challenge? And who would expect any escorting guiding arm in a crowd to occasion a diplomatic incident? When the Prime Minister of Australia showed his consideration for the

Queen of the British Commonwealth in such a manner, he was in trouble. The saying, "Even a cat can look at a king" derives mythically from a reprimand of George III to a person who dared to make eye-contact. All visitors to Greece should be warned not to order five coffees relying on hand-signs. In fact raising almost any number of fingers in Greece is liable to cause trouble.

Learning to develop and control NVC skills is associated with the issue of the distinctions between "self-expression" and "self-presentation," between "being authentic" and "attempting to pass as." As elaborated in chapters 11 and 12, at a societal level, questions about appearance and reality are now a salient and disturbing focus of concern. On the one hand, it used to be expected that novitiate teachers and doctors will be nervous when they are launched into their classrooms and surgeries. On the other, assumed identities can be treated as reprehensible. Whilst it is easy to understand why thieves posing as meter-readers or social workers are condemned, and exposed false claimants to glorious past achievements are prone to rejection by society, when such acting and deception is construed as being for the public good, for example military commanders and our spies it is commended. Notwithstanding this, it is also true that some false claimants have been famous (men), and provided that they are jovial and generous, then their misdemeanors (and even crimes) can be dismissed as eccentricities; expressions such as "charming rogue" or "bit of bounder" serving to mitigate culpability.

5.5 NVC in the Wider Context of Communication

The importance and special qualities of NVC as a component of communication more generally are discussed in the chapters where relevant functions are treated in detail, but it is clear that NVC in humans as well as other animals is heavily implicated in the following functions:

1 Encounter Regulation
2 Marking and Regulating of (i)   states
                            (ii)   personal identity
                            (iii) social identity
                            (iv)   social relationships

Here comments will be confined to two topics, both focussing on interpretation, one of which will re-appear in the chapters on marking. With so many NV cues available, what happens when they differ in what they are signalling? How do interpreters cope with NV cues displayed by members of other cultures or sub-cultures?

5.5.1   The Interpretation of Non-Verbal Cues

The simplest generalization would be that the whole array of NV cues is sampled, and if all are consistent with each other, no difficulties of interpretation arise. What is noticeable are any discrepancies from the general profile. When this occurs, the following diagnostic sequence would be typical:

1   Which cues are odd?
2   Why might they be discrepant? Are they cues which are typically within the control of the communicator? If they are *not* – and are involuntary leakage – then what is motivating the display that is controllable? Is the person trying to impress, manipulate, or deceive? If they are normally controllable, then is the communicator trying to keep up appearances whilst experiencing some kind of conflict? This can happen when private grief or exhaustion is being felt in a public situation that requires a cheerful and lively role enactment. In both cases the attention is on what is *least easily controlled*; this is what stands in need of primary interpretation, with the more controllable being viewed as what the communicator wants to be believed. (Some human performers are able to introduce a further level of misinterpretation into their performances – pretending that they are pretending. ("Victor Hugo was a madman, who thought he was Victor Hugo," – *Cocteau*.)

In the mundane world of the untrained, the general assumption is that what is said is under greater voluntary control, than both how it is said and the remainder of the bodily NVC, but this is not necessarily so. The use of the lie-detecting polygraph (see Robinson, 1996) is a terrifying and invalid application of this assumption, giving use to false positives and false negatives in serious criminal cases. Some people can lie without any NV indication. Some people sweat whenever they pass through customs. We can be trained how to avoid NV leakage, just as we can be trained to simulate emotions.

5.5.2   Intergroup Communication and Miscommunication

The essence of the concern is miscommunication at a variety of group levels: intergroup differences between sub-cultural groupings within a society as well as what are normally called cross-cultural differences. Following the observations about similarities between primates and humans, it is to be expected that some NV displays are recognizable by human beings everywhere, a generalization encouraged by comparisons in judging basic emotions across a wide variety of societies (Ekman, 1982). In addition to the core of commonality, a number of possibilities arise:

1   Irrelevant variable in one group being relevant in another;
2   Same relevant variable, but with different scales;
3   Same relevant variable, but with different meaning;
4   Same relevant variable, but with opposite meaning.

For the first exposed soles of the feet provide an example of a feature irrelevant in western societies, where persons can sit cross-legged or even with feet outstretched. In a number of Pacific Islands western visitors will be handed rugs so that the soles are not exposed. For Arab cultures also to show someone the soles of your feet is to register contempt for them.

Examples of some cues with different functional scales were brought to public attention by Hall (1959; 1966) with his vivid caricatures of intercultural communication at the United Nations. His descriptions were of Latins coming to stand so close to Anglo-Saxons that the Anglo-Saxons would step backwards to increase the distance, the reiterations leading to a strange dance. His observations were valid. Cultures differ in how comfortable they feel at different distances. The same is true of the amount of touching. Within a single society, Sissons' (1971) working class interpreters saw middle class expressions of gratitude as excessive to the point of insincerity, whereas middle class interpreters saw working class expressions as casual to the point of rudeness.

According to Morris (1978) the forefinger-thumb ring of "OK" in the west indicates money in Japan. In Malta it means someone is gay. In Greece it is just obscene. The fourth type is commonly exemplified via the vertical and horizontal head-movements around Macedonia in south-eastern Europe. The vertical "No" movement is in fact easily distinguished from the more common assent, unless you are a Macedonian waiter serving European social psychologists, for example. At least one conference of the European Association held in Bulgaria generated complaints about non-arrival of coffee and excessive deliveries of yoghurt, while those in the know remained sneakily guilty in their *Schadenfreude*.

When there is potential for miscommunication, what are the principles people use for interpretation? Not surprisingly they use those of their own culture, and then add a tendency to evaluate the outgroup negatively in respect of their differences. The negative evaluations of differences appear to be more common than the insight that cultures differ in their conventions. Even when the cognitive evaluations accept the differences as differences, the affective components are likely to remain negative. "I know they are not being rude, but I can't feel that they are not." "I know that the English are not being unfriendly, but they still feel unfriendly." These differences are conceptually and behaviorally important and are aspects of negative stereotypes of other social groups where the observations of behavior are reliable and valid, but the interpretations are not. So in Hall's study, Italians were disposed to see Americans as stand-offish and aloof, Americans to see Italians as intrusive and over-friendly. Many hand gestures are insults in cultures other than one's own. Internationally such misunderstandings must be very common.

The same misunderstandings can occur with language, but are not necessarily correlated in the same way. For example in the 1960s the Americans moved to first name terms very quickly (chapter 8), but kept their distance spatially. Certainly too, older English worry about the over-friendliness of the rush to first names.

5.6   To Carry Forward

It may be obvious to many readers why chapters 4 and 5 have been included in this text, but by their relative neglect of NVC, so many general beliefs about language held by linguists, psychologists, and sociologists can be interpreted to imply that language is *the* means by which human beings communicate, and is a sufficient system and resource in itself. Whilst it may indeed yield intellectual and communicative possibilities not feasible with NVC, as chapter 4 illustrates, NVC is necessarily, centrally, massively, and pervasively involved in the lives of non-human animals. As I have argued in chapter 5, the same is true about NVC among human beings. That so much of its operating is habitually out-of-consciousness does not diminish its centrality to human interaction. That language cannot be used without non-verbal features and that these cannot carry no information entails that for human experience and behavior the non-verbal and verbal have to be treated together. For analytic purposes it may be important to separate them, but they have to be treated as articulated and integrated when they are being considered in use in context.

Section 5.4 hints at their articulation in reducing and maintaining uncertainties and ambiguities in interactions. Section 5.5 draws attention to principles that have been found to operate in decoding "mixed" messages, an issue explored further in chapter 9, but already hinting how weighty the non-verbal features are for interpretation. Section 5.6 points to ways in which NVC can be misleading among human beings. When attempting to speak with someone when there is no shared language, most participants will recognize that they cannot communicate linguistically; monolingual English speakers and monolingual Mandarin speakers accept the futility of talking past each other in their respective vernaculars. They may however presume to communicate non-verbally. Section 5.5 notes that there are etic features of NVC that are not relevant to emic features across cultures. However, there are also features where similar variables carry similar meanings, but for which the scales of significance are not the same, and more unfortunate still, there are also some with unrelated and even opposite meanings. Failures to interpret the first are likely to be just puzzling, opposite meanings can result in friendly efforts being interpreted as hostile to the extent of being life-threatening. However, it is the second that most frequently give rise to misunderstandings and where intergroup differences are likely to be interpreted as negatively evaluated characteristics in the outgroup. These can have very serious consequences for intergroup relations, but so can language use. For example, it has become fashionable for groups who have suffered from massacres and other vicious forms of persecution in the past to demand that current leaders of the aggressing countries apologize for the evil doings of their national ancestors. One of the unrequited requests has been that from British prisoners of war held by the Japanese in the international war 1939–1945. I may be wrong, but it is possible that for the Japanese this has been "impossible," not because they are not ashamed but because they are too ashamed. Their official history books and pronouncements still ignore or deny their atrocities in Korea, Manchuria, and China. Their army organized slave labour and committed casual and organized rape, torture, and murder of civilians to an extent comparable to that of the Nazis in countries they occupied, Poland and the Soviet Union. Many Germans who could not have had anything to do with the Nazis felt guilty about these atrocities and said so. Their government and some companies made restitution to go with their apologies. But as the song has it, "East is east, and west is west," and communication may be easier within than between.

CHAPTER 6

Encounter Regulation and Conversation

6.1 Preliminary

By definition social interaction involves more than one person uttering a monologue or scribbling a note to self. How is the "inter" component of the action achieved? For oral dialogue, Speaker (S) and Listener (L) will not be the only role played by each person. How does S switch to become L and L to S? What signals do S and L provide for each other to indicate intentions to continue or to switch? '(Having or) holding the floor' has been the phrase used to refer to the role of S. If the floor is thought of as a ball in a throwing game between S and L, then the focus in this chapter is on the movement of the ball from end to end and not on the players or what or why they are throwing the ball. How does L know when S will be throwing the ball? The informal Face-to-Face (FtF) dialogue is taken by social psychologists as the archetypal interaction, but of course there is a great variety of types of encounter, more than one channel and mode of interaction, and more than two people can be participating. Interaction itself has to be agreed to, opened up, and closed down, and these phases have particular characteristics.

Questions about what is being achieved in interactions cannot and will not be excluded entirely insofar as they are integral to the signals effecting the regulation of exchanges. Both chapters 4 and 5 have offered examples of non-verbal and verbal features relevant to encounter regulation and conversation. Chapter 6 explores F1 specifically and its most common informal exchange context of conversation more generally.

⌐ 6.2   Introduction

Half a century ago, any review of work on the regulation of interpersonal encounters could have been confined to no more than a brief and idiosyncratic collage of personal observations, perhaps complemented with an agenda for future studies. A little later, any proposed agenda would have depended very much on its discipline of origin, but now there is a wealth of data, even if this is still without a satisfactory synthesis of the contributions from the quartet of anthropology, linguistics, social psychology, and sociology. The significant advances made in the mapping and understanding of FtF encounters have been enriched, but also complicated further by the new and unstable infotech world; this has created an array of fresh issues as new modes of communication open up new possibilities.

In the more tranquil 1950s, social psychologists were examining the classification, incidence, and sequences of speech in small problem-solving groups and were relating variations in these to variations in role differentiation, norm formation, sentiments, and productivity. The work had arisen out of practical problems: in times of war how to pick efficient crews for aircraft, tanks and other military teams and particularly how to select effective leaders, and in peace how to promote efficient decision-making in committees, and high productivity and job satisfaction in work groups (see Cartwright & Zander, 1960). In these studies, data were not analyzed from the perspective of how interactions functioned and what the reasons for and consequences of variability were, but it is possible to retrieve some useful ideas along the lines illustrated below.

The serious study of exchanging roles in social interactions *per se* arose partly from the study of group dynamics, and partly from a transposition of models of non-social sensori-motor skills coming to serve as a heuristic for examining social skills. What skills are involved in successful social interactions? What are the components and how do they function? In particular what are the elements of non-verbal communication (NVC), and how are they articulated in interactions (Argyle, 1988; Duncan &Fiske, 1977; Duncan & Niederehe, 1974)? Answers to some of these questions are offered in chapter 6, and they constitute some of the most well-founded advances in social psychology.

About the same time, and following Goffman's (1961, 1967, 1969) idiosyncratic but highly perceptive observations and interpretations, the 1970s also witnessed a Californian gold-rush from the freshly-labelled ethnomethodologists and micro-sociologists. A major concern of these enthusiasts was with the workings of the mundane. Everyday living is replete with interactions among people which involve both the non-verbal and verbal. It is orderly to the extent that how interactions are managed is, for the most part, not contested *in situ*. Surely this state of affairs was of interest to social scientists? What are the rules governing this orderliness? What are the "understandings" that participants share that enable them to operate the interactions? These two questions have led to two separable strands of research. The first has focused on language *per se*: the rules of sequence, substitution, and collocation in the management of verbal exchanges. The second has been more concerned with how we make sense of what is said and done in verbal exchanges and what presuppositions we need to bring to any encounter to make sense of what eventuates in one. In this chapter the emphasis has to be on the first, but cannot ignore the second entirely.

How the social psychological and the micro-sociological strands are to be articulated has yet to be tackled. Stemming as they do from separate disciplines and traditions, and given the hazards still facing those academics who attempt inter-disciplinary or multi-disciplinary work, comments here will be few and confined to the example of opening sequences for FtF encounters. While FtF interactions have dominated research in the past, the technological revolution in the world of Information Communication Technology (ICT) has been mentioned as opening up new modes of non-FtF, and the utilization of these and some of their consequences as alternatives, substitutes, and replacements have at least to be noted.

The previously sensible tunnel vision for FtF included a similar restriction and constriction on the types of interaction investigated, "natural conversation" being the main activity. Many of the investigators used university students, often "getting to know each other" – or university staff in domestic settings. Financial, logistic, and ethical as well as academic considerations necessarily entered into such decisions as to who could be studied doing what, where, and when. The need to open up this restriction will be discussed.

"Natural conversations" typically involve opening and closing sequences preceding and succeeding the central exchanges, but of course in real-life who comes to interact how often with whom and for how long is also relevant to encounter regulation.

Finally the two settings of police interviewing drink-driving suspects and TV presenters interviewing politicians are offered as different approaches to real-life issues in the regulation of encounters.

⌐ 6.3   Small Group Dynamics

How often convened small groups met was determined by experimenters, as were the tasks they were set to do. When investigators constrained who spoke to whom (see Cartwright & Zander, 1960) it was clear that the channels available affected more than how often a channel was used (Bavelas, 1950). Role differentiation was influenced by centrality of position in a group, but in turn emergent leaders also regulated who spoke to whom (Leavitt, 1951). Deviants from majority opinion received more communications than others up to a point where the group gave up and reduced or ceased interacting with them (see Cartwright & Zander, 1960; Schachter, 1951). It was in small groups that social psychologists first became aware of the ideal of alternative directions of causation; for example if channels are constrained role differentiation will be affected *or* vice versa.

These small groups were microcosms of larger and more formal groupings in which rights to initiate and have encounters were and are commonly prescribed in detail. This is true of grievance and complaints procedures in the workplace as well as to other work-related practices. The two social dimensions of relative power and social distance underlie much of the variance, with power achieving primacy in formal organizations and social distance in interpersonal interactions.

Much of the coding of observations of such groups could have formed the basis of conversational analysis (CA) or discourse analysis (DA). Bales (1950) experimented with various numbers of categories into which utterances could be located in, order to see which followed which, and how their use related to role differentiation, norm formation and sentiments, for example. Some schemes ran to 96 categories (Carter et al., 1951), others dropped to four, but the most commonly used featured twelve; this was judged to give the best returns for feasible recording. These activities pre-dated the invention of video-recorders, and contemporary tape-recordings could be difficult to transcribe. Certainly, adjacency pairs such as the unsurprising conjunction of question–answer were reported, as were more larger scale patterns of speech organization. Lacking a linguistically-based provenance or persistent pioneering advocacy however, the study of how turn-taking worked in such settings was not taken up. A social psychological approach to turn-taking arose out of the general study of non-verbal communication, and eye-contact variability in particular.

⌐ 6.4 Non-Verbal Communication (NVC)

The upsurge of interest in NVC in the 1960s included a particular interest in eye-movements in FtF encounters, and one set of questions which emerged in the area focused on how gazing related to turn-taking. Kendon (1967) initiated this work and continued to explore it for many subsequent years. He began with frame-by-frame analyses of films of pairs of British interactants holding conversations. His focal features were the direction, duration, and frequency of the gazes of each partner, and in particular mutual eye-contact. Were these systematically related to the exchanging of the roles of speaker to listener and back? Kendon showed that S and L were looking at each other about 60 percent of the time while S was in mid-turn. About three seconds from the role exchange point, S shifted the incidence of gazing at L to 80 percent, while L reduced the percentage to 20 percent. At the exchange point, both L and S moved back to a 60 percent rate over a five second period. Under these conditions synchrony of the exchange was achieved on 70 percent of occasions; without the increase, only 29 percent were achieved without pausing.

Criticisms of the details of this work were many, but did not relate importantly to Kendon's central claim to have found a systematic relationship between turn-taking synchronization and eye-gaze. Whilst it was true, that this was shown only for a small number of pairs of undergraduates at Oxford who were conversing to get to know each other, questions of possible generalizability are a separate issue from the fact that interpretable links between two variables had been demonstrated.

From these beginnings, work developed in a number of directions. One was the pursuit of other cues indicative of S imminently handing over to an L. By 1972 Duncan had listed:

1 a change in pitch in the last word of a phonemic clause;
2 an increase of the duration of an intended final syllable or word;
3 a reduction of gestures;
4 the use of sociocentric sequences such as "you know?" and "isn't it?";
5 a reduction in pitch and/or loudness at the end of sociocentric sequences;
6 the completion of a free-standing grammatical clause (namely a sentence).

By 1974 Duncan & Niederehe had begun to include more than speaker yielding cues and more than verbal and vocalic features and by 1977 Duncan and Fiske had created the contents of Table 6.1. There are of course cues that signal S's wishes to continue speaking, and cues from L displaying a wish to take the floor or a declining of an offer to do so.

Whereas Duncan was concerned with turn-taking *per se*, Knapp, Hart, Fredrich and Shulman (1973) analyzed correlates of closing sequences, concentrated on the final 45 seconds, and found that this period showed a peak of verbal and non-verbal indicators some 15 seconds prior to leave taking. In this study at least these signs appeared to be independent of the power differentials and degree of solidariness of the interactants. The Duncan and Fiske (1977) review is probably still the best introduction to ideas and details about turn-taking, with broader approaches being taken by Siegman and Feldstein (1979;1985) and Street and Cappella (1985).

Table 6.1   Speaker and Auditor Signals Hypothesized for the Turn System

Name of signal	Constituent cues	Related to subsequent:
Speaker turn	1. Intonation-marked clause 2. Sociocentric sequence 3. Grammatical completeness 4. Paralinguistic drawl 5. Decrease in paralinguistic pitch and/or loudness on sociocentric sequence 6. End of gesticulation	1. Auditor attempt to take turn
Speaker gesticulation	1. Gesticulation 2. Tensed hand position	1. Suppresses auditor attempts to take turn
Speaker state	1. Turning of head away from partner 2. Begin gesticulation	
Speaker within turn	1. Grammatical completeness 2. Turning of head towards auditor	1. Between-unit auditor back-channel 2. Speaker continuation signal
Between-unit auditor back channel	(5 different types, both audible and visible, observed)	
Early auditor back channel	(Same as between-unit auditor back-channel)	1. Speaker continuation signal
Speaker continuation	1. Turning of head away from auditor	

After Duncan and Fiske (1977).

The advances of the last 40 years have been prodigious. This has been made possible, in part, by technological advances in the capacities of recording and analyzing instrumentation, with the correlative consequence that not having such equipment precludes the microanalyses necessary for pattern detection and interpretation. One great achievement lies in the discovery of many etic cues available for use. One continuing difficulty is finding evidence relevant to the emics. Which are simply correlates and which are causally or consequentially related to interchanging the roles of S and L remains problematic.

The general conception of an orchestration in which size matters appears to be well-founded. Orchestration in this context refers to the involvement of the whole body and its actions, such that strong demands for change will be more likely to include significant and large body movements and gesticulation as well as fine changes in the vocalics. In lower key encounters, cues are likely to be attenuated in amplitude with the verbal features rising in importance. Such a profile approach may also serve to reconcile arguments about the differential value of semantic and vocalic cues (Duncan & Fiske, 1977; Slugoski, 1985) and reconcile findings contrasting telephone with FtF conversation (Rutter, 1987; Hopper, 1992). For further examinations of the relevance of verbal features *per se*, social psychologists need to refer to Sacks and his colleagues and successors.

6.5   Californian Linguistic Turns

It is customary to cite Harvey Sacks (1971) as the prime mover. There is a touch of irony that his influence was achieved mostly through lectures, of which dog-eared and yellowing gestetnered and photocopied versions circulated around the world prior to their formal publication in 1992. Informal conversation was taken as the point of departure for analysis. It was assumed to have the dual virtues of being historically archetypal and natural rather than invented. Its characteristics should therefore be independent of context, even if subject to locally negotiated rules! In the introduction to his collection, Schenkein (1978) mentions the novelties of using materials from actual interactions and of taking seriously the details of the interactions themselves. He notes that these materials are the tiniest sample of circumstances in which conversations are found and that they are for the most part conversations of the white middle class of North America and England. Investigators in the genre share an analytic mentality of a relatively unmotivated examination of materials, a concern with the details of interactions, and a preference for writing rules. The turn-taking paper can be used to illustrate the issues. Sacks et al. (1974) list 14 facts about conversation to which any model of conversation must accommodate. They accomplish this accommodation with two rules. The first five facts cited are:

1   Speaker change recurs;
2   Overwhelmingly, one party talks at a time;
3   Occurrences of more than one speaker speaking at a time are common, but brief;
4   Transitions from one turn to the next with no gap and no overlap between them are common. Together with transitions characterized by a slight gap or slight overlap, they make up the vast majority of transitions;
5   Turn order is not fixed, but varies.

To accomplish accommodation to these facts, two rules are proposed:

1   At initial turn-constructional units' initial transition-relevant place:
a   If the turn-so-far is so constructed as to involve the use of a "current speaker selects next" technique, then the party so selected has rights and is obliged to take next turn to speak; no others have such rights or obligations, transfer occurring at that place.
b   If the turn-so-far is so constructed as not to involve the use of a "current speaker selects next" technique, self-selection for next speakership may, but need not, continue, unless another self-selects.
c   If the turn-so-far is so constructed as not to involve the use of a "current speaker selects next" technique, then current speaker may, but need not, continue, unless another self-selects.
2   If, at initial turn-constructional unit's initial transition-relevant place, neither 1a nor 1b has operated and, following the provision of 1c, current speaker has continued, then the rule-set a–c re-applies at next transition-relevance place and recursively at each next transition-relevance place until transfer is effected.

The authors suggest that the model is a local management system and an interactionally managed system and that conversation itself probably marks one pole of a complex gradation of speech exchange systems, the other end being marked by ceremonial activities where who says what to whom (and to some extent how) is institutionally prescribed.

Many questions can be asked about the specific and general quality of this account. The facts may be generally uncontentious, at least within the subcultural and contextual constraints examined. They could have been collected by the random or systematic sampling methods used by social psychologists rather than through the unsystematic agglomeration of data collected for other purposes. How representative they are of the white middle class of North America we cannot know since the universe of situations of which they purport to be a sample is not closely defined. Such a criticism is attenuated however by an establishment of general facts. If the generalizations represent patterns within a plausible construction of reality, then the orderliness of that reality entails that the situations and people sampled are homogeneous in the relevant aspects, and they stand in need of explanation.

The initial work was extensive and early reviews (for example Schenkein, 1978; Sudnow, 1972) were able to make particular reference to analyses of turn-taking (Sacks, Schegloff, & Jefferson, 1974), sequences of summons-answer (Schegloff, 1968), closing sequences (Schegloff & Sacks, 1973), side sequences (Jefferson, 1972), insertion sequences (Schegloff, 1972), and adjacency pairs (Schegloff & Sacks, 1973).

It is not surprising that the carefully constructed rules set down by Sacks were found to have the weaknesses one would expect to be present in pioneering ventures. The generalizations were found to be too strong. Exceptions were easy to find. Limitations and elaborations were suggested. More important though was the successful introduction of a new agenda combined with a new methodology and new techniques of analysis for talk.

People from all cultures have been opening, sustaining, and closing FtF encounters for thousands of years, but these activities had not been studied systematically. Massive grammars and dictionaries have been produced, as have descriptions of the workings of sound systems. What the Californians initiated were the beginnings of considerations of the rules that appeared to govern how acceptable talk gets constructed.

To pursue one feature a little, once people have got into communicative contact they typically exchange greetings as opening remarks. In English, choices are made with terms of address and the small set of greeting markers, for example "Good morning," "Hello," "Hi," which may be followed by "How are you?" or "How's life?." There may be a prefatory "Excuse me, but . . ." There may be occasions to ask as in the film *Casablanca* where it is cool to open with "Out of all the bars in all the world, why . . .?" or to assert as one bumps into a fellow social psychologist on the summit of Mount Kilimanjaro "Dr. Giles, I presume!". If one begins to set out the range, the possible, plausible replies, and the moves from greetings to substantive conversation, it becomes possible to sort and classify greeting/

opening sequences in terms of occasions, relationships of power and social distance, and all the other parameters listed by Hymes (1967). Unfortunately the data would comprise very long and open-ended lists, but it will be seen in chapter 7 that sense can be made of the selections in terms of accounts such as that offered by Brown and Levinson (1987/1978).

Language is a resource in which breaking the rules of the system and instituting new ones is perfectly acceptable. This happens, and not infrequently. Hi, reader! How goes it? With greetings, there are of course all the vocal and physical components, which also offer choices at each step of the sequence, and they too are subject to innovation. These can be introductions and/or droppings of handshakes and kisses, wavings and hand-slappings. It can become smart to adopt foreign "Hellos" or sub-cultural rituals – *Ciao*! Not surprisingly what develops among pairs and groups is a matter of negotiation by the participants. The extent to which these idiosyncratic devices become markers of identity of the particularities of relationships is also a matter of co-construction by the participants.

What is true for opening sequences is equally applicable to the sustained phase of any interaction and to its closure. For all three, norms come into being and are established, and stabilize within a social unit, at all levels from pairs to cultures. Novitiates to any sub-culture have to learn and follow the conventions. Whether individual members attempt to innovate will depend how tight or loose the conventions are and how attempts to make changes are treated. Small groups of children may be free to devise new greetings to mark gang members, but woe betide the first ordinary mortal who attempts to include a kiss as a greeting for the Queen of England. A recent Prime Minister of Australia "appalled the world" – according to an Anglo-centric royalist BBC newscaster – by touching her (coat) with a light guiding movement. As with all behavioral features susceptible to criteria of fashion, would-be innovators run the risk that their novelty will be challenged, ignored, or dismissed, but once adopted by reference groups, it may well infiltrate its way into society. This kind of consideration will be particularly relevant to groups with shifting memberships, such as adolescent coteries. For example, no one has yet exited from an FtF *avec moi* with, "Stay cool, man." Neither have I been dismissed with, "See you in hell," uttered either seriously or ironically. And of course older academics have no idea what greeting sequences are now in use among contemporary youth groups. A recent undergraduate project found that unacquainted students in bars just started talking about a topic without even a minimal "Hi" and that in male-female FtFs initiated by males a variety of imperative verbs followed by an "off" were common female responses. Opening sequences are important socially and merit some special attention, but first one has to achieve communicative contact with the right person.

6.6 First, Catch Your Interlocutor

In the UK in recent years people at large have complained of a significant growth in difficulties of communication with public service and commercial organizations. Letters and files cannot be traced as would-be hospital patients wait months to be given dates for consultations, get on to admission waiting lists, and finally make it to operating tables. A recent TV programme documented six cases of persons trying to find out by phone when they would be seen or admitted by the National Health Service. There were problems of engaged lines. Operators were prone to re-direct calls to wrong sections, to persons who were on leave or out with no cover, to break off contact, and to promise that someone would ring back – who did not do so. The inefficiency was almost unbelievable.

Since such experiences are commonplace with public sector organizations, I decided to check out the commercial sector. I rang eight companies to say I wanted to discuss life insurance cover to an amount of £50,000, which would benefit the companies to an amount of roughly £200 a month. Only one rang back within their specified time to arrange an appointment, and this was not kept. One operator said their company did not offer such cover! Three operators put me through to the wrong section, for example claims. Three diverted the call to the right section, but the subsequent promise of a ring back was not kept within 48 hours. One said they only worked through professional brokers; ironically this was the company with which my life was already insured.

No single explanation will serve to account for the variety of ways in which interactions can be avoided. Understaffing and lack of training are clearly two factors, and lack of accountability is a third. The customary anonymity of telephone operators encourages the last. While such failed attempts at interactions are dysfunctional for customers and clients, they can also be functional for members of organizations. In addition to cutting operating costs and shifting effort to clients, who has not heard a secretary ask the boss if he or she is in, and then reported that he or she is out at a meeting? Signs proclaiming, "If you have a complaint, ring XYZ" do not add that XYZ is an unstaffed phone. In the early days of e-mail, denial of receipt was a commonly given justification for non-replies, just as it was in the earlier days of faxing. To counter this, e-mails can now be tagged and checked to see whether the receiver has opened them. The proportion of genuine failures and false recipient/sender claims remains unknown. Ways of avoiding encounters and the reactions of those denied the services or goods they were seeking are ripe for study!

For arranging to meet friends or would-be friends, obstructive or incompetent gatekeepers are not likely to prevent meetings, although those wishing to avoid contact can exploit failures to reply to invitations, unpunctuality, and other devices to indicate unwillingness to meet or otherwise interact. Straight refusals are also in order, especially in the face of harassment, currently construed as persevering to a third attempt at meeting the other. Harassment itself has become defined in law, especially but not solely in the context of inter-gender encounters. For most people most of the time, both the frequency and the nature of encounters with particular people are negotiated into mutually acceptable routines that together complete the life-space available.

⌐ 6.7   Greetings are Special

Greetings are special because, by definition, they set the scene. They make bids on behalf of their users about the identity they wish to claim for themselves and the kind of relationship they wish to define. In respect of the latter, the underlying dimensions of power and social distance are invariably implicated, although the particular varieties of relationships also have to be considered as equally important within that framework. And first moves and reactions to them can be decisive determinants of the initial role relationships, at least for the encounter in hand. For example, in a small group an immediate bid for leadership may be difficult to resist. A latecomer to a small assembly might arrive and announce, "Right. Follow me to the station," and find the rest following as they mutter among themselves that they are walking in the wrong direction. Once announced, confident and assertive claims can be countered, but this may involve offending against norms of politeness and agreeableness.

In such a case compliance marks convergence, and a rejection of the suggestion indicates divergence (see chapter 14) – and clearly threatens (attacks) the positive face of the speaker. The strong weighting given to first impressions can set both the power and affiliative frameworks for the future of the relationship, but these are dealt with elsewhere, and here the interest is on rules for sequencing who says what to whom. This can vary between an absence of even a hand-wave or "hi" to elaborated progressions of mutual enquiries about the weather and world, through to personally preferred or prearranged topics. As with turn-taking, it is the rule-breaking techniques of Garfinkel (1967) that are probably the most rewarding research approach to adopt for exploring the norms.

⌐ 6.8   Kinds of Encounters: Procedural Rules

The considerations of relevance to the hows and whys of encounter regulation are simply a sub-set of the etic possibilities of communicative acts. If one asks about turn-taking in particular, probably the most embracing useful metaphor is that mentioned in chapter 5 of an orchestration of the cues available for signalling. In FtF encounters more cues are utilizable than on a telephone link. Postural changes, gestures, facial expressions, and eye contact can be coordinated with extra-linguistic, paralinguistic and linguistic features to achieve smooth exchanges – in cooperative contexts. The orchestration will also be relevant to success in gaining the floor in competitive contexts. Telephone interactions involve a reduction in the range of cues available, but this can be compensated for with greater clarity of use of vocal and verbal indicators.

As previously mentioned, to date much of the social psychological work on encounter regulation has focused on informal interactions of pairs of peers, much of it with university students in the USA, supplemented by additional observations of domestic or work-based conversations. Institutionalized encounters might be considered to be beyond the level of analysis of concern to social psychologists, but even if that is so, it does not mean that we cannot profit from the adoption of such an approach.

Whilst growing members of a culture are generally expected to acquire the relevant norms of displays and skills without explicit instruction, socializing agents are likely to comment on "do's" and "don'ts," and immigrants and other outsiders may be taught explicitly how to conduct themselves if they wish to be assimilated. Guidance is available. Telephone directories may well give written advice on how to conduct opening sequences, both to facilitate communication and to avoid calls from abusers or would-be exploiters and salespeople. More formally law courts have strict rules of limits of what can and cannot be said by whom to whom, while religious services may well be ritualized with prescribed scripts. These latter ceremonies are sufficiently regulated to ensure that openings, middles, and closings are defined to predetermine specific turn-takings as well as what is said and how.

Such rituals do extend down into homes and work, both for particular forms of talk, for example certain kinds of joke, and for everyday set pieces of exchanges such as when spouses meet at home after work. "Went the day well?" Clearly the patterns of rituals found in ceremonials can form templates, which can in turn inform the study of everyday exchanges. The norms people have developed were intended to be functional rather than dysfunctional, and other things being equal, they are likely to be so. Insofar as asymmetries of prescription and proscription in formal ceremonials occur, then indexical characteristics are likely to be those that can be exploited to assert power and dominance. Who has the right to break the rules and thereby exercise dominance? Who behaves in such ways, even without any such right? If A frequently interrupts B by talking at inappropriate transition points, and then continues speaking until B is over-ridden and goes silent, is A condemned or is dominance conceded? If A is adept at seizing apparent juncture points, such presumptions can become acts of power and impoliteness combined, unless the Bs simply defer. Would-be leaders in small groups have utilized such knowledge and been judged accordingly (Bales & Slater, 1955; Borgatta & Bales, 1956; Leffler, Gillespie & Conaty, 1985). Those behaving similarly out of ignorance are judged and are likely to be judged as unpopular and avoided (Schachter, 1951). The social skills training model of Trower, Bryant and Argyle (1978) focused on informing and enabling those who had either not learned or forgotten the norms of turn-taking in everyday interaction.

6.9 Political Interviews

One well-studied case about whom uncertainties about motivation remain was the erstwhile Prime Minister of Britain, Margaret Thatcher, who had complained that political interviewers interrupted her. Beattie (1982) reported that Mrs Thatcher was indeed interrupted twice as often as her Labour opponent in televized pre-election interviews. He attributed this to her higher incidence of (false) turn-yielding cues, for example falling intonation and drawl on the stressed syllable in a clause. Beattie, Cutler, and Pearson (1982) then had undergraduates judge 40 extracts of interviews with Mrs Thatcher which were terminated at three different junctures: A. real turn-final, B. turn-medial, and C. turn-disputed, the last of which was where she was about to be interrupted by the interviewer. Undergraduates judged C as more frequently complete whether given visuals alone, the sound alone, or both.

Bull and Mayer (1988) pointed to weaknesses in the design and analysis used by Beattie and corrected and repeated the essential features at the succeeding national election. Interruptions were common, being present in 45 percent of answers, but there were no differences in the rate or percentage made by or imposed upon the two would-be Prime Ministers. Interruptions were not an apparent turn-yielding utterance for the most part for either candidate.

One analysis that did yield a difference showed that Mrs Thatcher commented on being interrupted 21 times compared with eight comments from the leader of the main opposition party. The most frequent type of interruption was a re-formulation of the question, which Mrs Thatcher was prone to interpret as an accusation, a personalization of issues, or a "put down." These claims created an impression of a plucky honest woman being misrepresented by a dominating male interviewer who was behaving badly. That these interpretations were not a valid interpretation of the facts was perhaps manifested neatly in one interview with the recently-knighted Robin Day, in which Mrs Thatcher called him both Mr Day and Mr Sir Robin. Subsequently, her disposition to describe the succession of resigning colleagues as individually guilty of betrayal and disloyalty personalized attributions to an extent that suggested she was deliberately exploiting what her competitors tolerated to win sympathy – and votes. That said, the very high incidence of interviewer interruptions – 45 percent of answers – could be seen as impolite attempts at dominance, especially since with Mrs Thatcher 73 percent of these were at non-turn yielding points of utterance. In turn, interviewers can become frustrated by the frequency of equivocation in politicians' answers (Bull & Mayer, 1993), which in its turn can be seen as a result of their insistence on asking closed questions to which any direct truthful answer cannot be sensibly given (see Bavelas et al. 1990).

Clearly this kind of interview is not the same kind of cooperative conversation that had characterized much of the work designed to expose non-speech, vocal, and verbal cues involved in turn-taking. It is however now the normative style of interviewing adopted by British TV and radio presenters: antagonistic, confrontational, disdainful, accusing, and intellectual in getting at "facts" and their explanations. Its characteristics are dealt with *in extenso* by Bull (in press).

⌐ 6.10   Legal Difficulties with DWI

Several years ago police in England and Wales were required to follow new protocols (performative function) for charging, arresting, and interviewing any suspect. These required assents from the accused that they had understood their rights and what the consequences of waiving any were. The scripts were difficult to learn and follow, and very quickly shrewd accused and their lawyers were escaping from prosecution because the commissive performatives (Austin, 1962) had not been followed verbatim. In the USA Shuy (1998, pp. 51–58) has documented some of the difficulties arising from what is required of the interaction between police and suspects when a charge is being made. Five constitutional rights have to be stated, and then since the right to remain silent is one of these, the police normally seek a waiver of this by the suspect. So what happens in DWI (Driving While Intoxicated) arrests where the police wish to gain a Breathalyzer sample? With a drunken suspect whose sober understanding might be lower than average and a police officer handling a script where *ad hominem* glosses may be required, the spectre of irresolvable dilemmas emerges. The rulings were designed to be legally comprehensive, and were presumably drawn up by lawyers whose criteria of acceptability would have suited their perspective. Shuy examined nine videos. His first observation was that just as the drafting lawyers had attended to their legal requirements, in handling initial encounters the police endeavored to ensure they followed the script as closely as possible. They need to be above criticism, and successful tactics to gain understanding were of lower priority, especially since requests for elucidation from suspects required police to be creative and adaptive and thereby expose themselves to risks of criticism. Such requests were typically met with re-reading of the exact words, a claim to have already explained, or a reflexive "What didn't you understand?" (Shuy, 1998, p. 53). Shuy goes on to show that in the legally constructed script the sequential ordering of rights read out is not user-friendly. He lists examples of a lack of cohesion within and between sentences in the protocol and how they could be improved, and his final somewhat alarming illustrations are of two embeddings of five and six layers respectively, when most people find three difficult to follow. Altogether Shuy found ten ways in which the language used was unnecessarily difficult for the suspect to understand and for the police to implement.

More generally police interviewing techniques of suspects and witnesses have changed greatly in the last decade as a result of psychological considerations. Encouraging people to offer accounts in a relaxed manner has become more common for two reasons. First, such open-ended enquiries are more likely to yield significant initially unreported details and second *de facto* guilty suspects are more likely to generate inconsistencies in their accounts (Memon & Bull, 1991). There have also been moves to protect witnesses in court from the threats and accusations of their abusers, in the interests of discovering whether a crime was committed and if so by whom. Children who may have been abused can now be videoed outside the courtroom. Accused rapists may soon be prevented from cross-examining their putative victims. Such approaches might be adopted towards any kind of interaction in any setting, for example patient interactions with medical practitioners, or classroom activities in schools. The list could be extended, and much research has been conducted in these settings and others. What is missing is a classificatory basis for contexts that would serve as a framework for describing and explaining similarities and differences across contexts, an issue taken up in the final section of the chapter.

Whither Next for Encounter Regulation

It is dangerous to predict what will not be advantageous to follow up, because one can never tell what might emerge. Counting, sorting, and classifying grains of desert sand are unlikely to be fruitful activities unless at least some prior reasons for doing so can be advanced. It would be reassuring to have a classification of encounter types that might relate to different rules for who can and does speak to whom and how exchanges are initiated, continued, and ended. Whilst it is easy to dream up *continua* such as formal–informal or contrasts such as intergroup–interpersonal, it is not evident outside particular questions how any particular general classification might be justified. In formal settings and structured settings like law courts, political assemblies, or religious services, it is not difficult to relate turn-taking rules both to manifest and latent functions. That witnesses can be required to answer inappropriate closed questions with "Yes" or "No", whilst politicians are allowed to evade appropriate closed questions can be explained in both social psychological and sociological terms, but to say that rules are more structured in formal settings would simply be to comment on the meaning of "formal." That an interpretation of the first case might be that courts allow demonstrations of power to override elucidation of relevant facts, and hence subordinate principles of procedural justice may be objectionable, but has been empirically observable from the beginnings of formal judicial institutions. Likewise, demonstrations that turn-taking in competitive or conflictual relational encounters is different from those in cooperative ones, with more interruptions and overlappings, would be most likely to be seen as symptoms of the definitions, rather than as empirical surprises standing in need of explanation.

In terms of what might be, perhaps the first point to note is how much of the work reported has been done in the USA and UK. What is more, the data have been collected mainly from the middle classes, whether from students or non-students. This narrowness sets two kinds of limits to what can be claimed so far, etic and emic. Etically the listing of relevant features of behavior may be too short with other groupings within the UK and USA and other cultures picking up additional cues which might or might not have similar significance. Emically features may have different meanings, just as they do with NVC more generally. Certainly rules of when and when not to make eye-contact, and hence its potential significance for turn-taking, differ greatly from society to society.

The one-person-speaks-at-a-time rule of Sacks is not an imperative of Italian conversation. It is unlikely that cultures which specialize in the art of meaning more than they display or say would operate similar systems to the UK and the USA. Even at the end of a month's stay in Japan, which had included a most enjoyable incidence of informal evening banquets, I could not detect how all the Japanese managed to finish and rise with the elegance and simultaneity of ascending geese; the rules guiding the closing sequence were enacted with surprising rapidity. More generally, the culture excels in minimalization of explicitness, relying on considerable indirectness in speech, mainly directed to face preservation or enhancement. Insofar as rights in turn-taking are themselves linked to values of politeness and both absolute and relational social status, the rules of opening and closing interactions are likely to be prescribed in ways consistent with these values.

For both settings and cultural variation, societies will have developed norms imposed or negotiated and whilst changes can no doubt occur with these, it is in the emergence of norms for the new modes in ICT that social psychologists can expect interesting issues to emerge. Within the constraints imposed by programmers, decisions about norms are being made indirectly from the bottom up. At present with e-mail there is a diversity of views about rates of reply and appropriateness of mode for whatever purposes people have in mind. As Baym (2000) notes early in her text, internet communications were initially suspected of being impersonal, but with dating agencies claiming marriages being made in cyberspace initial expectations are clearly being confounded. The format of e-mails may have similarities to memo forms but how many users are restricting their use to memo functions? Early sociological studies correctly noted that industrial workers who could communicate easily with each other (for example coalminers, steelworkers) were more effective negotiators on pay and conditions than those who were geographically diffused (for example shop assistants, agricultural workers). However, the internet can eliminate the tyranny of distance and dispersal, as was shown by European lorry drivers organizing blockades in response to price rises of petrol in 2000. Politically and economically, while mass media are becoming increasingly consolidated in multinationals or remain in the hands of the state and hence are becoming more Big Brother-like, it is simultaneously now feasible for the ordinary people to organize revolutionary alternatives on a national or global scale.

Fascinating as such research will be, it will not advance the three main challenges yet to be met in the area of encounter regulation:

1   the systematic integration of the verbal, vocal, and physical etic and emic features associated with engaging in encounters, and then opening, maintaining, and closing them.
2   the classification of the associations as affordances, consequences, or simple correlates of turn-taking.
3   the development of explanations as to why the particular affordances have the roles they do.

6.11   New Modes of Encounter

Information Communication Technology (ICT)

The world of communication has been shrunk, so that neither time nor distance are the tyrants they were, even fifty years ago. Even for FtF encounters global travel resources have reduced the time it would take for A and B to meet to less than 48 hours. Non-FtF communication can be so fast as to be perceptually instantaneous. When James VI of Scotland became James I of England and Wales, an astute sycophant arranged to carry the message from London to Edinburgh in three days, which was half the time for the official intelligence to reach him. In 1815 pigeons (?) of the London-based Rothschild family carried the information about the outcome of the Battle of Waterloo to arrive days before the official communiqué reached London; this enabled them to anticipate changes to markets, reorganize their finances and secure a fortune. By the 1880s, the land line telegraph connecting London to Calcutta could transmit cricket match scores within 8 hours! In 1910, instantaneous wireless telegraphy from London to the SS Montrose ensured the apprehension of the emigrating wife-poisoner, Dr. Crippen. Bell's first telephone message from Maine to Vermont evoked the cynical enquiry from Emerson as to what Maine could have to say to Vermont, but simultaneously set the scene for another revolution.

Now there is wireless, TV, phone, fax, e-mail, scanning, videoconferencing – and the delivery of affordable interactive multi-media for the multitudes is imminent. The questions here are confined to issues of the regulation of encounters across the different vehicles.

Two main general consequences of these developments must be contrasted. Real FtFs are now qualitatively easier and faster to achieve than they were, and virtual FtF even easier and instantaneous. In contrast, the information-exchange need for FtFs is much reduced as a result of telephone and internet networks. But what is such use doing to the interpersonal relations? Within and between organizations, e-mails and faxes have reduced the use of memos and letters. Within and between people mobile phones permit instant audio links with other people, as yet still within geographical limits however. The current situation is (probably) transitional as individuals and organizations are still developing norms for which mode of communication to use when, with whom, and why. The use of mobile phones will prove to be an interesting social psychological phenomenon. The competing companies have proliferated their tariff systems, ostensibly to offer consumer choice but with the very expensive charges or costs for those who do not optimize their use of their target tariff. How many of the young persons who are making so many casual calls have budgets and records of their activities, and what will be the results of overspending? Will phone calls be reduced or income enhanced? (Are these phone calls replacing smoking cigarettes as five-minute break fillers?) Are they serving to increase the frequency of FtF meetings or to reduce them? Are the norms of use similar to those for fixed phones? What are the taboos about who should not be rung when and when and where should one be unavailable? With the exception of the life-style question in parenthesis, the others are relevant to encounter regulation: how frequent, with whom, and when?

Frequency

All people are used to regulating the frequency with which they meet with other people. Norms of what is expected differ from sub-culture to sub-culture. Rights to and the meanings of deviation from norms could be contingent on the expense and ease with which FtF encounters were possible. Relationships such as friendship will require certain frequencies of meeting or interaction to retain their label. Friendships from the past may be reduced to annual exchanges of cards. Typically the closer and more personal the relation the more frequent the encounters and the greater the pressure for those to be FtF, or where distance is a factor, phone. Daily or weekly such interactions may well be organized on a regular timetable or even a "drop in" basis. Both cultural norms and individual negotiations will set these frequencies. For phoning, who phones who will also be regularized. Where pragmatically sensible much communication at work is already on an e-mail basis. It seems that a 24 hour turn-around is the current expectation for replies whereas replies to letters can be slower without reminders being sent.

When to use which

One advantage of e-mail and fax lie in the facts that they can be sent when it suits the sender and attended to similarly by the recipient. There is no need to rise early or stay up late to make inter-hemisphere phone calls. Issues of turn-taking do not arise with written modes. For transmission of information in representational form, the written mode encourages carefulness in the reduction of ambiguity and reflection and revision of content prior to sending. For expression of sentiments however written modes lack the vocal information of phone calls. For making requests, written modes render it easier for the recipient to decline, and phone calls carry lesser force than FtF encounters. Hence e-mails are likely to save recipients from pressures to agree or to agree and subsequently withdraw.

With whom

The financial services industry has been transformed with phone-based and internet services. A great variety of commercial transactions can now be made online. Criteria of availability and ease of access are prominent factors in the switch from FtF and postal interactions. Concerns about unreliability and possible fraud remain as deterrents.

As already mentioned it originally seemed that for personal relationships the internet would be seen as impersonal and formal but its facilities have been exploited to make and maintain contact with like-minded others in fan-clubs and discussion groups that overcome the barriers of distance. Baym (2000) charts the development and subsequent fate of a soap-opera fan group over a five year period. She treats it as an online community with a focus on the medium, as an audience community bound by the soap opera of common experience, and as a community of practice in terms of who does what in terms of practice. As noted, this is but one example of thousands of such newsgroups in a whole variety of web realizations. New journals have sprung up, and reviews of interactive features of computer-mediated interactions have begun to appear (for example

Herring, 1996). Watch the space explode with articles about encounter regulation in the media! But in which media?

6.12 Old Mode of Encounter: Conversation

Progress in the charting of sequences and their significance for the beginnings and endings of FtF and other encounters has been considerable, regardless of the new limitations expressed in 6.11, but what can be said about the middle bit? Conversation as a title word has been in vogue since the Californian Linguistic Turn was initiated, and workers in the area have typically hurried over definitional issues but used adjectives like "informal," "casual" or "non-formal" to indicate that the encounters do not include institutionalized structures, but refer to whatever subcultural norms dictate as permissible in meetings between pairs or small groups of individuals in the home, the café or pub, in work breaks, or in the street.

Hence, any reader who is expecting a definition of "conversation" that unambiguously discriminates it from all other language-based activities has yet to appreciate that very common characteristic of everyday lexical items – their lack of preciseness. Just as Wittgenstein could set out a list of games which did not share any universal criterial attributes or clearly separate themselves from cognate activities, so it is with "conversation." How are we to discriminate between conversations and informal interviews, discussions, tutorials, e-mailing? Is it sensible to think of the typical conversation as involving more than one but only a few persons, talking informally about everyday topics? Slugoski and Hilton (2001) define conversation as an "orderly, jointly-managed sequence of utterances produced by at least two participants who may or may not share similar goals in the interaction." They are aware that this definition is so broad that it includes activities that would be more commonly referred to with more specific terms, but trust that an over-inclusive bias probably has fewer disadvantages than its opposite. It certainly suffices to ensure that some sensible empirical questions about conversation can be posed.

Given the broad definition, conversation is clearly a ubiquitous activity around the world, in all but a few specialized groups. It may in fact be the commonest waking interactive activity engaged in by human beings. Among western adults, everyday conversational partners are likely to include kin, colleagues, and friends, as well as strangers. Within those categories topics will cover everyday personal events such as what they and others have been and are doing, what is newsworthy in the media, with some topics such as sport and children probably being mainly divided along gender lines.

But is it worth pursuing such "commonsense" and personal experience more systematically? Is there any point in knowing how often who talks to whom about what – and why? Unfortunately until we have found out some answers to such questions, we are unlikely to be able to assess the value of such data. Darwin and Wallace would have found it difficult to support their arguments about the origins of species and the pressures of natural selection had they not collected and collated masses of ecological data first. Much less is known about the ecology of conversations. Among studies of topics, Emler's (1989) event-contingent self-recordings have highlighted one way forward. Over a seven-day period, 60 students tracked one of six given topics to yield some data about 22,000 conversations. The six topics were constraining and reflected a particular research interest in politics, which was in fact the only topic that yielded a sex difference, with the highest frequency in inter-male conversations and constituting 12 percent of conversations. The most common topic was the doings of known others, constituting 40 percent of all conversations for each sex. As Emler points out, the method requires considerable cooperation from participants and yields a massive data set. It has the strengths of reaching situations where unobtrusive but ethically contentious recordings cannot reach. It has the weakness of its reporting being under the selective control of the participant. Whilst it is not as quick and simple as questionnaire completion, it is more likely to achieve a higher degree of validity. The finding of the very high incidence of talk about third parties is sufficiently dramatic to imply that this could indeed be a dominant focus of much conversation. The result can be combined with some from earlier related studies at least to begin to establish a frame of reference. Czikszentmihalyi, Larson and Prescott (1977) bleeped students 42 times for a week and estimated that their participants spent an average of six hours a day in conversation. Wheeler and Nezlek (1977) arrived at a similar figure in their diary-based study, and like Emler and Grady (1987) reported that conversations *a deux* were the most common.

We need to hold in mind that university students are predominantly youthful and unmarried, follow flexible timetables, and may well be meeting large numbers of new peers on campus prior to joining the adult world of work. They may therefore have particularly strong reasons for talking about others, and ample opportunities. What was being discussed about others was not pursued in greater depth, but Emler argues more generally that one function of such gossip is finding out and checking hypotheses about the character and conduct of potential mates, friends, and colleagues. We need to check out whether our perceptions of others are valid, and the views of third parties are a major source of such intelligence. Students may be occupying temporary and transitional roles, but they are also form-ing social relationships that may establish networks that will last a life-time. It is important for them to form valid impressions. English-speaking students are a limited group on which to base even weak estimates, but personal experience points to a continuation of the heuristic functions of conversations throughout life, but one that goes beyond finding out about others, to finding out how to do things, and gathering intelligence for careers, clubs to join, schools for children et cetera et cetera.

It is also true that what we say and how we say it constitutes an impor-tant component of our own self-expression and self-presentation: how we wish to be seen by others. We also use conversation to regulate the affec-tive states and actions of others and ourselves. We use it to fill silences when silence is not acceptable. We use it to register and change group membership and social relationships. We use conversation for phatic com-munion. We use it to impart and receive and evaluate world knowledge. In sum, we can use conversation for any and all of the functions listed in chapter 3. That social psychologists, and more importantly their cultures, view ecologically valid studies of human activities as time-consuming and expensive and therefore to be avoided is unfortunate.

6.12.1   One Social Psychological Approach to Orderliness in Conversation

Among many others, Clarke (1977; 1983) has argued that social psycholo-gists need to describe and explain the temporal structure of the stream of interpersonal behavior. At least three main issues have to be tackled: the segmentation of that stream into appropriate units, the classification of those units, and the formulation of rules that will generate the orderly behavioral sequences which can and do occur. While these three prob-lems may be separable for initial analytic purposes, the projected solutions for any one are contingent upon concurrent and complementary specifi-cations of the characteristic features of the other two, and they must even-tually be synthesized to form a consistent whole.

Clarke and Argyle (1982) enumerated similarities between these prob-lems and those confronting linguists intent upon writing grammars. In each case what is needed is a "canonical generative representation of sets of sequences of discrete events arranged in time according to their type classes" (p. 161). It is necessary to maintain a distinction between the meanings of the units and structures and their lexico–grammar. Both the non-verbal and verbal behaviors are hierarchically organized systems in which higher-order plans generate the lower-order structures and units; the meanings of the latter can be inferred only from the higher-order plans. If this is so, then perhaps it is a sensible methodological approach to work from the top down as well as from the bottom up. To find out about plans requires the intelligent exploitation of the comments and judgments of competent members of the culture.

In certain respects lay native speakers may be able to be more helpful with supra-sentential than sub-sentential analysis. For judgments about the grammaticalness or sense of sub-sentential strings, ordinary native speakers may be confined to assessments of what can and cannot be properly said. They may only be able to offer reactive replies: "Yes," "No," or "Perhaps." They may be able to segment strings into words but are likely to experience difficulty both below and above this level. Further, they are not likely to have a command over the linguistic terminology necessary for classifying units or structures into sets.

In contrast, native speakers may well be able to comment about speech acts in some detail. They may be able to specify necessary and sufficient conditions for the successful enactments of promises, bets, requests, complaints, and apologies, and these specifications may include structural and sequential features. At still higher order levels, Everyperson may again be more likely to be incompetent. Determining what textual features make a sermon a sermon or a lecture a lecture may well require consultation with experienced practitioners rather than Everyperson, just as descriptions of literary texts will need the service of experts.

It is at the level of speech acts however that Clarke has experimented. Four main methods have been exploited:

Secondary experimentation. Natural conversations were collected and the recordings or transcripts are then mutilated in systematic ways. Native speakers can then be asked to perform a variety of tasks. They were asked to construct utterances to replace deletions or to choose items from a given array. They were asked to order utterances into acceptable sequences. They were asked to classify extracts in terms of similarities or differences. In-so-far as the native speakers agree with each other, the experimenter is entitled to draw inferences about the propriety and likelihood of sequences, the appropriate segmentation of units and structures, and the classes into which they can be formed.

Inductive Procedures. Utilizing samples of natural discourse, the experimenter, as a specially trained native speaker and culture member, can try to extract and classify units and structures, count commonly occurring sequences, and then infer the meaning and significance of these through the principle of communication – the rule that items that exchange for each other are of the same type. Clarke found the initial classification phase with this technique particularly difficult, since it presumes a knowledge of the relationships to be ascertained in the final phase of the sequence and, more important, because form–meaning linkages are so context dependent.

A priori modelling. It is possible to exploit current beliefs of experts about units and structures in various kinds of generative grammars in order to construct computer programmes which, when fed with units and structures, may yield outputs that simulate discourse. Clarke has compared the differential efficacy of finite state, push-down stack, linear-bounded, and Turing automata models to this end.

Analyses and modelling of case studies.   This strategy relies upon generating a system that takes a set of case studies and derives a predictive model for these at the same time as it takes account of significant discriminating variables, for example, possible situational determinants. Programmes can be tested against observed sequences.

Clarke suggested that the first two approaches yielded results more easily but that the results tend to be uninteresting and obvious, whereas the latter two were harder to make to work but yielded more unexpected results when they were successful. It is perhaps useful to illustrate these considerations by describing some of the studies conducted by Clarke and reported by Clarke and Argyle (1982). Using dialogues recorded in waiting rooms, each utterance of twenty-utterance extracts was typed on a single card and respondents were asked to sort these into a sequence that reconstructed the original conversation. The respondents were able to perform the task with massively greater-than-chance accuracy. Even when asked to do so with the relatively abstract level of Bales' Interaction Process Analysis categories (1950 & chapter 6.2) to rank order which of the 12 categories was likely to follow the emission of any particular category, the judgments of respondents correlated highly with the actually observed relative frequencies reported by Bales over 20 years earlier.

If utterances are in some measure predictable and themselves have predictive significance, over what span are these operative? Both Pease and Arnold (1973) and Clarke (1983) used the technique of providing respondents with one or more preceding utterances and require them to add to the text. The resulting texts were subsequently rated for plausibility. Both investigations found that plausibility ratings increased up to an order in which the respondents had a knowledge of up to four preceding utterances but not beyond.

A rather complicated design was used to try to define which features of earlier utterances were predictive of later ones. One group of subjects was shown the first 15 lines of a twenty-line dialogue and asked to write a précis that would enable someone else to construct the last five lines. Members of a second group then used the précis to construct the last five lines, while members of a third group performed the same task with the original 15 lines as a guide. Members of the fourth group were provided with the versions of the last five lines generated from the second and third groups along with the original five last lines. They were also shown the original first 15 lines and rated each of the endings for the plausibility of their closeness to the original final five lines. Versions resulting from the précis were rated more highly than those from the other two sources.

In an attempt to specify the important features guiding choices, 22 scales were constructed that referred to such characteristics as topic, setting, and temporary and more stable cues about the participants. These were rated for perceived utility and correlated for each summary and the plausibility rating. The resultant matrix was factor analyzed. The pattern and size of loadings were interpreted to suggest that the content and the social roles of the participants were the best predictors of successful continuation of the dialogue.

Other similar experiments have been used to infer that in conversation speakers first decide which of the previous remarks will be used as a springboard for their utterance and which of the possible reactions will be made. Narrative accounts by respondents of three conversational situations were used to extract a sequence of greeting–establish/relationship–task–re-establish/relationship–parting. When respondents were asked to name the units in the episodes, they tended to give labels for higher-order units, such as "complaining," but offered extended descriptions of lower-order units. (Presumably the existence or absence of such brief lexical labels has social significance.)

Why these secondary experimentation and inductive procedures ought not to be disregarded by lovers of natural discourse is that "artificial" as they are, the results are generated by human minds. Suffice it to say at this stage that insofar as respondents can perform such tasks with a high degree of consensus, they must in fact be relying on their own versions of two theory-driven strategies: a priori modelling and the analysis and modelling of case studies. To be theory-driven, there must be theories of two kinds, one that segments and classifies discourse and one that generates the set of sequences which can occur but not other sequences. Various classifications of discourse units exist, and Clarke and Argyle elected to work with speech acts deriving from Searle (1975). Simple labels of speech acts do not in themselves offer sufficient information for judgments to be made readily about likely occurrence; for this they need to be tagged at least with speaker identification and some semantic cuing. Labels do enable us to see some of the relationships between speech acts themselves; for example, "compliance" can be seen as a "command" or "request" followed by a performance. A priori (personal?) judgments were made as to which of 43 speech acts could or could not follow each other. Combined with distinctions between proactive and reactive speech acts and possibilities of speaker change, the model can generate dialogue. Judges in fact rated such dialogues as being more likely to conversations than random sequences.

The case study work has concentrated on question–answer sequences with their possibilities of nesting and recursion. It has shown that none of the four models seems to be adequate in itself, a combination of the pushdown stacks and linear bounding being necessary. This kind of activity encounters two difficulties not experienced by analyses of sub-sentential grammars. First is the difficulty of deciding upon levels of analysis and classifications within those levels. Second is the difficulty that none of the four generative models combines both recursion and nesting with the interactive qualities, both of which are evident features of conversation.

6.13   Conceptual Frameworks

Thanks to Grice (1975/1989) and Brown and Levinson (1987/1978, see chapter 8) two complementary frameworks have been advanced which have helped to give structure to thinking about some fundamental features of verbal interaction, whilst Giles and colleagues (Giles et al., 1987; Shepard, Giles & LePoire, 2001) have emphasized adaptations within interactions (see chapter 14). Grice put forward what he saw to be the basic presuppositions of representational communication in conversation, and used these as a basis to discuss the meanings of deviations from them. Interesting and important as the latter are, it is the presuppositions themselves that are most immediately relevant. Since one of Grice's objectives was to explicate how irony works, he would no doubt have appreciated the irony that his framework is likely to prove to be just as useful as his elegant demonstrations of how we can say more, or less, than we mean.

Grice: Conversational Maxims

Perhaps at a convivial New Year party, an exuberant friend might say, "I see Geoffrey hasn't gone to prison yet!." Given that Geoffrey is at the party and that no criminal charges have been laid against him, the remark would appear to be true but uninformative, so why bother to make it? To anticipate, the statement breaches Grice's first conversational maxim. Given that the conversation is amiable and cooperative, what is the point of the remark? It is of course likely to be followed by "Oh, what do you know that I don't?" and depart into rumors about Geoffrey's conduct that might be going to lead to charges being laid.

What then are these basic assumptions? Grice (p. 26) begins by limiting his frame of reference to conversations which can be included under his Cooperative Principle in which case participants should "Make [their] conversational contribution such as is required, at the stage at which occurs, by the accepted purpose or direction of the talk exchange in which you are engaged." Immediately then we can raise questions as to which kinds of exchange are excluded. First we might note that the primary antonym of "cooperative" is "competitive," and hence it is to be expected that the rules which Grice is concerned with may well not apply to competitive discourse, that is exchanges in which the goals of the participants do not mesh or more dramatically are in conflict. He does not pretend to cover conversations that are arational or irrational in the sense that the participants are not trying to coordinate their utterances. He is focussing too on statements apparently serving the representational function. This excludes much, but as will be seen the word "apparently" is a weasel word whose significance will be cashed hereafter.

With these implicit provisos, Grice suggests that contributions to cooperative conversations should follow prescriptions within the four Kantian categories of Quantity, Quality, Relation, and Manner.

Under Quantity come:

1 Make your contribution as informative as is required for the current purposes of the exchange;
2 Do not make your contribution more informative than is required.

Under Quality comes: "Try to make your contribution one that is true" which is subdivided into:

1 Do not say that which you believe to be false;
2 Do not say that for which you lack adequate evidence.

Under Relation comes:

1 Be relevant.

Under Manner comes: "Be perspicuous" that subdivides into:

1   Avoid obscurity of expression;
2   Avoid ambiguity;
3   Be brief;
4   Be orderly.

Provocatively, Grice appends a note that additional maxims might be needed, and helpfully mentions that "Be polite" is one such. Whilst his special interest was in what is implicated when a speaker blatantly flouts a maxim, and the conversational partners are both aware of this, for the present, it is more relevant first to comment on the rationality of following the maxims and secondly to note reasons why people may not follow them.

Both at first sight and after critical reflection, the maxims are so self-evidently rational that what is surprising is that they were not listed before 1975! Their rationality however is contingent on the conversation having *a cooperative purpose and being directed to the transparent and efficient exchange of propositionally expressible information*. Drop any one of these features, and the maxims can become irrelevant, and it has already been mentioned that conversations can have purposes and can perform functions other than those covered by Grice. This does not mean that Grice's analysis is unhelpful. What it may mean is that if other interactants do not invoke the speaker's failure to follow one or more maxims, then the primary purpose is other than the apparent one, and the problem is to work out which.

One answer which has received very little attention is speaker ignorance. I know of no syllabus in the educational systems with which I am familiar that cites Grice's maxims for conversation or any other communication and I doubt that many people could articulate them. Ideally the answer to any posed question should minimize the load on the questioner; the answer should maximize the shared knowledge and just fill the gap signalled in the question. Not too much information and not too little. Accurate and supportable. Relevant and presented clearly in the optimal order. And if this does not happen as it often does not, is it possible to invoke the maxims and suggest that the other person learn and follow them? It is instructive to invoke maxims explicitly and note their effects. When in a group that is discussing international conflicts or other current affairs, checking the extent to which professed opinions can be supported by evidence and argument can lead quickly to hostility and rejection of the enquirer. It is rude to challenge beyond some conventional threshold.

Even when people are implicitly or explicitly conversant with the maxims they may not be able to follow them. Their performance skills may be inadequate. States of anxiety or stress can reduce proficiency. We can know we are not speaking efficiently, and afterwards remember what mistakes we made.

As soon as more than one maxim or principle is operative, then the possibility exists that they can be in conflict with each other. "Be truthful" and "Be polite" can come into conflict with each other when the respondent has just been handed a gift that he or she does not like. Pragmatic solutions such as *white lies* are one compromise. *Equivocation* is another. Just as the Jewish Ten Commandments come into conflicts with each other which require real people in real situations to assign priorities as to which to disobey, so Grice's maxims have to be prioritized by individuals in contexts, with guidance from cultural norms.

These three factors operate separately and together to ensure that the Gricean model is not followed as closely as it might be. The fourth factor of deliberate flouting is a more sophisticated game requiring the listener to work out what is meant. The example of a driver saying, "I'm almost out of petrol" receiving a reply of "There's a garage just down the road" implicates that the garage is close, sells petrol, and is likely to be open. Not a difficult set of inferences to draw, but the suppressed assumptions do have to be worked out. The opening example implicated Geoffrey as being under suspicion of committing some criminal act, but avoided being slanderous or serious. It could also mean less than was said and be a mild joke. Implicature causes extra work for the speaker, and the calculation required by the listener may be too difficult. There needs to be appropriate shared knowledge and a common sub-culture for implicature to work. Without elaborating the idea at this point, we can note that a minimum effort principle combined with transparent representational transmission is just one function in communication. Bonding through shared understanding and joking, both to show shared understanding and to be mutually amusing, are common components of many conversations and it is important to remember that Grice's ideas are particularly useful as a challenge pragmatically when involved in a conversation and theoretically when analyzing those of others.

A final word needs to be said about competitive conversations. At the work-place perhaps competitive elements are always present, even within cooperative activities. When A and B are bargaining in commercial transactions each may well be trying to maximize their own gains at the expense of the other, especially in individualistic capitalist cultures. Whether it involves selling goods or oneself, "The higher the price the better" would seem to be a contemporary theme. This means hiding from the competitor what would in fact be acceptable, in the hope of getting more. It may lead to exaggeration and simple falsification if winning becomes sufficiently important. In a Darwinian world, inner wariness is a characteristic that facilitates survival and success. To imagine otherwise is to be lulled into a dream of a benevolent and just society that can change quickly into a nightmare, as many British citizens have found in their financial arrangements for pensions and savings. Bank managers and financial advisers are not paid to hold charitable cooperative conversations with potential and actual customers. In competitive conversations some of the maxims may well switch in directions, for example minimize information, be prepared to lie and make false claims about evidence, use ambiguity and other features of manner to maximize the chances of gaining personal goals at the expense of the competitor.

6.14 Commentary

The questions broached in chapter 6 do little more than introduce the diversity of topics and approaches that are available for initially analytic and subsequently integrative investigation. Contributions have come from each of the relevant disciplines and have ranged from the micro to the macro in terms of level of focus. There are significant omissions. Although the Californian Linguistic Turn is given consideration, the style of fascinating Conversational Analysis (CA) adopted by Antaki (1994) is not. The procedural rules across different kinds of encounters are confined to two illustrations of successful uncoverings in two domains. Much more could be made of the developments of norms for ICT modes, and gossip (Emler, 2001) as a common variety of conversation are not given proper weighting.

Perhaps it is timely to raise the question of how much everyday talk is doing what. Analyses of samples of conversation have been based on whatever interchanges academics chose to analyze. They may have been "natural" and therefore real, but of what population are they samples? At the present time there are very few estimates of the frequencies of even topics of conversation and what there are derive from undergraduates. Certainly these pioneering efforts are consistent with Emler's (2001) hypothesis that conversation has a high incidence of gossip which he sees as being a major means by which we find out about other people and make sense of their activities. These conversations are typically not spreading scandal or malicious untruths about others, but are providing interactants with the perspectives of others about mutual acquaintances. Serving as checks on reliability and validity of our own and others' beliefs about target persons, these interchanges are also of new information and news. They can save us from embarrassing or upsetting enquiries or comments. They can encourage wariness and suspicion. They can enable us to be manipulators and exploiters.

Reference was made to *phatic communion* in chapter 3.4. For those of us familiar with this phrase it is an excellent shorthand. For some others, it could be viewed as unnecessary technical jargon for referring to the chat, animated or desultory, that goes with enjoying the company of other people: talking that induces and maintains comfort in human company. It is not the agitated chatter of would-be cathartic coming to terms with the day's awfulness and stress. Neither is it the fun of witty exchanges and offering opinionated solutions to the world's problems satirized as dinner party talk. It is the talk around bed-time stories with children, the bedsides of the sick, the drinks in the café and pub, or the cups of tea before going to bed. Strictly speaking this could be classified as a special case of regulating states of self and others, with the particular sense of well-being being the objective, but of course the situations and occasions are not planned as tasks with well-being as an objective. It may well be that historically a reduction of regular occasions of phatic communion is in part responsible for the exhausted quality of life for modern men and women. Arousal reduction via phatic communion is no longer scripted into daily routines. Do those who continue to observe the practice sleep better?

While Grice has generated a helpful set of rules against which individual conversational utterances can be compared, there are as yet no classificatory systems for conversations *per se*, and for the present, it is difficult to see against what criteria any proposals would be evaluated.

CHAPTER 7

Regulation of States and Behavior of Self and Others

The components figuring in chapter 7 differ from each other enormously in the amounts of research so far devoted to them. The spontaneous reactive expression of states and people talking to themselves have not occasioned the same interest as getting them to change their attitudes to the People's Political Party or to buy Santa's Snowy Soapsuds. In these last two cases the focus is on controlling the attitudes and behavior of others with a view to them working and/or voting for the party, and buying goods; the relationship between the message senders and the receivers is of no concern or of secondary importance. Those studies which have focused on interpersonal relations and their management do involve regulating both the states and behavior of those in the relevant relationship, but changing or maintaining the relationship itself is the primary focus. Hence they are treated in a separate chapter 8.

7.1 F5a: Expression of States

States are expressed by laughter, smiling, glaring, crying. They can manifest themselves in screaming, shouting, whispering, stuttering. Swearing and noises that are labelled "Ouch!," "Gosh," or "Wow!" severally are reactive phenomena, spontaneous expressions of immediate experiences. It is *not* known yet whether they are functional for the person. They *mark* states and they may serve a cathartic function. Whether people do feel better after saying "xxxx!" has not been investigated so far as I know. The emission of "xxxx!" may simply be a product of an originally voluntary ejaculation that has become classically conditioned. Involuntary swearing does seem to be much more common than the research literature suggests, but since it is frequently an ingroup activity, apparently inhibited in the presence of outsiders, social psychology has yet to come to grips with the phenomenon.

⌐ 7.2   F2: Regulation of Self

F2a: Regulation of Self: States

There is a song which claims that whistling reduces fear. There is a belief that telling oneself that the current depression is not real, but just a consequence of the flu, will help to relieve the feelings. These issues of mind over matter do not appear to have been researched in spite of the advisory booklets persistently arguing for the powers of positive thinking, an activity which may well require verbal *sotto voce* instructions to oneself. Knowing under what conditions talking to oneself might alleviate negative states would be theoretically interesting as well as socially useful.

F2b: Regulation of Self: Behavior

Unlike speech regulating the behavior of others, that which is used to control one's own behavior has no unique label. "Talking to oneself" is inadequate, both because it might be premature to eliminate from consideration covert as opposed to audible speech, and because simple talking may involve other functions such as giving a commentary of ongoing action (representational).

While there have been studies of this regulatory function in developing children (see Luria, 1961), adults have been left alone. There are no reported studies of how cooks attempt to control their cake baking or gardeners their rose pruning. We cannot say with what frequency "talking to oneself" has an apparent instructional component, and, if it has, what its formal characteristics are. This is particularly unfortunate. It would be illuminating to know just what form the grammatical structure of the speech takes. Does it simply omit explicit references to features of the environment already understood, and therefore involve an extreme degree of contextual presupposition? Or is it "telegraphic" in the ways in which the speech of very young children is, that is omitting as many function words as possible and relying on the order of selected lexical items to convey the essence of the message?

Without the necessary empirical evidence it would be hazardous to venture guesses about what differences found might mean. With so little knowledge of the facts of the matter we cannot readily offer answers to questions about any possible increases in efficiency persons might achieve through overt speaking to themselves. Studies with young children led Luria to suggest a three-stage process in the development of the regulatory function: an initial one in which speech has no relevance, a second in which it accentuates the vigor of an ongoing activity, and a third in which the semantic value of the language units used becomes relevant. For example, a child at the intermediate stage with his hand poised to push a button will respond positively whether he says to himself "Press!" or "Don't press!," and while "Press twice!" will yield one push, "Press! Press!" will yield two. Claims to obtain such results (Luria, 1961) date from a period when Russian psychologists were prone to present their supportive evidence in an illustrative and piecemeal fashion; other investigators could not examine critically the methodology or stages between premises and conclusions of arguments. Jarvis (1964), after most carefully piecing together fragments of information to recreate and elaborate one of Luria's most quoted investigations, found no evidence to support the results reported. Random results can be obtained by bad experimentation, but such a criticism would not appear to have substance in relation to Jarvis's work. The field itself remains wide open. Klein (1964) has been able to show that speech to self declines with age, but that within that constraint, task-relevant mutterings increase and task-irrelevant speech decreases. There is variation among children, but high talkers do not appear to be either more or less successful at puzzles or button-pushing tasks than low talkers, although not all his results were random.

Both Jarvis and Klein suggest that certain parent–child variables may be relevant to how much children do talk to themselves, but they are not specific. Maybe highly dependent children being socialized out of close attachment to their parents talk to themselves to reassure themselves: talking could substitute for whistling when you are afraid of the dark. Whether or not, and if so how much, speech-for-self is controlling affect rather than sensori-motor skills, and whether it works, we do not yet know.

I have already mentioned that we do not know what linguistic structures are used, whether or not there is a high incidence of imperatives and modal verbs, whether a large amount of presupposition and abbreviation is present or what. As with states, so with behavior, a (rich?) mine waiting to be excavated.

⌐7.3 F3a and b: Regulation of States and Behavior of Others

All speech and writing addressed to others is intended to have (or may have) some effect on their states and/or behavior, and as with some other chapters (for example marking of emotions), this one may turn out to be informative at the level of speech acts, but no more than inchoate at a macro-level. As people, we can perform an alphabet of acts from abasing to worrying, from absolving to whitewashing. Whilst it would be boring rather than amusing for the reader to be presented with a dictionary of speech act verbs glossed with their linguistic and contextual conditions of use, any selection for consideration can be no more than arbitrary and minimal. Most of us know how to amuse, annoy, arouse, and bore others in general. We can distinguish between the kinds of utterances which would be expected to achieve particular effects, given the context of situation and the participants. We know how to give orders and extract promises. We know how to combine the arousal of states to actions – provoking others into shouting at us or laughing with us.

In the *New Handbook of Language and Social Psychology* (Robinson & Giles, 2001), the editors restricted coverage of such issues to four activities: accounting, deceiving, negotiating, and patronizing. The decision was heavily influenced by the topics that had attracted research. Here too coverage will be restricted and illustrative rather than comprehensive. The two selected are attitude change and persuading to help or buy.

Attitude change figures because it remains a somewhat muddled field where psychological writing can still be at variance with much real-world experience. Persuading to help or buy have figured strongly in the literature of social psychology and the mass media.

⌐7.4 Attitude Change

As M. Burgoon (1990) has pointed out, some authors have been prone to conflate social influence, attitude change, persuasion, and compliance-gaining into a single bundle, whereas more conceptually concerned psychologists would distinguish between changing beliefs about X, changing sentiments towards X, changing approval of X, changing action-orientation to X, and changing behavior towards X. Even around 400 BC Plato was distinguishing between cognition, affect, and conation, but not all social psychologists have taken these distinctions on board yet. The components of X listed are neither independent of each other nor in fixed relations, and changing beliefs may or may not change sentiment, for example. However, it is well established that professed attitudes and behavior are not perfectly correlated. Here this first section is focused on attitude change and 7.5 on compliance in behavior. In studies of attitude change, the actual mix of the four constituents mentioned is not usually made explicit; approval of X is probably the most common aspect represented.

The Yale School is credited with providing the impetus for attitude change studies (Hovland, Janis & Kelley, 1953; Hovland, Lumsdaine & Sherif, 1949, Janis & Hovland, 1959), and standard social psychology texts typically devote a substantial section to social influence, providing accounts of models of routes for change via different psychological processes, and giving results about source factors, audience factors, and message characteristics, the last being of particular concern here. Suffice it to say that the field has suffered from many very weak manipulations on serious issues, with the experiments yielding no or tiny effects. Students in a sophomore lab class reading single paragraphs which challenge long-held views about the death penalty or abortion are unlikely to bring about any change, however credible the source attributed. Too many experiments fall into this category of trivial manipulations. More substantial studies do find effects. All the factors one might imagine to have relevance can be shown to have influence: The credibility of the source, message, audience, and context have all been shown to be important. In respect of the messages themselves, studies have examined the effects of such factors as the amount of information relayed, the difference between the current stance of the receiver and the orientation of the message, the order of presentation of arguments, whether one or more sides of argument are presented, and the basis of the appeal, for example fear or empirical evidence. Each of these can be shown to be relevant under certain conditions for certain people. However, the review literature has an air of disappointment about the size and unpredictability of effects (Jaspars, 1978) and a sympathy with F.H. Allport's (1924) original suggestion that habits are the flywheel of society, meaning by this that they provide the inertia, in the original dynamic sense of this word. In unchanging environments we would expect adults to have relatively stable attitudes.

How then is the paradox to be explained that attitudes and behavior can be changed very fast? In 1981 the Argentinian military dictatorship invaded and occupied the Malvinas (the Falkland Islands). Within a few hours, the British media and individuals were suggesting that we "nuke the Argies." The rhetoric quickly dehumanized Argentinians to "Argies" and "dagos" in spite of the fact that most British probably had little knowledge about Argentina, were unlikely to know how unpopular the dictatorship was, and had no knowledge of the history of the islands. Members of the British government were abusive, and Mrs Thatcher had no difficulty in gaining support for the subsequent military action. In contrast, all the ingenuity of social psychologist consultants to the government of the day could not produce an advertizing campaign that gained more than 15 percent compliance for car drivers to wear seat belts, but a law for compulsory belting-up achieved 95 percent compliance within a week of its enactment.

Just post-Plato, Aristotle (1926/Fourth century BC) had provided the human species with an excellent introduction to the art of speech-making in the service of political persuading, forensic fencing, and funereal panegyrics. His text built on the accumulated folk wisdom of the Sophists, notably Gorgias, and the dialectic of Socrates. Aristotle advised speakers to remember that what would appeal to young men would not appeal to old men; young men were idealistic, optimistic, and courageous, old men conservative, pessimistic and fearful. He advised on the art of delivery. He wrote extensively about ideal structures and offered hints about influential details. Rhetoric subsequently came to make up one third of the trivium curriculum and remained there until the seventeenth century. As might be expected, over the centuries, the earthy grounded qualities of Aristotelian principles became ritualized into a multitude of rules emphasizing form rather than substance, ornateness rather than simplicity, and shifting focus from persuading listeners to displaying the erudition of speakers.

On political campaigns, evangelical crusades, and in courts of law however, the practice of rhetoric did not decline, and it remains a potent force today. Powerful dictators of the twentieth century did not rely solely on ruthless secret police and other special forces to enhance and maintain their power; these served to contain or eliminate dissidents. The masses of sympathizers for both Fascist and Communist causes were treated to rallies and rhetoric that made them feel great and believe great things about their future. In times of great threat to their countries, Churchill, de Gaulle, and Stalin were able to galvanize determination not to be defeated. Martin Luther King combined political rights and religious principles in his extraordinarily powerful speeches to establish the rights of non-whites in the USA. In similar style, Billy Graham attracted converts to his interpretation of Christianity. The list of great British legal advocates of the last century comprises people who combined great knowledge with powerful speech-making that could sway juries to bring in surprising verdicts.

For each of these contexts, the attitudes of the participating audiences have mattered to them. Hitler and Mussolini were offering orderly prosperity and positive social identities to populations that were suffering from economic and social chaos. Churchill's offer of "blood, sweat and tears" was less positive, but found its force in an unwillingness of the people to be conquered after what they believed to be a thousand years of not being invaded. Martin Luther King offered release from institutionalized racism manifested in dramatically unequal rights. Billy Graham offered eternal salvation. It is more hazardous to say what great lawyers offer juries; some might suggest they offer them an emotionally-based orientation to bring in the wrong verdict!

Such phenomena are on a qualitatively grander scale than handing out slips of paper containing information about phenomena of no perceived importance to the lives of participants. One line of argument would have to be that the main reason why many studies of attitudes and attitude change have yielded minimal results is that too few participants have cared about the target issue. Another is that they had considered matters thoroughly and were not going to be swayed by what they may well have seen was a small manipulation in a laboratory experiment. Yet another is that they see through the experiment. The list of such reasons could be extended.

⌐ 7.5 Compliance

Elementary texts in social psychology typically distinguish between "conformity," "compliance," and "obedience." All refer to actions not attitudes and and none immediately relate to the whys of the behaviors. Conformity is modelling behavior on that of others: doing the same as those around are doing. Compliance is concerned with meeting requests framed as interrogatives. Obedience is doing as ordered, with the transparent form of a command being an imperative. Here only compliance is examined, mainly because this is the one of the three that has been most investigated in terms of the linguistic characteristics of the message, and this has research links to the mass media discussed in chapter 12 and to attitude change studies already discussed.

Cialdini (1985) reviewed a series of investigations which he and colleagues had run on the relative efficacy of different kinds of verbal primers on subsequent compliance: the foot-in-the-door, low-balling, the door-in-the-face, and "That's not all folks!."

As its name implies, the first is referring to the stereotype of the door-to-door salesperson. The first hurdle for such a person is to gain entry to the house with some form of, "May I just come in for a moment to tell you something to your advantage?" – a small request. Freedman and Fraser (1966) used cold calling to homes to ask a few questions about the use of household products. A few days later they rang those who had complied and asked if the householder would agree to a number of men coming round to make an inventory of products in the house, probably taking two or three hours. A surprising 53 percent agreed. When the prior call was omitted compliance was much lower. Similar findings have been made across a variety of samples, situations, and types of request. The initial explanatory hypothesis was that those who comply with the large request have voluntarily presented themselves as helpful people, and are disposed to maintain this image in the face of a more burdensome request. Subsequent studies have checked and supported this information.

For low-balling, the would-be customer is offered a bargain of a deal, but having secured it, the salesperson checks it out with a higher authority and comes back with reasons for reducing the attractiveness of the bargain. Cialdini (1985) showed that securing the prior agreement followed by a renege secured more compliance than an open move to the second offer. Exemplified with buying cars in Introductory Psychology courses, this case invariably yielded stories from each category: victims, walkers-out, and those who claw back to the first offer. The explanations of the victims coincided with Cialdini's explanation of the power of the *commitment* to the purchase object leading to a differential attention to all its positive characteristics other than price.

Rather than building up to the sting, persuaders can use either of two tactics which begin big. The first is such a strong request that it is refused. It is then followed by a less burdensome request. This sequence elicits more compliance than using the second request on its own. Cialdini offers three reasons for this effect: the second request appears smaller if contrasted with the first, to refuse the second smaller request as well as the first suggests being selfish and unhelpful, and thirdly the concession by the asker merits a reciprocating concession. Burger (1986) extended this triad to the bargain-offering sequences of sellers in markets: "How much in Posh Shop? $200. But for you, here today, not $100, not $50, nor even $30. For a mere $20, you ..." and found he could sell more unpriced cupcakes at a fair if their price was quoted at $1 which he reduced to 75¢ immediately than if he quoted 75¢.

Each of these involves a two step communicative process. Each, either on its own or in combination, can be built up into more complex manipulative sequences. Each is a part of the everyday experience of the consumer and/or the good-willed cooperative member of society.

7.5.1   Compliance-gaining Units

Elsewhere (chapters 8 and 9) the politeness of requests is discussed, along with a model of determinants of selection. The lists used by Soskin and John (1963) and Brown and Levinson (1987/1978) were shorter than the options listed by students in Table 7.1 (Deaux, Dane, & Wrightsman, 1993). This list was not accompanied by indications of the degree of consensus and did not indicate variability as a function of other variables. There's not a lot of point of writing to a journal editor threatening to tell one's father, if you have had a submitted article rejected. On the other hand, no item on the list is surprising.

Not all studies of attitudes and attitude change in social psychology were unconcerned with issues of prospective behavior change, and since Fishbein and Ajzen (1975) first introduced their Theory of Reasoned Action, a wealth of research has been concerned with isolating the sufficient conditions for a positive attitude to be realized in behavior (Madden, Ellen & Ajzen, 1992). Approaching the issues from another direction, Marwell and Schmitt (1967a, 1967b, see Table 7.2) listed what they viewed as 16 distinguishable strategies for gaining compliance – which served as a frame of reference for Miller and his colleagues to launch a series of investigations to check the completeness and validity of the list, to examine how variations of situation influenced choice of strategies, and to ascertain whether or not individual differences among would-be persuaders affected choices. Burgoon (1990) provides a succinct and critical review of what happened subsequently. He concludes that the list cannot sensibly be divided into either empirically-based dimensions or clusters. If a unidimensional solution to the list is the best fit with the data then the three questions become redundant. This in itself is informative, if somewhat surprising. Burgoon has concluded that the items can be viewed as differing along the single dimension of instrumental verbal aggression, ranging from punitive threats at one end to promises and appeals to goodwill at the other. Utilizing Expectancy theory (see chapter 14 and Burgoon & Miller, 1985) he and colleagues found that people expect males to use more punitive threats than females, and subsequent studies of male doctors found that male doctors could achieve greater compliance with specific kinds of patients if less positive appeals were used.

⌐ 7.6   Accounting

Issues of accounting to others appear twice, once here and again in chapter 8.7 where interpersonal relations are explored. If called to account in

Table 7.1 Strategies for Obtaining Compliance

The following strategies for obtaining compliance are listed in the order in which a group of students at the University of Alberta thought it likely they would be used.

1. Ask (either directly or indirectly).
   Example: "Would you please. . ."
2. Invoke personal expertise.
   Example: "I read in *Consumer Reports* that . . ."
3. Offer a personal reason.
   Example: "I need . . ."
4. Invoke a role relationship.
   Example: "If you were my friend, you would . . ."
5. Bargain for a favor.
   Example: "If you'll do this for me, I promise I'll . . ."
6. Invoke a norm.
   Example: "Everyone is doing it."
7. Invoke a moral principle.
   Example: "It would be the right thing to do."
8. Invoke altruism.
   Example: "The health of other people depends on you."
9. Butter them up.
   Example: "You look so attractive today."
10. Bargain for an object (or bribe).
    Example: "I'll give you $100 if you will. . ."
11. Appeal to their emotions.
    Example: "I'm going to cry if you don't . . ."
12. Offer a personal criticism.
    Example: "You're so stingy, you probably wouldn't . . ."
13. Try deception.
    Example: "The boss told me to tell you . . ." (when the boss never said a word about it).
14. Threaten.
    Example: "I'm going to tell your father if you don't . . ."
15. Use force.
    Example: "Do it right now!" (accompanied by physical shaking).

After Deaux, Dane, and Wrightsman (1993)

court, defendants are unlikely to have a primary concern with their personal relationship to the magistrate or judge. What will increase the chances of avoiding or mitigating any penalty is more likely to be of uppermost concern. However, when called to account by a spouse or friend for failing to fulfil a commitment, the focus is likely to be on repairing any threat to the prior status of the interpersonal relationship. Typically it will be infor-

Table 7.2   Typology of Compliance-Gaining Strategies,

Strategy	
Promise	If you will comply, I will reward you.
Threat	If you do not comply, I will punish you.
Expertise (positive)	If you comply, you will be rewarded because of "the nature of things."
Expertise (negative)	If you do not comply, you will be punished because of "the nature of things."
Liking	Actor is friendly and helpful to get target in a "good frame of mind" so that he will comply with the request.
Pregiving	Actor rewards target before requesting compliance
Aversive stimulation	Actor continuously punishes target, making stimulation cessation contingent on compliance.
Debt	You owe me compliance because of past favours.
Moral appeal	You are immoral if you do not comply.
Self-feeling (positive)	You will feel better about yourself if you comply.
Self-feeling (negative)	You will feel worse about yourself if you do not comply.
Altercasting (positive)	A person with "good" qualities would comply.
Altercasting (negative)	Only a person with "bad" qualities would not comply.
Altruism	I need your compliance very badly, so do it for me.
Esteem (positive)	People you value will think better of you if you comply.
Esteem (negative)	People you value will think worse of you if you do not comply.

After Marwell and Schmitt (1967b)

mal interpersonal issues that have a prime concern with relationship repair, and formal institutional issues that occasion affecting the behavior of others, where others are likely to be defined by their social rather than their personal identity. Hence the initial foray into what some social psychologists would view as intergroup issues. This view would be correct in that it is the roles of defendant/judge, employer/employee, or teacher/ students that should be determining both processes and outcomes. (That no blatantly guilty female driver friends have been charged by traffic police when caught speeding, whereas my wholly explicable justifiable marginal offenses have all led to fixed penalties, might raise doubts as to the blindness and deafness of justice – but in theory. . . . The tactics implied by the results reported in 7.4 and 7.5 were used to no avail.)

Researchers in the area have argued for a differentiation between explanations and accounting that ordinary language, with its endemic fuzzy borders, does not quite afford (see Draper, 1988). Both are often implicit or explicit answers to "why" questions, but whereas explanations unpack reasons for events and actions which are morally neutral, accounts are more likely to be required in situations where the actions or events are seen to be inappropriate such that L is blameworthy if L is the person responsible for them. To explain is to render events and actions understandable. To account for oneself is to avoid or escape blame. For these latter circumstances, English does afford four distinguishable tactics: denial, excuse, justification, and apology. An accepted denial precludes a need to provide an account. An excuse admits performing the relevant actions and then blameworthiness, but attempts to offer reasons why the acts were performed (or not performed). A justification admits performance, but denies that this was culpable or seeks to diminish the seriousness of the actions. An apology *per se* admits the act, accepts the blame, and if sincere, expresses regret (see also F7). Within each of the four categories there will be more than one kind of denial, excuse, and justification, and of course they can occur in varied combinations.

As well as seeking useful typologies, investigators have reflected and examined data as to how many elements might be involved in an account and whether they have sequential characteristics. Schonbach (1990) summarised research in which he proposed that there must be a failure event, a reproach, an account, and evaluation of the account, but found that elements might be implicit rather than explicit, that the sequence was mutable, and that embeddings and other complications were normal rather than rare (see Cody & McLaughlin, 1990, pp. 232–233). Evaluations were found to vary with the qualities within a tactic and as a function of which tactic was adopted. A strong apology, with expressions of regret and offers of restitution, is more powerful than a casual "I'm sorry" offered *en passant*.

Within this customary complex framework, various investigators have sought to collect and interpret data. Here, it is the institutional data that will be summarized and discussed. Courts of law are one obvious context of situation for examining the operation of interpositional accounts and their efficacy. This may well vary as a function of type of alleged offense, and whilst neither the dispositions of judges nor the identities and self-presentations of defendants should be relevant, both experience and evidence show that they are relevant to outcomes (O'Barr, 1982, 2001; Penman, 1987). Both the latter could co-vary with the kinds of accounting defendants offer, but within these constraints there are studies that have examined outcomes for traffic offense charges. In an early survey of drivers in California, Cody and McLaughlin (1988) had found that apologies plus excuses were most efficacious for avoiding being charged but that apologies were irrelevant to outcomes once in court. In a sample of 375 charged drivers, Cody and McLaughlin (1988) examined outcomes in the 301 where the accused did not plead guilty. How did percentages of those penalized vary with kind of account? 91 percent were penalized after denial of being the correct person, 81 percent after denial that the offense was committed, but only 25 percent whose denial was based on empirical unlikelihood. Attempted justifications resulted in penalty in 91 percent of cases, and excuses in 75 percent. Within excuses, denial of intention to offend was more effective (30 percent) than ignorance, mitigating circumstances or personal state (75 percent).

Not surprisingly, Hale (1987) found quite different percentages for students accounting for late submissions of term papers, but it is not difficult to see why this might be so. Weiner et al. (1987) have raised the level of generality to argue that excuses which successfully cite reasons that were external to the offender, uncontrollable, unintentional, and unstable are likely to be more successful than those which do not exhibit at least one of these features. He could have added plausibility as a fifth factor. Once there are doubts as to the honesty of the pleader, this will begin to weigh.

In England and Wales, "being abused as a child" as a mitigating factor for a variety of crimes had a brief spell of efficacy – until the judiciary realized that not all defendants were being truthful. Also on one occasion at least, pre-menstrual tension served to reduce a murder charge to manslaughter and resulted in a conditional discharge outcome. That judge did not repeat such a sentence. Within Hales' ambit, a student whose Harley Street doctor inadvertently sent two sick notes citing quite different illnesses was not forgiven for her failure to submit a term paper.

The Los Angeles team pursued their enquiries taking a somewhat different set of attributions from that preferred by Weiner et al. (1987). They asked how the use of the various types of account impacted on judgments of the moral character of the offender (McLaughlin, Cody, & French, 1989). Selecting some of the accounts from their 1988 study, they had students rate the character of the offender in terms of dispositional and structural factors relating to blame. For speeding, justifications yielded the highest ratings for intentional wrongdoings while challenging the accusation attracted the same judgment for driving through a red light. As they point out, traffic lights can change unexpectedly, whereas speeding does not, and hence one would expect different accounts to vary in culpability as a function of the type of offense. More serious offenses have also been investigated from an attributional perspective (Carroll & Payne, 1977; Felson & Ribner, 1981), and the results found have generally fitted Weiner's framework in terms of sentencing, once judges' views as to what were "good reasons" were taken into account; females accepting responsibility, apologizing and expressing remorse for their conduct, and having other-centered justifications, for example feeding hungry children.

7.6.1   Public Service, Industry, and Commerce

Organizations employing people to do jobs have psychological as well as legal contracts with them, and these impose obligations on both parties. There are expectations about conditions of work and payments on one side, and expectations about hours kept and rates of working on the other. More basic expectations of fairness and considerateness apply to both sides. The most frequent occasions for accounts are changes to the expected, and the agents of deviation are those from whom accounts are required. In a series of studies, Bies and colleagues (for example Bies & Sitkin, 1992) have studied excuse-making for change by management, and workers' perceptions of procedural and distributive fairness. The causal attribution factors play their role as in forensic affairs, but additional factors of timing, adequacy, and sincerity affect workers' judgments and reactions. Of course, the workplace is replete with accounts that workers have to offer for absence, lateness, errors, and low productivity and the perceived value of these, but strangely this perspective has not apparently generated sufficient studies for a review. Neither have there been reviews of the massive accountability exercises required of personnel in organizations over the last ten years. With annual reviews of workforces in which targets have been set, what explanations have been offered for failures, and how have reviewers reacted to these? At a sociological level, it would be interesting to know the extent to which such central initiatives have been ignored, ritualized, and subverted and generated a mass of wordings that do not fit the world of action but are fit for the purposes of the bureaucracy.

More pertinent for the account of accounts here, these institutionalized texts were not reactions to a "failure event" of some kind and did not therefore evoke the four types of reaction that legal defenses do. The negative evaluations are only required when targets are not met or when unexpected events look to be blameworthy. Accounts are likely to be closer to explanations that are geared to making sense of events, as are more typical of questions arising within role relationships. Both managers and workers are being people with personal identities as well as occupants of social positions.

7.6.2   Commentary

As with certain other topics, the last decade has witnessed a switch in the approach of investigators of accounts. Buttny and Morris (2001) note that the seven reviews they refer to can be divided into those continuing to show social psychological preferences for "quantitative methods" and a concern with cognition, and those setting out from examples of talk arising in social interactions and where qualitative analysis predominates as a preferred means for answering different questions (for example Antaki, 1994). They contrast too in a shift of focus from accounts as justifications to accounts as ways for others to make sense of people's actions. This latter may involve explanations that explicate what a person was doing in terms that L will understand or follow a story-like approach now known as accounts-as-narrative. Particularly for others to make sense of apparent changes in personal activities or relationships, people can provide a (narrative) history just as much of history itself offers narratives, with or without explanations, so everyday talk makes use of stories. Buttny and Morris (2001) point out that one consequence of turning to an examination of everyday talk rather than institutional activities such as courtroom proceedings is to widen the domain of accounting. Accounts are not just responses to accusations or means of escaping from blame. They do not have to involve evaluation in terms of acceptability, but include making sense of the unexpected or mysterious. They can be initiated by the account giver rather than be reactive. They can function to regulate role relationships, and although they may include statements whose truth or falsity could be evaluated (F7), this is not done, in the interests of preserving particular role relationships.

Whose accounts of accounts are to be preferred? The short answer has to be "Both!." If the objectives are to describe and explain human experience and behavior with respect to language and its use, how can one deny the observations made, be they in courtrooms or kitchens? Are either of the two approaches making unreliable or invalid observations or analyses? If not, then we are obliged to point out any weaknesses in inferences drawn, but data are data, regardless of whether they are social constructions or "facts." There is at least one ground on which either approach might be misleading. Just as a physicist would not ask why each individual stone emptied from a wheelbarrow fell where it fell, neither would a zoologist ask why it took this fly 22.5 minutes to emerge from this milk bottle today. In both cases of course, the case study might serve to lead on to further observations. Social psychologists are concerned with the general in the particular, the patterns in the singularities. Language and its use have the additional danger and complication that its users are not all perfectly competent in its use and there is no ultimate consensus on usage. If one consequence of this is that many utterances have chaotic elements in them and misunderstandings of conventions and rules, we have to be careful not to treat such utterances as standing in need of the same category of explanation as other ones. This issue is taken up more fully for arguments and explanations in chapters 11 and 12. It just makes life more difficult for those interested in language and its workings.

Regulation and Marking of Social Relationships: Shaking Hands, Terms of Address and Reference, and Being Polite

8.1 Introduction

Three topics make up chapter 8: shaking hands, terms of address and reference, and politeness. They are linked thematically. Issues of politeness arise with both shaking hands or not and with choices of terms of address and reference. Shaking hands is performed or not in opening or closing sequences of FtF encounters, and terms of address are also likely to co-occur in these phases of an encounter. However, the main rationale for the joint appearance lies in highlighting differences of approach to problems.

Shaking hands is a distinctive and discrete activity, and it is proper to ask who shakes hands with whom, where, when, how and why? How can handshakes vary and what do the variations in the type of handshake signal? The same questions can be posed (see chapter 5 about other distinguishable human non-verbal acts and displays. In those cases references were made to systematic empirical studies, some observational, some based on questionnaires, and some experimental. So far as I know, there is no volume entitled "The Handshake," and I shall write out my own current views as a member of a culture in which the practice exists. As native informant "ethnographer." I am free to ask myself what I know and what I believe on the basis of my participant observations. Is this arrogance or naivety? It is neither. My observations will be heuristically less useful than those of some people whom I do not know, and more useful than many of those I do – I hope. But the propositions advanced are no more than ideas and points of departure for more systematic observation. However, it is as crazy to ignore personal experience and observation in human studies as it would be to ignore natural observations of other animals. Experiments may or may not be appropriate later, but first watch, listen, and reflect. Think of explanations. Try to see what might be wrong with them. Devise empirical checks. Carry them out.

Terms of address and reference have been taken much further in two important ways, one being codification and the other being systematic empirical observation. In the UK, books of etiquette and explicit rules have been codified as to how persons in various social positions shall be addressed and referred to. In many societies and languages the rules are much more elaborate and more strictly prescriptive and proscriptive. Alongside this have been the systematic empirical studies that have afforded the construction of the options available to speakers, and their conditions of use. A plausible interpretive framework has been devised and checked, now constrained by "facts" to an extent that the study of handshakes has not.

Part of this framework is infused with notions of politeness, and this is one of the concepts around which a broad theory has been constructed and evaluated, both conceptually and empirically. The same kinds of developments are beginning to take place with accounting, arguing, deceiving and other domains of communication, and such progress is to be welcomed. Both handshakes and terms of address and reference can be slotted into theories of politeness, along with the myriad other non-verbal and verbal features that have etic possibilities or emic realizations.

8.2   The Act of Shaking Hands

Who shakes hands with whom, where, when, how and why? What is shaking hands? Separated by a suitable distance two standing persons raise their right forearms to a horizontal position, hold hands palm-to-palm with the prehensile thumb being prehensile. A minimal handshake requires no more than a brief contact, but a few centimetres up and down movement lasting a further few seconds may succeed the initial grasp. On occasions quite vigorous shakings combine with the left arm round the other's shoulder, broad smiles and mutterings of "Marvellous to see you again." Both parties stand, when conditions permit. Right hands only are used, even by left-handed people, except under rare circumstances where this is not possible. The shaking of the hands cannot have too great an amplitude, neither can the grip be too firm; if it becomes too firm the meaning will change. It cannot go on for too long, although if asked to say what constitutes being "too long," most of us would reply, "You just know." (These two paragraphs are a neat example of how a verbal description can be inferior to video representation!)

Why do people shake hands? They do so upon greeting another person and on leave-taking, provided that there is a sufficiency of trust and goodwill between the participants in the encounter. In formal encounters it is transitionally taken as an indicator of cooperative good faith. Having made introductory comments about the two final interrogatives of how and why, it is probably sensible to switch to who does it.

No non-humans shake hands or paws. Most human beings did not and still do not. Most societies have other forms of greeting: mutual bowing, simulated kissing, hugging, testicle tugging, or right arm raising with the forearm going vertical with an open palm facing the other person. Shaking hands has been most common perhaps among the misleadingly labelled Anglo-Saxons and Norsemen, that is Northern Europeans who may have emigrated south to become Normans or south-east to become Slavs. The rise of the British and French Empires led to a wide geographical dispersion, and with the first country to escape from the British empire becoming the current superpower, handshaking is probably going to continue to expand internationally as a practice.

However, the handshake is an inter-adult phenomenon; young children are not expected to take part in the ritual, and future generations may decide increasingly not to adopt it. Historically, it was probably confined to the upper strata of feudal societies and then only used within a status rank. If any hand were proffered across a status boundary, it would be extended by the higher status person to the lower and then only in exceptional circumstances. That remains true in the Britain of today. It is more common, but far from exclusive, to male–male encounters. It is more common in formal settings and for introductions than it is for informal settings or regular meetings. It is more common as a daily feature in France than in Britain. In examining the who, answers have also implicated where and when: work rather than leisure, rare rather than daily encounters, introductory rather than repeating interactions. None of these statements is more than a speculative normative generalization, and what is normative can change with time.

There are however rules which do have a universal significance. To refuse to shake hands with someone who has extended a hand is a strong sign of rejection; an offer of goodwill is turned down. Two recent incidents both illustrate the significance and importance that can attend the ceremony. With the signing of one of the recent peace accords between the Palestinian Arab leader and the Jewish Israeli Prime Minister, the shaking of hands was reported by the American media as heralding a categorical change in the relationship between the Palestinian Arabs and the Israeli Jews; a change from confrontation to negotiation, from the assertion of irreconcilable positions to trying to find compromises. More recently, when the Prime Minister of Britain met the President of Sinn Fein (the main party advocating the incorporation of the Six Counties/ Northern Ireland/ Ulster into the Irish Republic), they did not shake hands in public, but almost certainly did so behind closed doors. Too many groups and individuals would have been offended by a public handshake and would have criticized its probable private enactment, but media mention of the event was extensive, so that all the interested parties believed they knew what had happened. In contrast to the British Prime Minister, the leader of the main pro-Unionist (with Britain) party was later seen to refuse to grasp the proffered hand of the Sinn Fein president, implying a doubt in the sincerity of the other's gesture.

Within the cultures that engage in handshaking there is a low probability of misunderstanding, and has been seen earlier, members of such cultures are prone to see this as the proper and sensible way of greeting, with other forms being odd or worse (chapter 5.5.2). For example, no-contact mutual bowing is likely to be seen by handshakers as stand-offish and unfriendly, even by people who would themselves bow in the presence of royalty. In contrast, the huggings and kissings of the Mediterraneans were liable to be seen as odd, unmanly, and perhaps insincere, but this habit seems to have become more popular in recent years. The phenomenon of interpreting differences from one's own habits as strange and indicative of negative characteristics is widespread. This is a common form of interpretation and misunderstanding, a point to be developed later.

A proximal answer as to why people shake hands has been given, but is there some deeper symbolic or pragmatic significance to the gestures? Certainly there is a story. In the days when those who could afford swords or daggers carried them, to offer an open right hand implied that one was unarmed and hence harmless. Rendering oneself vulnerable indicated that the meeting would be either friendly and cooperative or at least confined to verbal disagreeing. Whether this particular account is historically true is contestable, but its underlying principle is generalizable. Typically, greetings involve mutual vulnerability and indications that no weapons are being carried. The open palm of the raised right arm is very similar, and so is a double arm hug. Mutual bowing results in a loss of eye-contact and an exposed neck. A gentle tugging of the testicles could be rapidly transformed into excruciating pain, as a vernacular English expression exclaims. The importance of being able to signal to con-specifics that no threat is intended is of course a crucial component for minimizing intra-species inflicted injuries and hence reduced fitness.

In today's world there still needs to be a means of signalling trust, good faith, and a willingness to negotiate or cooperate, but mutual interpersonal vulnerability is less of an issue. Perhaps this is one reason why handshaking has become optional and rather unpredictable. We can now kill each other at a distance if we wish to do so, and claims to be trustworthy can be made with other indicators. The handshake is wholly symbolic rather than functionally indicative. We also learned long ago that an empty right hand did not prevent handshakers from drawing a dirk with their left hand, or from initiating throws of unarmed combat.

Finally we may note that handshaking not only serves to open or close FtF encounters and to mark relative status and the cooperativeness of the relationship. It can be interpreted as a marker of personality. A "good" firm handshake is often construed to indicate a strong decisive person, while a crushing grip or a little finger contact give rise to other analogical references. How valid such inferences are is problematic.

Commentary

As presaged in the Introduction, the omission of citations of references is deliberate. What has been written derives from the author's experience as a more or less competent member of the handshaking culture, and some experience and reading about other cultures. To become "scientific," the claims made would need to be subjected to systematic empirical enquiry and number crunching. Would such activities be worthwhile?

Estimates of the ecological distribution of who shakes hands with whom, when and where at particular times in particular places may or may not be useful. Repeated samplings would chart changes. Again, whether such surveys would be worthwhile cannot be answered *in vacuo*; it would depend on what could be done with the answers and why. Like the many other non-verbal and verbal acts, the meaning(s) of handshaking is/are conventional; it means what it means to the actors concerned and within limits can shift, as can the cultural conventions.

The differential patterns of who shakes hands with whom should be charted at least once in each culture to check whether the empirical claims made here are valid. Certainly they are not comprehensive. To be thorough, they would be checked by a variety of methods which would include observations, accounts, and experimental manipulations as well as quickie questionnaire estimates. These latter techniques might well reveal anomalies and insights beyond the comments made here. Doing the research might be intrinsically interesting, but would be unlikely to bring fame or fortune. A book entitled "Greeting and Leave-taking around the World" is not likely to achieve massive sales in the current capitalist profit-conscious climate or bring fame to the author, and as noted already, a general coffee-table version has already been produced and marketed twenty years ago by Morris (1978).

In the current context perhaps it will be most sensible simply to continue to categorize the kinds and varieties of signals along the traditional lines, illustrate their manners of operation, and move forward to their functions and, in general terms, try to specify why particular signals are linked to particular functions – but at this point the move is to a functional/structural analysis of a "verbal" signalling system, one offering an extension to handshaking and leading on to considerations of politeness.

8.3 S Addresses L or Refers to O

"Hi, reader! How's it going?" "Hello! I'm Amanda. How can I help you?" "A warm welcome to all sinners!" These examples each contain a conventional greeting word or phrase, a term of address, and an inquiry. There are variants of "Hi" from which to choose: "Good morning," "How do you do," etc. There are variants of terms of address: Your grace, Sir, Dr. Pain, Mr. Smith, Smith, James, Jim, Baldy. Whilst initial inquiries are frequent successors to the attention-gaining of an identified individual, the possibilities are infinite. At each point the initiator has a range of options (paradigmatic choice), but the sequence can also be varied (syntagmatic choice) – Sinners! "A warm welcome to you." Finally the combinations can be varied (co-occurrence or *collocation*), with "Hi, Your Majesty" and "Good afternoon, darling" being less likely to occur at British royal tea parties than the two other conjunctions. All three kinds of selection have semantic and pragmatic significance, and there are culturally prescriptive rules relating the significance to the selection.

Both because it is historically the best-worked example and because it serves as a reminder that languages differ both in what they afford and what they require of users, the first illustration of how terms of address and/or reference work will be the *tu/vous* (T/V) distinction common to most of the standard languages used in Europe. In French, speakers have to select *tu* or *vous*, in German *du* or *Sie*, in Russian *ty* or *vy*, etc. English has dropped its "thou," "thee" and the ambiguous "ye." (Word processing software dislikes "ye" so much that it gives it the red squiggle.) What are the rules of selection for T/V, and what do they signal about S, L, and the relationship between them? For the first review of studies, social psychology is indebted to Brown and his colleagues (see Brown, 1965). As Brown points out, investigations in this area can adopt a wide range of methods and materials. Historically, there is a mine of archival material scattered around the world: records of letters and meetings, reports and agreements, plays and poems, speeches and histories, stretching back to the earliest human writings. There are plays and novels and latterly films, tapes, videos and now CDs, all recordings in which persons may address and refer to other persons. The records are global in their coverage. Analyses of these texts afford both historical (diachronic) and cross- and intra-cultural (synchronic) comparisons.

Field studies with recorded observations of current usage can be conducted unobtrusively. People can be surveyed and asked what they call others under what circumstances. And finally experiments can be conducted in which hypotheses and rules are followed or broken and reactions of observers and participants can be sought. What emerge for the T/V distinction are strong patterns, with variations which can be explained within a slightly messy single framework. Three patterns dominate: V<->V, T<->T, and T<->V. In medieval Europe mutual V and mutual T marked the cleavage between the elite and the rest. The nobility exchanged mutual V, as did related persons in positions of authority. The "common people" and slaves exchanged mutual T. The nobility and others in authority addressed the lower orders with T, but received V. The Christian God received V from everyone, and was represented as T to everyone else. Angels and priests formed a second rank, other human beings a third, and animals a fourth. How God and the Popes addressed each other is not known. One myth about the T/V distinction is attributed to Diocletian and his division of the Roman Empire into Eastern and Western halves. Given the theoretical basic unity of the empire, anyone addressing the emperor in Byzantium was also addressing his equal in Rome, and vice versa. Another story links plurality with power, as in the Hebrew address form for God. Similar asymmetries occur in Turkish, Tagalog, and Tamil. The adoption of the mutual V form by those of high rank is attributed to kings recognizing others as powerful and in some respects equal (*vide*, in England, lords in the House of Lords are still known as peers). Whatever the origins, this simple linguistic device marked the distinction between the small elite and everyone else.

As feudalism gave way to the emergence of societies with merchants and craftsmen, with the centres of activity shifting from castles and abbeys to cities and towns, so the simple rules became more difficult to apply, and questions arose as to which aspects of a social relationship should be emphasized. Six examples can be considered. In three there was an initial V for upwards address and an uncertainty between T or V for downwards: officer–soldier, customer–waiter, employer–employee. The first two became resolved with mutual V, the last with T down and V up. In three cases it was T down, but V/T uncertainty up: parent–son, elder brother–younger brother, and master–favored servant. In these cases the uncertainties were resolved with mutual T, or so it is claimed. (It is to be noted that the situation for females is not included).

As already mentioned in chapter 3, Brown (1965) had no difficulty in arriving at a two-dimensional explanation, in which asymmetry of T/V marks a difference in power, with the receiver of V having rights to control the other in certain respects in certain situations, ranging from a one-time "right" to total disposal through to minimal contractual, conventional rights; this was labelled as the Power Semantic. The second dimension is more difficult to label. For mutual T, interdependence is involved, but in some relationships this includes strong affection, in others camaraderie. Brown called this the "Solidary Semantic," and this will be adopted here in that none of the three possibilities of cohesiveness, interdependence, or friendship captures what appear to be variable mixtures of emotion and mutual obligation. Mutual V remains the default for formal and routine exchanges where T has not become the norm. In the cases of mutual V or T however, it *cannot* be inferred that the social relationship is between equals; asymmetries may be registered in other components, non-verbal, verbal, or both, for example proper names of address. Why the T form won out over V as the index of solidariness has not been documented to date – so far as I know.

Brown and Gilman's (1960) extensive surveys and observations produced results consistent with the Power/Solidariness model. They noted cultural differences in that *du* was stronger in families in German, whereas it was in sporting teams that the French moved quickly to *tu*. What applies to T/V can be found with proper nouns, viz. names. In English the selection of names remains as a comparable means of discrimination with the asymmetry rule for power and steps to solidariness being taken down the stairway of Figure 8.2. Brown (1965) argued for the main distinction being made between Title Last Name – Mr. Jones (TLN) and First Name – James (FN) but as Brown and Ford (1961) showed across a range of studies, the stairway had 5 gradations, with increasing solidariness as the steps move from T$\leftrightarrow$T to MN$\leftrightarrow$MN (multiple naming). Brown suggested that steps to solidariness were initiated by superiors, but this was found to be less than the whole story. In an English department store (Staples & Robinson, 1974) the basic pattern held, but it was more junior staff who were reducing the verbal differentials, and it is of course true that whilst seniors may ask for more deferential terms, it is speakers who decide what they will say, and the more egalitarian and familiar atmosphere of the 1960s combined with full employment to reduce the earlier imbalance of power. A situational factor was also evident with front-of-store yielding greater asymmetries than out-of-store encounters. Forms expected and forms received were generally agreed (94 percent), but the discrepancies showed that those of higher ranks were trying to maximize asymmetries and those more junior to minimize them. The shift to a normative mutual FN at work in English-speaking societies has moved further since the 1960s. In British universities at that time undergraduates found it difficult to address academic staff with FN, especially older staff of 35 plus. In the 1990s there was no such difficulty.

But as a Serbian friend lamented, the rush to FN-ing, which he blamed on the USA, means that one cannot develop a friendship over a 20 year period and mark stages with graduated changes in the use of more familiar terms of address. It should be noted also that such findings as those mentioned here refer to the mainstream of people in North America, Western Europe, and culturally comparable societies. Even in some of these, members of social elites have highly differentiating titles, and some of the highest ranking persons hold many titles which are listed on certain formal occasions. In Japanese, Thai, and the Indonesian languages, distinctions are much more finely graded than in the English two pronoun/five proper name system, and includes whole verb systems and varieties within the language.

8.3.1 Evaluation of the Power and Solidariness Semantics Story

It is precautionary to ask questions about the quality of the data that the explanation is intended to fit. Whilst tests of reliabilities and validities have not been made formally, there is a sense in which the findings are unlikely to be inaccurate. Which words are being used does not require inferences on the part of the data recorder or categorizer. Textual data may suffer occasionally from their authors being ignorant about the matters in hand, as may spoken answers of participants, and indeed the speech and writing of individuals. However, if these linguistic units are to function efficiently in communication, then members of the community need to know how to use them properly, and in this case one might expect much of the relevant knowledge to be verbally explicable. Children being socialized into the community who use terms which are insufficiently deferential or condescending, too familiar or formal, are likely to have their errors commented upon, with corrective feedback if they are fortunate. If they are even more fortunate, the explication will be in terms of respect and politeness and/or kinship and friendship.

The relevance of the Power Semantic would appear to be unproblematic; asymmetries typically imply power differentials. Whilst historically, civic societies have reduced the number of ranks and the power differentials in terms of the arbitrary exercise of gross punishments by higher strata, and the demands for deferential bowing and scraping, these remain linguistically marked in the social stratification systems extant. In the Bolshevik revolution, the Soviet Union "abolished" the T/V distinction as well differentiation in uniforms, and quickly re-instated both as the functioning of the armed forces fell in efficiency. It is difficult to conceive of circumstances in which such a reform would be a vote winner for a political party.

The reduction in marked differentials cannot be attributed to the voluntary surrendering of status by those higher up that scale. Titles of jobs have registered continuing inflationary, differentiating, and distinguishing tendencies; managing directors have become chief executives, secretaries personal assistants, sales assistants sales consultants, rat-catchers environmental health officers. Bristol City has a Statutory Arboriculturalist who tells you which of your trees you cannot prune without local authority permission. These are the result of pressures from below.

The nature of the Solidariness Semantic is more problematic. The basis for the switch from V to T or First Naming may reflect values within the sub-culture, but that simply shifts the issue of explanation to another level. People from cultures that are resisting early shifting state that premature shifting shows that the social psychological significance of the shift has been devalued, and that its value as a marker of friendship, for example, has been eroded. Not surprising perhaps is that such people are disposed to interpret such premature movements as insincere. For those who accept the early shift, First Naming does become the routine norm and loses its marker status – another example of inflation.

If this is so, then interpretations of cross-cultural comparisons have to be carefully checked. The apparently informal, friendly societies may not be such at all. Their cultivated myth of egalitarianism is being exploited through the use of forms of address which are no longer indicative of ascribed or achieved cohesiveness; they no longer have contrastive significance.

That said, the significance of situation and form-switching has been relatively neglected. Multiple naming, for example, is not independent of situations, but indicative of them, just as switching of terms is. In business meetings when the chair (boss) switches from FN to TLN it is a signal to keep quiet and allow power to be exercised. In developing intimate relations, the acceptance or rejection of "darling" etc. is indicative of the intimacy that is wished for by the listener and speaker, in much the same way as touching operates. A long married Welsh wife claimed to have used the returning husband's name greeting as a valid marker for what kind of day he had experienced (and hence what mood he was in): Welsh for good, English for bad. The husband was alleged to be unaware of this. Do shifting terms of reference as a function of situation, mood, and state of relationship in close relationships map on to the isomorphic standing features found in less close relationships? If so, all is well. If not, why not? As Fitzpatrick (1990) concluded from her evidence on marital interactions, more generally a presumed openness about feelings (explicitness) and expressions of positive feelings were indicators of happy marriages. This may not be surprising, but it rings warning bells for those whose positive statements exceed what they really feel as well as for those who are open about their negative feelings. The "negotiated" indirect markers to signal temporary difficulties and downs arising from internal strains or external pressures might serve as non-threatening stabilizers, and avoid the spirals of derogation that can escalate into destructive tornados. As Laing (1965) pointed out, in a hostile exchange between two persons the ratio of insults may be n to n+one, where n becomes too large for the one to be pragmatically significant. (The same can be observed in intergroup conflicts with similar never-ending reciprocated antagonistic acts that prevent settlements.)

More generally, a charting of terms of address in an organization can very rapidly give a portrait of the likely state of social relationships within and between levels of seniority – with mutual extent of agreement being indicative of the morale of the organization, provided of course that there is variance to explain. This is not to imply that a high incidence of asymmetric pairings is indicative of low morale, but a high incidence of terms which are objectionable to receivers or users is. There has been a rapid reduction in the use of terms of reference and address for members of subcultures in multi-cultural Britain. "Nigger" disappeared half a century ago except as an amiable impertinence among male black youth. "Negro" disappeared too. Uncertainties prevail around the acceptability between and within societies of the terms "Afro-Caribbean," "African-American," "Black British," etc., for example. Members of the groups have yet to develop and agree on single stable preferences as to whether the ethnic social identity should take precedence over the national social identity or vice-versa. None of this is surprising or novel; such changes have been happening for several thousand years and take time to sort out.

In the field of gender, it might appear to be the case that there should be less difficulty with titles, in that it is feasible for individual women to decide on Miss, Ms, Mrs, or whatever. Individual women can also negotiate what terms of address and reference are preferred or rejected in the workplace. Unfortunately again, there is no consensus among women, and a resistance among some males to follow women's preferences. "Ms" still carries associative meaning for some men and women in some contexts. Even the female gender reference term is still contentious. Fifty years ago most women would expect to be referred to as "lady," "woman" was derogatory – linked to social class, as in phrases such as officers and their ladies, sergeants and their wives, and other ranks and their women. Now "lady" remains among the older generations of both sexes (also retained), and among certain higher social status groups. In both the UK and the US there are now laws about harassment that allow both objective and subjective criteria to operate to define the unacceptable, with "tart" or "whore" being illegal, and "Gorgeous" or "My dear" being negotiable by females. However, no Bristol male has dared raise the issue of female shop assistants continuing to use the dialect "What would you like, my lover?," but it can feel slightly unnerving for newcomers. One difficulty is that terms of amiability and affection have done service for being either friendly or patronizing or both.

For both ethnic groups and gender, asymmetries of "rights" to use derogatory terms of address and reference have a very long history, and discussion could be extended to questions of the de-individuation (Latané & Darley, 1970). They have been used to diminish and have been associated with intra-societal exploitation and oppression, inter-societal conflicts and wars, and genocidal killings.

In contrast to the de-humanizing is the option of distancing by euphemism. Companies have developed terms for deaths arising from dangerous products (for example Ford Pintos bursting into flames upon rear impact, Callahan, 1988). Armed forces refer to deaths of innocent non-combatants as 'collateral damage', and to killing members of their own armed forces as "friendly fire"! These fashions have yet to be studied in respect of people's understandings and attitudes, and very little has been researched about euphemisms more generally and what effects their use has on participants and observers.

To revert to social relationships and social interaction and a concept that impacts upon the power and solidariness semantics, it is appropriate to introduce politeness.

⌐ 8.4   Politeness

Reference has been made to Grice's (1989/1975) brief mention of the possible need for a "Be polite" maxim. In contrast, Brown and Levinson (1987/1978) have created a comprehensive and detailed model of when and how such an imperative operates and how considerations of facework interact with those of message perspicuity in achieving the optimal compromise between the two. Like Grice, they posit an ideal, and also like Grice, they assume rationality on the part of the speaker: a precisely definable mode of reasoning from ends to means that will achieve those ends. The second concept of *face wants* derives from Goffman (1967), who proposed two of these:

1 *Negative face* is the wish to be unimpeded in the pursuit of personal goals – freedom from interference by other people.
2 *Positive face* is the wish to be approved of by certain others in certain respects.

If these two components are put together and combined with *rational reasoning*, then interaction with others will need to be cooperative, because every utterance directed to another person must necessarily threaten their face as well as having repercussions for one's own. Saying "Hello!" obligates the hearer (H) to reply and impedes H's freedom at the same time as it indicates approval of a sufficiency to provoke the speaker (S) to make the effort required for the greeting. The strength of the threat and the associated personal vulnerability will depend upon a number of factors: what is being attempted (for example, a request or a promise and how burdensome this is), the nature of the relationship between the interactants (for example, power differential and solidariness), and the cultural norms deemed relevant to the interaction. It will also depend on how the speech act is performed; what is said, and how it is said.

What Brown and Levinson argued was that in selecting what to say and how to say it, S has options which involve a trade-off between perspicuity and politeness, in maximizing the chances of achieving one's goal whilst preserving face. Making yet another appearance, Soskin and John (1963) noted that taking without asking and "Lend me your coat!" are perspicuous and direct, as is the normative form of "Please could I borrow your coat?." The other forms are indirect and might well be misinterpreted by L as comments rather than requests; their indirectness reduces the threats to face, but the cost to S could be continuing coldness.

Brown and Levinson have sought to develop and systematize these ideas into a model that lists the range of expressions for a given speech act and scales them in terms of how polite they are, and then specifies the determinants that will determine which option optimises the chances of minimizing loss of face to either party whilst achieving the desired outcome. To scale the strategies Brown and Levinson chose a five-point hierarchy made up of four binary choices as shown in Figure 8.1.

Use of 1 involves following Grice's maxims in terms of explicitness, conciseness, and clarity, but because it is the most face-threatening to L (here referred to as H for Hearer, following Brown and Levinson) in the first instance, and to S if refused, its use is likely to be restricted to situations where urgency and efficiency are paramount, or where H is a clear beneficiary and costs to S are clearly low, or where the relative status/power relations of S to H allows S to ignore the face-wants of H. (H may be too young to have developed face-wants or treated as though too young to have them.) Redress implies an explicit attenuation of the FTA via one of two means. Positive politeness links to positive face by giving a positive reason for H to act in the way suggested, for example "I wouldn't dare ask anyone else . . ." – categorizing H as a person who is special. Negative politeness has hints of being a self-contradictory idea, and the choice of the particular verbal conjunction as a label was pragmatically unfortunate even if semantically appropriate. Use of such an option explicitly recognizes the impedance of H's freedom and excuses it. In the case of requests apologetic prefaces are one device for redressing negative face, for example "I'm very sorry to inconvenience you, but . . .;" "Can you spare a minute please?" Five of the six Soskin and John examples are off-record FTAs, each having possible replies from H that leaves S cold, either because H fails to see the point of S's comment or decides not to meet the indirect request. For these, H has a range of replies available however that would not threaten either person's face.

Not surprisingly one of the early criticisms of the model queried the ordering of options, especially that of positive and negative politeness. In using positive politeness, Brown and Levinson argue that S makes an assumption about H's personal and/or social identity, and is vulnerable to a denial of this particularity. A simple denial of the presumed identity leaves S with a loss of face and H free, but perhaps less approved of. Using negative politeness avoids the particularity, but already recognizes H's general right to freedom of action and, hence is less threatening to either. (For the moment we will do no more than note this rationale.)

Brown and Levinson extend the relevance of the model to all interactions, but draw especial attention to speech acts that have obvious links to

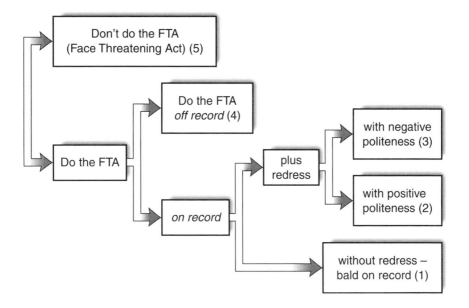

Figure 8.1   Brown and Levinson's 5-point hierarchy

the two kinds of face wants: freedom of action and desire for approval. There are three categories for the first. In the first category they include requests and orders, advice and suggestions, reminders, threats and warnings. In these S does not intend to avoid impeding H's freedom of action, and implicates H in some action. In the second it is S who is committed to an action, but that action may impose a subsequent obligation upon H, for example offering or promising to do something for H. In the third category are indications that H's person, property, or *significant* others are the object of S's desires for possession, insult, or injury, for example envy, lust, hatred.

Threats to positive face of H can be divided into those that evaluate H negatively and those that indicate indifference. The former include expressions of criticism, contempt, complaint, accusation, and insult, along with disagreements and challenges. Brown and Levinson list six indicators of indifference: temper loss, profanity, passing on criticism of H, raising sensitive conversational topics, interrupting or ignoring H's contributions, putting down H.

These listings are followed by categorizations of whether it is the face of H or S that is at primary risk. Among responses to prior H-originated FTAs are expressions of: thanks, apology, acceptance of thanks or apologies, excuses, acceptance of offers, promises or compliments, reactions to *faux pas* of H. S's negative face is threatened by S making promises or offers unwillingly. S can lose positive face through admissions of wrongdoing, stupidity, or thoughtlessness, and by physical clumsiness or failure to inhibit rude noises.

This precis can do no more than point to the breadth of verbal activities included, and the account of how selections are made among the forms available within any type of speech act will be similarly abbreviated.

8.4.1 Determinants of Option Selected

The general factors cited by Brown and Levinson as relevant to the seriousness of particular FTAs are three in number, with a fourth set of contextual variables moderating the effects of the other three, which are:

1 the perceived social distance between S and H (D);
2 the perceived power differential between S and H (P);
3 the perceived ranking of the kind of imposition involved in the particular culture (R).

The *seriousness* (Se) of the risks to the participants are represented as a multiplicative function of the risks to S and H respectively, which are then formalized as: Seriousness for S = D (S,H) × P (H,S) / P (S,H) × R Se.

Unfortunately the perceptions of S and H may not be in agreement with each other, social distance is not a simple unidimensional concept (see Section 8.3), and neither is power. There may be no reciprocity of face-concerns between S and H, and the multiplication signs in the formula are unnecessarily specific.

Generally, the implications for the selection of an optimal speech act are that explicitness is likely to increase the greater the social distance between S and H, the greater S's power over H, and the smaller the imposition. In so far as explicitness is correlated with politeness, the need to be polite is reduced as D and R diminish and as P (S > H) is heightened. Brown and Levinson point to complications that need to be incorporated into their account, drawing particular attention to the role of context of situation on the other three. Removed to a desert island, masters can become and speak like servants and vice versa (for example in the play *The Admirable Crichton*). Mateship can be indicated by the right to exchange insults. A deathbed request of one's spouse to pass on a message of good-will to an implacable enemy may be a great imposition.

The original chapter (1978) and the later book (1987) both offer many illustrations and applications of the ideas to a wide variety of speech acts both within and beyond the culture of the middle class English-speaking Caucasians from which many examples are drawn. The Introduction to the 1987 book offers a review of relevant research and criticism of the model. Holtgraves (2001) offers the most recent succinct and construc-tively critical appraisal, which includes references to many supportive find-ings and some less so. It is not surprising that Brown and Levinson were not and are not omniscient; it would have been extraordinary if their model and its explication were free of errors of omission and commission. (Whilst it is important that we are not unduly deferent in any evaluation, it is also important that we do not seize on trivial issues, exaggerate their signifi-cance, and abandon a massively constructive framework as a result of methodological or theoretical nitpicking. Deciding what is trivial and what is important is of course neither certain nor easy.)

8.4.2   Critical Evaluation

It was argued in chapter 3 that utterances are etically multi-functional always and emically very often so. It was also pointed out that the prag-matic significance of any utterance cannot be sensibly assessed independ-ently of the historical and current context of situation. Neither can it be treated as independent of what has just happened and what happens after it has been uttered. This being so, it is empirically impossible to classify any utterance unequivocally, and it can be dangerously misleading to as-sign a specific single function to it. In any text classification is necessarily provisional, and given the meta-games and meta-meta-games that hu-man beings play with language, it is simply wrong-headed to demand too much of any classificatory scheme, and that includes models of politeness. Hence, to demand that an individual utterance can be assigned a particu-lar function is to misunderstand how language works.

Another focus of criticism has been that the scale of politeness strategies is both incomplete and that reversals may be possible. Holtgraves (2001) offers an immediately plausible explanation of conditions under which positive politeness could be more polite than negative politeness. As he and Yang (1990) showed for directives (which threaten H's negative face), the original ordering makes sense theoretically and may be generally sound empirically. However, if the speech act threatens the positive face of H, the reverse will be true (Lim & Bowers, 1991). Hence, to order the strength of FTAs may require detailed consideration for each speech act; the order needs to be considered for any particular case. Finally here, the issue of the relationship between politeness and indirect speech acts can be raised. Brown and Levinson assume that a positive association exists, although they never claim that the correlation is perfect, and it clearly is not. "Please may I borrow a coat?" is perfectly polite and transparent. Indirectness based on evasion, equivocation, or ambiguity could well be impolite, just as indirectness based on false assumptions about the shared knowledge can be. Not everyone is *au fait* with the multitude of acronyms that now surround us, just as many of us would not know why we might have been at Augusta, Bayreuth, Cowes or Whistler. To assess whether an indirect expression is or is not polite, knowledge of the temporal, personal, and situational context are necessary. Again this issue requires more detailed examination. (For other criticisms and responses see Coupland, Grainger, & Coupland, 1988 and Brown & Levinson, 1987.) The final concern to be expressed here relates to the assumptions of the model, and in particular those of its universality.

8.5   The Role of Politeness in Human Behavior

Appeals to politeness as a first order explanation of socio-linguistic choices have an intuitive plausibility which is consonant with our everyday experience, but the social psychological story cited as underpinning it needs to be examined and elaborated. The postulations of the positive and negative face-wants of S and H being mutually satisfied in the manner suggested is a rational point of departure, but may be best treated as a default position of everyday interactions in a mythically egalitarian and cooperative society. If nothing more important is at stake, then a cultural norm of "Be polite" may operate, *à la* Brown and Levinson.

In reality however all human societies have a Darwinian competitive component, and the USA and UK are also individualistic in their basic orientation, relative to most other societies (Hofstede, 1980). At the present time, each individual has to come to terms with values such as "Look after yourself" and "Maximize your power, wealth, and/or status." Welfare systems may intervene to reduce the apparent incidence of premature deaths from factors associated with being jobless and homeless, but support for more than bare survival is rare. Above this level, competition is the name of the main game, and in that competition appearance rather than reality may count. Hence the rise of "impression management" as a social psychological concept – and as a training activity. In such a society, S and H may well give an appearance of being considerate and being equally other-centered and self-centered, but the underlying reality can be primarily self-centred. Pay-offs will be calculated in terms of how to exploit the cultural norms to one's own advantage, minimizing impositions on self, and maximizing power and other differentials where possible. This latter can lead to an appearance of temporary excessive deference or friendliness – even though the folk wisdom of the efficacy of flattering is not to be dismissed just because systematic empirical evidence on the issue has yet to be presented. In brief, ambitious individuals can exploit the cultural norms of politeness in the pursuit of personal success in a competitive society.

Whilst Brown and Levinson and Holtgraves rely mainly on empirical studies in the mid-range of the social strata of a society that has no feudal history to demonstrate the operation of the P component in the model, historical books on European court etiquette make quite clear how extreme the deference demanded of both the higher and lower orders towards the monarch was. Since breaches of such rules were classed as "rude," the implication is that lack of deference is impolite. These asymmetries in relationships of differential power seem to be something more than matters of politeness; they are consistent with other asymmetries. This power perspective can be seen to apply to most or all of the speech acts listed by Brown and Levinson and extends of course to rights to speak or reply. Just as with other social institutions, elites have defined the rules of interaction, and these have invariably been asymmetric. In these cases it would seem more realistic to see the invocations by higher authorities of rudeness by those of lesser formal or informal standing as more likely to be assertions of power, masquerading as demands for politeness. (A similar analysis can be utilized when the less powerful attempt to point out that the more powerful are lying; authority is more likely to comment on the impropriety of the challenge than offer evidence that there has been no cover-up.)

Both of the last two appear to be examples of the ways in which persons can abuse the Brown and Levinson model, in the first case in the service of personal ambition, and in the second in order to maintain power and status in stratified institutions. Neither should be seen as invalidations of the model, but if the arguments for their existence are valid, both instantiate this peculiar difficulty of social psychology that once human social systems are understood, there will be individuals and groups who exploit and abuse the systems to their own advantage.

As noted, Brown and Levinson extend their analyses to several non-Western cultures and languages, but they do not comment on social stratification within long-established and populous societies. Their data from English-speaking Caucasians look to reflect in the main the speech habits of the urban middle class. To the extent that this is true, the habits of the many ethnic, religious, and other socially defined sub-cultures are not articulated into the model. A consideration of the history of the last thousand years of European societies might lead to the entertainment of an inversion of the relation between power and politeness: the rules governing politeness were one means of keeping "rude people in their place." To ascend the social scale required a mastery of the etiquette of the higher strata which reached its zenith of elaboration in the royal courts. It might be demonstrable that the complexity of the rules governing what was polite was highly correlated with the flamboyance, wealth, and stability of the court. At the other extreme, in such societies peasants and the urban poor had to endure lives that were nasty, brutish, and short. In the middle, pretentiously wealthy merchants could still be excluded from the elite as inferior and rude beings, in part because they could not emulate the appropriate etiquette. Even in the newer societies such as the USA and Australia, "old money" excluded "new money" whilst "new money" read the books of how to pass in polite society (Anonymous, 1886; Elias, 1978; Vanderbilt, 1963).

Whether the sociological hierarchical exclusion function arose prior to the social psychological face-preservation function is a matter of almost certainly irretrievable history, but it is important to remember that both operate in present-day societies and probably with differential weightings and force across different societies. One of the oldest examples of a predominantly monolingual nation-state that preserved its isolation until 1866 is Japan, a society remarkable for the pervasiveness and subtlety of politeness markers and its indirectness of speech, both up and down, and within its hierarchical strata. Superficially at least it offers a portrait of the Brown and Levinson plus Goffman analyses, with face-threats being of paramount concern. By contrast, in England lack of politeness is invoked readily to perform an excluding and putting down function within similarly stratified institutions; it is also used as a device to hide mistakes and misdemeanors by those at the top.

To date, this last issue appears to have been neglected, and there seems to be only one study that has examined social class differences within and between evaluations of expressions of gratitude to someone who has helped by giving geographical directions. Sissons (1971) used an actor to seek directions to Hyde Park from Paddington Station in London from people standing in the concourse. There were subsequent debriefings and questions about occupational status. Middle class participants judged the actor to be polite in his Middle Class (MC) guise and rude in his Working Class

(WC) guise. Working class participants judged him to be polite as a WC speaker, but excessive in his thanks when playing the MC role. The WC role limited his expression of gratitude to "Thanks," whilst the other expanded to "Thank you so much." WC participants showed ingroup preferences, but for the outgroup judgments, it was the MC who treated a minimal "Thanks" as rude. Most or all of them probably used a similar expression only for a minimal service (Okamoto & Robinson, 1997).

8.5.1   An Alternative Approach

What can be said about the semantic network of 'polite'? Its contrastive cognates appear to fall into two groups: positive and deficiencies. The latter comprise words such as "uncultivated," "uneducated," "unrefined" and even "uncivilized," all of which indicate a lack of socialization into (higher stratum) cultural norms. The positive opposites would be "vulgar," "rude," and in some subcultures, "common." All three of these have social significance. The etymology of "vulgar" lies in the Latin for "people," and current terms such as "folk" or "*volk*" may have similar derivations. Peasants were rude people, and the common people could be classed as common. The implication is that the mass of the population was *not* polite. They were certainly not members of *polite society* or *le beau monde*. Gentlemen and ladies were. The royal courts were where courtesy was to be found in all its differentiating elaborateness, but with its greatest distinction being between the nobility and the rest. The duality of connotation is consistent with earlier analysis that politeness as a concept of harmony carries with it a clear component of social stratification, with implications of the superiority of the elite.

8.6   Grice and Politeness

It is unlikely that Grice (1975/1989) would have treated his own suggestion of a supplementary maxim of "Be polite" so casually if he could have foreseen how its working out would relate to his own contribution. Lakoff (1979) and Leech (1983) both append additional maxims to Grice's, and both seem to be thinking within an egalitarian cooperative framework that may now have more limited applications in our societies than they imagined (or was true in the 1970s). Lakoff (1979) adds: give options, don't impose, make the other feel good. Leech (1983) adds: Be tactful, be generous, give approbation. However, as Holtgraves (2001) notes, it is theoretically plausible to treat "politeness" as a common set of implicatures.

The answer to the question as to why a speaker has not followed the Gricean maxims with a remark, could be that S is being polite. If matters are as Brown and Levinson describe, many of us are in a position to interpret the implicature in terms of the face wants of S and H. (In part Goffman's great influence stemmed from the clarity with which he told us about what we already knew.) As soon as students have mastered the terminology of the FTA model, they typically raise questions about the detail rather than the framework. For the system to operate, each of us needs to interpret what is said to arrive at what is meant, to see that what appear to be statements of fact are requests, for example.

At present I can see no empirical or theoretical grounds or arguments that oblige any of us to prefer one conceptualization to the other. Lloyd-Morgan's Canon (1894) that fired "Thou shalt not proliferate entities unnecessarily" could be invoked to keep maxims to a minimum and treat sets of intentional deviations as implicatures. This would align being polite, with being humorous, ironic, and other such derivatives that have been developed to be parasitic on the maxims.

As an erstwhile biologist who finds sensibly applied evolutionary principles intellectually satisfying as foundations for taxonomies, Grice's maxims have the appeal of being a minimal basis for efficient (transparent) communication, where what is said is what is meant. Politeness in English has overt markers, such as 'please' appended to interrogative forms in the case of requests. To add further complexity and especially indirectness look to the constructions of elite sub-cultures in increasingly complicated societies, such complexities being retained and enhanced for as long as those societies (and their languages) are isolated from external influences or internal revolutions.

Such a line of argument is consistent with the historical changes from decentralized small rural communities in which encounters would be mostly with persons known personally to those of today in which the divisions of labor and complexity of organization bring people into contact with a diversity of strangers as well as friends and relatives. Some such historical perspective is also consistent with the diversity of functions that superficial politeness can have; exploitation is necessarily parasitic on a default function/structure relation.

⌐ 8.7 Accounting in Social Relationships

In comparison with the accounting chapter of Cody and McLaughlin (1990), its successor of 2001 (Buttny & Morris) devotes less space to social positional accounting and more to interpersonal exchanges, marking a decade in which approaches changed. It is not accidental that Buttny and Morris also adopt a language-and-social-interaction approach with a heavy reliance on examples of natural exchanges involving accounts. The theoretical stance emphasizes "making sense of events" rather than assessing blame. There may be no reproaches, no failure event to trigger accounts. Efforts by participants seem to be collectively geared to achieve coherence for all parties concerned. Exchanges are likely to be extended. The examples used make these distinctions clear. In part the differences arise from differences in agendas. Earlier, Cody and McLaughlin eliminated the mundane and minor from their frame of reference, but these provide the core examples for Buttny and Morris: declinations of invitation to take a coffee, apologies for late arrivals. Feelings and face are both prominent features of the events cited where accounts do take on a blame component.

As in other fields, neither conversational analysis nor field studies appear to be making invalid observations, and the long-term problem is to articulate the results of the various approaches, regardless of discipline of origin. Both are open-ended in that cultures and sub-cultures can and do change the rules of the game in terms of what counts as making good sense or can serve as an acceptable blame-seeking account. That said, there are likely to be considerable continuities: cultures do not change that quickly; killing other people for minor insults to face has not been excusable for ordinary citizens of any culture for some years now. In role relationships in the west there has been an unsteady move towards greater equalization of rights and obligations between men and women, which could be viewed as a qualitative shift over the twentieth century as a whole. Husbands are now much more accountable for many more of their actions, though asymmetries still remain; "just sowing wild oats" would not be an apposite phrase to accompany a nod and a wink about a young woman, at least not generally so.

For interpersonal relationships, friendship and marriage have been the most studied by social psychologists and extensive texts have appeared about both. Here in-depth comment will be restricted to just one component of marriage, the component itself offering an interesting solution to a dilemma. For most westerners, who will marry whom is decided by the couple rather than by their families. Typically, most western marriages are based on love rather than material assets. During the courtship phase and the early part of marriage, statements and gestures of love made by each of the pair are likely to have been genuine escalations of passion in contexts with novelty. If the relationship is to continue to be imbued with pleasantness and passion, how are these to be kept alive, over perhaps a

40 year period, in which the couple may become parents working to survive and to rear their offspring?

In respect of speech any pair is likely to have used the extremes of the positive range, for example "I will love you and you alone for ever!" How often and for how long can such sentiments be repeated without losing their original force? In contrast, on the negative side of verbal interaction, there are more opportunities for downward spirals. Initially the answer to "Did you pick up my shoes, darling?" may receive a contrite apology which is immediately closed with an acceptance. Ten years on the scenario could be expanded into an exchange culminating in "You are an inadequate father, an inadequate husband, an inadequate man!" To continue to carry force, it appears that insults and accusations have to be escalated to extremities, and in terms of preserving a role relationship, situations tempt partners into breaking the rules about what must not be said. Albee's play, *Who's afraid of Virginia Woolf?* epitomizes the ways in which the connivances couples may require to preserve their relationships can break down. (It was particularly poignant to watch Richard Burton and Elizabeth Taylor playing the lead roles with too strong a degree of realism – just prior to their marriage disintegrating.) Married couples know, or need to know, what can most hurt their partners – and be able to keep the knowledge secret to themselves and certainly never use it against the partner, if they want the relationship to survive.

Fitzpatrick (1988) noted the dilemma. For marriages to be happy and stable, couples should be open with each other and exhibit a preponderance of positive interactions within a shared set of *marriage schemata* (or scripts). If partners give priority to openness, this will mean saying negative things, occasionally. If priority is given to positive interactions, this risks charges of insincerity and hypocrisy. (Very few couples seem to have been seriously advized about ways of facing up to the realities of the up-and-downs, the dangers of downward spirals, and the impossibility of continuing escalation of positive experience in long-term intimate relationships.) For continued harmony what is entailed is that either pairs have to be very fortunate in their positive matching or that they negotiate ways of handling the negatives that do not lead to an escalation of conflicts, finally resolved by breaking up the marriage. Not requiring accounts and accepting accounts of the other provide one means of reducing the difficulties.

8.7.1 Realities in Close Relationships

There can be matters of character and conduct that partners might rather not know about each other, and not to render these explicit to each other is one way of conniving to keep these out of consideration. The same principle applies to others knowing, and others may well connive in the silence. Many partners and close friends of criminals must know more than they mention about them. Many partners and close friends of the great but bad must suspect that there are serious discrepancies between the self-presentation and the self behind this. Both the great but bad and criminals may have pictures of themselves that are quite different from their eventually-exposed characters. At least two subsequently discredited senior British politicians have maintained their innocence of alleged offenses, beyond the point where courts have decided otherwise – and their families have defended their conduct. How many married persons have no secrets from their partners, and "secrets" with which their partners are fully familiar but never mention? These may refer to small personal habits; they may be sinister. Many more such secrets are known than are revealed in the law-courts.

Data in this area are not easy to collect, and the validity of those extant is unknown. Miller, Mongeau, and Sleight (1986) found co-habiting students estimating very little deception in their own relationship compared with that in others, and believed they would be able to detect any that did occur. They were also concerned about the impact any such discovery would have on their relationship. Metts (1989) notes the primacy given to the preservation of the role relationship as a reason for concealment and lying to one's partner, and the relative absence of questioning in strong and satisfying marriages. The emerging picture is of behavior that is trusting in a variety of respects. This can be viewed as advantageous, regardless of whether the trust is well-founded or not, since frequent (suspicious) interrogation about actions is likely to undermine any close relationship anyway. The games within games that can be developed in close relationships have been illustrated by Berne (1966), and the advantages of delusions have been registered by Taylor (1989). What is important here is that such activities have implications for minimizing enquiries and accepting explanations of the Other to preserve the relationship and the face of both actors.

8.8   Complications

Unfortunately, in the quasi-democratic capitalist societies of the twenty-first century, the promotion of the individual as an individual with extensive rights and minimal obligations renders marriage preservation more difficult. As Fitzpatrick (1990) indicated, any pretence of all marriages following a traditional and well-defined set of reciprocated obligations has to be abandoned. She introduced two variants on this on the basis of a survey with her Marital Relationship Inventory and for her purposes, utilized three categories to typify models of interactive styles in marriage: *traditional, independent,* and *separate.*

> Traditionals hold conventional views about marriage and the family, are very interdependent in the marriage, and willingly argue over serious issues. Independents are more liberal in their orientation toward marital and family values, are moderately interdependent in their marriages, and are habituated to conflict. Separates are ambivalent about their family values, not very interdependent in their marriages, and tend to avoid marital conflict. (p. 441)

Clearly both Independents and Separates are stressing individuality of the partners, with Independents apparently trying to achieve powerful bonding via personal negotiated role-expectations, whereas Separates are stressing individuality, whilst reducing the intensity of the bonding. Fitzpatrick and colleagues conducted empirical studies examining the correlates of individual and pair characteristics on a grid in terms of time taken to recognize types of marital interaction, matching of accuracy and confidence of interpretations of feelings of S, and extent to which speech displayed shared implicit understandings (see Fitzpatrick, 1988). They found effects for characteristics of individuals, pairings, and gender in all three respects. Across types, pairs classified as Separates were prone to underestimate anger in the partner. Independents communicated both positive and negative feelings clearly and were confident in their interpretations. Traditionals showed gender differentiation, wives understanding their husbands' sexual interest but not his pleasure, husbands the converse.

The differences both between matched partners within the three types and between mixed partners extend into accounting and accounts. For example, matched Traditionals do not have to account for their accepted role enactments, but will be called to account for any deviations. Matched Separates have few issues on which they need to account. Independents are likely to have to negotiate mutual acceptability on many features of role-enactment and risk clashes on those which involve interdependent coordinations. There is a likelihood of behavior and accounts being acceptable cognitively but not emotionally. Freedom to engage in extra-marital sexual relationships on the basis of individual desires seems to be the least acceptable of the "liberal" components emotionally.

CHAPTER 9

Marking of States, Identities, and Settings: Issues

9.1 Conceptual Distinctions and Clarifications

Human beings may be unique in their capacity to communicate verbally with each other, but as seen in chapters 4 and 5, they share many vocal and other non-verbal communicative capacities with other animals, which can often serve as primary markers. For present purposes it is also apposite to repeat that the function of marking emotional/motivational states, identity, social relationships and settings are usually realized through multiple cues rather than single ones, and that links between *markers* and what they are marking *(referents)* can be complex, probabilistic, and contingent rather than simple, invariant, and deterministic. It would of course be neater as well as easier to offer bold diagrams of connections between single markers and single referents, but that is not the way things are, and there are good reasons for this. Simplicity of system is correlated with simplicity of creatures, and chimpanzees and human beings are even more complex than Eastern Phoebes and Great Crested Grebes, and it will be recalled that they had to negotiate relationships with each other. In the cases of marking emotions/motivation and personal identity, current knowledge is probably greater and more systematic for markers and linkages than for their referents in the sense that understanding of the ways the "referents" are to be organized is far from achieving consensus. For social identity, social relations and settings, knowledge about the markers, links, and referents are in balance, and this is because these last three are entirely socio-cultural constructions.

However, for all referents, it is necessary to pick a way through some points and some complications before plunging into empirical results and their interpretations. A first point to note about markers is that, if they are to be efficient, then they need to be observable by con-specifics, predators (at least from their perspective!), and other animals whose lives are in some way associated with the marked. This applies whether their colors are really warning colors, such as the black and yellow stripes of the stinging wasps or the empty threats of non-stinging wasps and bees. Likewise with human beings, naked kings are less kingly than those with crowns, orbs and sceptres. Markers can still be markers, even if their referents have only disjunctive significance: they may announce presence, and the possibilities of mating, fighting, or flying away, as noted for Eastern Phoebes alighting on the same branch as a con-specific (chapter 3). Different sequences of actions and reactions negotiate and resolve the ambiguities of an opening contact for Eastern Phoebes, just as they can for human males and females in a nightclub. More critical for survival is fast and efficient identification of emotions and motivation of possible aggressors and predators, and again this is true for human beings.

Whilst the psychologists have difficulty with taxonomies of emotions and motivation, both they and other people have extensive vocabularies to refer to specific emotions and motivations in everyday life, and this at least affords possibilities for basal level empirical studies. It is paradoxical that as human beings we can operate more or less successfully with elements which we cannot classify into systems! For emotions and motivation we can use words like "happy" and "hungry," "comatose" and "frustrated" effectively, but when we try to specify how the super-ordinate concepts of emotion, mood, and motivation are alike and different, initially easy distinctions become problematic. Perhaps no one would classify happiness as a motivational state or hunger as an emotion, but what about fear? We eat when we are hungry and we run away or freeze when we are frightened, yet "fear" is typically treated as an emotion. Are emotions more temporary than moods? Can someone be in a fearful mood? There are other lines of possible differentiation that could be pursued, but for the present, they do not yield clear solutions, physiologically or psychologically.

Similar hazards emerge when trying to classify emotions and moods independently of motivation. Whilst "happy," "sad," "angry" and "frightened" appear on all lists, and there appears to be a consensus that states can be blends of these, how to classify emotions and moods in terms of dimensions and/or clusters, and as hierarchical or single level phenomena, remains unresolved (Frijda, 1985; Lewis & Haviland, 1993; Planalp, 1999; Russell & Fernandez-Dols, 1997). Cross-cultural issues also arise. English is only one of the several thousand languages in which emotion words occur, and even within western cultures, English speakers have difficulties with identifying *saudade*, *élan*, and *Angst* with English vocabulary. Attempts have been made to argue for universal primary emotions that become differently differentiated and mixed at secondary and further levels in different cultures (Ekman, 1993; Ekman & Friesen, 1974; Russell, 1994; Ekman, Sorensen & Friesen, 1969). This is a plausible position, but one for further exploration rather than current acceptance.

An alternative line could be that psychology (and physiology) are seeking an orderliness that does not exist. Just as the creative imaginations of human beings have constructed strange mythical beasts, metaphysical entities, and diseases, and then relegated some of them to the rubbish heap, so in the future we may dispense with some but not all of the emotions to which we pretend. The Philosopher's Stone and phlogiston of alchemy and early chemistry have gone, but iron and oxygen remain, along with all their cognate chemical elements in Mendeleyev's Periodic Table, a late-arriving classificatory system which has proved to be of great heuristic value and whose constituents have consequently grown in number. Notwithstanding the classificatory difficulties, within culturally homogeneous groups, it has been possible to make progress in specifying both non-verbal and verbal markers of emotional/motivational states.

What has been argued to be problematic for the emotional/motivational is even more apposite for personality (see chapter 10.3). Some of the vocabulary for personality traits is virtually a lexicon of (dispositional) states. Someone who is generally happy across situations through time becomes labelled a happy person. In the Second century AD, Galen introduced the idea of four basic dispositions, in his case linked to the balance of different humours in the body, hence sanguine, choleric, melancholic, and bilious. Unfortunately the number of words in English that refer to personality traits has risen to many thousand, roughly 18,000 according to G. W. Allport and Odbert's (1936) count in Webster's Dictionary. How should these be organized? Many personality theorists have dispensed with them altogether and invented their own lexicon. The disagreements about emotion/motivation are minor compared with the diverse array of incompatible views about personality. There is something seriously odd about Hall, Lindzey, Leohlin and Manosevitz (1985) being able to include so many theories of personality in their volume. Two or three contestants might be expected, but such an abundance looks like theorizing running way ahead of empirical evidence. Further, with a few exceptions, all these theoretical constructions were generated by Caucasian males whose first language was English or German – and whose data were provided by smallish samples of ordinary people, undergraduates or clinical sub-groups living within western societies. Many of these theories have focused on general processes, development, or explanations for abnormality, whilst trait theories have continued to dominate concerns with individual differences. Most recently there has been a thrust towards synthesizing the diversity in the last, both conceptually (for example Digman, 1990) and operationally (for example Goldberg, 1992), and this has led to talk about the "Big Five." Goldberg (extraversion, super-ego strength, openness to experience, anxiety, sociable conformity) does not use the names that Digman proposed: extraversion, will to achieve, intellect, neuroticism, and friendly compliance (see chapter 10.3.1).

Again, as with emotions/motivation, it has to be repeated that similar criticisms might be made of the restricted samples in studies, and additionally in this case, the heavy reliance on self-report questionnaires as the major if not the sole means of measurement constitutes an additional limitation. One handicap of personality theorists has been their concern to abstract personality from situations (Mischel, 1994; Mischel & Shoda, 1995) and yet still hope to predict attitudes and actions. Another has been the assumption that personality will remain stable throughout life, as well as across situations. (N.B. In this text "setting" answers the question about where events are occurring. "Situation" includes answers to where, who, what, and how, namely the whole situation.)

A final constraint has been the neglect by social psychologists of situations. If behaviors were to be conceptualized as Sit x Pers or Pers x Sit, where are the taxonomies of Sit? (It has been noted already that any social psychologist who devoted a research career to settings or Sit would be seen by many fellow social psychologists as oddly neglectful of people.) As attribution theorists have repeatedly found, people of the western hemisphere display strong preferences for assigning causes of events to Pers rather than Sit, especially if the actions and events have potential for praise or blame – the so-called *fundamental attribution error* (Ross, 1977). For all sorts of reasons some societies have emphasized the *individuality* of persons along with notions of their rights and responsibilities, and these happen to be the societies where psychology has been earliest to develop as a separate academic discipline. And for these, the focus has been on *individual differences.*

Positively however, as with emotions, when questions are asked about markers of individual differences, provided that these are posed in terms culturally consonant with those of the participants, investigations can proceed sensibly, at least at the level of the mundane phenomenological. Individuals can also be differentiated into membership of social categories. Typically these differences are realized as answers to "What is this person?," as contrasted with "What is this person like?." Answers are likely to be in terms of nouns rather than adjectives. The nouns often refer to relevant statuses in the culture (for example gender, marital status, ethnicity, occupation), but will also include membership of groups (for example political, religious, sporting, leisure) and social relations (for example husband, daughter, employee). In all societies, some quantitative dimensions are rendered qualitative and categorical for administrative purposes, such as schooling, retirement, eligibility for benefits. These components are normally treated as matters of social rather than personal identity. The two are not always conceptually distinctive in respect of definitions, and neither are they empirically independent in the social structure. People normatively high or low on certain personality dimensions are more or less likely to be acceptable as members of particular social groups. Extraversion, for example, appears to be valued in many of the competitive occupations that capitalist societies have promoted, especially in recent years. Persons proposing vigorous changes and action appear to have been preferred for jobs, often to the detriment of their employers and everyone else. As noted above, some components of social identity are relational rather than categorical. Husbands exist only in relation to wives and vice versa; likewise employers and employees and a large range of both asymmetrical and symmetrical social relations. The nature of these relationships will be marked.

Finally of the referents, there are settings about which little will be reported because so little has been written. It is trite to note that the rules of procedure and interaction differ in churches, factories, homes and parliaments, and law courts. All have both non-verbal and verbal markers that identify them, in terms of locations and procedures.

The analysis so far can be summarized by stating that while the general task is to describe and explain which kinds of links there are between non-vocal, vocal, and verbal markers on the one hand, and the emotions/moods/motivation, personal identities, social identities, social relationships, and situations on the other, there are difficulties in defining or identifying each component, and especially referents more general than the mundane.

9.2   Stability and Change

A first addition to this essentially static frame of reference has to be the issue of change in individuals. We are sensitive not just to what is, but how things are changing. There are short-term and longer-term changes. Is Fred getting more irritated? Has John really reformed and given up lying? Is Leslie changing gender? Do Jill and James show signs of ceasing to be wife and husband? Will the presence of women in parliament reduce the amount of swearing there? (This was one of the questions posed in South Australia prior to women being eligible for election. The answer was that it did!). How can change be negotiated?

Neither is it just the referents that change. The markers change too. One of the inevitable referent changes we all experience is of growing older – and older. What is deemed appropriate changes in individuals with time, as dress changes with age as well as with fashion, and talk changes too, both because new phenomena appear and because fashions change. These two have combined in the world of sound transmission. Gramophones and wirelesses are now rare as reference terms, and so are ghetto blasters and trannies, yet radios remain. 78s are for the cognoscenti only as are LPs; CDs are buoyant, and DVDs surgent. Are the elderly expected to retain the vocabulary of their earlier days or vary their speech as a function of changing usage and the age of their interlocutors, and what are the differences between those who change more and those who change less? As seen already with terms of address and reference, results are prone to have components of discontinuity at a surface level and continuity at deeper levels, and these issues need to be considered both in the conceptualization and interpretation of research.

There is a second kind of change that is best considered separately as aspirations, and sub-divided into the acceptable and unacceptable.

9.2.1 Unavoidable and Socially Acceptable Aspirations

Children change as they develop. They have to adopt and grow into new roles and social positions. Learning how to enact new roles frequently requires pretending to be what one is not in order to become that to which one aspires. Whether it is for real or in playing games, practice is almost always a necessary condition of achievement and improvements, and coaching and training may also be required. The same is true of social roles such as friend and girlfriend, husband, and mother, and occupational roles such as teacher and truck driver. The substantive challenge in all such cases is to master the new roles without being undermined in the process.

The socially mobile have similar problems in emulating the behavior of the strata to which they aspire. As Labov (1966) demonstrated, would-be climbers are prone to suffer from hypercorrection in both their pronunciation and their verbal usage. They are prone to credit themselves with posher accents than they have, and may not recognize their voices when these are played back from tape-recorders. How we hear ourselves is not necessarily how others hear us.

All of the roles mentioned incorporate being able to generate speech and non-verbal behavior fit for the roles. In the jargon of social psychology these are exercises in *impression management*, and while development is occurring, there may well be a degree of dissociation between the markers manifested and their referents. In play-acting, emotions will be simulated so that there are markers without referents. In other situations attempts will be made to disguise underlying emotions of embarrassment, fear, and lack of confidence. These are socially acceptable simulations, presumably because they are seen to be necessary means to achieve socially desirable ends. There are other simulations that are not socially acceptable.

9.2.2 Unacceptable and Contestable Aspirations

Confidence tricksters are presenting acceptable social identities to their victims, as are other wolves in sheep's clothing. Liars may appear to be telling the truth, but are not (see 9.3). Both aspire to deceive for self-centered rather than socially desirable ends, and present problems for society of how to detect the falsity of their appearances. Courts of law are intended to expose the false markers of criminals in their search for the truth. Whilst many of these displays of misleading markers are clearly unacceptable, there is also a broad band of contestable discrepancies.

Present-day media insist on reporting about images of public figures, and in particular of politicians. Celebrities are now likely to have image consultants, who train them into personas popular with the people. The ex-Prime Minister of the United Kingdom, Margaret Thatcher, was professionally coached towards a vote-winning image. The discrepancy between Nixon on the White House tapes and on television cost him the presidency of the USA. At what stage image creation becomes unacceptable has not been resolved and will be presumably a never-ending issue. It is clear that the *spin* via which politicians persistently pretend to a better reality than exists is becoming difficult to sustain, but to date this seems simply to be alienating populations from participation in the political domain (see chapter 11). These are but two examples of discrepancies between appearance and reality that are contestable, and it is probably sensible to move to a more differentiated set of discriminations among levels of reality than a simple binary opposition between reality and appearance.

9.3 Circles of Reality and Linkages to Truth

Figure 9.1 notes the rings of discourse and data surrounding what is true about markers (and all other explicit or implicit beliefs about and representations of reality). All rings are real in that they are relevant to experience and behavior, but the bulls-eye is what scientists are trying to reach, and many hope that the outer rings will come to reflect "The truth" more and more. Two of the four central quadrants are labelled *etic* and *emic*, the distinctions between them being what could be used as valid markers and which of these are in fact used. The number of etic markers cannot be smaller than the number of emic ones. Both etic and emic knowledge can be represented as propositions about (knowing that) or as procedures (knowing how to). In the area of lying, Ekman has conducted microanalyses of certain facial muscle movements which he believes are indicators of lying. This etic possibility was not being considered twenty years ago, but now it is. The verbal formulation of the precise nature of the relations between these muscle movements and lying would involve the construction of a set of propositions, which will need to be supported by publically available evidence eventually. At this stage the idea has etic potential. Meanwhile there may be some people who know how to detect lying (valid emic), but cannot articulate the grounds for their judgments.

The circle of what the experts report as being true is included as a reminder that experts can disagree and can be wrong. Ekman (1992/1985) is very circumspect in his tabulations of possible cues that need to be followed up to facilitate accurate diagnosis; others less so. For example, 30 states in the USA permit screening of job applicants with polygraph testing, and there are several hundred polygraph experts employed in US government departments alone. About 9,000 persons have been trained to use polygraphs for lie detection. Convincing empirical trials demonstrating the success rates of lie detection using the polygraph have yet to be published. Is Ekman wasting his time and being too circumspect with his listings but justified with his claims about muscle movements? Are polygraph users deluded?

Out in the everyday world, millions of people are taking decisions about lying daily, both as deceivers and detectors. Some risk their lives because they believe what others say. Historically, many garrisons and civilians have been massacred, having been promised that their lives would be spared by their enemies if they surrendered. Also, in the everyday world there are many beliefs about the validity of certain cues, which are believed by many to be symptomatic of lying, but which have been shown not to be valid indicators, for example embarrassed smiles and a high incidence of pausing and speech errors.

These considerations about lying could be applied to *all* the indexical connections mentioned in this chapter: smiling and being happy, claiming to be hungry and being hungry, speaking slowly and being introverted, speaking with a particular accent and being a member of a particular social class, calling each other "darling" and being friends.

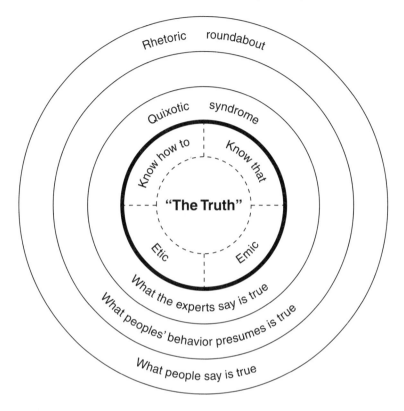

Figure 9.1   Some Layers of Reality

If markers are only or probabilistically related to their presumed referents, then their practical discriminatory utility may be zero. No precise criterion can be specified that will differentiate between usefulness and uselessness of a feature as a marker, but even an asymmetrical success rate of 95 per cent would lead to many Type 1 and Type 2 errors. This matters greatly to individuals if incorrect identification could lead to a violent attack, an arrest and trial, or a rejection from a job.

In contrast, if we consider strangers on a train negotiating whether or not to have a prolonged conversation, it may not matter that initial exchanges are associated with mistaken guesses about personal or social identity as the would-be sociable participants proceed to try to find topics of mutual interest, but some mistakes will be less serious or embarrassing than others. One of the virtues of the strong difference between the voice pitch of men and women on the telephone is that the embarrassment of gender misattribution is low – and usually immediately perceptible.

For many potential markers there are likely to be a number of small statistical differences between members of different social category that could serve as useful markers for experts trained in the relevant discriminations. In contrast, even for lay people, vocalic qualities, especially those combined into accents, can serve as reliable and valid identifiers of nationality, ethnicity, region of origin, and social class. The least equivocal markers are those where ingroups and outgroups have established deterministic and invariant criteria, such as the names to be used for particular places for example. If you wish to refer to that town in "the Six Counties, Northern Ireland, or Ulster", you cannot escape from saying "Londonderry" or "Derry". There was no doubt of the sympathies of an aging woman in a home for retired actors in the 1960s who said that she had been born in St. Petersburg, had survived Petrograd, suffered in Leningrad, and hoped to die in St. Petersburg. For ethnicity or political identification, clearer still is the use of a particular language either out of necessity or by choice. Most countries are multilingual and multi-ethnic, and which language is used where and when is a strong marker of identifications.

As a final point, and this arises out of these last observations, it should be noted that social markers serve different purposes for different people in different situations. People can wish to display their social or attitudinal position, declaring their identifications to others. Alternatively they can be concerned to hide aspects of their true social identity. Spies epitomize this latter, but in all hierarchical societies, the gatekeepers to valued memberships will be expected to be trying to detect persons unsuitable for membership, and to find excusable grounds for not accepting them. False negatives are preferable to false positives.

Weakness of association should not be confused with infrequency of occurrence. A rare event can be a strong marker. Talking once in one's sleep in the language of the enemy may be sufficient to ensure an accurate marking. Each instance of a potential marker has therefore to be assessed empirically and in relation to its value as a marker, and whilst a weak statistical significant association between cue and referent may not have pragmatic significance, a rare but deterministic one can.

9.3.1   Rings of People: Talk and Action

What people say and what they do can be dissociated, as demonstrated in an early study by LaPiere (1934). After enjoying a tour with two Chinese friends that included meals and accommodation at 251 (!) restaurants and hotels, and having suffered from only one ethnically based refusal, LaPiere wrote asking about the acceptability of Chinese people in each establishment. Of the 128 replies, 92 percent said that Chinese visitors would not be admitted. The reverse is also common with favorable verbally-expressed attitudes not eventuating in corresponding actions. In particular in multicultural societies denials of discrimination in opportunities on grounds of ethnicity, gender, and social class have been pervasive in the rhetoric of gatekeepers to openings but not evident in their practices.

9.3.2 A Ring of Experts: Talk

Expert opinion and reporting is not a perfect guide to truth. On simple matters where you might expect a consensus among reports – such as LaPiere's study – accounts across elementary (social) psychology texts differ. Further, some of the adverse criticisms of it are in respect of claims not made in the original. That experts disagree at the cutting edges of research is not surprising and that media versions of their statements may be distorted is to be expected in individualistic competitive societies in areas where there are no rewards for being seen to come second. That noted, the training of experts should have inducted them into a questioning attitude towards ill-informed opinions, but too often other factors override this. Following Grice (1975), they should only make statements which they believe to be true and for which they have adequate evidence. They should be careful in the limitations and qualifications to the claims they make. Many are, but some are not, and the media have no difficulty in finding a "rent-a-prof" to say something controversial. For a good example of the lack of circumspection on the point of academics, a trawl through the arguments about the "existence" of social class and intelligence and the nature of any relationship between the two would yield a diversity of nonsense. This point is being raised under markers, partly because of the still prevalent set of inferences linking accent, social class, and presumed intelligence and other personality traits. Accents do vary by social class, but each social class is heterogeneous with respect to any measure of intelligence linked to academic school achievements.

9.3.3 Truths about Language-carried Markers

The kind of summary statement that might issue forth could be: the pronunciation of post-vocalic /r/ has been found to be indicative of socio-economic status in the Lower East Side of New York City in the early 1960s among residents of two years' standing. It occurs with the highest percentage in the lower strata, and is particularly evident in informal situations (Labov, 1966). Whether members of the groups concerned and other groups actually notice this and use its frequency of occurrence as a marker of social identity has yet to be investigated.

This is just one example of a feature *available* for use (etic), but it is only available to those whose aural sensitivities and knowledge are sufficient to identify and estimate its incidence of occurrence. In fact, the boasting of Professor Higgins about his capacity to recognize accents by district within London is not absurd. Families who have lived in the same neighborhood all their lives may well be distinctive in certain phonological and other features. This is true of rural areas as well as urban ones, and the work of Orton, Dieth, and others gives some idea of what is involved. To chart dialectological maps of rural England took 11 years of recording around 313 villages. This yielded a data set of over 400,000 items. It was not until 16 years later that the *Linguistic Atlas of England* was published (Orton, Sanderson & Widdowson, 1978). (Four books had been issued *en route* to this climax.)

To be able to do such work requires extensive and intensive practical training. (I was amazed both at how much there was to learn about one small set of English sounds and how quickly appreciation of this could grow when well-instructed; I began to appreciate how phonetics and phonology could constitute a whole degree programme.)

Emic markers are those which are actually used by people to inform inferences from marker to referent. Emic possibilities are fourfold: wrong belief versus valid belief about it being a valid marker; a conscious awareness of using it as a marker versus an unconscious one. It is not odd to claim that someone sounds like a New Zealander without being able to verbalize the grounds.

9.3.4   Changes in Language and its Use

It is nearly time to ask how a sad voice differs from a happy one, but one last qualification is in order before that. The assumption that the personality of individuals does not change through history or individual lives is an assumption. That we can sympathize with why characters in Shakespeare's plays feel as they do implies that occasions for and types of emotion have not changed radically in the last 400 years, in England. How much longer more complex emotions/motivations such as duty, guilt, shame, and honor will make sense to younger generations is a perennial worry of parents and grandparents, but these concepts as experiences are certainly less prominent in education, the media, and the pronouncements of authorities than they were 50 years ago. (Plato made the same observation in Athens, although the Greek city-states were subsequently overrun by the Romans.)

Language is not a constant at any of its levels. Structurally the English of fourteenth century Chaucer is not that dissimilar to its twenty-first century equivalent, but the lexicon has changed enough to render much of it unintelligible, and much of it difficult to decode. A systematic analysis might show that the 750 words of basic English (Ogden & Richards, 1923) or the similar number of structural words listed by Fries (1952) have changed least in pronunciation, spelling or meaning.

However, the scientific and technical vocabularies have exploded. Our houses still have roofs, walls, and doors, but the new gadgets inside are many and generate their peculiarities of Newspeak. The computer/telecommunication (ICT) vocabulary is the latest example of a proliferation of new terms that have rapidly had their meanings extended beyond their technical origins. The specialist occupational activities have seen the greatest increases. It is not just the Graeco–Latin inventions for the medical, physical, biological, chemical, and social sciences, but also the worlds of manufacturing and construction. These terms will appear in published writings, and some are likely to be crunched into vernacular expressions in daily use; they leak out into the general population. Whether "geek" and "nerd" have such derivations I do not know, but expressions such as AC/DC signal their origins clearly. Once they cross the borders into slang, most will have a short life, just because they are markers of particular but temporary statuses. The fighter pilots in the Battle of Britain of 1941 rapidly developed an argot of camaraderie that set them apart from their less glamorous but longer-lived compatriots. The usage spread into the armed forces more generally, but much of it vanished with the ending of that particular phase of the war, and the rest once the armed forces were demobbed. "Wizard prang" is obsolete. Members of groups within the armed forces need to be members of strongly cohesive groups to be effective, and a special *sociolect* is a powerful identification tag for speakers and hearers. Such phenomena are frequently found in transient groups or continuing groups with changing members. In adolescent groupings those who drift out into pairs quickly fail to pick up changes and thereby identify themselves as passé.

More dramatically, in the last 40 years English has witnessed the 'Great Gender Struggle.' Paradoxically, the pervasive marking of gender pronouns in English was one of the most obvious linguistic weapons that women could use in their struggle to achieve greater equality of opportunity. The move towards replacement of the use of male marking of occupations and positions (for example fireman, chairman) with ungendered substitutions have also been helpful to the cause. Some of the changes are cumbersome (for the moment at least), and English is still stuck with a pronominal system that is proving to be a nuisance. Historical evidence on the role of language features as weapons will no doubt continue to be interpreted in more than one way, but there is no doubt that its marking of gender could be and was used to crystallize and render transparent the ethical and political issues to all users of English.

As chapter 13 illustrates, language varieties have always been powerful ethical and political components of the struggles of the victims of discrimination, just as it has been used as a weapon against them by elites. In all these circumstances it has served as a marker of social identity and social relations, as chapter 10.4 explicates for social class in particular.

9.4 Summary

Unfortunately, the various distinctions mentioned in chapter 9 are all valid and eventually will have to be incorporated into work on markers and their referents, but the analyses made so far have also to be re-integrated into the whole person. Each person is a combination of all of the features mentioned: emotions and motivations, moods and traits, personality and social identities, social relations and settings; what is worse is that each of these has fuzzy borders with its partners on either side. Practically, each of us has to make and take decisions for actions about ourselves and others in the light of each context of situation. We have to take account of changes with time over shorter and longer periods. We have to distinguish between actualities and aspirations, between masks and what is being masked. It is amazing that we manage. How we actually exploit the vocal and verbal features to these ends is dealt with in chapter 10.

CHAPTER

10

Marking of States, Identities, and Settings: Data and their Interpretation

10.1 Marking Emotional/Motivational States

10.1.1 Vocalic Markers

Scherer (1979; 1992) and Winton (1990) each review the substantive literature of the conceptualization of emotion, the methodological difficulties associated with this, and some of the language-related phenomena involved. Here is it is necessary to make some prefatory observations about non-language related cues, which are many, and then the issues of vocal and verbal markers will be addressed.

To ignore situation and context would be foolish. Funerals and weddings are typically respectively sad and happy occasions for the central characters, even though tears may be shed at each. Cross-culturally, outsiders are not likely to mistake the two, although they may well be prone to assimilative errors. Clothes are a cue, but they can be misleading. It is far from universal for brides to wear white at weddings. Similarly, it is far from universal for chief mourners at funerals to wear black. Neither will all persons present be experiencing the normative emotions. For variability in these we can note features such as *posture*, *gestures*, and in particular *facial expressions*. (see Argyle, 1988 and Morris, 1978 for a general and popular account respectively, and Ekman, 1993 for a recent review about faces.) Cultures may have required children to learn to mask their emotions or to perform the natural physical actions with a cathartic exaggeration, but these are matters for local enquiry and discovery to which answers are likely to be forthcoming and clear.

Davitz and colleagues (1964) conducted a set of studies that helped to define the field very satisfactorily in terms of hypotheses, but in fact did not check the extent to which the profiles on the eight voice characteristics they used were either heard as indicative by listeners or found to be characteristic of the voices of people experiencing the particular emotions. They had actors simulate each of the emotions whilst reading a passage, and also read it in a neutral tone. Judges rated the voices on loudness, pitch, timbre, and speech rate and did in fact find that their judgments correlated well with the characteristics listed in Table 10.1, but Davitz did not proceed to have participants try to identify the emotions. This investigation crosses the circles of the Russian Dolls of Reality (Figure 9.1) by having simulated performances checked against perceptions of the basic features of the emotions, as defined by the experimenters.

In a further study Davitz used tape recordings of semantically neutral messages read with ten different simulated emotions including anger, fear, joy, disgust, and affection. Independent judges were asked to identify the emotion expressed by the voice. In the first place judges agreed with each other and their agreements coincided with the intentions of the speakers. The generous conclusions would be that:

1 trained actors can simulate emotional states vocally, and that the acoustic characteristics can be specified by both experts (Davitz) and non-experts;
2 non-experts can identify emotions on vocalic qualities alone, as simulated by trained actors;

A skeptic might argue that these results are products of particular dramatic social conventions that both actors and audiences have learned, and that in real life, even if the experiences of the emotions have been subjected to conventional pressures, the cues, linkages, and emotions may be different. Certainly Davitz would have been on stronger ground had he included some genuine recordings and both analyzed these acoustically and had them assessed by judges of varied expertise. It is true that in such a study, the verbal content would almost certainly contain explicit claims about the states of the speaker, and the acoustic equipment would not be able to exploit this, and it would be possible to select segments which were not explicitly signalling the emotional state. It needs to be added that in the Davitz studies some emotions were more readily identified than others: amused, despairing, and disliking. The design could not locate whether this was a recognition matter or one of differential simulation competence or both. In another study (Davitz, 1964, chapter 7), Levitt contrasted the value of facial and vocal expressions and concluded that the gains of having the combination differed across the emo-

Table 10.1 Characteristics of Vocal Expressions Contained in the Test of Emotional Sensitivity

Feeling	Loudness	Pitch	Timbre	Rate	Inflection	Rhythm	Enunciation
Affection	Soft	Low	Resonant	Slow	Steady and slight upward	Regular	Slurred
Anger	Loud	High	Blaring	Fast	Irregular up and down	Irregular	Clipped
Boredom	Moderate to low	Moderate to low	Moderately resonant	Moderately slow	Monotone or gradually falling	–	Somewhat slurred
Cheerfulness	Moderately high	Moderately high	Moderately blaring	Moderately fast	Up and down; overall upward	Regular	
Impatience	Normal	Normal to moderately high	Moderately blaring	Moderately fast	Slight upward	–	Somewhat clipped
Joy	Loud	High	Moderately blaring	Fast	Upward	Regular	
Sadness	Soft	Low	Resonant	Slow	Downward	Irregular pauses	Slurred
Satisfaction	Normal	Normal	Somewhat resonant	Normal	Slight upward	Regular	Somewhat slurred

After Davitz (1964).

tions. His conclusion that vocal quality is a more important source of information for some cues than others is a legitimate hypothesis warranting further investigation.

Conclusions

Articulatory and acoustic phonetics are well established in terms of both the conceptual and empirical analysis of voice qualities, and technical instrumentation for analysis and production is now available. Arguments continue about the classification of emotions themselves, and about the extent to which the genetically programmed potential can be shaped and re-shaped by culture, but how we eventually classify states is a separate issue from how we use words like "anger," "fear," "happiness" and "sadness." Given that limitation, findings concur with lay experience that vocalic qualities provide reliable and valid cues to emotional states of people who are not disguising how they feel.

10.1.2 Verbal Markers

Children learn to use the vocabulary of emotion as they do other self- and other-referential terms, and their normal use of these appears to be expressed naturally with the vocal qualities mentioned, along with correlated facial expressions, gestures, and postures (Harris, 1989). Smiles go with contentment and happiness, tears with pain and sadness, and they do so from very early in life. The non-verbal and verbal reactions precede the vocabulary, but the modelling of comments of caretakers and observations of others lead to basic competence with the use of the four or five basic emotion words by age four to five in western societies. Versions of "I'm hungry" and "I'm thirsty" will have been constructed and scaffolded up from the demanding monosyllabic and nonsyllabic noises used earlier. Reactively and proactively, children of four or so have learned how to combine the verbal with the non-verbal which empowers them to mark their states for others. In parallel with these developments however there are two other related strands of events to be considered. The first is self-control of reactions to emotional/motivational states, the second is the capacity to mask and simulate states.

Very few, if any, societies allow young children to run amok with anger. In various ways children are constrained to limit their behavior when they become angry. They have to learn not to allow excitement to escalate into mania. They have to learn to wait to satisfy hunger and thirst, falling in with whatever the regulations of the family are. Delaying gratification of appetites and diverting or suppressing destructive impulses can have been well established by age four in those families and cultures that value and exploit efficient socialization procedures.

Masking emotion is a special form of self-control. Hiding fear, anger, and disappointment will be required to greater or lesser extents in different families in different subcultures in different societies, but all define ages and situations when such masking has to be exercised. When children learn to mask emotional experiences by pretending either to be unreactive or to be feeling some other emotion, they are simultaneously being afforded powers to pretend that they have emotions which they do not or will not have. In short they are learning to manipulate and deceive others, sometimes for selfish reasons, and other times, out of consideration for others (Broomfield, Robinson, E. J., & Robinson, W. P., in press). The limits of deception and simulation with emotional states have yet to be uncovered.

What is true of young children can be developed by adults so that we finally arrive at several variants.

1   For much interaction emotional and motivational states can be marked explicitly and sincerely verbally and non-verbally, both expressively and as a guide to other interactants as to suitable demeanor, topics, and comments. In either case self-marking is primary.

2   In other situations, persons will pretend to emotional/motivational states that they are not experiencing either verbally or non-verbally or both, but this can be for a variety of motives: encounter regulation (maintaining or breaking off interaction), marking self as considerate, concerned etc., or as ruthless, contemptuous, etc., or regulating others.

10.2   Impressions of Others

10.2.1   Vocal and Verbal Markers

Reference has already been made to the academic troubles in conceptualising and measuring personality and individual differences, more thoroughly reviewed elsewhere (Scherer & Giles, 1979; Furnham, 1990). To be positive, here the initial focus will be on the results and interpretation of a single carefully conducted comparative study. Scherer (1979) employed 28 American and 29 German adult males recruited from adult education files to take part in a jury study. Groups of six discussed a criminal case and were given about an hour to reach a verdict. They were told that the investigator's interest was in personality influences on jury decision-making, and before the deliberations of the case, they completed a battery of questionnaires and ratings. Peer ratings of each participant were obtained. Voice and speech analyses were conducted by trained coders and computerized digital speech processors. The five components of the acoustic speech signals of each individual to be mentioned here were: fundamental frequency (f_0) ($\bar{\chi}$ and σ), vocal intensity ($\bar{\chi}$ and σ), and energy distribution in the speech spectrum. The first two correspond to pitch and loudness, the third to the kinds of features listed in Table 2.1. Correlational analyses constituted the primary data set. To render the results readable in this context, some complexities are not introduced.

American and German data were analyzed separately. For Americans, mean f_0 correlated positively with self-report measures of achievement, task ability, sociability, dominance and aggressiveness, and with peer ratings of dominance and assertiveness. For Germans, f_0 had positive correlations with self-reports on adjustment, orderliness and lack of autonomy and with peer ratings of dependability and likeability. There was no suggestion of higher f_0 being associated with dominance/competence.

Why the difference? Scherer argues that for the Americans, higher f_0 is indicative of the heightened habitual muscle tone of higher arousal and energy, other things being equal. Beyond a certain level of f_0 the pitch would sound strained which would *not* be indicative of competence/dominance. (Subjectively the same could apply to intensity/loudness in Britain; within a range louder males may be seen as competent and dominant, but if greater loudness is heard as shouting, then the inference would shift to failure to achieve dominance. The principle of a reverse Poisson distribution where increases along the x-axis have a rounded cliff of decline is in fact a feature originally claimed for a variety of leadership qualities (Gibb, 1954).)

Scherer's own review makes clear the difficulties of work in this area and the huge amounts of data and painstaking analyses needed to create a coherent story about relatively homogeneous small groups of men from just two not that dissimilar cultures. And he is right to do so. But if it is so complex, is f_0 serving as a marker of personality for the other participants? Since the voices were recorded for a short time and in a single setting, is it sensible to ask people to pass judgments about personality? The answer to the first question may well be "Yes." The second question may be answerable in terms of the participants being willing to generalize from the sample of behavior *in situ*. That so many studies since Asch's (1952) pioneering work have been conducted with such judgments may be taken to imply that participants are comfortable with such decision-making. In the hope that this is so, a next step from Scherer's focus on the vocal can be to look at the vocal, other non-verbal, and verbal in combination.

10.2.2   Vocal versus Verbal Cues

Argyle and colleagues manipulated cues believed to signal the two fundamental dimensions of power and solidariness in studies to examine the relative relevance of vocal and verbal cues to judgments of others. In the first, Argyle, Salter, Nicholson, Williams, and Burgess (1970) exploited the newly arrived video camera to dissociate and create different combinations of an actor displaying indicators of interpersonal superiority, equality, and inferiority. Participants were told that several versions of a film had been made to show to students to entice them to take part in an experiment in the Psychology Department, and that it would be helpful if they as students would rate the performer in each of these. Superiority of the non-verbals was signalled by an unsmiling face with the head raised and a loud dominating voice, and verbally by telling the potential participant that there was no point in explaining the experiment; it would be beyond their understanding. (Note that vocal was included as a non-verbal here.) All non-verbal/verbal combinations of superior, inferior, and equal variants as performed by two female actors were presented. Ratings were made on ten scales, using inferior/superior and submissive/dominant as checks on the validity of performances, with the others including hostile/friendly, unpleasant/pleasant, insincere/sincere, unstable/stable, and confusing/straightforward. Both the non-verbal and verbal variants shifted judgments across conditions: the verbal having significant effects on six and the non-verbal on all ten. Following some adroit but questionable calculations, the authors concluded that participants were giving over four times as much weight to non-verbal as to the verbal information.

In a second study substituting friendly/hostile for superior/inferior, changing the performances appropriately, and amending the scales, Argyle, Alkema, and Gilmour (1971) obtained comparable results and drew the corresponding conclusions. Excellent as these studies were as potential points of departure for series of variants on the basic themes, this line of research was not pursued with the refinements and thoroughness that it needed to be able to draw better-framed conclusions.

Nearly twenty years later, Howe (1989) and Telfer and Howe (1994) were able to note a number of studies refining the original by, for example separating the visual from the vocal and reducing unnaturalness, particularly where credibility was lost by being unnaturally extreme; one study included the statement "You're a complete idiot." Telfer and Howe both simplified and refined the study using a similar paradigm, with professional actors saying either "Give me that book," or "Could you possibly give me that book?" in vocal superior/inferior ways and with contrasting facial expressions. Dubbing and splicing were used to create the tapes, and participants rated these on: respectful vs. disrespectful, self-effacing vs. overbearing, submissive vs. dominant. Under these conditions the vocalic quality was the most powerful, with the verbal second. The visual influence was much weaker. Very similar results were obtained with ratings on friendly vs. hostile, cordial vs. cool, and welcoming vs. unwelcoming for friendly/hostile manipulations.

Whilst it is a significant issue as to the weighting participants give to the various components of displays, it needs to be asked why results were as they were, and to answer that will require an account of how people draw inferences about others, and especially pertinent to that question is how they handle discrepancies among cues.

From the Argyle studies, it was trebly dangerous to infer that the non-verbals are more important than the verbals in such a context. Telfer and Howe give one set of reasons. It was true that in both studies Argyle and his colleagues made independent checks on the verbal and non-verbal performances separately and the range of ratings extended similarly across scales of inferior/superior and hostile/friendly respectively. Declarations of love and hate or liking and not liking may not be common in Oxford colleges in group settings, but they are essential and/or significant components of certain social relationships in certain settings. The relative weight approach is the wrong model. Where all cues are available, we expect consistency across the range, and when we are alerted by an inconsistency, we seek to explain the violation of the expectation. We may ask the other directly. We may reflect upon possible explanations.

In fact both experiments offer data relevant to this issue. When we see someone sweating and twitching, but making authoritative statements in a strained voice, what do we conclude? A lack of confidence springs immediately to mind. A newly trained teacher giving a first lesson to a new class. A student giving a first seminar presentation. The opening night of an amateur dramatics production. The verbal component can be well-prepared and rehearsed, but its delivery may well leak the nervousness, as may the other non-verbal components. If we believe that the performer has greater control over the script than the rest of speech components, then we have a ready explanation for the verbal/non-verbal discrepancy. Unfortunately no confidence scale was included among the ratings. The non-verbal superior/verbal inferior combination did attract high ratings on "confusing." If participants could not make sense of the performance, then "confusing" was an understandable assessment. In other situations, it is possible to interpret such a combination as being obsequious, syco-phantic, or "being a creep" – to approach more probable colloquial expres-sions for the phenomenon. With none of these adjectives being available and the situation not being a likely one for such conduct, "confusing" was a rational choice, but a reference to effects on self rather than a marker of the other. The friendly/hostile results with the conflicting messages yielded similar results, with friendly non-verbals and unfriendly verbals being seen as "confusing." The real life equivalent could be one where the performer likes the other more than is appropriate to the situation and is masking it with lies. For the unfriendly non-verbals and friendly verbals the strong-est effect was on insincerity, which accords with the same kind of inter-pretation terms of leakage of the least controllable.

Rules for initial interpretation might be summarized briefly:

1   If all markers are consistent with each other in terms of inferences to draw, interpret as normal.
2   If markers are sending different messages, then;
   a   Interpret for each set separately;
   b   Ask which sets are likely to be most difficult for the person to con-trol in this situation;
   c   Try to synthesize discrepancies in terms of motives of performer and/or reasons for the performance, for example lack of confidence, sycophancy, deceitful manipulation, delirious, exhausted.

10.3   A Taxonomy for Personality

10.3.1   Expert Verbosity

Issues about the conceptualization of personality were raised in chapter 8, and as with emotion/motivation earlier sections of this chapter have shown participants willing to rate personality characteristics *in situ* without commit-ment to whether such features were stable and general in the individuals concerned. Overall the English language has a very large number of trait descriptors. By 1967 Norman came to prefer a title of "2,800 personality trait descriptors" to Allport's much larger count. Grammatically, most of these are single lexical items in the class of adjectives. What do they presume? Why are there so many, and how do they function in everyday life?

One pervasive presupposition of these items is that human beings have relatively stable characteristics that may be attributed to them as individuals. In terms of scalar qualities, many are bipolar, often with an unnamed neutral point: happy–sad, brave–cowardly. Others refer to more or less. While people may use "stupid" as an opposite of "clever," this contrast only implies lesser cleverness and not its inverse. In either case, and especially when modified with "very," "quite" etc., both bipolar and unipolar adjectives, imply contrastive comparisons based on individual differences among people or variations in states of people across time and/or situations.

But why so many terms for this domain? Some of the world's languages make do with many fewer terms. How do these function in everyday life? Are they used reliably and do they correspond to a plausible construction of reality? It will be necessary to go somewhat further and ask not just what they mean, but what they presuppose and imply. More dangerously, questions will be raised about the use of such terms by psychologists. Are they descriptive or explanatory? Why have psychologists not been able to reduce the number of theories of personality from the array reviewed by Hall, Lindzey, Loehlin, & Manosevitz (1985)?

At the turn of this century the most popular classificatory system of personality descriptors revolves around variants of the "Big Five," (Digman, 1990) and it will be tactically reader-friendly to introduce some of the issues from this conception (see Wiggins, 1996 for some perspectives on them). The argument of the protagonists of the "Big Five" is that "these personality factors appear to provide a set of highly replicable dimensions that parsimoniously and comprehensively describe most phenotypic individual differences" (Saucier & Goldberg, 1996, p. 36). The model is "derived from lexical data" (p. 37). Digman (1996, p. 25) prefers to use the word "attribute" as the common name for these descriptors, on the grounds that it does not have the connotation of stability that "trait" has. However, "trait" is in common use, and the whole story is predicated on assumptions of the stability and centrality of the five hypothesized dimensions of temperament. It is true that many individual lexical terms serve also for reference to acute emotional states and moods as well as traits and can have implications for attitudes, values, and life-styles.

The "Big Five" listed earlier are: Neuroticism (anxiety, angry hostility, depression); Extraversion (warmth, gregariousness, assertiveness); Openness to Experience (fantasy, aesthetics, feelings); Agreeableness (trust, straightforwardness, altruism); and Conscientiousness (competence, order, dutifulness). The questionnaires used to measure these and variants of them have direct items such as "I am typically X" (where X is a trait descriptor) or behaviorally clear "I enjoy parties" with checking against a rating scale as a response.

Saucier and Goldberg (1996) have given eight reasons for endorsing the sense of a straightforward lexical approach to the issues raised by the concept of individual differences, and since a number of these are locked into the interface of language and social experience and behavior, they can quite properly be raised here, and be supplemented with questions and answers that will bring smiles to the faces of some discourses analysts and social constructionists.

10.3.2   Everyday Conversation

Do the advocates for the "Big Five" approach offer any corpora taken from everyday conversation to illustrate or support their case? The short answer is "No," and the immediately following question is, "Why not?" Saucier and Goldberg have been quoted as asserting that English-speakers would not have invented and preserved all these adjectives if they were not useful to us. They can of course be useful and invalid! As H. L. Menken reported, most of the names of the many gods devised by human beings are no longer in use. Neither are most of those from demonology, alchemy, and early medicine.

It has been argued that one of the great appeals of Freudian concepts was that they enabled psycho-analysts and subsequently the medical profession more generally to talk about each other. Freud provided not just an extensive vocabulary, but also dynamic explanations of how people come to be what they are. This has been a great boon to art critics and historians. It has provided jobs for analysts and listeners for those who wish to talk about themselves and their experiences to a captive audience. It has provided conversational tools for the café-bar intelligentsia and the dinner tables of the "chattering classes." But the correspondence of words to world (F7) is in greater doubt.

If the constituents of the "Big Five" are simply a more general and much older lexis for people to talk about people, questions about their validity are of lesser significance than the fact that they are now pragmatically indispensable, given the cultural histories and assumptions of English speakers. They may be replaced at a later point in time, just as Freudian terms may, but until technologically more valid successors appear, they will survive.

A weak but interesting example is the disappearance of "melancholy" and the emergence of "depression." Being melancholic was a respectable and acceptable condition in medieval times. Being depressed is liable to be treated as a psychiatric condition rather than a national stance to the state of *le condition humain*. Being "bilious" has changed its meaning, "choleric" is used but rarely, with "sanguine" still usable among certain sectors of society. These are no more than the guesses of one person, but more cannot be said because studies have yet to be conducted on the everyday use of personality trait words. That many of the lexical items are pervasive in such talk is true, but how they are used has yet to be investigated, and those studies might yield results of considerable interest to the following. Are the terms used most for referring to emotional states, moods, or personality descriptions? Are they used for descriptive or explanatory purposes and if both, what are the determinants of each?

10.3.3 Emotional States, Moods, Dispositions or Traits?

The difficulties of drawing distinctions among these three has already been discussed in this chapter. It would appear that states are the longest lasting and most frequent reactions to immediate circumstances. "Those flowers really cheered him up." "Failing her driving test made her very sad."

Reference to moods can use some of the same vocabulary ("You're in a cheerful mood this morning!"), but "You're in a sad mood" sounds odd. "He's a cheerful person" implies stability through time and across situations, as does, "He's often sarcastic". The empirical evidence for consensus in people's capacity for labelling core emotional states is reasonably strong, especially in familiar and genuine contexts. People are both frightened and surprised by unexpected loud bangs. Western people are disposed to become angry when their plane or train departures are repeatedly announced as being delayed. These can be considered as involving minimal levels of both inference and generalization, but the move to "He is a cheerful person" involves greater inference and generalization. To what extent do these trait ascriptions represent a wish to have a predictable and stable world and to what extent can these be delusional?

10.3.4 Description versus Explanation

Since the chapters offered in Wiggins' (1996) collection make no reference to everyday use, there is no basis for assuming that the trait descriptors are used for description rather than explanation. In courts of law in England and Wales, the defense can call "character witnesses" whose task is to point out that the accused has a character which is incompatible with him or her committing the crime in question. Typically the appeals are to honesty, integrity, and honor, and so often the appeals appear to be implausible in the light of the evidence adduced by the prosecution. These are clearly intended to serve as explanations as to why the accused could not have committed the crime. On other occasions, strong passions are adduced as justifications for crimes being committed.

Much more generally in social psychology, and in everyday living, the question asked of events relates to causes or reasons for their occurrence. Historically, one major contrast has been between person and situation as the origin of determinants and, when persons are cited, relevant evidence is evaluated against criteria of consensus, consistency, and distinctiveness. Would people agree that he/she is the sort of person who would do X? Has he/she done X in the past? Are there distinctive circumstances that would occasion her/him to do X? The first two are clearly person-focused, and both are serving as explanations (and perhaps excuses or justifications) of conduct. For authors such as Saucier and Goldberg (1996) to argue that the Big Five are solely descriptive is to impose their wishes on a world where person-related adjectives are frequently invoked to explain, justify, excuse, and commend.

10.3.5   A Hierarchy of Traits

If everyday utility is a criterion of the proliferation and retention of so many personality descriptors, why have people been so slow to develop a hierarchical taxonomy? In chemistry there were metals and non-metals, and gases, liquids and solids, prior to the construction of Mendeleyev's Periodic Table. In botany, there were hierarchical classifications prior to Linnaeus, and there were single lexical item labels for trees, mosses, and ferns. The Greeks (αρετη) and Romans (*virtu*) had high level ideals or codes of conduct for character, just as the Japanese (*bushido*) and the Portuguese (*brio*). The Big Five in contrast need phrases "Open to Experience," combinations of apparently independent concepts, for example competence and dutifulness, and potentially mutually contradictory same level and different level combinations; to be straightforward is not always altruistic, and neither is it agreeable.

And is it not odd that the Big Five are not clearly differentiated into single lexical items? If the accumulated experience of the English-speakers has generated so many useful lower level adjectives, it is surprising that they have not noticed which co-vary and combine to make up the Big

Five. It is also surprising that they have so far failed to generate any substantiated rationale for the differentiation. Galen's (1997/first century AD) idea of differential superfluity of four bodily humors was a good one, but unfortunately the differential presence of current hormonal candidates cannot yet be related to either specific emotions or traits. Recognizing this however does not mean that emotional states and moods are solely cognitively-based social constructions.

What to do

Issues of what to do about personality are even more serious academically and socially than are issues about emotions/motivation. The higher order taxonomy difficulties for the latter do not prevent people from operating in particular situations, in respect of markers, referents, and linkages. There are difficulties of cultural suppressions and distortions that may obscure the markers, but if we are cognizant with the cultural rules then judgments can take these into account. There are difficulties too of deliberate attempts to deceive others beyond what is culturally accepted as proper. At the present time expert knowledge is not sufficiently assured to slice through these masks, but as Ekman and others have shown there are etic possibilities which can be combined with enquiry techniques that can facilitate diagnoses of underlying emotional states and more. Particularly in cases of crimes and espionage we can expect continuing struggles between detectors and deceivers with relevant data on these not being made available in the public domain, just as the "secrets" of encryption and decryption for ciphers are too politically and commercially important or full disclosure of results (Singh, 1999).

Issues of speech markers of personal identity present essentially similar problems as markers of emotional/motivational states, with the complications but they differ from the personality problems in one respect that needs a special commentary.

10.3.6 Personality Markers: The Big Issue

Hawk-eyed readers may have noticed the switch in section headings at 10.1. In the studies reported about judgments of others there is no independent evidence about the accuracy of the judgments of others. In the case of the Scherer studies judgments are being about different individuals on the basis of their behavior *in situ*. In the Argyle studies judgments are about the videos of the *same* individuals acting in more than one guise. In one strict sense many of these judgments are ill-founded since two different judgments about the same person cannot both be valid. Such a point can be extended to all those studies which have relied on matched-guise techniques from Asch (1952) through Lambert (1972) to Giles (Giles & Powesland, 1975). Of course the crucial objective in these designs was to control for all characteristics of the people to be judged except for those of interest, but while the observation here in no way invalidates the claims about markers and referent behavior, it does invalidate the idea of persons being invariant in the impression they create across and even within situations. This does not lead to a further inference that personality is too variable to be pinned down; there is nothing odd about personalities having a *range* of possible behaviors, a range that may have limits. Some people can have narrower ranges than others, and at present we have no idea about adaptability to dramatic changes to life-situations, but the predominant western conception of adult individuals having a stable set of traits that are not subject to considerable flexibility is a strange construct. It clearly serves to give people illusions of the predictability of others. It clearly serves an administrative function of being able to hold individuals to account, but evidence from significant conflicts show nice people can become killers and torturers given appropriate induction procedures (Haritos-Fatsouris, in press; Zimbardo, 1970).

10.4   Marking of Social Identity

Personal and social identity are not independent of each other, as already hinted. Selection for certain achieved social identities may require personal identities that are consistent with the role expectations. Professional soldiers are expected to behave in a tough and brave manner. Nurses are expected to show compassion for patients as well as competence in health care. Social groups which people try to join voluntarily are likely to be initially self-selecting in terms of personal characteristics and subsequently filtered by contemporary group members. Ascribed social identities may nevertheless involve socialization procedures that encourage or require the appearance of particular personality characteristics. Here the concern is not with inferences of selection boards, about fitness for particular social identities, but with inferences from speech to social identity, and from social identity to personality.

Are speech markers of social identity reliable and valid? If persons are group members, whether ascribed or achieved, and if they wish to be known as members, then they will need markers of distinctiveness, and speech is likely to be a constituent of this and may even be a necessary condition of the identity. Clothes, adornments, and other non-verbal markers may take precedence, but presidents and premiers do not speak like the poor, and those in poverty do not speak like national leaders. This will be true for self-appraisal, intragroup identification, and possibly extragroup identification as well. Social categories with clear boundaries are most likely to fit this profile, and in quasi-democracies these are particularly likely to be in respect of achieved statuses: occupational, recreational, and educational, etc. (see Scherer and Giles, 1979, for reviews of studies).

The more general social categorization by gender retains distinctiveness in the same way, with additional speech differentiation in terms of audible fundamental frequencies of pitch, and historical divergencies of style, with female speech being less assertive and aggressive, more polite and uncertain, and in female/male interactions more deferential (Lakoff, 1975). The dramatic shift towards equalization of rights, expectations, and opportunities have led to corresponding reductions in such speech markers (Kramerae, 1990; Coates & Johnson, 2001), but then the original gender differences in style were indicative of role expectations and role relationships rather than markers of a norm-free social identity. Age-related social phenomena can be categorical for administrative purposes, and divided into rough phases such as infancy, childhood, adolescence, and adulthood, with labels such as "teenager" or "elderly" also being used. Just as these have no set boundaries, so speech markers do not. Vocalic features such as fundamental frequency have been shown to yield a negatively accelerated decline with age for females, which is similar for males, but with those post-75 showing a reversal (Helfrich, 1979). There are changes in extra-linguistic and paralinguistic features in both the early and the later years, just as there are with grammar, vocabulary, and colloquial expressions, but in FtF encounters vocal and verbal speech features would not be prime identificatory markers for age, and on telephones would only provide rough indications. In recent years there has been a growth of interest in markers from receivers rather than senders where the encounter involves a younger and an elderly person. This has exposed a high incidence of *patronizing talk*, reviewed by Hummert (1994) and Hummert and Ryan (2001) and illustrated in discourse by Coupland and Coupland (2001). Paralinguistic features of raised volume, slowness, and carefully articulated pronunciation, terms of address such as "dear" and "love," along with simplifications of grammar and lexis, are a few of the indicators of assumptions about linkages between social identity and personality characteristics analogous but not homologous with those inferences associated with social class and ethnicity. In the case of age the assumptions are likely to be those of reduced auditory and cognitive capacities and other decrements.

With social class the messiness becomes greater. Administrators, advertisers, and sociologists have constructed ranked categorizations based on variable mixtures of occupational prestige, income, education, and education of parents as bases for dividing societies into variable numbers of strata. When the indices are highly correlated assignment of individuals to a class is less problematic than when they are not. Classifications were simpler when males still predominated in the workforce: the upper class did not work, the middle class men wore white collars and ties to steady employment in offices, and the working class did manual work in whatever clothes were available; and earnings were correlated with the gradation. As investigators such as Labov (1966; 1972) and Shuy, Baratz and Wolfram (1969) showed, differential prior identification of phonemes and accents were markers of social class. Labov's New York data noted variability as a function of formality of speech (situation) and that the incidence of post-vocalic /r/s differed quantitatively rather than qualitatively by social class. English data have shown regional and prestige status variability in accents and dialects with a coming together of Received Pronunciation and Standard English among the upper middle strata. Such data have been found in other countries: Australia (Mitchell & Delbridge, 1965), and Canada in both English and French (Lambert, 1972).

At the level of individuals, their social class of origin may have a mongrel mix, and their adult social class of presumed achievements may not be consensually endorsed by others, but at least the bases of contention can be rendered explicit if necessary. Ethnicity is a trickier issue. Whilst the concept of "race" has been a hazardous one for both good and bad reasons, its lower level descendant of ethnicity still contains the seeds of dispute between biology and culture, especially when grandparent ancestors are invoked. Perhaps for societies such as Bhutan or Sikkim, into which few migrants have moved and which do not have invented or real ethnic cleavages, biology and culture are consonant to an extent that has saved those societies from that kind of internal conflict, so far. The USA presents an horrendously more complex picture, with its indigenous survivors, imported slaves deprived of knowledge of their cultural origins, and a manifold of voluntary migrants, whose descendants have varied in the extent of their negotiated melting into the "American" national construction and their retention of ancestral roots. Given the freedom to marry across cultures over the years, the extent of mix is prodigious, and it is mostly in the social/ethnic groups that have chosen to retain their countries of origin (for example some Jews, Irish, Poles, Hutterites) or have been obliged to remain separate by dominant groups (Southern states African-Americans, Puerto Ricans, Hispanics) that speech markers will reflect social identity. This can be at the level of language (Hispanics) or variety (Ebonics, or African American Vernacular English). Where individuals have chosen to retain a hint of culture of origin it is likely to be in the accentedness of their speech.

10.4.1 Inferences from Social Identity

If it is conceded that, in spite of the definitional problems with ethnicity and social class and the non-categorical dimension of age, social identities are typically registered reliably and validly in speech markers, in itself this need have no implications for behavior towards members of groups; it is the beliefs associated with such memberships that are relevant to the behavior of others. Consider beliefs such as "All A's are lazy slow learners and are likely to present discipline problems in classrooms." Combine this with certain values and the seeds of a self-fulfilling prophecy (sfp) are ready to germinate.

The speech, reading and writing of children entering school are taken as markers of both educational performance and potential. Research in the 1960s and 1970s was strong enough to demonstrate how such matters become associated with sfps leading to under-fulfilment of potential. Of course factors other than speech, reading, and writing can be and are involved as initiating and mediating concepts entering into the beliefs and pressures that act to eventuate in the practices leading sfps, but for many children from the lowest SES strata, the following flow is likely to represent their school career, with social class and ethnicity being the most prominent social identities involved in sfps and language features being major indicators of predicted failure rather than challenges to meet. Relevant research is reviewed by Edwards (1989), Robinson (1979), and Williams (1970).

Generalizations about teaching in school classrooms:

G1 Efficient teaching depends upon teachers engaging teachable pupils in relevant activities for sufficient time.

G2 Generally, but not universally, teachers perceive pupils in terms of individual and/or *socially based differences*.

G3 Generally, but not universally, teachers make *inferences* about pupils in respect of characteristics which are believed to be predictive of eventual academic success and failure.

G4 Generally, teachers value success in relation to norm-referenced standards of academic achievement.

G5 Teachers have at least implicit theories of teaching and learning.

G6 Teachers distribute both the quantity and quality of their interactions unevenly.

G7 Differential treatment of pupils by teachers affects the educational development of the pupils.

Self-fulfilling prophecy

The preceding generalizations enable us to specify two of the conditions under which sfp will operate. It will occur among teachers who make and maintain:

> *either* relevant *false* inferences about particular children (G2) *or* relevant *true* inferences where these are linked in the teachers' minds to false beliefs (G2) about the inevitability of the eventual academic success and/or failure of these children (G3), provided that such teachers also:

1 define success and failure in terms of non-referenced standards (G4);
2 conform to these standards (G4);
3 act on implicit or explicit theories of teaching and/or learning which are sound (G5); and
4 distribute the quantity and quality of their interactions in the classroom (G6) in such a manner as to render their predictions true.

Programmes of sustained attempts to break such cycles of poverty and underachievement have been successful both in the short (Brophy & Evertson, 1976; Stallings, 1975) and long term (Schweinhart et al. 1993; Schweinhart & Weikart, 1980), but it has to be recognized that the persistence of these differentiating activities in schools represents a discrepancy between the rhetorics of governments and the school systems they maintain.

Whilst the particular sequence of speech markers → social identity → presumed characteristics → behavior of perceivers is the one illustrated, it is quite possible for the chain to be unconscious rather than conscious and either intermediate stage might be omitted if simple classical or instrumental conditioning have been central to the perceiver's experience.

⌐ 10.5. Marking of Setting

At present "situation," "scene," and "setting" might be treated synonymously and all three carry implications of more than where and when. People present as participants or observers are a component of a situation.

The activities being engaged in are a component. Setting as place and time can have no influence if there are no people doing anything, and as soon as people are present then identities and relationships will come into play as part determinants of speech.

It is also true that the idea of speech marking a setting has an air of being the wrong way round. It is the location that influences the speech, and typically there are more salient markers than the speech itself. A large sign with the word hospital, school, or café, is indicative of the type of location, and once inside it would be the activities rather than the speech that visitors would find most noticeable. To hear someone say "Did you hear what she said? This must be a hospital" would be unusual. Hence, while settings will generate talk that is distinctive, the talk itself would not normally be used for recognizing and identifying the setting. Early reviews by Brown and Fraser (1979) and an edited collection by Furnham and Argyle (1981) have not led significant progress in the area.

Time of day likewise can determine the appropriateness of greetings and farewells, but as markers of and not markers for. Place as setting can have much greater ramifications, determining which language, which language variety, and how what is selected is spoken. Ferguson (1959) used the term *diglossia* to refer to communities where there are two languages or two varieties each with its proper sphere of use. The contrast was most commonly connected with a binary opposition between formal and informal settings. So in Paraguay Guarani was normative in formal settings, Spanish in informal ones. Having distinctive High and Low dialects was true of European countries such as Norway (Blom & Gumperz, 1972), Switzerland and Austria. Typically, imperial powers would require formal judicial proceedings to be handled in the colonies in the imperial language. In Europe Latin was the lingua franca of scholarship for many centuries – seventeenth century scientists and philosophers were still using it for their writings and Catholic church services have continued to utilize it. Churches also have a reverential plain-song style of speaking (intoning).

The frequency of kinds of utterances will be distinctive. Schools and courts of law are likely to have a higher incidence of question/answer exchanges than hospitals, and in all three the objectives of such exchanges will be different. The vocabularies will be indicative of the purposes of the setting.

A catalogue of norms for all settings for all communities would not be of immediate value for this text, but for social psychologists it is worth drawing attention to the consequences for those who find themselves in settings where they cannot meet the normative expectations or requirements. First, they can be identified as outsiders. Second, they cannot participate properly, and thirdly the consequences for them can be life-threatening or life-chance-threatening.

Being tried in a court of law without being able to understand what is being said is an extreme case, but not having the strict conventions of what should or should not be said is hazardous. Witnesses are easily trapped into admissions of faulty or false memory of event X which can be used to cast doubt of their remembrance of event Y. The answer to "Have you never felt the urge to hit your husband?" could be used to encourage a misrepresentation of the specific relevant event. Rape trials in England have achieved notoriety for the manner in which the replies of women witnesses have been misconstrued disadvantageously. The impropriety and unusual usages in medical discourse can lead to difficulties with those unused to such settings. Women from certain social groups may only be permitted to talk about certain problems with women doctors. Questions about lavatorial matters can still be phrased in terms of "motions" and "stools" to the bewilderment of patients.

The potential of schools as a setting for educational opportunities and the consequences of not taking advantage of these are not realized equally by all social groups (see 10.4.1).

10.6   Inference Processes: A General Comment

The initial summary set of rules for drawing inferences about persons from the vocal and verbal behavior provides a helpful point of departure for fuller discussion, but it will not be possible to escape from the concentric circles of the umbrella of Figure 9.1. It is easiest to start with the simplest case of a person who is simply expressing herself/himself without disguise or dissemblance.

For emotional and motivational states there are likely to be both reliable and valid markers, both vocal and verbal, at least in terms of the labels for such states in common usage. For personality variables the issues are muddied by the failure of psychologists to agree on the conceptualization and measurement of personality, and lay presumptions of relative invariance of dispositions across situations and through time. With those reservations, the extremes of the extrovert/introvert dimension are marked by a variety of vocal and verbal markers, although these are in some degree components of the definition of the dimensions; it is difficult to conceive of an outgoing sociable person who is not talkative and when roused to speak talks only slowly. Likewise, to be agreeable implies not disagreeing with conversational partners. For social identity, it will be important for individuals to identify themselves, especially for ingroup members, and for such factors as gender, age, social class, ethnicity, and region of origin/domicile, there are vocal and verbal features which are reliable and valid. Social relations and settings need also to exhibit clear identifying speech markers if communication is to be successful. It would of course have been very inefficient of human beings to devise cues for communicating those features which were unreliable, invalid, and difficult for others to recognize and identify.

It may be added that it is important for relevant cues to emerge early in any initial encounters with strangers. The language spoken and the variety of that language are immediate indicators of identity. Within a language vocalic features such as pronunciation of phonemes are readily available as soon as interaction begins. Forms of greeting and terms of address are necessarily attempts to negotiate the nature of the social relationship intended, with convergences or divergences (chapter 14) providing subsequent negotiating tactics.

Complications arise when participants are not following the same subcultural rules, as has been noted in chapter 5, but also manifest themselves when participants are engaging in impression management of one kind or another. If participants in an interaction are trying to hide information about themselves, then the first possibility is that they are able to suppress relevant markers. They can appear to be happy when they are sad or distressed when they are not. They can pretend to competence and confidence whilst being neither. They can claim group memberships which they do not have.

Other participants may become aware of oddities of different kinds, and may then try to make sense of these in ways mentioned in section 10.2.2. Are the discrepant components of the profile those least easy to control? If so, for what reasons might the speaker be trying to suppress such markers? The experiments in section 10.2.2 gave some answers to such questions in respect of emotional states and interpersonal attitudes, but more dramatic examples are professional confidence tricksters and spies, both of whom will have trained themselves to simulate what they are not. Skills of simulation can be acquired very quickly. It is amazing how persons charged with criminal offenses can lie their way through their trials in thoroughly convincing ways, until some critical evidence such as a DNA test or a CCTV camera tape destroys the plausibility of their accounts. The impression management skills of tyrants denying that they are guilty of massacres, murders, rapes, and a host of other crimes are extraordinarily effective in fooling many of the people most of the time.

The case of social identity marking has been taken up at some length to illustrate how speech (and writing) can enter into inference processes that lead to self-fulfilling prophecies adversely affecting the educational achievements, especially for lower social class and certain ethnic minority children, but stereotypes more generally can have more hazardous effects on the life chances of those stigmatized. Typically, language spoken will not have been a primary identifying marker in the long-term history of persecution of groups such as the Gypsies and Jews in Europe, but in limited areas it has almost certainly played a role, for example Serbian versus Croatian, Macedonian versus Bulgarian, with negative consequences for the speakers of the outgroup tongue.

10.7 Articulating the Comments

There are many vocal and verbal features correlated with other variables whose values may be indexed in some measure from the features, but for many of these they are not the primary markers used by people. This is particularly true of settings, which have no vocal or verbal features independently of their being used by people. Once people are active in settings many markers will be manifested to inform participants and observers about the kind of activity being pursued, and in institutional settings, these will be mostly of the non-verbal kind set out in chapter 5. The non-verbal markers are also of primary potential in situations where the array being sent is one of mixed messages, and those persons trying to make sense of what is happening need to focus on those features they believe to be least under voluntary control as a lead to gain an interpretation. This will be both when people are trying to hide their feelings for some socially acceptable reasons and when they are trying to deceive to protect themselves from reproof or gain advantage over others.

More generally it can be noted that because non-verbal features are both immediate and pervasive in their manifestation in any encounter, they can serve as reliable and valid markers through their extra-linguistic and paralinguistic features and their structuring into such phenomena as accents. This is true for emotional/motivation states, social identity, and social relationships and personal characteristics activated in the ongoing situation, but is contingent upon the concordance of appearance and reality. Such facts should not be understood as diminishing the importance of the verbal markers. When individuals are expressing themselves sincerely and identifying themselves clearly, their displays will combine both non-verbal and verbal elements. It is important not to ask which is more important and by how much, but to realize that the values of different cues add up to a profile that needs interpreting as a whole.

At the present time, there does not appear to be general empirical evidence that well-trained actors cannot simulate each of the types of referent beyond the unaided detecting powers of ordinary people. We can detect bad actors, but not good ones. Whether Ekman's micro-analyses mark the beginnings of the development of techniques by which experts can penetrate simulations remains to be explored. That governments have vested interests in not revealing what can be achieved is true, but if they are better than they admit, it is surprising how inept they are at detecting espionage. The issues are different from the issues of cryptography and in particular the struggles between code-creators and code-breakers (Singh, 1999), to the extent that for the latter the stories eventually surface as each escalation of sophistication is rendered obsolete. With interpersonal deception there has been no apparent development in detecting skills from the times when bizarre and lethal tests were employed to diagnose witchcraft. Already mentioned is the lying potential of ordinary people evidenced by the performances given by *de facto* "guilty" persons who are pronounced innocent *de jure*.

One surprising continuing aspect of these phenomena is the perpetuation of myths about the detection prowess of police interrogators, customs' officials and parents. To sustain such myths sociologically can serve both as deterrents against would-be criminals, smugglers, and deceiving and malingering children respectively and as accusations that may evoke confessions from the guilty. Some of us may have had great difficulty in child rearing in sounding convincing with a parental "Before you answer, remember I'll know if you are lying to me." Clearly the practice continues, although its incidence and efficacy remain unreported, and an authority needs to be defeated only once for a deceived antagonist to realize their impotence (see Gosse, 1970 for childhood autobiographical insights).

To keep these myths alive is greatly strengthened by the existence of a correlated mythology of cues, which is presumably why those listed by Ekman and those exploited by polygraphy users continue to be part of the traditions passed down the generations. As noted here the false "guilty" smiles and sweatings are plausibly valid cues that have alternative plausible explanations, as many innocent travellers continue to experience when they walk through customs. Knowing that one is innocent does not necessarily preclude feeling fear or worry that the relevant officials will not check one's baggage. (Or is that only true if one has endured particular contexts of classical conditioning as a child?)

That people have difficulty with probabilistic relationships between markers and referents is itself an index of more general socio-cognitive phenomena of several kinds. One of these is a genuine ignorance of probabilistic reasoning: confounding of asymmetries, tendency to overestimate and underestimate true rates of association for rare or frequent concordances as well as the socially-related attribution biases. As Gigerenzer (1991) pointed out some of these are not functions of ignorance of statistics. Some are sensible risk-assessments given certain premises. Probabilities of being run over by a bus may be greater than the probabilities of being an accidental victim of a shooting incident in Belfast, but it may require more considerable changes of lifestyle to avoid roads with buses than to avoid a trip to Belfast. In Australia, not picking up an injured snake of unknown toxic powers to save it from being run over is less risky than picking it up. Likewise if you have an irrational antipathy to members of social group X, it is less threatening to personal schemas occasionally to judge a non-X as an X than the other way round.

Of these errors in reasoning, it is the generalized *illusory correlation* that has been most investigated. This is the case when a genuine correlation becomes exaggerated in size, leading to a considerable over-estimation of false positives. This was documented in respect of the self-fulfilling prophecy arising from accurate identification of social group membership followed through with discriminating behavior that ensures the prophecy becomes true. Such phenomena may be based on cases where the illusory correlation is itself an artefact of historical discriminations. It is not so long ago that the female brain/mind was believed by many to be of inferior potential for studying scientific subjects to the male equivalent. Now in the post-industrial societies at least the educational outcomes at all levels have shown that the previously "illusory" correlation was itself an invalid premise on which to base the belief. Unfortunately it needs to be noted yet again that it is the stated beliefs about the lower capabilities of members of other social groups are at their strongest among the power elites of societies – and have always been so, particularly in respect of gender, ethnicity, and social class. Such stated beliefs have traditionally served the interests of elites by denying to members of other groups political and legal rights along with economic opportunities, and to justify low wages and poor working and living conditions. They still serve the same functions but are more likely to include "meritocratic" justifications among the arguments. Eventually the more spurious arguments in this arena may be encouraged to disappear, but no such prospects are even a glimmer at the present time, either internationally or nationally.

Ingroup/outgroup attribution biases are supplemented in most European languages and cultures by more general emphases on persons rather than situations as causes of events. The rich vocabularies for emotion, motivation, and traits afford references to persons rather than situations.

Japanese and Chinese cultures are more disposed to cite situations as having greater influence and take this into ascribing reasons to behavior. Whether they have a richer vocabulary for differentiating situations has not been studied in depth, and these attempts at grand cross-cultural contrasts may be intractable, unless translated into tests utilizing comparable individuals posed with equivalent tasks that were more ecologically plausible than the commonly used vignettes with forced multiple choice response arrays.

To ask why societies tolerate this messiness transcends not only the social psychological, but also the realms of questions to which empirically checkable answers might be given. It may be noted that the functioning of societies and their constituent members requires a constant stream of decision-making in respect of actions. These are pervasive and perpetual pragmatic imperatives. Had human beings not acted until they were sure of the truth–value of the propositional knowledge implicitly or explicitly underpinning their decision-making, the species would have disappeared long ago. Within such a framework, human beings need to be able to make sense of themselves in terms of emotions, motivation, and personality. That being so, an inaccurate set of constructs could still be better than not having any sets at all and such constructs would need markers whose utility would be more important than their validity. Once established rhetorics within such a framework are likely to develop great inertia and to replace them will require revolutionary shifts in paradigms, just as the revolutions in understanding the physical would have. Until the human sciences can come up with well-founded taxonomies of human experience, our current schemes will remain operative.

The Representational Function (F7)

11.1   Setting the Scene

As stated in chapter 3, the representational function is realized by Searle's "representative" speech act. The critical point of uttering a representative is to commit S in some measure to believing that something is the case – the proposition expressed being true rather than false. The "direction of fit" is of "words to the world:" that is, the expressed proposition corresponds to what S believes to be the most plausible construction of the world. The words fit the world. The psychological state being expressed is Belief (that p). The transparent simple syntactic verbal form for this is I *verb* (that) + p: for example, I state that the cat is on the mat. There are many verbs that could replace "state" and/or add complexity or specificity to it, for example conclude, contend, boast, hypothesize.

Unfortunately this account will not enable identification of a representative. There is a requirement of sincerity that is problematic. If a statement is a deliberate falsification, it fails to meet the sincerity condition and is therefore not a representative. If it is intended to spur L to action is it still a representative?

The semantics of a statement are evident, but to work out the likely pragmatic significance on any particular occasion of utterance would require more information than its form. Both the vocalic qualities and the context of situation in which the utterance is made will be important. Has S found the missing cat – and is now talking to self ? Has L asked where the cat is? Has L just denied that the cat is on the mat or expected it to be under the mat? Except for the first, these examples imply that S's utterance is intended to have L believe what S says, and this will be treated here as the default interpretation. It might be claimed as a limiting case that L's beliefs are irrelevant and the characteristic of representativeness has no entailments beyond S's own belief commitment. If this position is adopted, it is difficult to see why S has made the statement. If the former, then has the function become F3: Regulation of belief state of other? If L believes S, then the effect does appear to be a case of F3, but can be treated as F7 from S's perspective. S is not obliging L to adopt the belief, and any change in L's belief can be seen as mediated by L's evaluation of S's statement, and L should know criteria for challenging the appropriateness of any of the words and/or the truth value of their combination.

Here a sentence with a declarative form will be treated as serving the representational function, if three conditions are met: there are no grounds for doubting the sincerity of S, the truth–value of the statement is of primary importance, and L is under no pressure to adopt S's belief. Whether or not L does is up to L. Where the focus of any inquiry by L is on a fact rather than on S's belief, L is presumably hoping to act on S's reply.

The idea of the direction of fit being from words to world also raises questions. The relationships between statements and their referents have exercised the minds of philosophers, linguists and psychologists for a very long time. Beginning with the lexical units, philosophers since before Plato have worried about the reference of "cat." Was there an ideal form of "catness" in a World 3 of ideas? If so, what kind of existence does "catness" have? What are the denotation and connotation of "the," "is" and "on?" How does S know that his/her perception is veridical, and not a delusion, a dream, or a deception? Just what is the nature of the relationship between the words and the world? Is the combination of the words "a picture of a fact?" Is it a matter of *correspondence*? If it is a correspondence, what is the correspondence in respect of the units "the," "is,", and "on," or for mythical cats, or the smile of a Cheshire cat that has just disappeared?

The tutorials of my first term as a philosophy undergraduate were devoted entirely to questions arising from the cat on the mat; none were answered. Unfortunately, in those days the idea of some questions being inappropriate was only just arriving on the philosophical scene, and that most useful concept had yet to be divided into types of inappropriateness, for example false presuppositions (What did you do with the murder weapon?), improper demands for certainty (Are you absolutely sure that you left home at 12.30 on July 31 last?), or infinite regress – questions of a succession of causes running back to the beginnings of time and out beyond the limits of space. Suffice it to say that I no longer find the epistemological issues of the words/world combination a profitable distraction. Issues of meaning as denotation and connotation, were raised in chapter 2 and will not be pursued further here, for either words or combinations of words that are used to make up a declarative form of sentence which is used to make a statement. The issue of correspondence will be examined further below, but this will be for language as language. Consideration of statements will be dealt with in sub-sections of 11.2 and related to the criteria of evaluating claims to truth.

Why the statement is being uttered is an appropriate question not answered by Searle. Customarily, the conduit theory of communication invokes the idea of transmission of information from source to receiver with the idea of the receiver being able to decode and store the information with a view to immediate or later reflection or action. Representations in one head becoming representations in another head clearly have potential social utility, and although this is normally contrasted with deliberately persuasive and other influential social functions, no utterance of S to L can be stripped entirely of its social significance, as has been mentioned already. Nevertheless, this kind of functioning can be contrasted with those in which declarative forms of utterances are used for clearly social functions and their truth–value is pragmatically irrelevant. If S says to L "Nice little girls do not pick their noses," it is a brave daughter who treats this as a simple representative rather than a directive. If S says to L, "That is our lowest price," it is a naïve L who treats that as a fully-fledged commissive. Insofar as S intends that L shall come to believe what S said, the reason lies in the veridicality of the utterance and not in characteristics of S or the social relationship of S and L.

That granted, it is also the case that representative forms often do not have truth-telling as the primary concern. Many daily or weekly encounters involve exchanges that are best considered as examples of phatic communion, norm following, or silence avoidance. What form is the conversation likely to take? It would be easy to invent a family or friend script whose core structure might be repeated week after week with only minor variations – reciprocated enquiries about the health and activities of selves, family, and friends, comments about the weather, news, and TV, jobs to be done at home, followed by routinized farewells. Most of the declaratives will have stated facts, but to suggest that the primary function of the statements in such a conversation was to reveal and exchange factual information would be an implausible hypothesis. More plausible would be suggestions of phatic communion, defining an affectionate social relationship, and bringing pleasure to the participants. Within the conversation, it is likely that established norms will have been followed as to what should and should not be mentioned or said. There may have been awkward silences, so that some of the questions or statements functioned primarily to reduce embarrassment or anxiety. A case study from the 1960s that examined family conversations (Phillips, 1973) found high levels of routinization serving primarily social functions. While it is not fruitful to speculate on how much of conversation in families and among friends comprises statements whose representational significance is secondary to their social functions, it is salutary to wonder how often the truth–value of what is said is important, and how often the specialized phatic communion of F2 and F3 is of greater importance.

The grand issue of the correspondence between languages and what they are referring to is a final issue to be discussed before entering the smoother discourse on domains of knowledge. Of course languages and their categories are massive social constructions dissecting human experiences of the world in ways decided by earlier generations (see chapter 14.5). However, although the constructions and lines of dissections may be conventional, they are not arbitrary, the units and structures are those which their inventors and users found to be useful in the past. The ways they have been and are used in discourse may be misleading as a result of individual and species ignorance and/or individual or social group intentions to control and manipulate others. It is necessary to check and evaluate. Deconstruction has proved to be valuable in what it exposes, but deconstruction without reconstruction results in destruction and chaos, not reform or revolution. For some of us, these matters are too serious for frivolous games or conspiratorial insanity. In my opinion states of anarchy and solipsism are not to be preferred for either academic or social matters. As a value position, I endorse efforts to facilitate the developments of language as a system whose resources can be deployed to afford the construction of communities of responsible persons in which there is less ignorance and false belief, less deception and delusion, less injustice, and less unnecessary suffering than remains extant today. As a consequence I am saddened by the re-emergence of ideas which are, in their extreme forms, parasitic on the structures and advances whose value is denied, and are incompatible with the daily lives of their protagonists.

Social constructivist ideas about the nature of science are often cited as having an earlier origin in Thomas Kuhn (1962/1996), but via Derrida (1972; 1984) they exploded with those of Foucault, Latour, and their Parisian colleagues. (For critiques, see Gross & Levitt, 1998 and Sokal & Bricmont, 1998.) Some of these set up odd criticisms of the positions set out in *Conjectures and Refutations* (1972/1952) and especially *Objective Knowledge* (1972), where Popper endorses the contingency and provisionality of all claims to empirical knowledge, but does argue for the advantages of positing a World 1 which is not just a social construction or a mode of discourse, even though human beings can never know if their current constructions map on to that World 1. The constructions themselves constitute World 2, with World 3 comprising all the propositional claims stored outside human heads in artefacts and archives.

The views adopted here are that:

1   Even though all descriptions and explanations of the physical world (World 1) are provisional and fallible, not all World 2 views are equally at risk for rejection or revision.

2   For any rejection or revision of a contemporary belief, evidence appropriate to its domain has to be advanced and the change in belief shown to be an improvement on the contemporary beliefs and formulations.

3   There are no grounds for claiming that all symbolic systems, including languages, are equally useful or valid for describing and explaining human experience of World 1. As the various branches of logics (including mathematics) and the sciences have found, it has been necessary to invent specified, well-defined, and systematic sets of symbols and rules for their combination in order to achieve their purposes. Likewise, other academic professional, and technical activities have generated their own jargons.

4   To comment in respect of the particular language of this text may help to illustrate what is meant by the idea of categorization being conventional. As a so-called natural language, English has both strengths and weaknesses in its affordances. Like all other languages, the ways in which it dissects the world into categories and relationships is but one of the (infinite) number of ways possible. As with other languages, some of its strengths are also its weaknesses. For example, its sentence structure affords ease of making statements of the form "X causes Y," a great everyday convenience. However, this very convenience does bring with it oversimplifications, both in terms of construing X as an absolute agentive single feature acting on a passive victim Y, and in focusing on the here-and-now. Whether the thrown stone breaks the window in fact depends on the characteristics of the window, the throwing, the glass and the stone etc. Further, while this agentive feature of the S–V–O structure does not encourage allocation of credit or blame *per se*, the combination of the British culture and the language structure renders it very easy to ask "Whose fault?" rather than "How is this kind of event to be prevented in the future?" or "How should restitution be made to the victim?" That this is the preferred reading is taken up in chapter 13.

Table 11.1 sets out some binary contrasts which may help to locate parts of the profile of English and its strengths for simple intercourse and its weaknesses for complex analyses. As Whorf (1956/1927) argued specifi-

Table 11.1   Strengths and Weaknesses of English as a Scientific Language

Strength if World	Weakness if World
Causal	Co-variant
Absolute	Relational
Deterministic	Probabilistic
Linear	Non-linear
Simple	Complex
Causes unidirectional	Causes bi-directional
Effects conjunctive	Effects disjunctive

cally for Hopi views of time, its grammatical structure afforded ease of verbalization of relative and relational propositions – relative to English with its ease of focus on the absolute and the categorical. English can be used to express "relations of relations," but the constructions quickly become cumbersome and difficult. This has been evident in difficulties in communicating statistical information. In recent years, governments endeavoring to hide bad news have begun to issue figures that refer to the rates of increase of prices slowing down (inflation, wage rises, crime). Interpretations of such statements are typically simplified to an actual reduction. Similarly, ideas of probabilities, uncertainties, and risk require modifications and qualifications to basic English that have not been customary usage heretofore. People are still demanding risk-free foods and medicines, error-free operations, and transport systems. Time is represented as linear in English, just as cause/effect sequences are, again setting limitations to non-linear appreciations of phenomena. Within psychology, we have known for years that many relationships among variables are non-linear, yet still the majority of statistical analyses continue to be conducted on the assumption that relationships between variables are linear.

English has been selected for these comments for two reasons. First, English is the language in which this text is written and read. Second, I would have difficulty writing in a language that carved up the world along strongly different lines, for example Japanese or Hopi. Lucy (1992a) has reviewed some of the Whorfian issues (see chapter 14).

Advancement of knowledge in all specialist fields leads to the development of new specialized symbols and symbolic systems, and the achievement of understanding the relevant phenomena requires learners to master the symbolic systems in relation to the phenomena in focus. Everyday English cannot be expected to cope with many developments and cannot be used as a vehicle for communicating with non-experts. It will change as shared understanding in the community increases, but much more slowly than the cutting edge of knowledge.

Hence, in the most technologically advanced societies, we have the biological and physical sciences, along with their technological realizations, apparently directing their development towards better and better correspondence between the empirical evidence they have about the phenomena they are trying to describe, explain, and control, and the symbolizations they are using to represent these, be these in special codes and equations, or in specialized word-based language. Mismatches between observations and the symbolic representations are the driving force for further investigation and reconciliations between the two. This is in line with truth-seeking aims and the dialectical approach of Socrates, although the conflicts to be resolved and the uncertainties clarified are between statements and systematic observations of phenomena. In terms of making sense of the world we live in, many of these advances are beyond the knowledge and understanding of all but the specialists, and while attempts at fraud occur, and the checks against fraud are not foolproof, in the long run the accumulated empirical evidence sets limits to the plausibility of particular descriptive and explanatory symbolic representations. This is fallible, but it is the best that can be done, and it is dotty to point to the fallibility and its causes to undermine the whole enterprise (see for example criticisms and their rebuttals in Deanne Kuhn, 1991).

To put it simply, if people wish to understand any of the logics, sciences, or any other disciplines, they have to gain the relevant experiences and become competent with the symbolizations of the subject. This is not to be dismissed as elitism. That arises when protagonists pretend to social superiority by creating jargons that are intended to separate ingroup members from outgroup members, or in fact do so unnecessarily. I do not know to what extent legal language and judicial customs are designed to ensure that ordinary people have to pay professionals for help. Likewise with some philosophy and sociology. I do know that experts in differential and integral calculus and nuclear physicists cannot help but exclude me from understanding their work, unless I take steps to learn those subjects.

⌐ 11.2   Domains of Representation

With the reservations made, it is not difficult to see why the representational function should have assumed such importance. As has been seen in earlier chapters, the social functions of language such as regulation and marking can be carried out by non-verbal means, but it is the representational function that has underpinned the development of the accumulated wisdom of human beings as encoded in the texts that have filled archives, museums, libraries, and homes from the beginnings of written records, and was stored in the collectivity of human brains long before those inventions. The social functions of language realize a vast set of "knowing how to" (relevant to social behavior or presumptive know how), but all the "believing/knowing that" is in propositional form, as are so many of the products of the processes of imagining, thinking, learning and remembering. It is via representational heuristics that human beings have been able to imagine and construct alternatives to contemporary accepted views about the world – and to use appropriate means to check these. It is a never-ending process, but to date it has got rid of a lot of nonsense, and replaced this with better stories.

For present purposes it is better to be conservative and use 'well-founded beliefs' rather than "knowledge about." Philosophers have typically distinguished between knowledge and belief by defining knowledge as veridical, and allowing beliefs to be erroneous, but requiring them to be sincere. On such criteria, "beliefs" is safer here. However, following Grice, and anticipating the issue of deciding upon criteria for the evaluation of beliefs, "well-founded" is used to modify "beliefs." Whereas many of the millions of beliefs of most people are well-founded, many are not. Prominent among the latter are those that have not been personally checked against direct experience; these comprise much of the formal learning from educational establishments as well as the hearsay and gossip of everyday living. Typically, such beliefs are a rag-bag of transmissions from other people and other sources. None of us has direct experience of anything before we were born, and only a very limited sample of what we have experienced since.

The division here into four domains (see Figure 11.1) is not arbitrary, and neither is the further division of the domain of empirical matters into three sub-domains. The main justification for the separations arises from the differences in the criteria of evaluation appropriate for application to each domain. When evaluating the truth–values of statements, it is important to use tests specific and relevant to the particular domain. Historically, the most common error philosophers have made has been to apply tests appropriate to the domain of logics to the other domains, an error that should not have been made after Kant (1934/1781) used the contrasts of analytic/synthetic and a priori/a posteriori to categorize statements. An analytically "true" statement is one where its truth follows *deductively* as a result of the definitions of the primitive terms of the system. Hence, given the axiomatic definitions of primitive terms in mathematics, $2 + 2 = 4$ – and not 5 or 3 or 22. It is an a priori proposition, because, given the

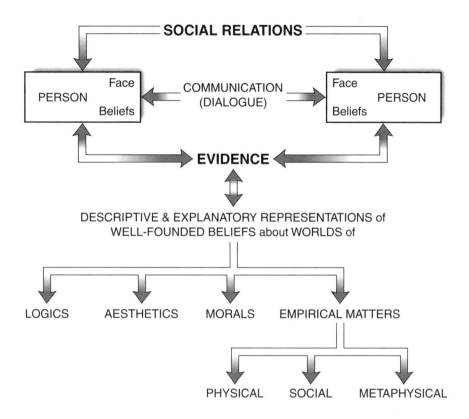

Figure 11.1   Issues of Precedence in Discussions about Constructions of Realities

definitions of the system, it is impossible for the human mind to conceive of other answers that can be justified. In contrast what are necessarily synthetic a posteriori statements about the physical world are not true by definition or deduction, and whether particular and concrete or general and abstract, they can be challenged and submitted to tests of an empirical nature.

What such tests are varies with the type of statement. One of Kant's (1964/1785) claims to fame is he argued for domains made up of synthetic a priori propositions, i.e. statements that were not true as a necessary consequence of deducible conclusions from definitions, but are true because the developed human mind could not sincerely believe in a world where the opposites of the propositions were true. He believed that matters of what is right or wrong were synthetic a priori issues, along with matters of what is beautiful or ugly; certain propositions in these domains were not true or false as a result of axiomatic definitions and their entailments For example, it is impossible to imagine a human society in which the arbitrary killing of other persons was right. If societies are to exist as societies, the normative framework must outlaw individuals killing other individuals at will. Stealing does not qualify, on the grounds that the concept flows from a prior notion of personal property, and a truly communist state might have no private property, and hence stealing would not be possible. These two examples are intended to be illustrative of the kind of claims that might be adduced, and should not be seen as definitive. Aesthetic claims may come to be viewed as synthetic a priori one day, but consensus on any candidates for such a status is not yet in sight. Taking these considerations into account, arguments can be elaborated to yield different tests for evaluating the truth or falsity of statements within the different domains.

11.2.1   Logics

For propositions in any of the many types of *symbolic logics*, questions of truth/falsity are contingently resolved in terms of the validity of the steps of reasoning relating the axioms of the system to the derived propositions. No questions of matters of fact arise. Examples of such systems are arithmetic, algebras, geometries, statistics, and the propositional calculus. The propositions do not represent anything outside the system. This does not prevent them from being useful in arriving at truths in other domains. On the contrary, the rules of logic act as a necessary constraint on sets of claims organized into arguments in all other domains.

11.2.3   Aesthetics

In respect of aesthetics, it is easy to demonstrate great cross-cultural and intra-cultural diversity in judgments of what is beautiful and what is ugly. Human judgments have also changed with time. It would be difficult to defend the proposition that there is a move towards consensus in the domain, and equally difficult to argue that there can be no universal principles. Historically, the field has suffered from the unnecessary presumption that there should be single principles of beauty rather than a disjunctive multiplex. The Ancient Greek love of the ratio of 1.618: 1 as a defining feature of beauty for people and for the artefacts they manufacture may eventually be universally accepted, but if it is, most likely it will be joined by other ratios and other criteria!

The field also offers great opportunities for research by social psychologists and the human sciences more generally in that matters of taste have been defined and used by ingroups to render themselves distinctive from and superior to outgroups, and in particular by elites to denigrate "rude" people and barbarians. Issues of beauty have been a pervasively central component in the pursuit and maintenance of power, wealth, and status. Is it strange that rarity and hence price becomes valued against norm-referenced criteria? That proposition would be hard to defend in the natural world. Aren't most flowers beautiful regardless of rarity? Likewise the rhetoric of disputations about high art offers exciting challenges to the social psychology of language, especially if enquiries are made about the foundations of critics' judgments. If the common sense of *de gustibus non est disputandum* is suspended in favour of a permissible alternative to the effect that as a matter of fact there can be rational disputes about taste, then how sound and well-founded are the arguments of art critics, and on what grounds do they disagree with each other? Certainly, much of the rhetoric and action in the world of high (valuable) art looks like, and functions like, a social phenomenon of conspicuous collection and possession (Bourdieu, 1977; 1991; Veblen, 1912/1925). Perhaps in the future the human species will take sufficient time to develop and enjoy its aesthetic susceptibilities to find global criteria of consensus, which may or may not include that golden mean of 1.618:1.

More significant economically, sociologically, and psychologically has been the commercial promotion of standards of personal beauty. The multibillion industry offers clothes and other adornments, youth-preserving and shape controlling promises, that encourage people to spend their money striving for the impossible. As with high art, the standards set are such that only very few can sensibly aspire to achieve them, and then only for a few years. Societies simply accept the suffering of those fated to be defined as ugly or inadequate when evaluated against such standards. Historically, it is particularly women who have suffered from such socially constructed phenomena, and rich males and females who have displayed their status via such means (Veblen, 1912/1925).

(The aesthetic function of language was omitted from this text only as a matter of space allocation.)

11.2.3   Truths of Ethics/Morals

On the issue of claims to *moral knowledge*, Kant's (1964/1785) concept of synthetic a priori statements seems to be the least indefensible position, and his principle of universifiability is helpful. Is it better that nobody ever kills anyone else or that people are free to kill whoever they wish when they wish? Whilst Hume's argument that there can be no logical justification for moving from what is to what ought to be the case, and he is correct, psychologically the idea of a "good" society where arbitrary killing is permitted defeats the imagination. It is also true that no human society has yet adopted the second freedom, and most claim to be concerned to minimize departures from the first. Rawls (1971) adds helpful examples of criteria for arriving at principles of distributional justice. For example, members of groups should endeavor to arrive at rules for dispositions of resources in societies without knowing what their own fates will be. Ideas such as these point to criteria of guidance such as "Do as you would be done by" and "Love they neighbor as thyself," which in turn might push "Goodwill to all" to the top of any pyramid of ethical principles.

It is alleged that Kant's position traps him into situations where wrong actions cannot be avoided because as soon as more than one principle is applied to any particular situation, then there will be occasions when they will inevitably come into conflict with each other. This is so, but it does not invalidate Kant's analysis. What it entails is that we have to accept that the best we can do is to minimize the wrongness of what we do. To achieve this will require some rank-ordering of principles and intelligent analyses of the consequences of the priorities accorded in particular cases. Once consequences of actions are brought into consideration, empirical probabilities come to be components in evaluations of what is to be done. It is only in an ideal world that principles might not conflict, and only people who strive for the impossible who might not be able to accept the constraints of reality.

To illustrate the issue, the French Revolution can be of service. Its leaders proclaimed the virtues of *liberté*, *egalité*, and *fraternité*, but how are these to be reconciled when they conflict? The revolutionaries themselves pursued the second at the expense of the other two. In its rhetoric, the United States appears to have given primacy to the first, and within that concept of liberty has been criticized for giving too strong a weighting on *freedoms to* at the expense of *freedom from*. If *fraternité* were to be construed as "goodwill." then its inclusion into arguments could resolve, or at least moderate, conflicts between the values of *liberté* and *egalité*. Again, the study of such arguments has great potential for social psychological investigations. For the foreseeable future however, it has to be accepted that there are no codes of conduct that can be imagined to provide recipes for wrong-free action. Agreement as prioritization of principles appears to be beyond the best willed intellectual efforts of the species. Calculations of the eventual effects of individual actions are certainly beyond individual or collective powers.

Whether and how these issues might relate to cultures which can use their languages to emphasize the pursuit of ideals of perfection rather than progress from less evil and less wrong is not explored here, but as with aesthetics, and more seriously for the mass of humanity, the moral/religious domain has been exploited by king/priest elites to the disadvantage of everyone else. Within the orbit of Christianity, very few kings or queens have been Christ-like in their conduct. Too many of its churches' leaders have appealed to special pleading to justify luxurious and decadent lifestyles, apparently related to the pursuit of and maintenance of secular power, wealth and status rather than the spiritual well-being of themselves and their flocks. It would have been interesting to challenge some of those leaders whose self-indulgences and abuses of their positions have been so contrary to their purported religious beliefs, captured in such injunctions as "By their fruits ye shall know them", but no relevant data have been handed down.

11.2.4   Claims to Describe and Explain Empirical Matters

In each of the three domains mentioned so far, it would have been feasible to distinguish between statements which are particular or general, concrete or abstract, descriptive or explanatory. This was not done, and will be side-stepped for the most part here too. However, so much everyday talk is concerned with the particular and concrete, the checkings of which are likely to use rather different procedures from those of scientists whose concerns will involve both descriptions and explanations that will include more general and abstract considerations. Testing the plausibility of these of these is likely to follow different and more systematic procedures. Since all the statements in this domain are synthetic a posteriori, checkings of them will have in common that they will not reach any chimerical ideal of certitude, and will always include inquiries based on observations.

(i) Everyday talk for everyday matters

In cooperative contexts, the default expectation is of truth being told. When answering questions, people may make mistakes of various kinds, but they do not generally deliberately mislead askers of questions about persons, times and places. When recalling the day's events in the evening, facts typically predominate over fictions. It is only once wariness has entered into relationships that interactants check for consistency and validity of the particulars. Evidence of invalidity comes from inconsistencies among stories from different sources or the same source on different occasions, and direct observations of suspicious or incriminating events or items.

Much of everyday talk can include brief encounters in which greetings are quickly followed by short question–answer–acknowledgment exchanges. Is the Number 9 bus running today? Is it going to rain today? Is my order in yet? What compensation are you offering? Is he nice or is he a smarmy rat? The most likely function of L's replies to these will follow the conduit model of communication and transfer a belief from one head to another. Exchanges where information is transferred in this is a common activity, as evidenced in chapter 6.12, and it has long been recognized that one of the powers of language as a communication medium is to transcend the here-and-now in this way. Its powers afford reference to the past and future, as well as to the present, and to distant places and absent persons as well as to those present. It can rise above the particular and concrete to the general and abstract. It can describe and explain, narrate and argue. Since utterances are etically multifunctional, without further information about the context of a situation it is not possible to interpret the primary function of any statement, but for many the simple appearance will correspond to the reality.

In competitive situations, the same principles do not apply: the wise are wary *ab initio*. To distinguish between truth and deviations from this, the evidence to be collected is empirical, and matters of fact are central to evaluations, even if these are collected unsystematically. As mentioned earlier, people check for consistency of information from different sources and across time, and within the profile of non-verbal and verbal cues, they look for and assess the possible meaning of discrepant cues (see chapter 10). Historians, archaeologists, and the police follow similar principles but more systematically.

(ii) Physical and (non-human) biological sciences

The vast literature of the physical and biological sciences comprises best efforts to generate best-fit descriptions and explanations of phenomena within whichever branch of science the phenomena fall. The propositions generated within these sciences are checked empirically with observation and experimentation by persons trained to be dispassionate and systematic in their observations and circumspectly sceptical in their preferred explanations. If propositions are not checkable, they are not scientific. The position adopted here about the status of representational claims has the following similarities with and differences from the views expressed by Popper (1959, 1963, 1972):

(2/1)   Although all empirical claims are synthetic a posteriori, checks on their plausibility can be used to evaluate their likely correspondence to a best guess construction of reality. Tests within the various sciences can be evaluated within established methodological frameworks that have a history of serving their purposes well.

(2/2)   There is no harm in positing a real world about which human beings can aspire to be informed. It can however be a mistake to be so confident about the current status of even the most strongly founded beliefs that contrary evidence is ignored or dismissed.

(2/3)   Popper's emphasis on the asymmetry of falsification and verification may be psychologically valid, but can be over-emphasized. Like all other language units, the words "true" and "false" are contrastively useful, but neither should be viewed as a ring-fenced absolute category. Deviations from a mythically ideal "truth" can take more than one form (Bradac, Friedman & Giles, 1986), and decisions about each are best viewed as pragmatic shorthands for guiding current beliefs and actions.

(2/4)   Those without extended experience of the physical and biological sciences are prone to over-estimate the extent to which scientists are victims of social constructions rather than their systematic and dispassionate observations. Much of the post-Popper post-modern writing about science is very seriously flawed (Gross & Levitt, 1998; Sokal & Bricmont, 1998). That scientists are fallible and may underestimate their fallibility is not to be doubted. That yesterday's descriptions and explanations may be discarded and replaced tomorrow does not give grounds for ignoring or rejecting them today.

(2/5)   That "expert" opinion can be divided and diverse is to be expected, particularly at the frontiers of advancing knowledge, and these frontiers can be at any level at any point where doubts or difficulties can be shown to be present. The extent of such doubts can be over-estimated about matters, especially those which the media deem to be in the public interest, and where policies can dictate that the presentation must be excitingly controversial, and experts are pressured towards making claims beyond what would be acceptable in academic journals. Likewise, business groups and others with vested interests in products or pronouncements under scrutiny or attack for being dangerous or injurious may adopt scientific positions whose tenability is implausible or worse. The effects of cigarette smoking are a very long-running example of this, and the BSE/CJD affair in Europe is a recent scandal for secretive governments in more than one country (see Robinson, 1996 for other examples).

(iii) Human sciences

The more social of the social sciences are still at a primitive stage of development in respect of their failures to achieve consensus about methodology, terminology, and epistemology. Social psychology is afflicted in all three respects, and social psychology of language and communication is not an exception. It must be accepted that four severe handicaps are endemic to social psychology, and always will be:

(3/1)   *The person objects of its study can have agentive properties.* This creates a double jeopardy. Insofar as their conduct is fully determined by combinations of external and internal causal factors, possibilities of accurate predictions are increased, but insofar as agentive possibilities are involved predictability is decreased. Insofar as people's own understanding of themselves and their worlds grows with their experience, the predictability is lessened further.

(3/2)   *Diversity among people of the extent of perceived agency is relevant to diversity in their life-chances.* A strong version of this arises from differential access to well-founded beliefs about people and possible motivation to exploit this in one's own interest. Confidence tricksters and fraudsters exemplify this at an individual level. Advertisers attempt to persuade businesses and other organizations that their special knowledge about how to persuade people to buy goods and services is a good reason for businesses and other organizations to employ advertisers. The whole commercial sector is dedicated to persuading people to buy goods and services. The political imperatives of governments in quasi-democracies are re-election to power, again an exercise in persuading the electorate to act in a specific way. Historically, the exploitation of the relative ignorance of others to the advantage of those with power is nothing new.

(3/3)   *Cultural evolutionary changes have been the norm for human societies.* Changes can be of greatly different durability and significance, but as shown in chapters 6–10, even in less than a generation descriptions of regulation and marking have had to change to take account of new modes of interaction and cultural shifts in relationships of power and solidariness. New kinds of social relationships have emerged in both the public and the private domains, as have new social identities. Conceptions of the structure and substance of emotions, motivation, and personality have changed (but not as much as psychologists would prefer). Hence, whatever the continuities relevant to social psychology of language in communication, there are also changes in what has to be described and explained. Notions about the constitution of "good" descriptions and explanations have also changed and may do so in the future.

(3/4)   *Complexities come to mask transparency.* Civilizations that are not destroyed seem to drift towards the greater elaboration of their institutions and that includes language and its use (Elias, 1978). It is not an accident that Byzantium gave rise to the adjective "byzantine.". In a culture in which norms followed Gricean maxims, all verbal communication would be transparent. The declarative form would be used to make statements only. People would only utter statements for which they had evidence. It would be optimistic to expect only the truth to be told, but there should be no implicatures to work out or indirect politeness forms to select. In reality of course elaborations have built up layers of subtleties through which conversations can be totally misconstrued by outsiders. Numerous figures of speech have proliferated. People have enjoyed playing with allusions, ambiguities, and ironies that challenge social psychologists trying to develop analytic schemes that relate pragmatics to semantics to lexico–grammar to phonetics and phonology.

Of the four hazards, both the third and fourth include many of the puzzles that render research challenging and interesting. Some psychologists would rather the issue of agency disappear, but it will not do so.

(iv) Metaphysical beliefs

Metaphysical beliefs are empirical claims which are necessarily synthetic a posteriori. Either there is a spiritual world or there is not. If there is, and there is one or more spiritual powers, then it may well be that human understanding is and will be incapable of apprehending and comprehending this power. Attempts to do so have been universal to the human species, and they have been diverse in their realizations. Changes from animism to polytheism to monotheism have occurred, and for some religions the conception of the divine has become less anthropomorphic. That said, to date each individual person who has ever lived is and always has been in a minority in whatever beliefs they have subscribed to, be these agnostic, atheistic, or religious. Attempts at generating epistemological criteria for demonstrating the existence and *modus operandi* of spiritual powers have been clear examples of the category errors already exemplified in other domains.

Thomas Aquinas (writing between 1267 and 1273) offered profound logically based arguments which "proved" the existence of God, as a prime cause, prime existence et al., but God as a first cause is as beyond human comprehension as the absence of a first cause to those of us accustomed to causal views of the empirical world. Those who have generated arguments that human beings would have no sense of right and wrong or of the beautiful and the ugly if it were not for a divine guidance can be challenged by those who deny the universality of subscription to the necessity of ethics or aesthetics, and challenged further by the diversity of actual codes of ethics and aesthetics across societies. Social surveys of religious faith and practice cannot answer metaphysical questions. This probably leaves the psychological contribution back with William James (1902), who emphasized the relevance of the interpretation of personal experience and faith as sources of evidence. As Pascal (1692/1982) pointed out in the seventeenth century, human beings trying to make sense of the world and their role in it have to place explicit or implicit bets on the questions of God's existence and essence and should then act in the light of their decisions. We may never find out whether or not the propositions to which we assent are true, but we may find out whether or not they are false!

It has been argued that the reduction in the varieties of religious belief and in adherents to particular religions in the twentieth century is a reason for predicting that they will all wither away. A similar argument could be used for science and technology, where there has also been a reduction in the variety of beliefs and of appropriate means for testing their validity. Systematic observations in its various forms are central to the sciences, but this has been a relatively recent phenomenon that is still not a universally accepted orientation. Human beings in the UK seem to have greater difficulty believing in a spiritual world than they did even 50 years ago, whilst happily agreeing that brains are not minds. It can reasonably be asserted that it is as wrong-headed to apply scientific criteria to the investigation of spiritual beliefs as it is to apply religious textual assertions to matters scientific. If human beings can communicate spiritually with a transcendent power, then the criteria of validity may be neither more nor less than individual faith in the emergent construction of this reality. William James set out to simulate paranoia and quickly gave up because he was begin-

ning to believe in his delusions, and subsequent psychologists have argued for the value of acts of will to change behavior as a mode of eliminat-
ing dispreferred activities. To give up wanting to smoke cigarettes, it may
be very useful to re-conceive of oneself as a non-smoker and just stop
smoking them – and persevering. There is no reason why individuals should
not use the same strategy of "behaving-as-if" to explore the possibility and
validity of spiritual experiences.

Over-riding principles

Having compared the domains in terms of similarities and differences in
the appropriateness of criteria of evaluation to be applied to propositional
claims in each, it is necessary to include an additional note on the peculiar
status of the logical domain. The essence of the note is to suggest that
within all domains relationships between propositions constituting an argument should *not* be illogical; that they should not be inconsistent with
each other is a minimal necessary condition.

Just as Aristotle distinguished between formal logic and practical reasoning, so his successors have wrestled with the core difficulty in scientific
arguments which take the form: if propositions A and B are true, then C
should be true. Empirical checks can then be made on the truth–value of
C, and if the evidence is inconsistent with it being true, investigators are
required to reflect on the reasons why. If consistent with C being true, the
investigators may be happy, but propositions A and B are *not* more likely
to be true – logically.

Questions about least unethical causes of action in human conduct
present different kinds of difficulties. Questions about the empirical relationships between particular human actions and outcomes present similar
uncertainties. These have given rise to the growth in attention to that
quantification of risk assessment and the acceptance of the probabilistic
nature of human predictions across the whole range of human physical
and social concerns, from issues of the control of economies, disease, and
crime to those of meteorology and global warming.

As well as the move to the developments of these necessary complexities, there has been an associated growth of concern with human fallibility
in decision-making (for example Sutherland, 1992), and an independent
emergence of explorations of what has been entitled *informal logic* (for
example Walton, 1989). Walton refers to the work of Fischer (1971) with
its catalogue of some 111 types of fallacy utilized by his fellow historians,
but omits the classical 38 dishonest tricks exemplified in Thouless's *Straight
and Crooked Thinking* (1974/1930).

Whilst it is possible to list errors of various kinds, as the sources already referred to do, listing of types with illustrations is as far as the logic has gone. Psychologists have begun to offer possible and plausible reasons as to why people unwittingly or intentionally make or try to exploit particular errors (Sutherland, 1992). Deanne Kuhn (1991) claims to have demonstrated empirically how disastrously inadequate various samples of people were with their handling of arguments about three contentious issues in social science, for example why released criminals are prone to recidivate, why children fail at school, and what causes unemployment The only group to emerge with proficiency were the professional philosophers, but then it is their trade to be skilled with argumentation. The educational systems in the USA do not train students in the general handling of argumentation and confine any engagement with rationality to specialized domains. Where then should the argumentational experience of the general population have come from? The arguments offered in the popular media are typically simplistic and naïve to the point of becoming insults to the human intellect. More seriously Kuhn gave people arguments to evaluate that masked the issues with pragmatically improbable examples; respondents gave precedence to sense rather than logic. Kuhn gave her respondents questions whose status as questions could have been queried, and in any case referred to matters about which whole books could be written and are. Such books would be unlikely to draw firm conclusions and would certainly not cite single causes. For those with an interest in human rationality, questions about the appropriateness of questions and about biases and invalidity are exciting fields to explore, but such work is still at an exploratory stage (Oaksford & Chater, 1998). Not that rationality itself is an unproblematic term. It is surprising how many texts with "rationality" or one of its cognates in the title somehow never quite get around to defining it. The immediate contrasts are with "arational" (matters where rationality is not relevant) and "irrational" (matters where S believes rationality is relevant and that the actions of the person in focus are not rational). Irrationality may be said to stem from insufficient reflection and consideration leading to the adoption of means that will not achieve the intended ends, but by shifting frames of reference what is irrational within one frame may be viewed as rational within another. As already noted, standards of formal reasoning may be set up that are inappropriate for practical decision-making, and as Gigerenzer, Todd, and the ABC Group (1999) have shown, generating a concept of *bounded rationality* with a cost benefit/analysis adds to rather than reduces the difficulty of human brains calculating rational solutions. Notwithstanding such difficulties, human beings manage to differentiate among degrees of irrationality, as argued in Section 11.3.

11.3   Extended Representations: Arguments

Arguments are collections of claims that may be offered in support of a focal claim; the supporting claims themselves are individual representational statements that should be coherent and consistent with the concluding focal claim. They are frequently referred to in everyday discourse as "reasons" or "justifications" and as premises in more formal settings. Arguments can occur within the head of a person or between two or more people. Their force is evaluated in the light of the perceived truthfulness of each claim and the extent to which they converge as the particular conclusions rather than other conclusions or no conclusions.

Arguments are most easily confused with explanations, partly because each can include components of the other and occasionally because it is only a detailed contextual analysis that can elucidate the situation. Explanations answer why questions about a putative fact or event. Frequently they involve causal accounts as to the prior necessary and sufficient conditions that occasioned the event, but can take other forms. An event is not a conclusion, and the conditions for its realization are not premises. However, the word "reason" could be used for each, and both explanations and arguments are likely to include words such as "because," "since," "therefore," "so," and "for." When people disagree about preferred explanations for events, the debate may well take the form of an argument. Explanations are directed towards better understanding, arguments are focused on the reasons for believing conclusions to be true.

The word 'argument' in English is used in more than one way. Billig (2001) offers a speedy zigzag around the opposing poles of a slalom of distinctions, an exercise performed in greater depth and at greater length elsewhere (Billig, 1996). Taking a basic opposition of argument-as-quarrel versus argument-as-reasoning, he demonstrates their interdependence in that in trying to win arguments-as-quarrels, the qualities of consistency and cogency can be relevant to outcomes and arguments-as-reasoning may well include theses–antitheses and other forms of proposal–rebuttal. Law courts which rely on the adversarial format are alleged to be founded on the principle that this structure is most likely to lead to a recovery of the truth, whereas those that espouse the inquisitorial format are prone to involve accusation and denial. Billig also exposes the self-contradictory dilemmas of those who use arguments to rebut arguments that take an extreme position of objectivity/idealism or subjectivity/relativism.

Is it then an admission of defeat to settle for pragma-dialectics (Van Eemeren & Grootendorst, 1988), a viewpoint that suggests that persons agree the evidential rules against which theses or antitheses are to be evaluated and debate towards conclusions within these? Not surprisingly, Billig also rehearses some of the variants of Aristotle's original oppositions between dialectics and rhetoric, one of whose present-day realizations contrasts how people argue naturally in speech, as exposed in conversational and discourse analysis (Antaki, 1994; Edwards & Potter, 1994) and how they present arguments in formal contexts, such as academic journals. Pragma-dialectitians might be tempted to call down plagues of noisy bees to drown the absurdly illogical and otherwise unsound arguments that dominate competitive "discussions" in which the participants are ill-willed competitors trying to win, regardless of the plausibility of their case. Much media activity in western societies now revolves around attack and defense, whether this be interviews interrogating individuals in the news, audience participation programs arguing on controversial topics, or presidential candidates criticizing each other. Confrontational verbal gladiatorial contests seem to reflect the media controllers' beliefs about maximizing audiences, and hence ratings success and/or advertising revenue. An assay into trying to analyze TV audience participation discussions failed because the discourse was so fragmented and inconsequential that it was not possible to note the incidence of types of logical error; there was no coherent framework within which to note logical flaws. It may be noted, of course, that such discussion programs are in fact serving social purposes of entertainment of audiences. They do not accord precedence to any educational function, and they provide a clear example of a concatenation of declarative forms used to make statements whose truth–value is not of primary concern. Since this text is concerned with psychology rather than genres of communication, the qualities of greatest interest in arguments are the errors.

⌐ 11.4　Arguing Crookedly

Crooked roads are not necessarily to be condemned, but crooked arguments do need to be straightened. Whether or not their protagonists should attract disapproval will be a matter of contextual morality. Deliberate abuse of logicality is more likely to be seen as blameworthy than accidental oversights are. In either case the task of classifying illogical steps remains the same. Here is not the place to do more than note contributions to the topic.

So far as formal reasoning is concerned, Aristotle himself generated an extended list of errors in syllogistic reasoning. If the sun shines today, we shall go for a picnic. The sun is not shining. The conclusion that we shall *not* go for a picnic is not a valid inference from the premises. Aristotle classified truth values of deductions of this kind for simple statements about all Xs and Ys, some Xs and Ys, no Xs and Ys, some Xs are not Ys, and the relations "are" and "not." (See Strawson (1952) for a summary on logical consistency and the propositional and predicative calculus and Govier (1985) for a practical analysis of arguments and their logic.) The development of arguments of such kinds is the essence of logics, including mathematics.

Arguing about aesthetic, moral, and empirical matters, however, will rely on criteria of less exacting stringency and be open to conflicting evidence. For example, when the issue is a matter of which action a person should take, then if more than one moral principle is involved there are possibilities of conflicts between them. People may argue that it is less wrong to lie than to tell the truth to X if that will prevent X from killing Y and Z. How to assign weights to different positive values in policies and practices is a continuing nightmare for both well-meaning politicians and individual people. Likewise with the values of "freedom from," "freedom to," and "social justice," two reasons might be offered for the human failure to achieve consensus on what is right and what is fair. First, the members of the human species genuinely cannot agree on what is right and fair, and second, those members of society who have the power, wealth and status generally behave to maintain or increase their privileged status – and argue that they are justified in doing so. But it is not just these arguments that may include improper premises or faulty linkages. Thouless (1974/1930) sets down a selection of crooked appeals and invalid inadequate connections.

⌐ 11.5   Crooked Arguments in Different Domains

Is there no way out of the various dilemmas? My personal view is that there is. The first and most important issue is the motivation of the participants debating any issue. If their primary concern is finding the least implausible solution or the least unjust outcome, then the linkages as well as the propositions in any dialectic can be evaluated against the criteria appropriate to the type of well-founded belief(s) involved (see Section 11.2).

Such motivation is rare, unfortunately. The mere existence of disagreement is likely to be indicative of a conflict over outcomes. Outcomes in terms of personal or group benefits easily over-rule concerns for truth or justice in conflict resolution, and hence the indifference to or the deliberate denial of any truths that may weaken a personal or group position. The logics themselves and the physical sciences and technology are the two domains of knowledge least afflicted by vested interests in that, although the academic professionals in these fields are typically and sensibly conservative, their views are subordinated in the final analysis to the results of applications of those checks for internal and/or empirical validity that have proved to be efficacious filters in the past. Hence the great advances in these areas of knowledge, in contrast to the never-ending wars and manoeuvrings for ingroup and personal power, wealth and status in the struggle to control values and resources in the other domains.

In the history of these latter, the truth–value of representational statements and their organization into arguments seems to have been generally of secondary or even lower significance. They have also been much more difficult to convert into consensual actions. The discoveries in the physical sciences are formulated in representational statements, and either immediately or subsequently, people have chosen whether to use these to change some aspect of the world, but there are no imperatives to action in arriving at the truths themselves. In contrast, even for aesthetics the search for truths has been somewhat of a side-show sociologically in terms of any thrust towards serious development of theories of aesthetic criteria or experience. How to appreciate beauty in everyday experience or even the arts is not central to formal educational curricula. As mentioned in 11.2, "high art" has multiple functions, one of which is to generate and sustain an ingroup that can claim distinctiveness and superiority to outgroups in terms of its sensitivities (Bourdieu, 1977). This category overlaps heavily with another ingroup that can make similar claims, but can also manifest its wealth through the collection of such artefacts. These activities are parasitic on the creative energies of the artists generating their particular representations, and on those who are seriously concerned to gain insights into art and disseminate appreciation to wider audiences. This is not a wild denunciation of the sincerity or goodwill of many critics and collectors; it is just that they are mixed in with others who are more concerned with impression management than art appreciation.

More significant economically, sociologically, and psychologically, has been the commercial promotion of standards of personal beauty and the investment that women and men in capitalist societies make in impression management through clothes, adornments and beauty enhancing products. Just as the promotion of high art has a strong component of rarity inserted into its values, so the promotion of personal beauty is linked to rare forms and expensive accoutrements and adornments. The forms vary from culture to culture and era to era, but they invariably require considerable personal spending for their attainment. Indeed most are unattainable for the vast majority, with the female sex having been the main victims in the last century, at least.

The criteria of morality and justice have followed a different but comparable historical path. Thrusts for basic human rights have become more global and have been distorted in different ways. The United Nations and the European Union both have lists of such rights, and items from these lists are invoked from time to time in civil and criminal cases. Since these rights do not specify obligations to other individuals or to communities, they provide a single rather than a triangular matrix perspective, and they are being contested currently by governments from less individualistic societies. It may well be the case that to date the decisions of courts administering justice in such terms, for example the European Court of Human Rights, have been unrealistic mainly in enabling affluent villains to escape true justice. These cases are the obverse of the abuse of judicial processes on grand scales by dictatorial regimes, for example the Soviet Union show trials of the late 1930s in which so many innocent people "confessed" falsely to crimes against the state. Such examples of "might being right" are in line with the position advocated by Thrasymachus over 2000 years ago, but as already mentioned, it is not only procedurally that justice can be corrupted. It is those with the might who have formulated the laws in the first place, and a cursory examination of any legal framework will yield many gross examples of power and wealth having its privileges enhanced or sustained in arbitrary ways. Why should certain categories of persons such as aristocrats or members of parliaments have been exempted from the laws governing everyone else?

Finally, it is no accident that the serious study of the Human Sciences only makes a public appearance after The Enlightenment, and then only slowly. They help to provide the descriptive data of the human condition in terms of variability in life-chances between and within human groups. The statistical distributions show selected and filtered facts about rates in the areas of health, education, housing and consumer goods as a function of various demographic groupings. Whilst income figures are reported for many groups, and some spectacular individuals, what does not get public attention are the individual details of the Inland Revenue returns of the very rich. These are matters of privacy in Britain, but that privacy is not applied to the wages of most of the population. This point is raised, not as a matter of prurience, so much as a question of perceptions of what is just and fair, and the extent to which the arguments used to justify the distribution of life-chances are or are not examples one "law" for the rich and another for the poor.

In the last thirty years, neither of the two largest political parties in Britain has done anything seriously effective to rescue those most chronically in poverty. In contrast they have made many tax changes advantaging the rich: reductions in income tax, elimination of inheritance tax for family businesses, raising of capital gains allowances. Again as a contrast, the raisings of levels of Value Added Tax for goods and services is proportionately heavier for poorer people, as are taxes on insurance premiums, fuel prices, alcoholic drinks and tobacco.

If it is accepted that discriminations of various kinds in terms of social categories such as race or sex are unjust, then ought not the list of social categories include the one that has been the most pervasive in all countries down the ages, namely class and caste? A contemporary issue provides one example in the discussion surrounding the concept of a minimum wage. It has taken years to introduce such an idea into legislation and its first setting was £3.70 per hour. Who argued against its introduction? On what grounds? And how did these arguments differ from those about a maximum wage? Employers at all levels argued against the introduction of a minimum wage, and the voices given most media exposure were those of leaders of industry and commerce, who were quite possibly receiving £370 an hour for their work. On what grounds? Workers' wages must be kept low so that British industry and commerce can compete in global markets. Workers who succeed in raising their wages drive themselves out of jobs as well as "damaging the economy."

Who was giving voice to the idea of a maximum wage? That idea has certainly not been advanced in the media alongside the minimum wage arguments. As top "salaries" have been escalating, the argument of those receiving these *were* given voice; in order to attract persons with the necessary skills it was necessary to pay such sums. In the meantime, manufacturing itself was being shifted to the low wage economies of Europe, Africa and Asia to minimize labor costs, regardless of whether the British factories were still profitable.

When those with power introduced comparison groups into their arguments, it was with workers in China or Morocco, and not workers in Finland or Switzerland. When they made comparisons for themselves, it was with the United States and not Sweden or Japan.

In short, arguments in the public domain were presented almost entirely by those who were being most heavily rewarded for their labors already, and their arguments were clearly biased to their own advantage. The process continues, with the media being united in its criticisms, since its own bosses and substantive owners are among the highly paid. The current Labour government has leaders who seem to be concerned not to offend those among the wealthy elite who could damage their prospects of being returned to power. Some senior members of the Labour Party itself have promoted their own wealth and incomes to surprising levels.

These points are *not* being made as ethical arguments, but as issues where the arguments advanced in support of cases can be shown to be clearly self-serving and hence crooked. In itself this would not necessarily render them irrational or invalid; what evokes wariness is that the same comparators are not used for other persons or groups. If middle and lower range jobs in the public sector have to be open to competition via advertisements and selection procedures which are demonstratably non-discriminatory against members of social categories, why is this not so for senior appointments by government ministers or private companies? If public sector organizations have to produce budgets and accounts for public scrutiny, why are central government and its ministers not equally accountable?

Other examples have already been given earlier. Perhaps the biblical advice quoted earlier can be re-phrased into a second suggestion: By the logic of their arguments ye shall know them.

The same forces have exploited religion-based biases in rhetorics that have helped to ensure that the meek shall not inherit the earth and that the poor man will remain at the rich man's castle gate. Not all religions have been anti-science, but when they have come into conflict with the sciences on empirical matters, they have not hesitated to assert their pretentious hegemony – for as long as they have been able to do so. For the most part now, the separation among domains of knowledge and their different criteria of epistemological evaluation have become sufficiently institutionalized in the quasi-democracies for the physical sciences to be developed in accordance with the priorities of the values of those controlling those societies. Insofar as those societies value their economic prosperity, and science offers the basis for the technological means of supplying this, then it is not surprising that it is the capitalist societies that have made the most significant contributions and developed the specialized languages to represent the realities most compatible with their observations.

11.6   Pro tem Conclusions

Each of the domains of knowledge presents different problems for students of social psychology and language in communication. Many of the theoretical disciplines under the umbrella of logics are so specialized that their development continues to proceed without complications over and

above the intellectual difficulties of the topics and whatever personal disagreements might do to retard the progress of the enterprises. The role of
logical considerations in everyday life is problematic. Although the "positive" qualities of rationality remain misty, lists of fallacies and predispositions to error have been drawn up, and both cognitive and social
psychologists have been able to offer explanations for the use of some of
these. Cognitive psychologists have specialized in errors arising from ignorance of statistics or propensities to overestimate or underestimate frequencies or amounts. Little attention has as yet been given to the ways in
which governments and business misrepresent statistics, although beginnings have been made with motives of monetary gain or blame-avoidance
being prominent in such explanations (see Crossen, 1994; Robinson, 1996).
Self-enhancing and other-debasing explanations are prominent in the arguments offered about bias in causal attributions (Weiner, 1994).

Sociological and psychological considerations both have clear relevance
to the rhetoric of aesthetics, ethics, and metaphysics. In these three areas,
the intellectual, affective, and cognitive endeavors of humanity have been
obfuscated by intergroup aspirations to superiority and privilege. Rhetorical propaganda directed towards the exploitation of consumers anxious to
beautify and display themselves is one example. The delusion that laws
made by elites are for the equal benefit of all rather than the law makers
has been another powerful construction of a contingent reality serving
the interests of their inventors. The practice, if not the premises, of religions have been similarly used and abused in the interests of preserving
and enhancing the privileges of elite groups.

One of the awful ironies for those trying to study delusions and decep-
tions and the roles of fallacious arguments in their creation and maintenance is the overwhelming ubiquity of data illustrative of such abuses of
the representational functions of language (see chapter 12). Almost every
news broadcast or documentary provides illustrations, as do newspapers
and magazines, television and radio. Films and books re-write history in
starkly misleading ways, and the oral traditions of cultures and societies are
also replete with false representations. One definition of a nation refers to a
collection of people who have invented a false history about themselves to
justify their current conduct. Social psychologists of language in communication can point to the examples and offer plausible explanations of them
that relate to the motivation of participants via attribution and identity theories proximally, and beyond these to sociological concepts of power, wealth
and status. Both the descriptions and explanations seem to make sense.
What further is to be done beyond pointing to continuing examples is not
obvious, a selection of which are provided in chapter 12.

CHAPTER
12

Mass-Mediated Communication: Spirals of Spin and Broken Swords of Truth

12.1 The Truth–Value of Statements and the Validity of Arguments in the Public Domain

In chapter 11 it was stated that the criteria of evaluation to be applied to a claim need to differ according to the domain of knowledge in which the claim is being made: logical, aesthetic, moral, empirical or metaphysical. It was also mentioned that the declarative form of a sentence can be used for a variety of functions other than representation. It can serve as a question or command. It can serve as a joke or an admonition. Primacy may be accorded to its beauty. Here, consideration is restricted to claims to its role for representations of an empirical nature, where these can be evaluated in terms of correspondence between the matter being referred to and the wordings used for reference. In Searle's (1975) terms, they are representative speech acts about which we require that S's perceived plausible constructions of reality should determine the wordings used. Departures from conventional views of what a truthful statement should comprise can take a variety of forms and vary with the context of situation. Being vague or equivocating to the point of being misleading are common tactics. Omitting relevant information is another. Simple falsification is a third. Presentations can be selective in terms of perspectives and can introduce evaluative words to influence reactions. Arguments can be incoherent and inconsistent. At various times the word "rhetoric" has been used to label speech designed to persuade rather than inform.

In chapter 12 a number of contexts in the public domain are selected to illustrate the operation of some of these factors. Examples are selected from politics, commerce, and the law, but with particular emphasis on the mass media. They range in scope from micro-analyses of sentence structure to the suppression of whole languages. Inevitably, if examples are described in terms of departures from Gricean and other ideals, the contents themselves can take on a negative overtone and convey an impression of a world where deception and swindling are normative, and that is especially so in a final section that takes on qualities akin to Wagner's *Gotterdamerung*. En route prophylactic reminders are inserted to alleviate any developing gloom, and an initial inoculation is in order too. Throughout the text winning in life's competitions is presented as the major temptation that seduces people from the truth and from cooperative living generally, but it needs to be remembered that competitions in the quasi-democracies take place within co-operative contexts. Many politicians are concerned to create better societies. While commercial enterprises are designed to maximize profits, most of the goods they sell are fit for their purposes and do endure for reasonable periods of time. Banks do not steal our money. Both the police and the law courts are presumably generally happier if the innocent are found not guilty and the guilty are condemned. To a considerable extent, the media provide what their audiences want; audiences decide what to listen to or watch, and the media continue to play their historical role of exposing corruption and venality. Many of their biases are both understandable and discountable; Pokemons like to hear news about Pokemons and they like it to show them in a good light. It can certainly be added that if you think the country you are in is awful, consider the conditions of your ancestors when life for the great majority was nasty, brutish, and short.

Some of the issues selected for consideration are currently high profile, others have been around from time immemorial (which, by an eccentric English quirk, is deemed to be 1189 AD). Throughout the history of the human species, tyrants of societies have invariably tried to impose their representations of reality on the citizenry they control, and they continue to do so today. Currently, the populations of a substantial minority of the member countries of the United Nation Organizations are dominated by one person/one party rule, which is sustained and enforced by armed forces and secret police. Most people living in less oppressive regimes, including readers of this book, must find it very difficult to imagine what it is like to live in a state of constant vigilance, distrust, and fear of arbitrary arrest and violence, even if they have spent some time living in such a tyranny. In fact, however, direct forceful suppression of questions about the justice of the status quo and criticisms of it have been normative for most of the people for most of historical time. Even in the apparently more tolerant quasi-democratic societies of today, any serious threats to their structure and functioning rapidly lead to the adoption of forceful measures being taken "in the national interest." The post-1945 anti-Communist movements in some of the quasi-democracies of the West revealed ideological zealotry and cruelty similar in attitude, but not in scale, to that of the Soviet leaders to whom they were so opposed and who were described a presiding over an "evil empire." Moreover, whilst maintaining a rhetoric of commitment to truth and justice, the societies pursuing forms of individualistic capitalism, with periodic binary-choice elections, are far from free of cover-ups and corruption (Etzioni-Halevy, 1989; Rose-Ackerman, 1999), deceit and delusions (Robinson, 1996). Empirical evidence shows a decline of public trust in the truthfulness of many forms of authority over the last thirty years, in both the USA and UK for example (Dionne, 1991; Lipsett & Schneider, 1983; Robinson, 1993, 1996). At the same time, government propaganda to create and enhance the "feel good" factor in their electorates has been serviced by the new breed of *spin doctors*, who have been added to the erstwhile advertisers and public relations personnel. Supported by the broadcasting power of TV, radio, and newspapers, the relevant elites have had implausible constructions of reality about particular topics created and sustained for them by their public relations personnel. On media news, it seems that every event that might reflect badly on the government is spun to minimize the responsibility of ministers and their associated authorities, whilst every accident of good fortune is seized upon and presented as being a result of their deliberate action. Committees of Inquiry take months or years to report. "Action plans" are formulated, but like the "Task forces" that are often used to implement them, the outcomes of these are not evaluated or called to account.

These comments are not intended as comparisons with a mythical past of a Golden Age in which truth, justice, and happiness prevailed in human societies. The protagonist of one such false myth was also the writer who first polarized policy positions about truth in speech. Plato (1979; 1973/ fourth century BC) contrasted the views of Gorgias the rhetoritician with those of Socrates, the dialectical pursuer of truth and justice. Socrates argued for the primacy of arguments as a means of discovering truths and insisted that statements be used to represent truths, both at the conceptual levels of principles and the factual levels of discovering particulars. In contrast, Gorgias was set up to present the case for learning to use language to persuade the relevant audience to adopt any set of beliefs that serve the purposes of the orator, and, if necessary, to make the weaker argument seem the stronger. This requires the development of oratical skills that can also be used in criminal cases to secure the conviction of the innocent or to enable the guilty to escape. It implicates the learning of skills that can enable political or military authorities to lead their people into unjust wars. The Gorgias position prizes persuasive skill above all else;

morality is not an issue. For Socrates discovering the truth was the prime aim and was a important moral issue. In the Gorgias and Phaedrus dialogues, Plato (1979,1997/fourth century BC) set down techniques appropriate to each cause. Aristotle (1926/fourth century BC) both expanded and systematized classifications of rhetorical devices. Additionally, he formulated rules of formal logical and practical reasoning. Cicero (1971/first century BC) defended the position that rhetoric and logic were complementary rather than opposed, and that for the effective functioning of society, both needed to be used by persons of *virtu* in just causes. Nero cut short the writings of Cicero, reminding the Romans that the sword can ensure that the pen ceases to write, and so it has always been.

The four qualities of rhetoric described by Cicero were correct usage, clarity, appropriateness and ornament, but from his time forward, it was the last that took centre stage and became more and more elaborated: particularly for literary rather than political ends. Schools of rhetoric reached their apogee in the Europe of the sixteenth century, with heavy tomes cataloguing types of rhetorical devices, preferably realized in Latin rather than the vernaculars. The numbers of figures, tropes, and schemes had grown to almost 200 in Peacham's "Garden of Eloquence" (1577), whose very title is indicative of the triumph of form over substance.

Whilst the convoluted complexities, as well as the decline in the use of Latin, may have been implicated in the demise of this kind of rhetoric, the more earthy pragmatism of Aristotle and Cicero continued and continue to operate in politics and jurisprudence. Today no national leader relies solely on Socratic dialectic to present preferred policies and practices. (It would be interesting however, to compare the logical fallacies in their criticisms of others with those detectable in their presentation and justification of their own actions. My guess is that it would also be found that explicit references to the untruthfulness and injustices of opponents are more frequent than expressed concerns with the truth of their own assertions.)

Another factor contributing to the decline of rhetoric may well have been the rise of science. Bacon (1855/1625) was a strong advocate of things (*res*) being more important than words (*verba*), and the idea that empirical evidence based on observation and experiment should be the basis for claims about the factual truths. Certainly the seventeenth century witnessed the triumph of chemistry over alchemy and the ascendancy of physics over metaphysics as sources of knowledge about the nature of the physical world. In the terms of this text, the truth–value of statements about the empirical world became subject to testing against scientific criteria rather than against the edicts of religious or political leaders – within limits – in some countries. Not that these battles have ceased. Consideration of Darwin's views of evolution by natural selection and the genetic theories associated with these were banned from school syllabuses in the Soviet Union by Stalin and more recently in parts of the USA by certain Christian fundamentalists.

More generally, readers of newspapers, listeners to news, commentaries and discussion programs on radio, and viewer/listeners switched on to TV are exposed to a steady stream of inaccurate information and ill-informed opinions about a wide variety of issues: scientific, moral, political, and factual. As mentioned in chapter 11, it can be instructive to record a discussion program in which claims about facts are made, and then to analyze the conversation against Grice's (1975/1989) maxims of quantity, accuracy, relevance and manner, and the logic against criteria that can be used to evaluate the validity of arguments (Fischer, 1971; Thouless, 1974; Walton, 1989). In news broadcasts, the reporting of sports results meets the Gricean criteria. If this were not so, there would be public outcry. About most other events, it is worthwhile asking why the topic was selected, what other perspectives might have been adopted towards it, whether any evaluative slant is made explicit, – how the arguments stand up to a logical analysis. This last is interestingly difficult because TV news in particular has such a high incidence of short snippets in which just a few individuals are asked to offer instant but brief personal opinions to a microphone; there are very few sustained arguments to evaluate. Fowler (1991) and Jucker (1986) both offer systematic analyses of press items.

These considerations do not necessarily imply that sinister purposes underlie what the media report and how they present items. Commercial enterprises are intended to make profits, and if profits depend on numbers of viewers, listeners, and readers, then management is likely to maximize audiences. If more rather than fewer people will watch victims of disasters and tragedies giving distressed personal accounts, then these will be broadcast. If aggressive confrontational arguments attract higher ratings than truth-seeking enquiries, then these will be offered. If entertainment demands are greater than those for information, then more entertainment will be broadcast. Along with the wishes of the proprietors, it is the preferences of the purchasing public that are the major determinants of what is presented by commercially-based media. In present-day Britain, the BBC has also become sensitive to ratings, presumably being under covert political pressure to keep its audience figures high.

It is possible to compare and contrast issues of truthfulness and consistency of argumentation in any of the domains of pretending knowledge referred to in chapter 11. Such an enterprise could be conducted in particular and institutional domains, such as politics, the law, business, and education, and yet further in fields within these, for example history, science, or literary criticism. Coverage here has to be limited, and it is restricted to some idiosyncratic and partial comments on politics, commerce, and the law and on data relevant to that great innovation of the twentieth century – the mass media. These can now reach everywhere on earth, and are the major medium of constructing and disseminating social realities beyond the here-and-now experiences of people. Finally, as a reminder that these policies and practices are not new, there is a minimal sketch of how power elites have used language throughout human history to sustain its privileges.

12.1.1   Truth in Politics

Richard Nixon resigned his presidency, but was neither disgraced nor punished for authorizing criminal acts and then lying about his involvement in these. No repentance, no restitution. Biographies of both Kennedy and Johnson reveal the extent of the gap between the public mask and the private person. Clinton survived being economical with the truth and saw through a second term of office.

On the other side of the Atlantic, France, Germany, Italy, Spain and the UK have had multiple exposures of dishonest dealings and cover-ups by senior politicians, some of whom have resigned some of their offices, but few of whom have been subject to criminal charges and trial. The European Union had its 20 Commissioners resign, as a result of a whistleblowing about corruption. No charges have yet been brought.

In the UK, some 20 ministers of the last spell of Conservative administration resigned their offices over issues where they were also deemed to have covered up their indiscretions or offenses. Most continued to draw their salaries as MPs, and all but one of those who have stood for parliament again or taken up other high offices have been permitted to do so. Whether the occasions for resigning their ministerial offices should have been seen as actions requiring resignations is not the concern here. What is to be noted is that heads and members of elected governments and other senior political figures can:

1   willfully make false statements about their conduct;
2   deny that these statements are false;
3   resign only from a minimum of offices;
4   be unlikely to be charged with criminal or civil offences;

5   profit from fees for publishing autobiographical accounts;
6   find it easy to return to public office after a year or so of absence;
7   make no voluntary restitution;
8   show no publicized signs of repentance.

It is not just at the level of personal conduct that politicians mislead the public. President Bush Snr suggested that the electorate watch his lips to find out about future rates of taxation for the US citizenry. They were wrong. In Britain the last Conservative and current Labor governments promised that "tax" would not be increased. Whilst it is true that both either reduced or retained levels of *personal income tax*, they both invented new taxes, raised other forms, and both substantially increased the general burden of taxation.

Government statistical calculations for public health, education, crime, and unemployment have had their bases changed frequently, all showing apparent improvements. National educational attainments have "improved" year on year, but empirical evidence on standards imply correlated lowerings of standards. Waiting lists for hospital treatment have been reduced, but it has become more difficult to get onto waiting lists!

As a third set of examples, in the UK there has been a succession of governmental statements about food-related and environmentally-related illnesses: salmonella, listeria, E coli-B, and Creuzfeldt-Jakob" disease (CJD) for the first category, and for the latter the carcinogenic risks from nuclear power plants, asbestos, and lead fumes from traffic. The linkages between CJD in humans, spongiform encephalitis in cattle, and scrapie in sheep were denied by ministers for a number of years. The minister who offered a never-refuted statistic on the incidence of salmonella in chicken eggs was obliged to resign very quickly.

Such then are a few illustrations of some political evasions, obfuscations, and falsifications, all functioning to protect the careers and reputations of those in office, and to enhance the image of the government presented to the public. A second category of potential beneficiaries included the companies and businesses involved. The well-being of affected workers and the general public seldom figured as the major concern.

There are of course many circumstances where the practices described will not occur. When the truth is about desirable news or neutral, it will be told. If news is bad, but the government cannot be blamed the truth can be told. If party members, the opposition parties, or the media keep up pressure for the truth to be told, governments may cease to cover-up or lie. It may also be the case that a government tells the truth as a matter of principle. In a society which was prepared to recognize that mistakes are inevitable and forgivable, governments might be encouraged to be more open and honest.

12.1.2 Commercial Highlights

The division of labor in our societies requires the buying and selling of goods and services. It would be odd if those doing selling emphasized the weaknesses of their products in their advertising, and the phrase *caveat emptor* has been around for many years. But from what *caveats* has *emptor* a right to be protected from? Misleading advertising can rely on omissions of information, exaggerations in the form of jokes or metaphors, and empirically false claims.

If we focus briefly on the last we may note that in the UK for a number of years sales-people of insurance companies have sold personal pension plans that were not advantageous to the several million people who purchased them. Most of the companies are still trying to minimize their liabilities. No senior managers or directors have either resigned or been dismissed as a result of these malpractices. A great bureaucracy of supervisory bodies has been set up to protect the public from financially misleading recommendations, but their effectiveness has not been evaluated. Many recent and current savings plans mention their low charges, but not their high ones in their advertisements. They are prone to put any unpalatable conditions in unreferenced small print. The publicity selects time periods which maximize historical success. Opacity for the negatives, transparency for the positives! This is apparently legal. So are the claims of the numerous beautifying and medicinal products on the market.

The willingness to sell is not always supported by a willingness to handle complaints. Seriously debilitating side effects of toxicity in work environments or pharmaceutical products are not always investigated thoroughly and dispassionately. For nearly 50 years, the respiratory and carcinogenic risks of smoking have been notoriously dismissed or diminished by tobacco companies – and ignored by tax benefiting governments. Design weaknesses in cars, ships, and planes have been denied, beyond reasonable doubt. The denials are often combined with assertions of commitments to giving people the freedom to choose to die of lung cancer. In accident investigations, design and operational procedure weaknesses have typically been treated as less important than possible proximal operator errors (Reason, 1990).

The public relations spokespeople of companies can make extraordinary claims about the missions of their companies. Are GM crops really intended to help the impoverished farmers and famine-prone populations of South Asia? What are the advantages to farmers using seeds that yield one crop and no fertile seeds for the following year?

My suspicion is that the invention of the limited liability company will eventually prove to be one of the most globally devastating organizations yet devised by people. Constitutionally, they are required to aim to make profits, and their annual reports are written in that spirit; increasing earnings per share and profits overall are the primary aims. For whose benefit? Typically the answers by company spokespeople and the media are that shareholders are the primary beneficiaries, but increasingly the salaries and other perquisites of senior management appear to be rising at a much higher rate than the dividends or capital value of the shares. In short, there is a double rhetoric, each strand of which is at variance with reality. The next version of Orwell's (1949) *Nineteen Eighty-Four* may well present the villains as international cartels that have grown beyond the control of national governments as well as their own managers.

Given the structural drives of individualistic capitalism, companies that do not form cartels are under continuous pressure to minimize costs and maximize profits, and those that do not are at risk of bankruptcy. Individuals running companies are victims of a system that punishes those who are not ruthless. Most of the time most of the products are fit for purpose and are rendered affordable; consumers are beneficiaries of industry and commerce as well as being occasionally open to exploitation. *Caveat emptor*.

12.1.3 The Law

The legislative arm of government is expected to make just laws and develop procedures that maximize the chances of justice being done and seen to be done. Since laws and procedures are coded in written statements, and writing in itself cannot capture the spirit of goodwill, they will not be adequate to the ideals they are intended to formulate. This last is one argument for having discretionary judgments and case law as well as statute law, since "cases" which appear to be moving towards unjust outcomes can be re-directed. So runs the theory.

Claiming the need for objectivity and transparency, the professionals within the legal system have constructed a concept of "legal truth" to embrace what is true within the law. A verdict of "Guilty" is then not synonymous with stating that the defendant committed the offense, but only that after due legal process a verdict has been delivered and any sen-

tence appropriate can be passed. Once the concept of legal truth is con-
joined with a notion that the paramount duty of the defence is to obtain a
verdict other than "Guilty," with the prosecution simultaneously pursuing the "Guilty" verdict, the scene is set for a verbal tournament.

An earlier tournament in any prosecution in an adversarial system will
have been between the investigating police team and the person charged.
And prior to that, the police have had to arrest and charge the suspect.
This procedure now has a complex wording, and trivial variations from
the correct formula are one possible technicality that may be exploited by
the defense. The same fate can apply to the succeeding rules about proper
conditions of interrogation, and in particular what is recorded of what is
said and made available to the defense. However, it is not only an alert
defense that can (ab)use failures to follow precise procedures laid down.
The police can create and sustain conditions under which people get confused or exhausted and utter statements that can be construed later as
attempts to mislead or deceive or even as confessions of guilt. An adroit
selection of extracts from any interrogation can be used to create false
impressions in the minds of those in the court.

In court itself, the jury, the witnesses, and many defendants are ama-
teurs whereas the court officials are professionals, familiar with the procedural rules and customs, the law itself, and the tricks of the trade. Again,
the professionals can exploit the situation to generate false impressions of
the un/reliability of witnesses (O'Barr, 2001), just as skilled witnesses can
lie with panache. Success in the verbal dueling is the aim of both the prosecution and the defense; persuading the jury and judge taking precedence
over the exposure of the most plausible construction of the true history of
the crime. The "great" lawyers are those who can win weak cases; their
fees are high and access to their services depends upon the wealth and
influence of their would-be clients.

Very few citizens have experience of participation in the process as jury,
witnesses, or observers. Perhaps it should be compulsory. And they could
have sets of questions to consider. Is this an honest and efficient enquiry
into truth? Is justice the paramount concern of all present? Is the procedure in line with the advice of Socrates or Gorgias? Each set of persons
participating has their own vested interests in either acquittal or conviction, and since the law itself sets up the trial as a gladiatorial contest, it is
not surprising that the truth is liable to be a chronic casualty. Correcting
this would still not overcome the crucial difficulty that the boundary between what is just and what is unjust cannot be captured by words, and
the principles of justice cannot be expressed exhaustively in words.

As with joint stock/limited liability companies, societies seem to have designed legal systems with weaknesses that were not foreseen and then are left uncorrected. If police are given performance-related pay (PRP) on the basis of arrests made, they are being encouraged to arrest. If PRP is related to convictions achieved, they are encouraged to strengthen convicting evidence. If barristers' fees and reputations depend on maximising cases won, then they have to try to win cases. If justice is to be served, incentives have to be geared to the convictions of the guilty, while leaving the innocent untroubled. What this may mean is encouraging more personal pride in getting the right answers and trying to ensure that securing freedom for the guilty is as damaging to reputations as gaining convictions of the innocent. Meanwhile the hope has to be that enough of the professionals have and retain such attitudes.

12.2 The Mass Media

Standard texts of social psychology are as unlikely to have sections on the mass media as they are to have sections about language and communication, even though ironically, the related topic of social influence almost always captures a whole section. Media are now very diverse in sensory channels, modes of representation, audiences, and scale. The channels can be visual or auditory or both. If visual, they can be pictorial or graphic or both. The form can be paintings, photographs, videos, small screen or large screen. If graphic, the presentation may be in writing. If written, the text can be in books, magazines, comics, pamphlets or posters. If auditory, is talking or singing involved? Is the audience a crowd in a square, a smaller group in a cinema, opera house or music hall, an even smaller group at home watching TV or listening to the radio, or a solitary individual working through *War and Peace* – or filling a tax form?

Media are also diverse in accessibility and management. Which media are available to which communicators and audiences in terms of provision and cost? How are decisions taken about the kind of content that is forbidden and the kinds of functions the media are permitted or encouraged to serve? Are their owners and managers concerned to amuse, educate, sell goods and services, or are they creating and sustaining a cultural ideology within which people are expected to live their lives? Have their audiences alternative information sources? If so, are these real or only apparent alternatives?

With such a variety of possible projects available, perhaps social psychologists are wise to avoid exploring so much of the unknown. More especially, they may be wary of becoming involved in questions that have already been posed and answered within other disciplines. However, as we shall see, other disciplines do not always follow through hypotheses with collecting the empirical evidence necessary to check whether what may be plausible hypotheses are in fact consonant with systematically evaluated data. As intimated in chapter 2, although a multitude of semiotically sensible projects can be devised very quickly, the collection and processing of adequate data can be very expensive and time-consuming.

To begin then with caution and care. Most people now have enough experience to be aware of the manifold functions and modes of operation of the media. They know that media are necessarily selective in what they present (Glasgow Media Group, 1976, 1980, 1982). They know that they can be deliberately biased or deceptive in their selections. They hold beliefs about the effects media have on audiences, in particular their relevance to violent and sexual conduct and to the purchase of consumer goods and services. However, systematically collected and processed empirical evidence on such issues has not so far yielded publicly endorsed consensus on "effects." Partly this is because there are many vested interests at work. Pressure groups may wish to ban broadcasting on particular topics and issues for a variety of reasons. Companies wish to sell their products. Advertising companies wish to persuade companies to advertise. Media companies wish to sell space to advertisers, and currently appear to believe that stories and documentaries replete with sex, violence, and suffering will attract the large audiences that will boost their profits. The inter-company competitions ensure that commercially collected data are not accessible to the academic community or to the public generally. The owners of the media have interests beyond the profits they can make. So have politicians and governments. Whereas evidence about the influences of the media may be sparse, the data about the "consumers" and especially about the characteristics of the media are in overwhelming supply.

If we take the word "media" to refer to mediated messages, and not just to what are frequently treated as the mass media, then we can note that information about them extends backwards in time across several millennia, extends geographically around the globe, and is in continuous and continuing production. A bad poet writing about the media would probably use a series of watery metaphors to generalize about present day human experience – awash with, bathed in, drowned in. TV has become the largest ocean for most people to bathe in, but radio and newspapers are omnipresent, as are books, magazines, and comics. Throwing away junk mail is a daily chore for the victims of advertisers. The rising tide of the

Internet must be threatening the time-management resources of its increasing number of its users and addicts. How to stay abreast and afloat could become increasingly difficult. At work, people used to read letters. Now they additionally check for faxes, voice-mail, and e-mails.

Unfortunately for present purposes, most of the social psychological research of the media has focused on TV, which includes pictures with its words, and it is language and its use that is supposed to be the principal concern here. However, just as it would be foolish to dissociate verbal from non-verbal communication to the extent of not mentioning NVC, so it would be myopic to see media using more than language as irrelevant to the brief. What research has been done is guilty of sins of omission as well as sins of commission. As indicated already, some of the reasons for this relate to unsinister commercial interests. The income of commercial media depends on advertising revenue or audience subscriptions, both of which are directly related to the numbers of users. Hence the need for research into program characteristics that keep audience figures high. In contrast, very few books have advertisements scattered among the pages. How the reading of Bill Bryson's *Notes from a Small Island* has affected foreign attitudes to the English remains unknown. How history textbooks for teenagers affect beliefs about the past and present remains unexamined. Radio speech might have attracted much more research, but has not done so. TV is another matter.

12.2.1   Two Perspectives, a Complication and a Resolution

Early social psychological work focused on *effects* of media messages on attitudes and behavior. Such work assumed that the way the creator of the messages defined their meaning and significance would match the audience's interpretation, i.e. that the meaning was in the semantics of the message, as it would be interpreted by a dispassionate observer. This assumption was combined with naïve expectations of finding substantial main effects, either with tiny manipulations in the laboratory or mass main effects on whole categories of people (Hovland, Lumsdaine & Sheffield, 1949; Himmelweit, Vince & Oppenheim, 1958).

The second phase is now called the *uses and gratifications* model (Blumler & Katz, 1974), and this served as a reminder that audiences are typically voluntary; they decide which radio and TV stations to listen to and watch, which books, newspapers and comics they will read. Insofar as one medium serves an individual's needs and desires better than another, it will be preferred. Radio remains pre-eminent for music listening, but the combined vision and sound of TV have obvious advantages for sports events. Of course the two approaches can be combined without conceptual or empirical difficulties, but a third perspective has to be introduced to render work anchored to plausible constructions of reality.

It is principally to cultural and media studies (see chapter 2) that we owe the insistence on the openness of many texts – that typically more than one interpretation can be imagined both of the text itself and of the reasons for its appearance. The inferred intentions of the creators and the disseminators are but one of the possible interpretations of the text. This is normally referred to as the "preferred reading," and as Hall et al. (1980) have emphasized, in the mass media sampled by the majority, this reading typically celebrates the virtues of the political and social status quo. Alternative interpretations of both the media messages and the social structure may well be the dominant stance of those people who are critical of contemporary society and its normative culture(s). Alternative readings are not necessarily confrontational. Liebes and Katz (1990) illustrated this in respect of the enormously successful 1970s/1980s TV soap opera, *Dallas*. What the audiences from different countries focused on was different. A dispassionate (sic!) initial analysis by Liebes and Katz identified some standard themes of such epics: extra- and intra-familial conflicts and alliances, concerns with power, wealth, and status, etc. Recognizing that their interpretation was just one reading, they asked other viewers about an episode. They found that Americans focused on individuals and what they were trying to achieve and how. Moroccan Arabs focused on the flow of the narrative. Russian Jews emphasized the moral and political themes – the struggles between the right and the wrong. In this case, all three were selective and partial perspectives, which look to be guided by cultural norms, but each was consistent with the presentation.

As was hinted in chapter 2, imaginative academics (and others) can devise large numbers of perspectives and levels of interpretation of forms, substance, and context. How many of these possibilities are realized by how many perceivers under what conditions and to what effects? These then become the bigger and more appropriate frame of reference for guiding research: Imaginable possibilities are not the same as empirical realities. It is likely that there will be normative preferred readings within homogeneous sub-cultural groups, but any modern society is likely to be made up of large numbers of such groups.

Another feature emphasized in later research has been the interdependent nature of media/audience relations. The media themselves collect audience reactions as a basis for planning the future, but this information is no more than information. It is the media managers and owners who decide what to disseminate and how. They decide whether or not programs are intended to persuade or inform, entertain or delude, and which values are to be represented with what spin. Governments and sponsors can also, and do, exert their influence with licenses and money. At the present time it is probably most helpful simply to select some examples of recent and ongoing work on political activities and news reports to exemplify what can be achieved.

12.2.2 Micro-analyses

Given the constitutional requirements of a balance of interviewers and spokespeople on British television, natural experiments are created, and realistic comparisons can be devised and made. Detailed transcriptions of the video recordings, combined with painstaking fine taxonomies have afforded the extraction of some very informative results, with some surprising interpretations.

Bull (in press) in particular has followed the news interview veins previously explored by conversational analysts such as Clayman (1988, 1992), Greatbatch and Heritage (see Heritage and Greatbatch, 1991), who have severally examined disagreements, formulations, neutrality of replies, openings and closings, supplementary questions, topic organization, and turn-taking, and very successfully so. Bull's model links results on equivocation with the theory of Bavelas et al. (1990) that associated equivocation with answers to Yes/No questions, where either answer would be dangerous for the questioned person. He argues the case for the primary concern of politicians in news interviews being the preservation and enhancement of positive face with as wide an audience as possible (Bull, Elliott, Palmer, & Walker, 1996). Hence their especial need to avoid giving offense. When politicians spoke to live local audiences, they could deliver different speeches to different constituencies and emphasize their particular identification with the needs and aspiration of those they were addressing. Now, audiences are national and realize that the cake of government disbursements is finite, and they can readily see that promises of fatter slices for one group entail thinner slices for the others. (Adopting a related but different self-protecting perspective, one of the droller ironies of the annual budget speech of the British Chancellor of the Exchequer is the register used to refer to his generosity; he is reported as giving away money, making grants, helping particular groups much like Santa Claus. It is our taxes not his wealth that he is re-distributing.) Since the cost of any particular policy has to be met from somewhere, it is vital that their talk does not identify any group that may be disadvantaged by a policy and thereby lose votes. Empirical studies of such talk require detailed analyses of minutiae, followed by the constructive linkage of these to functional benefits or costs. Whilst testable against external criteria of audience reactions, the research relies heavily and sensibly on naturally-occurring phenomena for the strongest data. This is also true of studies of both interviews and speeches to large audiences.

Earlier work on rhetorical techniques and their association with applause at party conferences was initiated by Atkinson (1984a, 1984b) and Heritage and Greatbatch (1991). What are the determinants of invited and uninvited applause (uninvited applause being unscheduled and unexpected)? Three categories of remark accounted for most of the applause: favorable references to persons, favorable references to 'us,' and unfavorable references to 'them.' Rhetorical formatting increased the likelihood of these references being applauded: combinations, contrasts, headline–punchlines, lists, position taking, pursuits, and puzzle posing with solutions. Of these features, contrasts and listings accounted for nearly 50 percent of the applause. Work continues.

12.2.3   Sequences in Representations of Violence

In *Deciphering Violence*, Cerulo (1998) offers an elegant story about storytelling. According to her, storytellers typically use one of four basic structures for their basic message (see also the Linguistic Category Model in chapter 14):

1   Performer sequences prioritize the perspective of the person who commits the act, using active indicative verbs;
2   Victim sequences prioritize the victim, and use passive verb constructions;
3   Contextual sequences prioritize the circumstances in which the act occurred;
4   Double casting structures provide both performer and victim information about an individual.

Cerulo links these to three different attitudes of presenters to the violence. The first to what she calls "normal" violence, but that might be better referred to as legalized violence, i.e. that performed by institutionalized forces of law and order. (Such violence is deemed acceptable by the storytellers, but not necessarily by the audience, especially in cases where inter-group identifications become salient.) In the second, the sympathies are with the victim. In the third and fourth, judgment is held in abeyance. The extent of these associations are illustrated by her analysis of newspaper stories, which gave modal percentage frequencies of 90 for 1, 71 for 2, and 85 for 3 and 4. In a separate study, with both written press and oral TV reports, Cerulo showed that readers and viewers generally concurred with such preferred readings, but with reservations and complications affected by initial general attitudes and identifications of individuals towards the events portrayed. She also showed an influence effect, and pointed out that such message structure choices will be influencing listeners, readers, and viewers pervasively, and probably for the most part unconsciously. Other things being equal, and this is why Cerulo selects the phrase "normal violence." this is the violence that we are expected to find acceptable.

The lack of overlap in source referencing between Cerulo's and Turnbull's (1994) analysis of how the thematic structure of narratives of violent events influences perceptions of responsibility is not atypical of media studies. Turnbull anchors his work in the linguistic and social psychological literature. He selects the theme/scheme contract but notes that he might have chosen topic/comment, given/new or agent/patient or even subject/predicate distinctions as a basis for discussion. The default rule in English is that the theme is mentioned first. It is the grammatical subject, and if it is not realized as a proper noun, its nominal head may well be modified with the definite article or a demonstrative pronoun. Engelkamp and Zimmer (1983) observed that people pay more attention to processing theme-related information, and a succession of studies has shown psychological co-variants consistent with this. Does this covariance extend to judgments of responsibility for the violence in two-person conflicts? In the experimental situation of undergraduates assigning responsibility to characters in vignettes, the short answer was "Yes" – but there were complications. These studies offer generalizations that need further exploration, but look to be firmly grounded in their basic claims of linkages between structures and functions of passing moralizing judgments, as was suggested earlier by Fowler, Hodge, Kress, and Trew (1979), and demonstrated by Sigman and Fry (1985).

12.3   Raising the Stakes

These examples may suffice to show that at least four of the major institutional orders in individualistic capitalist societies such as the UK and USA do not always place the highest priority on the truth of representational statements in circumstances where one might expect that to be the priority. Although the citizenry condemn falsification by authorities, including the media, their behavior generally shows little evidence of serious dissent, especially in respect of their participation with the media. There are signs of growing alienation from the political process, particularly in the lowering voting turn-outs in the USA and now the UK. The law passes most citizens by.

Elsewhere I have suggested (Robinson, 1996) that in situations where *winning* is what is most important, and the penalties for cheating and lying are slight or non-existent, then it is to be expected that success will often be predicated upon deception. In the extreme case of military conflicts, being able to deceive the enemy is treated as praiseworthy, and in international competitive sports, cheating and deception that are missed by referees and other officials, but are clearly recorded on video, are not penalized *ex post facto*. Politics, business, and courtroom proceedings are competitive, with the end being to win, so it is not surprising that cheating and deception occur. Only if politics and legal proceedings were constituted as co-operative activities intended to unravel the truth would truthfulness be valued. Only if business and its associated activities could be treated as a sensible division of labor intended to benefit society as a whole and as an arena where broad criteria of fairness of reward could be agreed would truthfulness achieve primacy. There is probably a measure of consensus among the population of ideas of fairness of payments and limits of wage differentials, but most countries remain a long way from applying Rawls' principles of social justice (1971).

For present purposes however, such possible reforms are not the immediate issue. What is of concern is that claims and arguments should be seen for what they are, and that untruthfulness, distortions, and irrationalities be described and explained. For example, to claim a right not to be interfered with if one chooses to hunt foxes is a position that can be asserted and argued. It is not the same as saying that fox-hunting is necessary to keep down a pest (community benefit and moral stance). To claim that it has been a rural institution of great longevity (tradition) is nonsense; only the aristocracy were allowed to hunt until after the eighteenth century (Gilmour, 1992). The pursuit of foxes only became fashionable in the nineteenth century because there were too few deer left alive for stag hunting to be continued nationally. No one has yet produced the financial accounts showing that hunting is cheaper than shooting (cost/benefit analysis), or that unemployment would be increased significantly (community benefit). Many fox-hunters may not know or may not believe these propositions, but if they are false, why not drop them? Why not simply say to the anti-hunting people, "We enjoy fox-hunting. We pay for the pleasure it gives us. Killing foxes is necessary for farmers, so we are being useful. If you wish fox-hunting to be banned, use the proper channels to get such legislation passed. We will likewise lobby to oppose you?"

This example has been selected because the fox-hunting controversy in Britain is a good case of an issue which has given rise to considerable passion on both sides and has witnessed extraordinary accusations and counter-accusations at much more general and personalized levels, with much ill-founded and irrational argumentation. What are the full agendas of those opposed to hunting foxes? Are all fishing and shooting on some lists? Is keeping farm animals for human food also on the latent list of activities to be banned? Zoos? Pets (companion animals in modern-speak)? Are the protagonists of fox-hunting wanting rights to do as they please on their own land in ways in which urban citizens cannot?

Societies are permeated with such genuine issues as to the kind of culture their members would like to live in. What is relevant here are the premises and logics of the arguments that are the foundations of the positions adopted about such issues. As Deanne Kuhn (1991) showed in her samples, people's beliefs and arguments about the causes of unemployment, of school failure, and of criminal recidivism were fragmentary. Her participants were simply expressing their views. What has been illustrated here is complementary to this; deliberate falsification and spurious argumentation by authorities is common practice. Some of this is encouraged by the general value structure we have created (namely individualistic capitalism) and some by specific institutional structures (for example adversarial law courts). Both are predicated on an implicit superordinate value position that elevates winning above truth-telling and valid argumentation.

This chapter has been relatively devoid of references to experiments in social psychology and fairly short on references to surveys and other systematically collected data. In the main it has been a collection of specific facts, but a collection which affords plausible interpretation, at least in terms of formulating hypotheses as to what is happening by way of verbally-based deception in the public domain and why. Experiments may come later, but given that the perspectives have necessarily been societal and cultural, manipulative experimentation may not be either feasible or necessary. The emphasis has been not on individuals *per se*, but individuals occupying certain positions in certain kinds of institutional structures. These structures exist in societies that are stratified vertically in terms of class, status, and power. They are also and simultaneously partitioned horizontally into diverse divisions of labor, with each of these divisions having small elites and many workers in the lower strata. The peaks of these pyramids are connected by kinship and acquaintance, with offspring being socialized into these, initially through family ties, common schooling and university education, and subsequently through social networks of societies and clubs (Sampson, 1965).

The social psychology of language and/in communication has hardly begun to look either at intergroup communication between these horizontal and vertical cleavages in societies or at intragroup communication in most social categories. Studies to date have focused on isolated topics such as doctor–patient communication (Hinckley et al., 1990; Street, 2001) intra- organizational communication (Gardner et al., 2001), politicians in the media (Bull, in press) and the ways the law and courts function (Tiersma, 1999; O'Barr, 2001).

The issues raised here about the truth-status of representational statements have either not emerged in such studies or have done so only peripherally. They have been raised in the direct national surveys about the perceived trustworthiness of various categories of occupants of various social positions and the media (for example Dionne, 1991; Gallup Polls, 1993), and they have been discussed in a comparative cross-cultural analysis of trust (Fukuyama, 1995). Fukuyama asks about the groupings within which individuals trust each other and how these differ across cultures. He is particularly interested in how these differences relate to the kind of commercial collectivities that societies are likely to generate. Here the questions have been posed more negatively, emphasizing lack of trust arising particularly out of situations where winning is more important than adherence to the rules, and with special reference to the rule of being truthful.

The concept of *trust* is central to these issues, as is the loss of trust realized as either wariness or distrust or both. It has been suggested that the default condition in social interaction is to believe what the other says. What is meant by "default" needs to be considered, if only briefly. To believe that statements encountered are sincerely uttered is easier than working out alternative interpretations and checking these for their plausibility before replying. To accept sincerity does not imply subscription to the truth of what is said, but does presume that deliberate deception is not intended. In a basically cooperative society trusting the sincerity of others in relevant ingroups is probably the default position.

Insofar as this default does not give rise to subsequent experiences that give cause to doubt the sincerity, it can continue to operate. If doubts are entertained and then check out as valid, *wariness* is likely to become a wiser default stance in the future, at least in the absence of an acceptable mitigating account. Within our networks of association, we learn who to continue to trust about what kind of matter, and one of the functions of gossip (Emler, 2001) is to check out doubts with third parties when these arise.

What is happening at the interpersonal level in terms of trust and wariness has also to be studied systematically, but it is clear that at the intergroup level there is strong evidence of wariness and distrust, especially up and down the social stratification ladders. In US organizations the salient question for superiors about inferiors is "How competent are they?" For inferiors it is "How trustworthy is the boss?" (Hogan, 1983). Not surprisingly the answer to the second question is frequently, "He's/She's not." Bosses are seen as liable to pass blame and responsibilities down, but retain power and take credit for the successes of their underlings.

More broadly, it is also clear that the majority of the citizenry of the UK and USA have lost faith in their politicians; they see them as ambitious people who enjoy the fruits of power, wealth and status rather than as dedicated servants of the needs of the population. "Big business" is seen as similarly exploitative, but then its *raison d'être* is to buy as cheap as possible and sell as dear as possible, at least within a framework of individualistic capitalism. As elites are increasingly seen as serving the interests of their ingroups and themselves, so also Simmel's stranger (1950) is liable to be seen as a threat. Homes have become fortified with CCTV, alarms, dogs, heavy duty locks, window bars and other security devices. These were not in evidence in residential areas in Britain 50 years ago. People are increasingly afraid to open their doors to strangers, even if they wear uniforms. Hitchhiking has almost disappeared.

The disposition to trust others and to accept the sincerity of what they state is probably contracting towards more tightly defined ingroups. The social psychology of such a trend is being driven principally by the perception (construction) of current sociological and cultural realities. Although social psychologists might correctly diagnose this retreat as having similarities with prejudice, and although cognitive psychologists might see this as exaggerating the risks associated with rare events, the "kernel of truth" hypothesis might have relevance. Gossip about people being robbed or attacked themselves and knowing of others who have been appears to be much more common than it was.

I know of no data which show that people are becoming more trusting at an interpersonal or intergroup level, and it is difficult to observe any current grounds why they should be changing in that direction. The proverb "Once bitten, twice shy" is apposite as far as the credibility of authorities is concerned. Both the classical and operant conditioning paradigms are clear in their evidence that avoidance learning is much more difficult to extinguish than approach learning. Public health concerns are one area where governments have been "mistaken" more than once, and each of their "mistakes" has been in the direction of exposing the public to risks and preserving the financial interests of government and businesses. In the aftermath of the Chernobyl radiation leaks, the government in Moscow issued advice to those living close to the nuclear power station. They were advised not to drink locally produced milk or eat local butter or cheese, but to use supplies of these sent from Moscow. When interviewed, the affected people said that they ignored this advice, believing it to be some scheme to benefit Moscow and to disadvantage local farmers. They also ignored warnings about eating local mushrooms, again on the grounds that this was devious propaganda. There have been two hints of similar reactions in Britain. When the Conservative government announced that women on high progesterone contraceptive pills were at higher risk of heart troubles than their low progesterone peers, some came off the pills immediately, in spite of advice not to do so. They believed that the increased risk must be high for the announcement to have been made so peremptorily. There was a jump in subsequent pregnancies associated with abrupt cessation of taking the pills. More recently, Belgium announced troubles with food contamination as a result of a chemical mistake. The British government issued a statement saying that no imports to Britain from Belgium had been affected, but nevertheless sales of unaffected paté and chocolate still plummeted.

Central government sets specific targets for regional authorities in health, education, crime, housing, etc., but does not provide the necessary resources. However, if targets are not met, resources may be cut further. So targets have to be met, either by real but devious means or by fixing the books – both of which breed corruption.

⌐ 12.4 Tyranny and the Media

Originally *dictators* were temporary leaders appointed by the Roman republic to counter acute threats to its existence, usually an invasion or rebellion. However, this is not what is meant by the term as commonly used today. 'Tyrant' is not in common use, but its root meaning of an absolute ruler whose powers are not restricted by a constitution is an apposite label for the leaders of a substantial minority of UNO members and will be preferred here. In the twentieth century, most of these have been gifted orators. Tyrannical rule can be achieved and sustained without mass rallies being addressed, but especially those who have been concerned to assert national pride (and launch imperialist military campaigns) have arranged and spoken at such comings together, for example Hitler and Mussolini. Although the Fascist and Soviet societies of the last century were not fully totalitarian, they did not tolerate voiced dissent from party policy, even in the form of jokes and certainly not in constructive criticism. While the speeches of leaders promised a greater and/or brighter future, the listening and reporting of the secret police or its equivalent were also ubiquitous. Children were encouraged to denounce parents, friends to denounce friends. It was not possible to tell who were wolves in sheep's clothing, and who were wolves in wolves' clothing, and it was a matter of life and death to mistake a wolf for a sheep. As already mentioned, it is difficult to imagine such an existence without the benefit of personal experience, even if this last is restricted to being a visiting observer.

Clearly in such societies most survivors have been circumspect about uttering statements that might deviate from the Party line decided by the leader. Two points only will be made here, both referring to Soviet Russia, but at different times. The first concerns the so-called "show trials" of the purges in the 1930s, during which a significant number of government ministers and military leaders made public confessions of being Trotskyites, enemy agents, or otherwise saboteurs of Stalin's Russia. Why weren't such people simply shot – as were many others? One answer would be that these trials were demonstrations of ultimate power. To be able to get such important and committed communists to confess to activities that were clearly incompatible with everything they had worked towards all their lives was an ultimate demonstration of the power of Stalin. In an interpersonal context and with a hint of irony, a similar point was made by Shakespeare in *The Taming of the Shrew* in which Kate signifies her submission to Petruchio by calling the sun the moon or whatever her husband tells her to call it. The issue itself is older than that. The Soviet situation has been the common practice of rulers throughout history, particularly where the political/military orders have combined with a priesthood that has defined the important truths about life and living. It is no coincidence that it was in the democratic and basically secular small cities of Ancient Greece that there was an explosion of hypotheses about almost everything about the world and the human condition. It is not an accident that this chapter began with some Athenian contributions.

The subsequent history of Europe from Rome until the eighteenth century was dominated by alliances of absolute monarchs with church leaders in which what was cited as Christian love was frequently expressed through wars and killings. Conformity to authority signalled preservation and continuity of the status quo, and successfully obliging people to say what they believe to be untrue was an ultimate sign of submissiveness – often prior to killing them, for example The Holy Office of the Inquisition.

The second point arises from demands to conform to the impossible, but relates to central planning and the setting of targets. In the Soviet Union, Moscow set targets for coal and oil production, for tractor manufacturing, for crop yields, for all production. The penalties for not fulfilling targets could be death or labor camps or both. If targets could not be met, then they had to appear to be met, and a world of paper grew up to authenticate these achievements. By the mid-1980s, the discrepancies between the worlds of reality and paper were so great that systems began to break down. Tractors that existed only on paper could not plough fields, and seeds confined to a written existence could not be sown. The infrastructure staggered into collapse. This example of worlds of words becoming detached from their referents in the real world dramatizes what has been noted in the previous sections as a growing tendency about target setting in Britain. Accounting procedures can be devised that show gains, when in reality no gains have been made. School registers can record pupils as present when they are not. Hospitals can fix records on costs per patient. Police can avoid recording crimes to reduce their incidence or collate them conveniently to improve clear-up figures. What the consequences are of such practices for the individuals concerned and for society at large have yet to appear. To date, however, the pertinent social psychological questions have yet to be posed, let alone investigated.

The first feature may not apply to the quasi-democracies, but it is the condition under which millions of human beings continue to live their lives. The second is unlikely on a national scale to apply to federally organized countries, but can certainly afflict centralized ones such as Britain. Recent British governments have boasted of policies of de-centralization, whereas the reality is of de-centralized responsibilities and increasingly centralized powers and resources.

⌐ 12.5   Differential Access to Wisdom and Knowledge

Societies differ in their social structures, but vertical stratification in various forms has always been associated with differences in power, wealth, and/or status. The number of strata and the possibilities of movement for individuals from one to another have differed from time to time and from society to society. The range of hierarchies (for example political, military, religious, judicial, etc.) have also differed in number and complexity, ranging from the ancient absolute power of a single monarch (often in association with a chief religious figure), to the multiple but pyramidally converging structures of capitalist quasi-democracies. If the leaders of these hierarchies are labelled *winners*, then as with war, it must be remembered that it is the winners who write the history and give accounts of the contemporary activities of their society. Historically, those with the power have used it predominantly in the interests of enhancing and sustaining themselves and whomever they have defined as their ingroups or allies. Collectively they have acted to prevent the spread of knowledge of any kind that might have threatened their ascendancy --and in particular ideas that present and offer justifications for alternative divisions of power, wealth and status. So it was. So it is. And so it will continue to be. In Europe there have been various eruptions of ideas questioning the contemporary status quo, notably in Ancient Athens, the early Christianity period, Renaissance Flanders and the Netherlands, and the Enlightenment in pre-Revolutionary France. The relevant ideas and books from these periods now circulate freely in many countries, but that is only a recent phenomenon. How then has language and its use functioned as a device for the suppression of knowledge and ideas and the perpetuation of hierarchies and élites? Five political/military mechanisms can be listed, as can several commercial ones:

1   Prevent or delay the development of a written form of the language. Documents can be copied and circulated. Why have the Irish a cultural foundation mythology of some substance and the English not? Davies (1999) notes that the Irish developed a written version of Celtic, and documents from the relevant period have been handed down and copied. The English druids preserved their power by remaining the source and arbiters of an oral culture, with no independent source of wisdom available to the people.

2   Encode the laws and norms in a language other than the vernacular of the people. In England, from 1066 until the middle of the fourteenth century, the political/legal language was Norman French and the religious language was Latin. Translations of the Bible into English were grounds for persecuting the translators. The Roman Catholic Church retains Latin still. The Vatican has remained the supreme authority of interpretation, in contrast to those Protestant churches that transferred ultimate authority to their readings of their translations of the Bible. Typically (imperial) powers have used laws and regulations expressed in and implemented through their own language to run their empires.

3   Prevent printing and distribution of texts. Censorship by the authorities is a longstanding tradition in Asia and Europe. Pre-Revolutionary Russia

and the post-revolution Soviet Union dictated what could and could not be printed, as have most dictatorships and strong monarchies. More recently, jamming of radio broadcasts from overseas has been a common practice for tyrannies. Throughout history, potential tyrants have acted swiftly to burn books and dispose of libraries, as well as silencing members of any intelligentsia that might interfere with their supremacy.

4   Forbid reading and discussion of texts. Men and their families were transported from the British Isles to Australia for reading Tom Paine's *Rights of Man* and/or holding discussions about such ideas. From the seventeenth century, Roman Catholics were forbidden to read any book on the Index.

5   Ration access to or abolish schools. It is no coincidence that access to schooling has been correlated with changes in social structure and the rights of élites. In England and Wales universal primary education began only in the late nineteenth century. Ethnic separation and language separations have been common practice. The English forbade schooling for Catholic children in Ireland for most of its centuries of occupation. Women have been disadvantaged educationally from the beginnings of civilizations. Social class continues to be the great variable of differentiation, with competency in certain forms of speech and writing still serving as bases for rationing access to and promotion through the educational system – and subsequently the higher ranks of occupational and social system.

6   Control what the media report. Whilst it is universally acknowledged that governments censor the media in times of war (Knightley, 1975), one of the current interesting peacetime oddities is that the Japanese continue to censor history texts of their wars in the 1930s and 1940s. It is not just the massacres and torturing of foreign troops, prisoners and civilians that remain hidden. The mass importation of Korean girls into Japan for sexual exploitation by and for their armed services is still not acknowledged. Denials that the German Nazis tortured and murdered millions of Jews, Slavs, and Gypsies are extraordinary but continue to surface. (This is especially incredible to people like myself, who saw Auschwitz in all its horror before it became partly sanitized as a macabre tourist spectacle.)

Selection and control of media production without formal censorship are ubiquitous (for example Glasgow Media Group 1976), and the points of view adopted are clearly represented in the choice of evaluative nouns and adjectives, verbs, and adverbs employed. "Vicious terrorists slaughter unarmed soldiers" does not convey the same impression as "Undercover agents killed by desperate freedom-fighters." Cerulo (1998) offers an elegant study of how simple variations in sequencing conveys the moral stance of the reporting of violence – and that people react in line with expectations. The active/passive verb contrast can in itself focus intended blame (see 12.2.3 and chapter 14).

7   Concealment of evidence. There are two analytically separable kinds of concealment, one of which was also implicated in the Watergate cover-up. The activities of whistleblowers often relate to companies and other organizations not revealing evidence that they have collected that would have reduced profits or even bankrupted the companies. Litigation against asbestos (but not tobacco) companies has been particularly successful when written evidence could be adduced that the company had known of the dangers of their products, concealed this evidence, and taken no steps to warn possible victims or in any way mitigate the harm being done (Callahan, 1988; Crossen, 1994). Recent dramatic commercial cases have been with asbestos, tobacco, automobiles, and various pharmaceutical and surgical products. Governmental malpractices along the lines of destroying files and other records appear to be universal and endemic (Rose-Ackerman, 1999).

In contrast, commercial organizations that are in competition with each other do not publicize the secrets of their successes for other reasons. If phrases like "*Vorsprung durch technik*" can boost sales of VW Audis, then one may reasonably expect the company to arrange for evaluative studies, but keep the answers to themselves. The research to find out the reasons why particular advertising slogans work or fail will not be published in open journals. We have already mentioned the further complication within the marketing world; advertisers have a strong vested interest in claiming great successes and persuading customers to part with money. Market research companies need to be credible to their companies. The whole field of marketing is setting out a research base of massive academic value to social psychologists, but permissions to tap into it are not likely to be given.

8   Control who has voice. By preventing the broadcasting of alternative views or by discrediting dissidents, those who control the mass media of TV, radio and the press can endeavor to ensure that their interpretations of events prevail. Passing over the strong and clear forms of such censorship, since these are obvious, two more insidious forms can be used to illustrate the device.

On a studio-audience participation program, the radio/TV station might hire a scientific expert to comment on the shape of the earth, which he/she duly does. One question from the audience generates an alternative view that the earth is a flat sheet. After consideration of some other comments, the chair sums up, suggesting that one opinion is as good as another and that the earth's shape remains a matter of dispute. (That is a genuine example.) In this case the potential effect is to trivialize scientific knowledge and elevate uninformed and strange opinions to a defensible status. A variation on the theme is to have experts propound opinions far beyond current evidence. Newspapers are currently replete with reports that unnamed scientists at the University of Nowhere have isolated a gene for almost anything. Evolutionary psychology is currently being cited as a basis for justified raping of females by human males and for females liking to grow vegetables and arrange flowers.

A second device is the one commonly used against whistleblowers by their organization heads, be these political, industrial or commercial. Those who have pointed out dangerous design faults, health risks of marketed products, and forms of corruption are not given access to the media to the same extent as those who try to define the whistleblowers as mad or bad. Further, media persons who try to get at the truth by giving whistleblowers voice are likely to be suppressed (*vide* the efforts of the Washington Post Journalists who persevered with the Watergate cover-ups) or sued (*vide The Guardian* newspaper by Jonathan Aitken, Harding, Leigh, & Palliser, 1999).

More generally and pervasively, the management and owners of the mass media control both who has voice and what is broadcast, and these are increasingly massive joint stock multinational companies. Any idea that such companies have come into existence to service the interests of the general public is just dotty, and should be discarded immediately. The substantive owners and senior managers have personal and group interests that are pursued, both in terms of what is disseminated and how it is presented. What particular profile of power, wealth, status and aspired-to lifestyle underpins the activities of such owners is at their discretion.

It would be cynical and misleading to imply that all media owners and controllers always sacrifice truth, rationality, and informativeness to achieving high audience ratings and maximizing their own returns. Historically, individual owners and employees of particular media are the persons who have campaigned against injustices and have acted as exposers of corruption and deception by authorities, Watergate being but one recent example in the USA. Insofar as the citizenry subscribes to the values of truth and rationality, and agrees as to what constitutes virtuous codes of conduct, then the media can be the primary resource for informing the public about news, history, and other forms of socially-relevant-information and ideas. Unfortunately they are also the primary source for much misinformation. If it is asked whether the forces of service or of violation and exploitation will dominate in the future, the prognostications are not propitious.

Two large-scale recent developments of media companies are relevant: their consolidation into a small number of national multi-media organizations and their diversification into the manufacturing, promoting, and selling of media-related products. More significantly, they control what is relayed about international and national politics and economics. It is not surprising if those who control the media promote their own individual and sectional interests. Such analysis leads naturally to a sympathy with the arguments and evidence advanced about the dangers of such a concentration by McChesney (1999) in *Rich media, poor democracy*. In earlier times the mass media acted to police government, but with the shift in the balance of power towards media corporations and away from government, who is now to police them?

Presentations can be checked for plausibility and rationality via a wide array of questions, and the answers to these can indicate whether wariness can be abandoned or should be maintained or increased. If statements have been made, have they been structurally loaded to indicate responsibility or blame? Are the questions posed answered unequivocally, precisely, concisely, and relevantly? Do arguments offered exemplify any of Thouless' 38 dishonest tricks or Fischer's 121 fallacious moves? (See chapter 11) Is the evidence offered fit for the purpose and sufficient for the case? Are plausible alternative perspectives and accounts aired and shown to be less plausible than the one advanced? What are the likely outcomes of the argument, and who stands to benefit? What happens if one applies the biblical injunction of "By their fruits ye shall know them?

Much could be done to raise standards of presentations before it became necessary to progress to questions that would challenge more fundamental issues such as oversimplification, flawed notions of causality, and lack of understanding of probabilities and statistical distributions! At the present time such critiques appear in communication journals and at social gatherings of the chattering classes, but these do not exert influence over the media. More regulatory conditions could be drawn up and applied to limit the power of the media and their "freedom" to present what they choose and how they chose to represent the relevant realities. To date however, British committees appointed to preserve standards have not acted, even to ensure that advertisements are "truthful, honest, and decent." Reprimands to companies are verbal, fines minimal, sackings non-existent, and restitution to victims derisory – except in high profile libel actions. Just requiring that statements made in news broadcasts meet Grice's maxims would transform reporting. European countries have passed legislation curtailing rights to incite hatred of social groups, but have not enforced these against the media. The USA has accorded primacy to "free speech," whilst permitting prosecutions for "hate" speeches or writing (Leets & Giles, 1997). Will either achieve its ends? McChesney addresses the more serious issue of a small band of media moguls becoming Orwellian Big Brothers, but seems to be overly optimistic about the effects of non-commercial media counter-acting such oligopolies; historically, governments have been the Big Brothers. Now the fraternity is larger.

12.6 Endpiece

The coverage may have been skimpy, but the illustrations probably suffice to trigger realizations that each mechanism referred to could be accompanied by very long lists of examples. Such cases have had very profound consequences for the rise and fall of cultures and the exploitation of their majority and minority members by small elites. As is frequently pointed out, the future is indeterminate, and "liberal progressive" scenarios are no more likely than variants on Orwell's *Nineteen Eighty-Four*. (I suspect that they are much less likely and that the exploitative communicative power of the media will play a critical role in defining realities for most people.) Meanwhile research can proceed and if suitably disseminated may be used beneficially. If this is to happen, then social psychologists will have to begin to widen their methodological horizons, and media studies will have to reduce their incidence of wild generalizations way beyond the empirical evidence to hand. The two might cooperate, to the benefit of all.

13

Representation and Regulation: Their Relevance to Social Class

In chapter 12 there was an upward shift in the level of analysis from the social psychological to the sociological, with illustrations of how considerations of power, wealth, and status come to impact upon the general population via the institutions of politics, commerce, the law, and in particular, the media. The concerns were with such issues as differential access to information through its rationing, selection, and distortion, and the consequences of these. Included at the end was a list of some of the techniques used by those with power to keep those without it in their lowlier positions. Having asserted and argued the case with a reliance on general historical, combined with what might be called common, knowledge it is necessary to pursue at least one example of such social stratification to explicate how such processes operate at the social psychological level. But which group to choose? In some respects gender is the most interesting, in part because so much research has been done on the topic generally and in particular on the ways in which language and its use have acted as determinants and consequents in discrimination. In part it is interesting because the last 50 years have witnessed significant social changes towards equalization of life-chances for women and men. However, with space for only one topic and the extent and quality of the literature, it will have to suffice to reference some recent examples more detailed reading (Coates & Johnson, 2001, Tannen, 1994; Tavris, 1992; Wodak, 1997).

Considerations of complexity as well as space and personal ignorance militate against the selection of ethnicity as the social cleavage to select. With ethnicity's linkage to race easily extendable into questions of mass murder and institutionalized discriminatory exclusions, it is simpler to note that in important ways ethnicity overlaps with social class, and select social class as the category for coverage.

Social class is contrastively interesting in relation to gender partly because although both issues achieved considerable salience in the 1960s as matters where the provision of equal opportunities in education were seen as important necessary conditions for reducing the much lower life-chances of women and the working classes respectively, the implementation of relevant educational and occupational policies and practices were only sustained for females (Robinson, 2001a). Social class disappeared as a research issue in the 1970s in the UK and USA, and has not re-emerged under that title to date. This is in spite of the fact that social stratification has widened in both societies, to the extent that in the UK, the term *underclass* is now being used to refer those trapped in the lowest social stratum in terms of wealth, income, and prospects (Hutton, 1996). Chronic unemployment, drugs, and single-parent families are severally implicated and over-represented in this category. To begin to answer questions about the ways in which language and its use are relevant to these circumstances, it is possible and desirable to refer back to research conducted in the 1960s and earlier. The coverage will be divided into three sections: a synopsis of a variant of Bernstein's views about the linkages between language use, education, and social class, their application to mother–child interaction, and a set of propositions about one set of mechanisms by which schooling perpetuates or accentuates the differentiation between pupils of different social classes.

13.1   Bernstein

Bernstein (see 1961;1971, 1973, 1975) transposed and adapted Whorf's hypothesis (see chapter 14) to link differentiating pragmatic priorities within a single language to social stratification within a society. In essence he argued and adduced empirical evidence for the middle classes being predisposed to orient themselves to the various functions of language as a function of the context of situation, and in particular to utilize the representational function as and when appropriate. In contrast, members of the lower working class were hypothesized as giving undue precedence to the social functions, and in particular to the regulation of behavior and social relations. Since so much of the knowledge necessary for full participation in society is communicated via the representational function, a relative lack of the development and use of this is likely to be predictive of remaining in the lowest stratum of the society. This will be especially true in a school system geared to norm-referenced criteria of success, norm-referenced expectations about development and a norm-referenced view of the distribution of general intelligence. How this can translate into self-fulfilling prophecies has been set down in chapter 10.2.1. Here the concern is with mother–child interaction and the mechanisms by which this may set the scene for differential school achievement if no special steps are taken to equalize opportunities by socializing children into realizing when the situation is one in which the representational function (and learning what it is being used for) is required.

Accounts of the range of studies are published or referenced in the series of books edited by Bernstein and published by Routledge, Kegan Paul under the general title *Primary Socialization, Language, and Education*. With gender and verbal IQ controlled, a factorial sample of five-year-old children was drawn from a larger population so that socio-economic status (SES) differences could be compared. Criteria of occupation and parental education were applied to extract clearly middle (MSES) and clearly lower working (LSES) families. The speech of the children was sampled over a two year period, and they also engaged in a number of recorded activities. Mothers were interviewed at the beginning and end of the research.

13.2 Mother–Child Interactions and the Representational Function

The relevant comparisons are from two contexts, one where one might see communication of information via representational statements to be prioritized – children asking "wh" questions of their mother – and the other where issues of regulation might be expected to be paramount – children being subject to maternal re-actions arising out of various misdemeanors. In accordance with Bernstein's hypotheses, the main predictions were that, relative to MSES mothers, LSES mothers would emphasize regulation and control rather than the provision of information, both in answering "wh" questions and in dealing with misdemeanors situations. As well as representing and regulating, some mothers were clearly teaching their children, and a third category of study was designed to encourage teaching and examine how this was done. It must be held in mind that the categories are not discrete. To answer an inquiry from a child may involve deliberate teaching. To instruct a child efficiently how to play a game will need to involve both the representation of facts and regulation of behavior. In the regulation of behavior an adult may supply information or emphasize instruction. However, other things being equal, children's questions appearing to solicit information about the world require the addressee to attend to representational content, and discipline problems require behavior to be regulated in some way.

13.2.1   Mothers' Answers to Children's Questions

Mothers of 5 year olds were asked how they would answer a number of "why", "who" and "where from" questions, assuming that these had been asked by their child (Robinson & Rackstraw, 1972; Robinson, 1973). Compared with low SES mothers, middle SES mothers were more likely to answer the questions, and to give more, and more accurate, information, with fewer "noisy" irrelevant linguistic extras. More claimed to be concerned about the truth of what they said. They made explicit more similarities and differences among objects and events. In answer to "why" questions, they were less likely to repeat the question as a statement, for example "Because they do" or to make a simple appeal to regularity, for example "Because they always have done." They were more likely to mention causes, consequences, analogies and categorizations. The middle SES mothers appeared to be competent and willing to exploit these opportunities to represent the world as a constellation of persons, objects, and events, related and organized in space and time. Low SES mothers appeared not to use these opportunities to the same extent; in some respects they were containing rather than answering questions, and answering in such ways that follow-up or repeat questions could have been construed as challenges to authority rather than earnest inquiries.

If it is accepted that there are SES differences in the way mothers in fact answer their children's questions, and if these constitute differential learning opportunities for their offspring, then it must be predicted that there will be SES differences in the way children answer similar questions.

Two years after the mothers had been interviewed, their children were asked to answer thirty "wh" questions, the answers to which they might be expected to know. Essentially, the SES differences in the children's answers reflected the maternal differences in both quality and quantity; the simplest explanation for the results is that the maternal data were valid, and that the children had learned in proportion to what had been made available to them. This interpretation is strengthened by the results of a secondary analysis of mother–daughter pairs *within SES* (Robinson, 1973), which yielded significant predictability across the generations.

The final investigation in the series (Robinson & Arnold, 1977) moved to direct observation of mothers and children interacting with each other in response to a variety of familiar and unfamiliar objects. SES differences in both mothers and children were consistent with the earlier results, but the main purpose was to examine within-SES co-variation. Two main indices of child behavior were used: number of information-seeking questions asked of mothers and verbally mediated knowledge offered by the children about the materials presented. Scores on both variables were strongly associated with an index of "provision of cognitive meaning" by the mother, both within and across SES groups. This index included answering questions with semantically appropriate answers, extending such answers beyond the minimal request, and setting them in a context of shared understanding.

How surprising these results are depends upon the initial stance of readers. They would not be so to a psychologist who recognized the simultaneous and complementary utility of Piagetian, Brunerian, associationist, and observational principles of learning. The units of linguistic analysis were semantic and pragmatic rather than syntactic, but this does not mean that they were not linguistic.

13.2.2   Regulation of Children's Behavior by Mothers

Work on the language of apparent maternal control has shown comparable results at the same three levels of analysis: SES differences between mothers in relation to their children; SES differences between children; within-SES mother-child co-variation. Relying on mothers' reports of how they would handle a number of discipline problems such as a spilt drink or a refusal to go to bed, and with the same sample as Robinson & Rackstraw (1972), Cook Gumperz (1973) used a coding frame for analysis that distinguished between three main bases of appeal: imperatives, i.e. *non-verbal means* or *threats* that focused on obtaining compliance but without recourse to explanations; *positional appeals*, i.e. statements that located the reasons for compliance in terms of social status categories of age, sex, or family relations, *personal appeals*, i.e. statements that referred to the behavioral and/or emotional consequences for named persons that would result from non-compliance, e.g. "You will be tired tomorrow." While positional appeals were the most commonly used appeals reported by mothers overall and their incidence did not discriminate between the SES groups, the other two tactics were differentially distributed. Low SES mothers more frequently employed imperatives, a result commonly reported in the literature (see Hess 1970); middle SES mothers were more likely to make personal appeals. Only middle SES mothers used appeals that referred to both the behavioral and associated emotional consequences for the child.

Turner (1973) exploited Halliday's (1975) concept of 'meaning potential' to derive a number of hypotheses about likely SES differences in children's use of language to regulate the behavior of others. His hierarchical taxonomy first separated imperative from positional control, and then divided imperatives into commands and threats. Positional controls were separated into rule giving, disapprobation, and reparation-seeking and further sub-divided into nine, twelve, eight, nine and eleven categories respectively. Each of the forty-nine categories linked specific functions to specific linguistic forms. He was additionally able to cut across and combine categories from this classification to extract options that were "more forceful" and less forceful, explicit and implicit, more specific and less specific. He applied the derived coding frame to speech samples of the same factorial groups of five-year-olds used by Cook-Gumperz and Robinson and Rackstraw and to the 127 of those children from whom similar speech was collected at age seven. The speech analyzed came from stories told by the children in response to a number of questions asked in respect of four-item picture story sequences. In one three boys are kicking a football around in the street. It breaks a window of a house. A man with a shaking fist appears, and the boys run off.

The results are most simply summarized by saying that middle SES children used more specific, explicit and less forceful options; they used more personal appeals referring to the states of participants and fewer imperative commands, threats and verbal punishments. In this sample, with these materials, the regulatory speech of low SES children was significantly different from that of their middle SES peers. (However, although the differences found by Turner were in the direction predicted by Bernstein's thesis, they were also compatible with a developmental lag hypothesis.) In this case no subsequent search was made for direct associations between the speech of children and that of their mothers, either within or between SES groups.

For the third aspect of linkage, it is necessary to switch to data from the United States. Bearison and Cassel (1975) utilized reports of mothers of six- to seven-year-old children as to how they would handle the child control problems used by the Bernstein group in order to classify them as relatively position-oriented or person-oriented. They predicted that children of mothers who used a relatively high proportion of person-oriented appeals would be more adaptable and versatile communicators than those of the other mothers. They tested this by having the children teach another child how to play a simple board game, having first taught the child how to play by a non-verbal modelling technique. Each child did this twice, once for a sighted and once for a blindfolded listener. Their protocols were scored against five measures: the amount of information relayed, the incidence of inadequate referents (i.e. terms that could not be decoded by a listener), the number of words, the number of verbally explicit referents, and the number of vague gestural referents. The major predicted interaction was supported: the increment in verbal description scores from the sighted to the blindfolded listener condition was greater for the children of person-oriented mothers; these children additionally manifested a greater decrement in gestural encoding, i.e. encoding that relied on the observer being able to see what the child could see and was doing.

13.2.3   Mothers as Instructors

Some years earlier, Hess & Shipman (1967) had mothers of different SES groups teach their four-year-old children how to sort blocks varying on two of four possible dimensions of variation and how to cooperate in the etching of five patterns on an "Etch-a-Sketch" machine. Frequencies of various categories of maternal activities related both back to SES and forward to variations in the behavior of the children. For example, control strategies appealing to power ("Because I say so") were more frequently used by low SES mothers, whereas those appealing to reasoning and feeling were relatively more common among middle SES mothers (see Cook-Gumperz, 1973). The latter form of control was positively associated with successful sorting of blocks by the child. Although middle SES mothers did not give more information than low SES mothers when teaching their children how to sort the blocks, they did indulge in more attempts at motivating and orienting, they demanded a higher ratio of verbal to physical responses from their children, they required more specifically discriminatory speech, and they gave more positive than negative reinforcement ("knowledge of results" should have been the term used). Four of these variables predicted success at sorting by the children.

Similar associations were found on the Etch-a-Sketch task. Use by the mothers of precise and specific verbal instructions during practice and production periods and showing the children the designs to be copied gave a multiple correlation of 0.64 (N=140) with an assessment of success in copying the target designs. Adding SES and intelligence test scores of both mothers and children into the predictive equation increased this correlation by 0.03 only, and on their own these three correlated 0.47 with assessed success. The teaching tactics and not the SES or IQ of the child or the mother were the important variables. Hess & Shipman also suggest that the quantitative results reported miss essential qualities discriminating between the SES groups, of which one of the most important was the apparent "lack of meaning in the communication system between mother and child" in the lowest SES group. Neither did the interaction have the warmth of phatic communion, since the low SES children were frequently reprimanded for not succeeding.

Hartmann and Haavind (1981) developed the design, materials and procedures of Hess & Shipman, and dropped the SES contrast. In the first place they demonstrated that mothers used the same techniques to teach their own child and an age peer. For the main study the investigators taught mothers how to play a board game and then had them teach a slightly younger child of a relative or friend how to play. The experimenters meanwhile taught the mother's child how to play the game, observing reactions during the teaching. In this way they separated possibly misleadingly high co-variations resulting from observing mother and child interacting. Informing, anticipating, demonstrating of alternatives, mentions of the competitive character of the game, emotional support, infrequency of giving orders, infrequency of restriction, and infrequency of imperative feedback by mothers correlated positively with planning, decision-making, rule-mastery, alertness, involvement, activity, and absence of task-irrelevant behavior in their own children in the independent but identical learning situation.

Hartmann (2001) has now replicated this research some 30 years on with 30 of the original children (C1) who are themselves now mothers (M2) of six- to eight-year-old children (IC2). The various correlations within and across samples are impressively stable. Summing the aspects listed in the last paragraph to yield a maternal tutorial score and child learning score yields the following correlations:

1 M1 r C1 = .61, M2(C1) r C2 = .53
2 M1 r M2 = .46
3 C1 r C2 = .36

The effects of maternal tutoring styles remain constant across the generations. How mothers taught their daughters correlates highly with the ways the daughter/mothers tutor their children, and the learning patterns of the two sets of children are likewise correlated. The results are a remarkable indication of intergenerational continuities, with the corollary that for those who were were learning least as children have not been helped to do better for their own children in the respects studied here.

While Haavind and Hartmann did not make direct tests of hypotheses derived from explicit theories of learning or instruction, they demonstrated that mothers can differ in the efficiency with which they combine verbal and non-verbal means of instruction and that these have consequences for the learning by their children.

13.2.4   Summary and Conclusions

For the verbal mediation of both representational knowledge and the regulation of behavior, the results are remarkably similar. There are differences as well as similarities between mothers of middle and low SES children in what they report they communicate to their five-year-olds. These reported differences correspond to what has been observed directly in other studies. The reported and observed differences in the behavior of the mothers are *reflected* in the speech of the children, once allowance has been made for the generally lower level of complexity in the children's speech. However, these differences have also been shown to occur within SES. Thus, it is what mothers say and do that is relevant to the children and not their SES membership. In summary, the children's speech is most parsimoniously explained in terms of differential opportunities to learn through observation, with the learning being conceived of as an active rather than a passive process. Such an account does not explain why, generally speaking, there is a tendency for middle SES mothers to behave differently from low SES mothers, but that is beyond a frame of reference that has to account for similarities and differences among children.

Such differences as there are between the orientations and emphases of researchers who have worked from linguistic interests in variations in maternal input and those who began with SES differences have not precluded their arrival at mutually consistent conclusions about the identification of some of the factors likely to facilitate development of proficiency with the representational forms language in young children. Perhaps the main common ground lies in the demonstrated relevance of mothers taking steps to establish and maintain effective communication in conversation with their children, whilst simultaneously making and taking opportunities to stretch the child's communicative competence by offering ideas and speech somewhat in advance of his understanding (Robinson & Arnold 1977). Such extended conversations were clearly found to be associated with accelerated development in both formal lexico–grammatical features and such activities as the number and structural complexity of questions asked or the range and type of meanings expressed in statements regulating the behavior of others. Likewise the results of Hess & Shipman (1967) and Hartmann and Haavind (1981) point to the importance of systematic structuring of instructional speech in relation to the relevant tasks and they have also highlighted characteristics that should render discriminations easier and materials more readily assimilable.

However, simply reporting quantitative differences in speech features between social classes and among individuals may be obscuring a qualitative difference in orientations and dispositions to facilitate development of (and enjoy interaction with) one's children. The construal of situations as affording the use of the representational function of language is a prerequisite of such activities. The provision of the kind of propositional information to young children by some of the mothers was equipping children with information and principles from which they could form their own judgements in other and subsequent situations. The kinds and amounts of information were clear learning opportunities, even though not always formulated as teaching, and the consequences of this were evident in their children. Such policies and practices are in fact also correlated with reading to children which in turn is related to children learning to read, which in turn relates to learning to write, with the development of these last two skills being driven by the children not the adults (see Wells, 1985; Wood, 1998).

13.3 Commentary

Along with many other findings, those assembled here should have had a profound influence on the policies and practices in education for any society that was concerned to promote equality of opportunity for young children entering its school system, but that is not the issue of immediate relevance here. What will be raised are the possible consequences for the development of persons exposed to different language-mediated socialization practices. There are issues of general communicative interest, such as persons checking for the understanding of the other when formulating messages, both to ensure an initially shared basis and a continuing checking on the extent of understanding of the new, with some mothers observing such rules for efficient communication much more than others. However, the focus will be restricted to a speculative consideration of the long-term effects of the three kinds of control and the extended answering of questions.

What might a child or adult learn from non-verbal means of control? Assuming that those being controlled are problem-solvers, then to minimize costs (punishments etc.) and maximize benefits (rewards), they need to work out the rules that are determining rewards and punishments, calculate how they might be applied to any situation, and act accordingly.

The calculations will work only so long as the contingencies do not change. Consideration for others is irrelevant, and so are questions of truth and logical consistency.

For positional appeals, two aspects need to be distinguished, first the type of position and second the rationale for its justification. Rules about gender can last for a lifetime. Rules about family might do so. Rules for an age category apply for defined periods only. These last are common in socialization, and many have durations of a year, for example five-year-olds. All of these are therefore up for challenge each birthday. None of them require any thinking to apply, since they all relate to the social identity characteristics of the individual and not to the individuality or situation, or to consequences for others. They may of course contain situational and other kinds of limitation built into their specification, but that simply requires matching rule to context. There is no rationale for the rules, and presumably any questions about such rules may simply be met with appeals to authority; it is likely to be the authority of the institutional framework rather any other type of morality that is invoked.

For personal appeals, it is most informative to take an idealized (etic) example, just to illustrate the possibilities. "If you don't go to bed now, you will be tired in the morning, and that means you'll be grumpy and won't eat your breakfast. That will annoy me and spoil my breakfast. Your father will be angry with me that I didn't make you go to bed, etc." The possibilities are wide, even open-ended! What is available for learning? First, it is consequences for individuals as individuals that are invoked. Second, persons other than the self are included. Third, the consequences refer to both states and behavior. Fourth, a reflective recipient might spot a general principle of "Don't cause trouble to yourself or others unnecessarily!" underpinning the message. This last has possibilities of transfer to all situations for the rest of life; it can be re-formulated as a question to ask about any action being considered. If accepted, the person has to calculate what will happen as a result of action decisions, but in terms of moral principles rather than cost–benefit analysis.

An enterprising developmental psychologist might immediately be tempted to relate these via some additional arguments to schemes such as Kohlberg's stages of moral development (Kohlberg, 1969), with the non-verbals combined with promises or threats being predictive of sticking at Stages 1 and 2, positional appeals linking to a ceiling at Stage 4, and personal appeals having possibilities of moving to Stages 5 or 6. A more circumspect approach would ask about the mix of the three, in so far as socializing agents are unlikely to use only one type and can change the mix as children grow older. In the adult world, one can see the three strands at work in society. Since 1979, both the governments of the USA and UK have constructed a rhetoric that appeals to "market forces" as justifications for an occupational wage structure that rewards elite ingroups and minimizes benefits for outgroups, within a value system that emphasizes extrinsic rather intrinsic motivation as the dominant incentive for work; only fools and horses work – except to maximize wealth, income, and prestige, and the pleasures that result from the exercise of these. The administrative and judicial systems work on positional appeals, with occasional exceptional cases. A cooperative community requires a strong component of the third kind of reasoning.

Whether this kind of analysis has a core of sense that is worth pursuing is not within the current remit, but it can be noted how language is functioning in the three strands. Its only relevance to the reward/punishment strand is through the performatives (F6) and their realizations, and whatever role it can play in the necessary calculations. Its main role in the second is in codifying the bureaucracy and implementation of conduct regulation, a constellation of prescriptions and proscriptions focused on regulation of behavior (F3b). In the third, the representational function (F7) serves to inform and provide a rationale for the moral principles relevant to the reflective decision-making resulting in self-regulation in the interests of self, others, and the community (F2a & b, F3a & b, F5).

The differential handling of "wh" questions provides an interesting complement to this analysis. Put simply, the most efficacious ways of answering appear to stimulate curiosity and the learning that results from this. Learning based on intrinsic motivation can be contrasted with learning related to external incentives of various types of reward or punishment. This meshes more readily with personal appeals than the other two. The use of the appropriate combination in the family and the educational system should help to develop that self-reliant but cooperative agentive general problem-solver that figures in the putative aims of the governments of the quasi-democracies. The master key for opening up this prospect would appear to lie in the use made of the representational forms of language for its transparent representational function.

CHAPTER 14

Five Theories and a Representation-as-Default Thesis

⌐ 14.1 Introduction

Many of those of us schooled in the natural sciences were probably surprised by our socialization into psychology. At school in zoology, I was told that intelligent observation was the key skill to develop for describing and explaining animal behavior; observe what the creatures are doing, when, where, with whom, and how – and try to work out why. Watch and listen! Interpretive hypotheses were to be checked against further observation and, if feasible, sensible experimentation. The dynamic dialectic between observation on the one hand and description with explanation on the other was to be controlled ultimately by the observations. (The writing of this provokes memories of watchings and wonderings about the nature of the honeybee dance and the feasibility of tracking them from hive to food destination – follow that bee!)

In contrast, undergraduate psychology insisted on the primacy of experimentation, mainly with rats, to test hypothetico–deductive theories from which falsifiable hypotheses could be derived. Hull's (1943) majestic theory of learning was one ideal, replete as it was with quantifications in its equations. Theories of shape recognition were another, notwithstanding the fact that in their natural environment vision is not a prime sense for the rat, and the clicks of the apparatus and the smells humans created handling materials were ignored as possible stimuli, by the experimenters if not the rats. In like manner, ideals in social psychology were of similar theories and experimental manipulations. As undergraduates, none of our practicals involved any observations of extra-laboratory people, and it would be interesting to see the results of surveys conducted about extra-lab person-observing in current undergraduate practicals.

Just as experiments cited in this volume are generally confined to topics where both casual and systematic field observations have preceded, so the exposition of theories has been contained to those with solid connections to language use in the extra-laboratory world. Grand explanatory theories which are so general and abstract that they have lost touch with the mundane have not been included. Theoretical concepts and investigated hypotheses have been used as a basis for building up from observations to synthesizing theoretical frameworks, as in NVC for example. For language use, Brown and Levinson's Politeness Theory (1987/1978) and Grice's (1975/1989) maxims have been cited frequently, and it is apposite at this stage to present other theoretical contributions that have been useful for the stimulation and synthesis of relevant work.

Two expectancy theories have each focused on particular domains: M. Burgoon's Language Expectancy Theory (LET) on suasory forms (persuasion) and the conditions under which they are influential, and J. Burgoon's Expectancy Violations Theory (EVT) seeks to explain and predict conditions mediating positive and negative deviations from normative communications. Both have been built up from field studies and experiments. Both have maintained connections between behavior and explanations (J. Burgoon & M. Burgoon, 2001). Likewise, Giles' Communication Accommodation Theory (Shepard, LePoire, & Giles, 2001) has been developed to accommodate to the empirical results obtained. Under what conditions do interlocutors become more similar or more different in which of their communicative acts – and why? As will be seen, these questions grew enormously in scope.

All three are concerned with speech in action; the Burgoons' selecting L's reactions as their primary target, while Giles has paid attention to S and L together in extended exchanges and considered them in terms of both personal and social identity.

Neither of the further two theories considered is immediately concerned with inter-action. Both are interested in how language and its use structures experience. Semin and Fiedler's Linguistic Category Model (1991) selects the limited domain of interpersonal verbs and adjectives, categorises them in terms of interpretive implications, and checks the cognitive consequences. Whorf (1956) aspired to a comprehensive story about the influence of language structure on human experience. It is included partly because it is an example of a grandiose aspiration which, although it suffered from serious misinterpretations, was nevertheless productive. Latterly its main thesis has been clarified and examined in a strong empirical study (Lucy, 1992a; 1992b). The main reason for including it is that it does raise fundamental questions about the relationships between modes of representation and the workings of the human mind.

Likewise, the Representation-as-Default Hypothesis re-visits the issue of what people are doing with what appear to be statements of fact. It sets out questions arising out of the long-used separation of social and non-social functions of language, and the peculiar neglect of the relations between the two. The last of the pre-Socratic philosophers for whom fragments of his thinking remains is Protagoras (Plato, 1991). He was alert to the dangers of analytic separations that do not return to integrate the whole subsequently. In different ways and different areas, Plato and Aristotle made analytic separations that have lived distinctive lives since their time. Plato's takeover of Socrates' focus on truth and relationships between statements and reality led by default to a neglect of language in and as action. With Aristotle's double division of logic into formal and practical reasoning and language into grammar and rhetoric, the scene was set for an unnecessary and unfortunate formal and informal curriculum that can still be found today. These concepts have changed since those days, but the social, action-oriented, practical reasoning, rhetorical functions of language disappeared from academic attention from the late sixteenth to the twentieth century, and the articulation of the functions and structures remains relatively unrefined and under-researched still – as this text exemplifies too well! Discourse Analysts in particular have tried to challenge some of the analytic separations (Potter and Wetherell, 1987).

The Representation-as-Default Hypothesis is a mild excursion into these challenges and a reminder of Protagoras and his pragmatism, and asks what the consequences are of erecting the social functions to the default status in studies of language use. As will be seen, this is not a bid for a social constructivist hegemony or a dictatorship of discourse, but an attempt to explore an alternative perspective to achieve a more balanced view.

14.2.   Language Expectancy Theories

Expectations/expectancies are infinitely variable in terms of possible classifications, but Language Expectancy Theory (LET) and Expectancy Violations Theory (EVT) have each focused on limited domains.

Language Expectancy Theory (LET)

LET was first rendered explicit by M. Burgoon and Miller (1985) and was most recently reviewed by Burgoon and Burgoon (2001). LET has focused on language use in persuading others (F3) and self (F2) and in resisting persuasory attempts. People of any culture in any society have expectations and views about the efficacy and propriety of persuasory acts and these are determined and in part shaped by cultural values and standards. Attitudinal or behavioral reactions to messages intended to influence people can be within or outside the band width of expectations and the reactions can be positive or negative – that is in line with or contrary to the advocacy. Whilst attitude change has been a significant topic in social psychology, especially since the inspirations of the work of the Yale school (Hovland, Janis, & Kelley, 1953; Hovland, Lumsdaine, & Sheffield, 1949), the forms of language used have not been foregrounded as a significant factor *per se*, and the focus in earlier work was mainly on achieving change in particular directions, rather than in asking about the general conditions under which what happened and why. M. Burgoon demonstrated the role that expectances can play in a succession of investigations that showed, for example, that females using aggressive verbal forms reduced their efficacy relative to males for whom such forms were seen as within the band width of expectations. For females, the use of verbally aggressive appeals was judged as improper. It may be noted that if proprieties are differentially linked to particular social categories, this militates against some groups having societal influence whilst allowing others extraordinary powers, for example presidential powers exemplified in Nixon's switch of US policy to China and Reagan's U-turn on the "evil empire" of the Soviet Union. Burgoon and Burgoon (2001) have summarized Michael Burgoon's position with nine propositions and the derived research is now heavily involved in the reduction of tobacco and substance use, and in-sun safety behavior.

Proposition 1: People develop cultural and sociological expectations about language behaviors which subsequently affect their acceptance or rejection of persuasive messages.

Proposition 2: Use of language that negatively violates societal expectations about appropriate persuasive communication behavior inhibits persuasive behavior and either results in no attitude change or changes in position opposite to that advocated by the communicator.

Proposition 3: Use of language that positively violates societal expectations about appropriate persuasive communication behavior facilitates persuasive effectiveness.

Proposition 4: People in US society have normative expectations about the level of fear arousing appeals, opinionated language, language intensity, sequential message techniques, and compliance-gaining attempts varying in instrumental verbal aggression appropriate to persuasive discourse.

Proposition 5: Highly credible communicators have the freedom (wide band width) to select varied language strategies and compliance-gaining techniques in developing persuasive messages, while low credible communicators must conform to more limited language options and compliance-gaining messages if they wish to be effective.

Proposition 6 : Because of normative impacts of source credibility, high credible sources can use low intensity appeals and more aggressive compliance-gaining messages than low credible communicators using either strong or mild language or more pro-social compliance-gaining strategies.

Proposition 7: Communicators perceived as low credible or those unsure of their perceived credibility will usually be more persuasive if they employ appeals low in instrumental verbal aggression or elect to use more pro-social compliance-gaining message strategies.

Proposition 8: People in this society have normative expectations about appropriate persuasive communication behavior which are gender specific such that (a) males are usually more persuasive using highly intense persuasive appeals and compliance-gaining message attempts, while (b) females are usually more persuasive using low intensity appeals and unaggressive compliance-gaining messages.

Proposition 9: Fear arousal that is irrelevant to the content of the message outlining the harmful consequences of failure to comply with the advocated position mediates receptivity to different levels of language intensity and compliance-gaining strategies varying in instrumental verbal aggression such that (a) receivers aroused by the induction of irrelevant fear or suffering from specific anxiety are most receptive to persuasive messages using low intensity and verbally unaggressive compliance-gaining attempts but unreceptive to intense appeals or verbally aggressive suasory strategies.

Michael Burgoon with Miller (1985) reviewed the coverage of the theory in relation to issues of appeals based on fear, opinionatedness, and their extremity/intensity, and later extended this to compliance-gaining research (see chapter 7.5.1). He argues that although LET emerged from a synthesis of earlier work, its propositional format gives it predictive powers that will ensure a linked dialectic between empirical evidence and theory of the kind recogniZed as a virtuous interdependence in the introduction to this chapter.

Expectancy Violations Theory (EVT).

EVT can also be summarized in propositional form (Burgoon & Burgoon 2001, p. 95) and differs from LET in its targets of emphasis rather than its underlying principles. With less emphasis on conditions for compliance and more on attitudes *per se*, with more concern for the operation of non-verbal factors (especially violations – see chapter 10) and a stronger focus on the reward valence of highly regarded communicators, the many experiments and field studies within its compass have covered judgments across a wide range of interpersonal and intercultural phenomena, including lying, sexual harassment, guilt or innocence of defendants, attitudes to health professionals, and marital satisfaction. The five claims are:

1   Expectancies do guide behavior and have persistent effects on interaction.

2   Communicator reward valence exerts both main and interaction effects on communication patterns and outcomes such that;

a   highly regarded communicators (for example those having higher socio-economic status, reputed intelligence and expertise, purchasing power, physical attractiveness, similarity to partner, or giving positive feedback) elicit more involved and pleasant communication from interaction partners and receive more favorable post-interaction evaluations (for example on credibility, attractiveness, and persuasiveness) than those who are poorly regarded; and

b   actors with higher reward valence have more favorable meanings ascribed to their non-verbal behavior than those with lower reward valence.

3   Some violations, such as deviations from normative conversational distances and use of touch, are ambiguous or polysemous and susceptible to reward valence moderating their effects; other violations, such as gaze aversion and substantial increases or decreases in conversational distance have fairly consensual social meanings that directly affect their status as positive or negative violations

4   Non-verbal violations heighten attention and create orienting responses.

5   Non-verbal violations often (though not always) alter responses relative to confirmations such that positive violations produce more desirable communication patterns and outcomes, and negative violations produce less desirable ones, then behavioral confirmations.

As well as organizing and synthesizing results in its own domain, EVT has helped to spawn two further theories: Interaction Adaptation Theory (J. Burgoon, Stern, & Dillman, 1995) rivalling CAT (see next section) in its concern to predict and explain stylistic adaptations of participants in dialogues, supplementing expectations with desires and requirements, and

Interpersonal Deception Theory (Buller & J. Burgoon, 1996) whose title indicates its domain of coverage.

14.3   Communication Accommodation Theory (CAT)

SAT (Speech Accommodation Theory), out of which CAT grew, began life as a succession of field studies and experiments that illustrated adjustments in speech style as a function of interlocutor. *Convergence* was used to refer to speech of L becoming more like that of S, *divergence* less like. Changes were interpreted as signalling motivation to increase or decrease the approval or liking by the other. In respect of convergence this was shown to be so in respect of pausing, utterance length, speech rates, accents, and even language spoken (see Giles & Powesland, 1975, for an introduction). An extreme example of this last was displayed in an interview on Canadian TV in which a French-speaking interviewee switched to English at the same time as his English-speaking interviewer switched to French. The phenomena appear in both interpersonal and intergroup encounters. As noted in chapters 5 and 8, social distance can refer to differences in status and power as well as familiarity and closeness, and both upward and downward convergence and divergence occur. This skeletal outline does not begin to do justice to the breadth or depth of the developing ideas, nor does it indicate the large number of studies arising from them. Shepard, Giles, and LePoire (2001) provide the most recent review of CAT in which they add to the reasons why people might converge, diverge, or not shift at all. They note, as LET and EVT would imply, that there is a band width of adjustments beyond which the other person might become wary of or surprised by the behavior of S and begin to consider alternative hypotheses. If convergence is too extreme, doubts about sincerity may arise. Increasingly too there has been expansion in the kinds of accommodation studied, upwards versus downwards, part-full-crossover, narrow versus wide, uni-modal versus multi-modal, symmetrical versus asymmetrical, and objective versus subjective.

The heuristic value of SAT and CAT has been considerable, and the incremental expansion into the areas of social identity and the socio-historical contexts in which issues of identity have been realized in linguistic phenomena and beliefs about and attitudes towards these have enlarged its scope geographically and historically. The ideas have been investigated to the benefit of understanding in many contexts, (for example the media, business, courtrooms, classrooms); its relevance to intergroup communication has incorporated interability, intercultural, and intergenerational adaptations.

As its primary author notes, it differs from LET and EVT in its concern with motivation; it draws attention to one or more levels and to the types of reasons *why* people adjust their speech to others. LET and EVT focus on Ls' reactions, CAT on S's motivation. They meet in the non-verbal and verbal qualities of S–L interaction. That said, neither SAT nor CAT proceed to a further stage and examine *why* S wishes to gain or reduce the approval or affection of L, and studies have not utilized to the full the accounts of S and L as to the reasons underlying Ss' behavior and Ls' reactions to it. One of the early findings in this connection were the relationships between character attributions and accents in Britain. The highest prestige accents were seen as indicative of expertise, presumably because of perceived connections between accent and amount of education rather than social stratum or origin. The lowest in prestige were seen as indicative of trustworthiness. How then are politicians to present themselves to an electorate? Would they rather be seen as untrustworthy but competent or incompetent but trustworthy? Analyses of voices of the most successful British politicians over the last 50 years would probably reveal that expertise is primary on the way up the political ladder, but once established, vocal indicators of greater trustworthiness begin to appear or re-appear. The same dilemma has applied to commercial financial service enterprises seeking to lure people's savings into their funds. In England these have played the Scottish card with accents and other stereotypical characteristics presumed to be indicative of canniness with cash combined with Presbyterian honesty.

As with other forms of professionalized impression management, simulations of being both expert and trustworthy should last only so long as they reflect reality, but people's faith in such stereotypes appear to have inertia well beyond their demonstrated loss of validity.

SAT/CAT is also now of sufficient longevity to have some of the instantiations but not the principles of its propositions changed. In particular, what has come to be called Estuarine English, allegedly indicative of coastal London overspill into Essex and Kent, has risen in its status; celebrity status in one's field of expertise becoming sufficient to do away with upward convergence. The new rich and successful are retaining their regional and/ or ethnic accents, just as radio and TV have diversified regionally and ethnically. An Oxford accent is probably a bar to being selected as a newsreader in twenty-first century Britain. It is therefore an opportune time to repeat some of the relevant studies referred to by Giles and Powesland (1975), with a view to checking the hypothesis of *plus ça change, plus c'est la même chose*, at a significant psychological level with some formal phonetic reversals.

14.4   Linguistic Category Model (LCM)

Semin and Fiedler (1991) make reference to the Sapir–Whorf Hypothesis in their review of the characteristics and success of LCM, and although it was constructed to account for links between linguistic forms, their (associative) meanings, and the cognitive consequences of these forms and meanings within a single language, some of its results are neat examples of the operation of Whorf's key idea. The model also helps to explicate various biases in human attributions. It therefore provides a clear example of language-based theorizing linking to the behavior of its users.

Semin and Fiedler initially developed a categorization system for person adjectives (ADJ) and interpersonal verbs (V) that differentiated between verbs referring to: State (SV), State Action (SAV), Interpretive Action (IAV) and Descriptive Action (DAV). They classified the cognitive properties of each, and then set out their expectations for the differential use of these for attribution processes (including biases), intergroup relations, and cognitive processes, including memory. Fiedler and Semin ranked DAV, IAV, SV, ADJ in that order from low to high on five properties: how revealing the focal quality is and how enduring; how much disagreement the statement would be likely to generate; how difficult it is to verify the statement; and how little it reveals about the situation. They suggested that each reflects the dimension of concrete to abstract. (Why this labelling is preferred to particular–general is not evident to me.) Semin and Fiedler checked the validity of their assumptions utilizing a principal component analysis of respondent's ratings of exemplifying verbs in each category, and found evidence of a concrete–abstract factor. Including SAV as well as SV verbs in a further study and adding questions about inferences that could be drawn about affect and causality of the subject and object of each statement; in a factor analysis of the data these inferences defined a second factor. When associated personal adjectives were subsequently subdivided into the same categories as the verbs in terms of their constituent morphemes, results were found that showed the IAV, SAV, and SV adjective equivalents more closely followed the subject/object inference pattern rather than the concrete–abstract component.

Here further reference will be confined to what became known as *implicit verb causality*. If Jim helped John, participants are likely to treat Jim as causally implicated, whereas if Jim dislikes John, features of John are more likely to be causally implicated, at least in the absence of additional information. The "Agent–Victim" pairing fits the first but not the second. Elsewhere (chapter 12) reference is made to the way active and passive sentence structures are differentially linked to causation and blame. Comparable arguments obtain with the actions verbs IAV and SAV, in contrast to SV verbs. Most of the many attribution experiments have treated language as a transparent medium through which causality can be studied, but this is not valid. How questions are framed affects outcomes, and this includes the categories of interpersonal verbs used. Both Au (1986) and Fiedler et al. (1990) have shown that if participants are asked to infer consequences rather than causes, action verbs are rated to imply consequences for the Object (O) not the Subject (S), whereas state verbs imply consequences for S not O. Fiedler et al. argue that it is the discourse contexts inferred which bias the selection of the significance of the verb. In other studies, characterized particularly by imaginative manipulations, Semin, Fiedler, and their colleagues have shown how the fundamental attribution error (Ross, 1977) the actor–observer bias (Jones & Nisbett, 1972) and the ego-centric bias (Ross & Sicoly, 1979) can be related to their Linguistic Category Model. Comparable results are found when questions are shifted from the personal/individual level to intergroup relations, in respect of ingroup favouritism/ingroup/outgroup distinctiveness, outgroup denigra-tion, and ingroup heterogeneity/outgroup homogeneity, which together embrace much of the work on stereotypy. For those who like to see social psychology retaining its links with the extra-laboratory world, it is gratify-ing to see LCM applied to the Palio racing in Siena (Maass et al., 1989) and extended to attributions for football outcomes intra-nationally and inter-nationally (Maass et al. 1995, 1996).

LCM has a treble relevance, as Fiedler and Semin appreciate. It has value in its own right as a basis for examining relationships between language structuring, language use, and cognitive processing, but it also has impor-tant implications for data collection in social psychology more generally. It raises questions of the extent to which the findings obtained in person perception, event interpretation, and intergroup phenomena have been structured by the verbal forms of the questions posed to respondents. Con-versation and discourse analysts were early critics of the oddities and un-realistic nature of some of the questions posed and the response options allowed in abbreviated and emasculated vignettes (Antaki, 1994). Whilst Heider's (1958) insightful observations about human beings making causal attributions to moving geometric figures were interesting and plausible, these could not be sensibly extended with simple closed questions to com-plex events, where "reasons" rather than "causes" would have been a more natural way of talking about such matters in any case. Hilton (1991) ex-emplifies this with his conversational model of causal attributions, but this also has limitations (see Antaki, 1994). Thirdly, as noted at the beginning of the chapter, the experiments targeting psychological processes look to have provided elegant support for a variant on the Whorf hypothesis and will perhaps encourage others to exploit variations in particular intra-linguistic structures to examine links with psychological processing, much as early work exploited lexical labelling to influence perceptual judgments (Carmichael, Hogan, & Walters, 1932). These ideas are expanded in section 14.5.

⌐ 14.5   Linguistic Relativity and the Whorfian Hypothesis

In chapter 4 it was observed that unaided human experience of the "real" world is limited by the ranges of our sense organs. Our perceptual world lacks the variety of smells so important to dogs and dogfish. The sonar apparatus of bats define a world for them beyond our capacities. For human beings, it is very difficult and tedious to try to view wooden tables as mainly spaces with a variety of molecules holding together the table shape. Switching down to a sub-atomic level and then re-creating the table is beyond the imaginative picturing of the human mind. We can marvel at the technologically-based extension of our sensory powers via microscopy and telescopy and via X-ray crystallography and MR scans, but these levels of acuity are not useful for habitual human activities. As Rosch and Mervis (1975) and Rosch (1978) argued and illustrated, both our psychology and our language utilize "basal" categorizations. Chairs are more frequent referents than furniture or Chippendale dining chairs, potatoes more frequent than staple carbohydrate, root vegetable, or King Edward's. These basal levels are not defined by level of structural analysis, but by customary utility. Just as human beings can switch their sensory conceptualizations and experience with the aid of technology, so they can switch their conception of a chair from something to sit on to a source of heat, a weapon, or an umbrella.

But how are the conceptualizations related to language and languages? Do the structural characteristics of the language of a culture set limits to the habitual modes of the thinking of members of that culture? The fast thinker will immediately detect many more similar questions to this by substituting other adjectives for "structural," "culture," "limits," "habitual" and "thinking," and by wondering how being multilingual is relevant. But Whorf (1956 – original writings 1927–1941) was the prime mover in investigating the question as posed, and that will be the point of departure adopted here, although a number of observations in earlier chapters have some relevance to the specific and general issues.

In chapter 5 brief mention was made of NVC rules and conventions differing across cultures, and the observation was made that, in the absence of accurate information and an awareness that much NVC is culturally conventional rather than biologically specified, members of a particular culture or subculture were prone to evaluate the NVC of other cultures in terms of deviations from their own conventions, and for these evaluations to be negative. If culture A has conventions about the frequency of making eye contact in dyadic conversations, then a culture A member is likely to judge a culture B person whose norms are for more frequent (habitual) eye contact as being too friendly or too intrusive whereas a culture C person whose culture has a norm for a low frequency is likely to be judged as unfriendly or evasive. Ingroup biases may be applied to whole languages and certain varieties of a language as well as to NVC systems, one's own language being taken as the standard of what is sensible or proper.

In chapter 12, eight ways in which power elites can exploit language to maintain and enhance their power over the rest of their societies were listed. Some of these function to prevent people from having access to texts that would present conceptions of societies less differentiated in power, wealth and status than the ones they are in. The texts can be in non-vernacular languages, people can be excluded from literacy, books and people can be burned – and have been. Questions about these matters are related to that posed by Whorf, and certainly the power elites have long believed and acted upon assumptions about language access and power.

That different languages do not share conceptual mappings is quickly experienced in learning foreign languages. The Portuguese *brio* and *saudade* do not fit with comparable categories of English. English itself is remarkable for its recognition of its own limitations with its borrowings from other languages: *élan*, *Schadenfreude*, *mañana*, *karma*, *yin* and *yang*, etc. As a colleague once remarked, with a double irony that he missed, its richness and piracy is to be wondered at, and it is not surprising that it has become the global lingua franca. These borrowings are lexical/semantic. Grammatical failures at mappings can be more tortuous as Whorf (1956) demonstrated with Hopi. Japanese pronunciation would not have the strong differentiating stress features of the English utterance. Agent actions and causes have less prominence than in English; events unfold and flow. Unable to exchange more than pleasantries in Japanese, I tried, with bilingual Japanese, on occasions to converge conceptually via an abandonment of the SVO sequence typical of English structures. This was highly acceptable. It appealed to their sense of humor, as well as being registered as my inadequate attempt to appreciate approximately to their *Weltanschauungen*.

For many readers these examples will be trite and will simply echo their own experiences, but for some they may begin to open up the idea that any particular language dissects a presumed reality along its own peculiar lines into its own particular categories, be these phonological, lexico–grammatical, semantic, pragmatic. What are the consequences for ways of thinking, given a command of a particular language? As already mentioned, this grand question can be broken into a number of formulations of questions about languages and ways of thinking. Do different languages facilitate or constrain basic categories of thinking in cultures? Does human thinking facilitate or constrain languages? Are language representations and conceptual categorizations and processes independent systems? Do different components of language (phonology, lexis, grammar and semantics) have different relationships to different components of cognition (perception, reflection, decision-making, decision-taking)? Do individual differences in competence with a particular language influence thinking? Do social differences in cultural orientations and norms of language use influence their psychology? Strictly speaking, only the first was of concern to Whorf, but the others can also be asked about language and psychology.

In a comprehensive review and a seriously relevant empirical study of the Whorfian hypothesis, Lucy (1992a, 1992b) traces the origins of the hypothesis and its subsequent fate. The root idea of language structure constraining habitual thinking is usually traced in anthropology and linguistics to an origin in von Humbolt, and charted through the antitheses of Boas and the theses of Sapir (1921) to Whorf. The probably truthful myth is of an alert Whorf in his role of working in fire insurance noticing a high incidence of fire insurance claims being associated with lighted objects being discarded into "empty" petrol drums. This is alleged to have inspired a life-long study of and devotion to comparative studies of indigenous North American languages and their cultures, mainly in comparisons with English and the psychology of the then dominant WASP culture of the USA.

The most exploited quotation from Whorf is:

> We dissect nature along lines laid down by our native languages. The categories and types that we isolate from the world of phenomena we do not find there because they stare every observer in the face; on the contrary, the world is presented in a kaleidoscopic flux of impressions which has to be organized by our minds – and this means largely by the linguistic systems in our minds. We cut nature up, organize it into concepts, and ascribe significances as we do largely because we are parties to an agreement to organize it in this way – an agreement that holds throughout our speech

> community and is codified in the patterns of our language. The agreement
> is, of course, an implicit and unstated one, but its terms are absolutely ob-
> ligatory; we cannot talk at all except by subscribing to the organization and
> classification of data which the agreement decrees. (1956, pp. 213–214)

This leads on to:

> From this fact proceeds what I have called the "linguistic relativity princi-
> ple," which means in informal terms, that users of markedly different gram-
> mars are pointed by their grammars towards different types of observations,
> and different evaluations of externally similar acts of observation, and hence
> are not equivalent as observers but must arrive at somewhat different views
> of the world. (1956, p. 221)

Whorf was primarily concerned with the macro-picture of grammatical
structuring presenting both a particular world view and constraining the
habitual cognitive frames of reference of the individuals speaking the language. His preferred mode of investigation was to compare whole cultures. His most famous example was the similarity between the grammar
of Hopi and English in their language and conceptions of space and the
corresponding differences for time: two languages and two cultures with
descriptive accounts that did not set one culture above the other. This is of
course an apparently ideal basis for comparative study, with two languages
alike in one fundamental respect and different in another.

As Lucy points out, it is inescapable, however, that any account is written in a language. Ideally the language should be equally able to express
both the linguistic and the cultural differences in terms that make sense to
the reader, which in turn requires that the reader has the experience and
the competence to apprehend and preferably comprehend the account.
There is a risk in any case that the greater familiarity which the reader has
with his or her own language will render the conceptions in the other
more difficult to appreciate and raise questions of which language is "superior."

In post-Whorf work, disciplinary divisions have acted to limit the credibility and relevance of studies. Lucy observes that typically studies by
anthropologists and linguists have been strong on the language side, but
weak in their assessments of the psychology of the members of the culture. In contrast, developmental psychologists and psycholinguists have
been stronger on the psychological and weaker on the language side, particularly in their emphasis on the lexicon rather than the grammar. The
topic has yielded the impressive results with the color lexicon (Berlin &
Kay, 1969; Kay & McDaniel, 1978), but as Lucy concludes (pp. 127–187)

that interesting as they are, these studies do not focus on frames of reference for thinking as a function of grammatical structures. They do not help to explain why Kikuyu-speaking children might colour the sky red when they are first introduced to painting! Unfortunately the critical evaluation that Lucy provides of other domains and approaches lead to a conclusion that Whorf's own formulation of his hypothesis has not in fact been examined by most of the studies conducted. This does not in itself render the results obtained unimportant, but it does mean that care has to be exercised in the inferences drawn from them, especially in terms of their relevance to Whorf.

Number and Material in English and Yucata Mayan

Lucy (1992b) chose to work with Yucata Mayan because it has both a critical grammatical similarity with and a difference from English within the same semantic issue, i.e. marking a plural in the noun phrase. English marks plurality in a number of ways: inflections of the suffix, types and forms of modifiers, and verb concordance. In terms of semantic markers, English can differentiate between animate and inanimate (with pronouns for example) and between "count" and "mass" nouns, for example "dogs" and "mud," and it can also mark plurality of a third category of non-animate discrete objects which have inflectional plurals, for example cake, stone. Yucata Mayan can also differentiate among the three, but in everyday use most nouns are not marked for number. Such marking is reserved for animate nouns, where 'animate' is stretched to include such objects as cars and shrunk to exclude some animals. Enumeration of these requires the addition of a noun classifier word whilst the noun remains unchanged. For this intermediate group of nouns such as tools, for example axe or shovel, or containers, for example buckets and bottles, the use of number classifiers is optional. Hence, if these have psychological relevance, Yucata Mayans and English-speaking Americans should not be different in respect of reference to animate count or inanimate mass objects, but Yucata Mayans should be less likely to pluralize inanimate discrete objects, which may affect their cognitive processing. In contrast to English, with its variety of numeral classifiers, Yucata Mayan is obliged to "unitize" mass nouns as well as count nouns, but some classifiers have some equivalents to "little" or "much" in English, with the complication that they can also graduate the meaning within a core semantic category, for example a banana, a banana leaf, a banana tree, a bunch of bananas; these are all aspects of banana material. This kind of device implies a focus on material as a basis for categorization, an extended analysis of which leads Lucy to a second study with contrastive categorizations as its core, and expectations that if given triads of objects to sort into two sets of similar/different, the Yucata Mayans will give primacy to material of composition and the American English speakers will prioritize shape.

Lucy's own derivations are more explicit and detailed than those given here. It is not easy to follow Lucy's account of the workings of Yucata Mayan and this is probably in part a function of English-speakers' language-related habitual categories of conceptualization! The empirical studies themselves encountered difficulties in methodology, technology, and administration, but if these can be ignored pro tem, the evidence is clearly consistent with the derivations from the Whorf hypothesis. Verbally-based measures of attention/perception and immediate recall of the content of pictures of scenes from village life do show the Yucata Mayans' comparatively less frequent pluralization of inanimate discrete objects, for example shovels and buckets. Likewise with non-verbal tasks of sorting, discrimination, and recognition memory. Further, the differences found in the similarity/difference triads was consistent with the idea of a Yucata Mayan focus on material rather than shape, both as a straight comparison and relative to American English speakers.

Too often the Whorf hypothesis has been extended or generalized into absurdities, just as its various oppositions have. Lucy's analysis sticks to the original formulation and tests it at the level of the cognitions of individuals. (Whorf left the checking at a cultural level.) Any psychologist examining Lucy's study will be disposed to ask why so few participants, why such strange matchings, how standardized were the procedures and how dispassionate was the scoring of the protocols? Such questions run the risk of ignoring the fact that Lucy not only spent a long time with the Yucata Mayans, he also learned the language; he invested time and energy on a scale seldom devoted to any single set of psychological experiments in a laboratory. If my principle that difficulties of conducting investigations are more likely to lead to random rather than significant results in the hands of conscientious investigators, then the findings have paradoxically greater claims to validity than might otherwise be suggested. The implications of variations on a Whorfian theme are pursued more fully in chapter 15.10.

14.6 The Representation-as-Default Hypothesis

In chapters 11, 12, and elsewhere, questions have been raised about the idealized status of the representational form essentially serving to utter propositions corresponding to S's construction of reality. However, why utter any if the utterances simply record a belief? Can an utterance have semantic value, but not pragmatic significance? Can S reveal a belief to L, just to show that he or she holds this belief? The answer is presumably "Yes," but this could be a rare occurrence, with most utterances in the declarative form more obviously serving a combination of Functions 1 to 6, so that interpretation as pure representation is a default option when no other function can be apprehended. One can ask whether or not S is being sincere, and that question relates to S's relationship to the belief and not to the truth of the belief itself. Whilst interesting questions can be asked about the evidence S has for the belief, and whether or not S is deluded, here the focus is on the conditions under which the truth of the belief itself is secondary to one of the social functions 1 to 6.

At least five arguments are consistent with the idea that one or more of the social functions should be accorded priority in evaluating whether the truthfulness of any propositional utterance is of primary importance, which will leave at least three contexts where its truth could be the primary hypothesis.

Chapters 4 and 5 rehearsed the similarities between non-human and human non-verbal communication and also demonstrated how five of the six clearly social functions of language rely on NVC in non-humans and how all six typically involve NVC in human interactions. Some NV features are clearly iconic. Other features of NVC are superficially clearly conventional among humans can still be interpreted (in hindsight) as having iconic relations to their functions, for example hand-shaking and bowing. Moves to symbolism and metaphor would allow a graduation to a hypothesis that in evolutionary terms language-like noises were first developed to serve social functions: marking identities, regulating the self and others, establishing, maintaining, and dissolving relationships are all activities necessary for community living, and language can certainly facilitate the efficiency and efficacy of inter-person and intergroup interaction. In such a story social action will have had primacy over representation.

If the argument that ontogenesis in part replicates phylogenesis retains any credibility, it may be noted that Halliday's (1975) case study of the speech development of his son found that the representational function of statements (informative) was the last to emerge, well after the regulatory, instrumental, interactional and personal. Then came the heuristic and imaginative. The ideational was the last. (This was also true for my own far less systematic paternal observations.) In my view, Halliday's description and account remains one of the clearest and most convincing yet produced of the earliest speech. Bowerman and Levinson (2001) offer a collection of more recent research, while Wood (1998) comments on subsequent linkages to thinking and learning.

A more dubious and contestable variant of the phylogenetic argument might try to exploit myths and legends. The variety of world creation myths is extraordinary, but only one or fewer of those extant can in fact be true. Whilst these stories offer accounts that can give sense and meaning to human existence, it is noteworthy that many of them go beyond descriptions and explanations of origins to offer prescriptions and proscriptions about human conduct. Those imperatives typically give particular privileges and powers to princes and priests, and still do. These are regulatory rather than representational. Likewise with legends. The truth–status of stories of the lives and deeds of heroes was perhaps less important than the functions these stories performed in socializing successive generations into acceptance and emulation of the virtues valued by the culture, be these of saintliness, other-worldliness, or the perfect warrior. In such legends the evil deeds and lives of the vicious received their just desserts – often in a just hereafter. Such stories were more powerful and extensive variants of the injunctions that "Brave little boys don't cry" and "Nice girls don't pick their noses." These points are in no way inconsistent with the claims about kinds of knowledge in chapter 10. What they implicitly pose are questions about the status of answers to enduring metaphysical and moral issues that all human beings implicitly or explicitly answer through their lives. We can ask however whether or not the implied truths of the messages of these myths and legends offer answers that will stand the tests appropriate to their domains as set down in chapter 11?

A similar approach can be adopted towards histories. Some religious faiths root their origins in historical rather than mythical claims. Most states in the UNO teach the secular and/or religious history of their own society through history texts used in their school systems. Historically, these texts have been notorious for their ingroup biases. Thucydides (1971, written fourth century BC) appears to be the first historian to observe that the surviving histories of events are more likely to be recorded by winners than by losers of conflicts. This remains true today where states pretend to their own virtuous justifications for waging war on others. They claim adherence to standards of decency in their own conduct, whilst ascribing badness and madness to their enemies both for promoting conflicts and for their uncivilized behavior in prosecuting wars (Robinson, 1996). Much of such histories is clearly at odds with the evidence, but the misrepresentations persist and are endorsed by governments, whilst the UNO draws up recommendations of questions to be asked of texts whose truthful answers would reduce ingroup aggrandizement and outgroup denigration.

Ingroup-serving delusions apply to current affairs as well as to past ones, and as noted in chapter 12, all mass media appear to give priority to audience and readership figures either for political or commercial reasons. Audiences prefer to hear and see how much more civilized they are compared with their enemies especially and others generally. Outgroup denigration and ingroup favouritism are pervasive and massive.

These then are five arguments pointing to the pre-eminence of social action over information giving in respect of metaphysics, myths and legends, history and current affairs as presented to people at large. Even rules of politeness can be instantiated as mechanisms to prevent people from pursuing enquiries into the actions of authorities. This is a significant expansion of Marx's restricted comment that religion is an opiate for the masses. The propositions about the origin of the human species, the idealization of one's own society, the laws and norms governing behavior in those societies, both in terms of privileging elites and preventing questioning of the rules, all seem to be geared to the preservation of the status quo, whilst providing positive delusions about the self in societies where injustice and dishonesty flourish (see Gilmour, 1992 for a frightening account of Britain in the eighteenth century).

The essence of this delusional system is the perverted exploitation of the representational function of language to regulate behavior under the guise of being informative. The reasons why such a perversion should be pervasive have been given at a number of places in the text, namely to maintain and/or enhance the power, wealth, and status of the elites who already have these in abundance. Whilst this view is promoted in terms of winning in the continuing competition for resources, it is simultaneously true that there is cooperation among the winners. Just as the aristocratic families have cooperated with each other to preserve their positions, cartels of multi-nationals in oil, chemicals, pharmaceuticals, and banking have ensured that inter-company competition is more apparent than real; they do compete at the margins, but cooperate *vis a vis* their customers.

Whilst the "pure unvarnished" truth may be a dead metaphor as well as an impossible aspiration, transparent and direct truthful statements are rarities in statements by authorities, and challenges to provide these are seen as rude or pernicious at the individual level, and unpatriotic or revolutionary at the societal level, which they can indeed be. However, how and why has it come about that societies have created layers of linguistic indirectness or implicatures to serve as politeness devices or codes of ingroup interaction? In short, why are the face threats of Goffman construed as face-threats *unless* they are true? Indirectness, whether in the form of politeness features or implicatures. Politeness can be viewed as considera-

tion for the feelings of the other and the importance of not causing unnecessary suffering or giving offense. But the tactical devices of telling "white
lies" is a step down the decline to telling real lies. Believed white lies create delusions in others. As Taylor (1989) summarises in *Positive Illusions*,
these can help to maintain self-esteem and a sense of well-being. They
figure prominently too in unsustainable ideals about cohabitation in close
relationships. How it has benefited societies and their members to base
their lives on delusions as to what is possible both for individuals and their
relationships is difficult to comprehend.

These norms and their exploitation have become endemic features of life in
quasi-democracies at all levels: intrapersonal, interpersonal, intergroup, and
institutional, but this is of course what is to be expected in individualistic
capitalist societies whose *de facto* dominant values appear to be the pursuit of
power, wealth, and status and the self-indulgence these afford. The competitiveness for resources inherent in such a system is of course constrained by
values associated with aspirations to promote the well-being of the members
of a cooperative community, which leads on to a consideration of the contexts in which the truth of representational forms becomes the basis of their
evaluation. First, it flourishes in the cooperative world of people being helpful
to each other in the provision and exchange of information, and the pervasiveness of this should not be under-estimated. Second, it survives in World 3,
that extraordinary fund of knowing how to and knowing that which is stored
around the globe in its varied forms. These are of course in perpetual use to
educate and inform, and to promote well-being through the reduction of the
consequences of poverty, disease, and ignorance. Third, in its ethical and
metaphysical realizations, it keeps alive criteria for the improvement of individuals and the communities in which they live.

Given that these contexts co-exist with competitive ones, representational forms are still serving social functions, but the rationale for their use
is different. Perceived truth is told in order to be cooperative: to do unto
others as you would be done by.

As mentioned in chapter 11.2.4, many informal and institutional exchanges are requests for information, services, and goods. Why give someone false directions or the wrong bus number? Why would a sales person
state that a plentiful item was not in stock? There could be reasons, but
other things being equal, expectations would be for truthful replies to
questions and requests. Likewise in everyday conversation, the default
option can be truthful whether narrative, descriptive or explanatory, provided the person is well informed on the topics of focus.

Even here, however, the social considerations can override accuracy. In
Japan I learned after just a few trials not to approach people to ask where

the rail station was. On the first occasion, it transpired to be within 50 metres after making a single left turn, but the request in my "Japlish" met with directions taking me further away from my original target. I should not have approached anyone, but just waited to be helped. Once asked a "helpful" reply had to be given, to save face. Similarly, as mentioned in chapter 4, contexts of phatic communion, situations where cultural norms prescribe talk, and escaping from dispreferred alternative behavior can severally generate conversational exchanges where the avoidance of too much silence has the highest priority. That being so, the truth of statements becomes important in the mundane, only where false statements would inconvenience or mislead others.

Writing this text is an example of an activity propelling what is intended to be truthful to appear on the page. The intra-mental world in which takes place the learning and remembering, creative imaginings and stumbling hypothesizing, spasmodic insights and their dismissing rebuttals, is characterized by struggles to make sense of the world and to take appropriate action. This applies as much to writing out shopping lists and deciding what to tell the doctor about one's symptoms as it does to writing books, but it is the accumulated and accumulating knowledge and beliefs in logics, aesthetics, ethics, metaphysics, and the sciences and technologies where representational propositions have been so significant for the development of human societies. (In this context "science" is intended to cover all systematically evaluated claims to knowledge that would include all philosophy, history, biography, and all sincere attempts to offer valid descriptions and explanations of the phenomena of the universe.) That statements within this universe of discourse are devised with abusive social purposes in mind is irrelevant to the sincere endeavors of persons operating within the temporal, spatial, and cultural frames of reference within which their lives are led.

Whatever personal drives have been responsible for stimulating these apparent advances in knowledge, their acceptability has depended in the long run upon the evaluations of others where the quality of arguments and evidence has provided the basis of those evaluations. Ideally in these areas influence is mediated by others acting as agents not victims, by consciously reflective minds that have come to accept the contemporary "rules of the game."

14.7   Discussion

None of the theories described here has used equations with algebraic or numerical variables. All offer contingent and probabilistic predictions, but when their hypotheses have been tested empirically, and found to be wanting, the propositions have been modified and elaborated. Their contingent qualities have given them heuristic value. All provide frames of reference from which further studies can be suggested. All are well grounded in empirical data, obtained by a variety of methods.

What can be claimed about their explanatory power? None have been elaborated to a hypothetico–deductive format with falsifiable derivations that would oblige their authors to abandon their theories if their predictions were confounded by empirical evidence. At the present time each offers mainly first-order explanations. So LCM can be viewed as a fascinating example of the Whorfian hypothesis in which language structure and content influences cognition, but leaves the puzzle as to why liking should be seen as a feature of the liked rather than the liker – in the context-free illustration. Of course, by varying the stress, any of the components can be picked out as the major contrasting term. Do verbs and adjectives in families other than mainstream European yield the same contrasting characteristics, and if not, are the cognitive consequences different? The grander question of why particular languages have divided their features up along the lines they have is way beyond social psychology, and is probably an unprofitable as well as unanswerable question.

The expectancy theories have predictive power, and give reasons for compliance/non-compliance and attitude change, but they do not carry the explanations beyond the concept of "cultural norms," although these may well have understandable socio-historical antecedents, and human inertia has already been cited as a reason for norms remaining unchanged. Social psychologists can pass the issue on to sociologists, but at some point reasons and motivation have to be included in the explanations. So many cultural and sub-cultural norms are irrational and/or incompatible with the pretended values of societies and yet they survive, the difficulties of agreeing international calendars being one example (Duncan, 1998). And how and why do all the relevant particular linguistic structures link to differential efficacy and propriety for different social categories of persons as Ss and Ls?

CAT has rendered its motivational basis explicit at a first-order level, but does not indicate why Ss should want to be liked and approved by Ls. Interestingly too, whilst it has checked the attitudinal consequences for Ls of adjustments by S, it has yet to probe into the extent to which Ss are aware of and deliberately adjust their speech and communicative styles. Why are which features selected for adjustment? Features differ in their roles as social markers and ease of change. Within limits, rates of speaking are relatively easy to change and do not mark social identity to the same extent that accents do. It was noted in chapter 10 that to be efficient markers of states, personality and social identity need to be displayed as soon as possible in encounters, and it follows that adjustments need also to be signalled early and unambiguously whether conscious or not. At an inter-country level one can observe the workings of CAT on a daily basis as leaders set up divergences or rush to convergence both in what they say and how they say it. That said, the power plays remain.

Whorf presents a more problematic scenario, especially when sociological transpositions are made to his analysis of between-languages phenomena. Given Searle's (1975) sincerity condition for representative statements, then what is written in chapter 12.5 about elites cheating the rest of society and using their rhetoric to support their privileges commits me to a variant of the Whorf hypothesis. The triumphant Zeitgeist of individualistic capitalism in combination with the globalization of multinational companies probably ensures at least another century of obscene and de-humanizing suffering for the poor in all but a few countries. As the final section implies my current view is that most of the rhetoric provided by elites and authorities is self-justificatory rather than informative, and succeeds both by means of crooked and biased arguments, backed up by armed forces when necessary.

CHAPTER 15

Retrospect and Prospect

15.1 Introduction

As Gilbert and Mulkay (1984) have pointed out, scientists in the lab do not talk or behave in the same register as they write and present their formal papers. The sequence and orderliness of a presented text is a conventional format, facilitating ease of reading, an account including what are believed to be all the important details in a reader-friendly sequence; the whole provides a basis for critical evaluation, replication, checks, and developments by colleagues and other people. Practitioners are aware of this, and to most of us the procedures make good sense.

The writing of books has similar characteristics. The chaotic windmills of the author's thought processes outpace the possibilities of committing those ideas to paper, which is just as well. In many cases, however, there is a serious difference between what is written and the details of what is thought. If the text is to be readable and read, current conventions require that mental reservations, qualifications, and hedgings are kept to a tolerably low rate of intrusion in the public text. The beliefs expressed are offered in good faith as best estimates of the current state of affairs, but that state of affairs may not be well advanced, yet to keep repeating this would be tiresome. Social psychologists working with language and communication are not writing with the professionally accumulated wisdom of 200 years of systematic empirical study and explanatory endeavor. We still lack the established frames of reference that have facilitated advances in botany and zoology. As pointed out in chapter 2 and elsewhere, our person "objects" of study are changed and change themselves through time, and with the added twist that publically available results from psychology are themselves utilizable for additional changes to be possible. Language as system and resource is also changing and being changed. There is as yet no consensus about the contending epistemologies and methodologies. But perhaps most frustrating is that so much of the relevant material is already within the operational and even the reflective competence of the people being studied. The section on how hand-shaking works (chapter 8) could have been written by most literate adults from a hand-shaking culture, as could some but not all of the gaze section (chapter 5). In contrast, a systematic exposition of the current propositional (but not the procedural) knowledge about forms of address and reference (chapter 8) would be beyond the competence (but not the understanding) of most. Table 3.2 is probably beyond the experience and training of most social psychologists.

That table itself offers a good example of the unevenness of current understanding. Phonetics and phonology are already advanced much more than the table suggests, and have established far more coherent and comprehensive frames of reference than semantics and pragmatics. To support research, there is advanced technological instrumentation for generating and analyzing sounds, and there are anchorages for evaluation in both physics and psychology. Since most of the topics addressed here involve the pragmatics of language, the claims made here are less well founded than is desirable. The concepts, hypotheses, "theories," and frames of reference offered are some of those which have justified their utility in sufficient measure to merit further exploration. The propositions linking the concepts for descriptive or explanatory purposes are the least implausible constructions of reality, given the evidence currently to hand.

This orientation of tentativeness should not be interpreted as being a form of implicit criticism of colleagues who are not so tentative. The discipline also needs those who are bold enough to make strong claims and even outrageous claims about language in communication and its study. They are not fools who have rushed in where angels fear to tread. Their enthusiasm is an inspiration to find out more about their claims and the empirical limitations of their ideas. Being constructively wrong is far more useful than being rendered impotent by doubts. Unfortunately, individualistic competitive cultures do not seem to be geared to appreciating the value of errors for the learning and development of persons or the culture as a whole, and individuals making mistakes are liable to pay a heavy price if they admit to them. One consequence is that the defense of lines of scientific enquiry whose utility has been exhausted can degenerate into the exploitation of the invalid arguments referred to in chapter 10 when what began as scientific questioning turns into ideology. I write these words facing a small placard inscribed, "May we be protected from the unshakeable certainty of the misinformed!" (H. L. Mencken) and a badge with the inscription "No more heroes," given by students, subsequent to a very animated and protracted discussion about the applicability of Brecht's "Pity the land with a need for heroes" to 1960s' work on children's developing competence with language. It is the peculiar propensity of disciples of heroes who have become ill-informed or mis-informed that is particularly unfortunate. Social psychology of language has yet to suffer seriously from such retarding influences, but communication itself is at risk from the three-isms of anarchism, nihilism, and solipsism, if it continues to be over-influenced by the gurus of the various post-Xisms of valuable ideas taken too far – and way beyond the evidence cited to support their validity.

The general absence of such theoretical positions will have been noted. The exciting ideas of Barthes (1969) and Habermas (1984, 1987) have not been followed with empirical work that has been fed into the social psychology of language and communication. The names of Foucault, Latour, and Kristeva appear but once here and without comment (see Gross & Levitt, 1998 and Sokal & Bricmont, 1998 for some reasons why). In contrast, most of the work quoted here has been developed out of mundane concepts which are familiar to us. On the psychological side, it has been easier to work with happiness, sadness, anger, and fear than with yet-to-be formalized higher level affective–motivational concepts. Many colleagues have chosen to work with "accounting," "arguing," and "patronizing," and can fill books with each.

The broader theoretical frames of reference that have been developed had and kept their roots in lower level phenomena. Communication Accommodation Theory (CAT) (chapter 14) grew to achieve a breadth of coverage that embraces international conflicts and the decline and fall of whole languages, but it has retained its foundations in studies of the dynamics of accent shifts in everyday FtF encounters. Conditions under which convergence or divergence of vocalic and verbal features proved to link well with predictions derivable from Social Identity theory. CAT is one of the clearest examples of a dialectic becoming established between empirical evidence and social psychological explanations. Expectancy Violation Theory is another (chapter 14), and Politeness Theory (chapter 8) a third. The prognosis would have to be that the exploration of empirical realizations of concepts within everyday experience are likely to provide the firmest foundations for future developments, with subsequent theoretical analyses of similarities and differences among the operations of these providing the infrastructure for more abstract and general theoretical frameworks. To encourage movement in this direction it may be useful to comment upon some of the issues whose resolutions would facilitate progress: cultural contexts of research, conceptual consensus, frames of reference and explanations, methodological minefields, the data, and a widening of Whorf.

⌐ 15.2 Cultural Contexts of Research

Nineteenth century biology in Britain began as the preserve of gentlemen who did not have to work to live. Darwin had an income of some £10,000 a year. Members of the Church of England were over-represented in amateur science. In the second half of that century, professional biologists began to create societies, jobs, university and other courses for students, and by dint of considerable evangelical work achieved a division of labor along the epistemological lines described in chapter 11. Evolutionary ideas replaced the two different stories in Genesis as the dominant account of the operation of species development, differentiation, and disappearance (Desmond, 1994). Biology was thus a late arrival in university studies and was itself a survivor of a struggle.

What is the cultural context in which most social psychologists of language and communication are working at the beginning of the twenty-first century? Most hold positions in universities and comparable institutions, mixing teaching, research and administration in varying proportions. In the last 20 years research has been squeezed by increasing bureaucratization in both administration and teaching, at least in the countries where English is the university lingua franca. To ensure promotion and tenure and departmental funding, academics need research grants and a stream of publications in high "impact" journals. Actual impact is unimportant, and new journals have proliferated so rapidly that regular reading for many is now confined to recent American and own country subject specialist journals. Computer searches with a trio of key terms can yield several thousand articles. As psychologists who have looked at assessment have demonstrated, the aspiring are increasingly assessed and disposed to conform to the rules of the game by concentrating on the indicators not the substance.

Rewards for achievements in publication are only one mode of reinforcement. Conference papers are another, with invited keynote lectures at top-flight international conferences carrying the greatest weight. Prizes are scattered around: for best papers overall, for best paper in section, best paper by a recent Ph.D. or postgraduate. The CVs of the successful are littered with these awards. Most are matters of sponsorship by recognized authorities, who are likely to be conservative in their evaluations. Hence, working within established frameworks and ensuring endorsement by high status sponsors is the safest strategy for rapid promotion. Sociologically, extrinsic motivation can come to be the dominating motivation. Intellectual curiosity is a luxury that only the famous and the alienated can afford to indulge. There is no suggestion of changes in the current climate that will afford escape from the reinforcement schedules of the assembly line to which current generations have become accustomed. The excessive professionalization combined with bureaucratic accountability is destroying the very virtues that are necessary for significant research.

What place have such comments in this text? They are a warning. Institutional frameworks that set up the wrong kind of reward systems generate impression management rather than substantive commitment. If long-term serious research and scholarship does not fit the institutional framework, then progress is retarded not advanced. If I were to be giving advice to bright young persons committed to the study of language in communication, I would suggest that they become financially independent as soon as possible, and then attach themselves to one of those few institutes where research can still be driven by academic curiosity. Back to the nineteenth century! In the meantime, those trapped on the treadmill have to conform sufficiently not to get into time-wasting trouble, whilst pursuing serious work in secret! It is necessary also to be very selective in what one spends time reading. Drowning in databases is becoming too easy.

⌐ 15.3   Conceptual Concerns

Why social psychologists cannot agree on how to use the word "X" has been a continuing complaint of undergraduates and other students of social psychology. *Prejudice* and *stereotype* spring instantly to mind as suffering from a multiplicity of meanings, and with no good reason for the variety. For the uncertainties surrounding the use of "emotion," there are better grounds (chapter 9). Chapter 7 referred to the difficulties with the core concept of *attitude*. Perhaps social psychologists need to generate a dictionary of recommendations and hope that a succession of editions will begin to cure this disease of diversity. Desiderata of good definitions have been around for over 2000 years, as noted in chapter 3.2.

That achieved, social phenomena will not necessarily fit into neat discrete categories. They will suffer from fuzzy borders in both horizontally and vertically ordered taxonomies, but there is also a requirement that good definitions should not create misleading distinctions. Examples in this text where clearer definitions and consensual use would be welcome are "accounts" versus "arguments" versus "explanations" versus "justifications." Everyday usage is not helpful, and colleagues working in these areas have recorded faithfully the multiple meanings and ambiguities. In the past philosophers have used superscripts (argument[1]/argument[2]), and perhaps that could be a practical solution. Billig (2001) is correct in noting the tensions between "argument" as a rational constructive mode of ascertaining truths and "argument" as a mode of contest between competitors striving for dominance, but analyses of events in committees, courts, and other contexts would benefit from knowing when which is being intended by which participants. If hearers decode constructive refutations *en route* to the truth as demeaning aggressive personal attacks, this does not facilitate progress. Likewise treating interested enquiries for explanations as disapproving demands for justifications can affect outcomes of interactions.

Linguistics suffers from similar difficulties in semantics and pragmatics, but is in a much happier state in both phonology and lexico–grammar. There may be strong divergences of opinion about how a grammar should achieve whatever it is meant to be doing, but the use of labels like "interrogative," "morpheme," or "free clause" do not appear to be topics evoking indifference or conflict. Part of the more general difficulties with semantics and pragmatics derives from the lack of a consensual explicit epistemology as to what is to count as grounds for preferring one descriptive system to another. There were mini-attempts to order certain words in terms of defining componential attributes, as with kinship (see Silverstein, 1987 for a challenging foray into semantic markers). The possible epistemology was the manner in which such terms were stored in human brains. That line of thinking was also put forward in transformational grammars in which the deep structure of the simplest free clause in English was held to be the active affirmative, with passivity and negation being first order components for change (Chomsky, 1957).

These academically derived thrusts contrast with Roget's (1952/1852) Herculean thesaurus, which has undergone elaboration and development, but not to nearly the same extent that phonetics, phonology and grammar have done. Whilst phonetics and phonology can anchor themselves in physics and psychology, grammar cannot and does not, and in large measure its norms have been driven by allegedly descriptive grammars becoming prescriptive via educational systems. The standardization of English grammar (and lexis and spelling) has been continuing self-fulfilling prophecies of successive generations being socialized into a relatively uniform and stable code of communication, over the last five hundred years. The epistemological bases of the system(s) are a mix of past precedents, cur-

rent usages, and current novelties. Whatever is done, the subsequent users of language are likely to "subvert" the efforts of social scientists. As
noted in chapter 2 and Table 2.2, languages are resources as well as systems.

15.4 Approaches: Functional/Structural versus Structural/ Functional Approaches

Using functions as the primary frame of reference for this text has not
been a satisfactory device, but it is difficult at present to see what would be
better. Taking units and structures of language as primary would have
several disadvantages for social psychologists. First the nature and operations of these features have been the provinces of linguists and philosophers, and whilst disciplines are essentially divisions of expertise that have
developed into the social and administrative categories through which
pretending knowledge is channelled, they have also accumulated inventions and discoveries that take years to master. Linguistics in particular
has most of its foundations rooted in the auditory not the visual medium,
and is therefore inadequately represented in written texts. Although it is
true that speech can be scored, just as music can be, and it can therefore be
transformed from a written to an auditory representation by someone competent to manage this, social psychologists neither can nor do display their
data in such formats. Here it has been pointed out how the practice of just
writing down sequences of letters and words without their phonological
characteristics has seriously misled semantic and especially pragmatic analysis. How utterances are delivered and the influence of the other components of Hymes' SPEAKING all have etic and emic features for accurate
interpretations of speech. It is probably inevitable that in the future social
psychologists for whom speech is relevant will have to use multi-media
texts from which it will be possible to hear and "read" speech scores. However, even these possibilities will not necessarily provide better frames of
reference and run the risk of diffusing into collections of details. The use of
units and structures as the foundation would simply mean massive texts
on each of the "units" of a language, where units will range from the
micro to the macro in all components. There is no reason why texts should
not appear with titles such as the social psychology of: pauses, intonation,
whispering, demonstratives, qualifiers, relative clauses or the imperative.
The semantic and pragmatic components pose their own difficulties.

Linguists have succeeded in some measure in developing consensual
technical terms and will no doubt continue to do so. Social psychologists

seem to be more concerned with prioritizing empirical data at the expense of developing conceptual consensus, and communication scholars have difficulty in disciplining their creative imaginations to conform to the empirical requisites of scientific enterprises. Just as technical terms need to be defined consensually, so different frames of reference need to be articulated. Currently unanswerable issues about its units and structures, and perhaps the bottom–up tactic of the kind adopted by Horn (1989) for negation is the best way forward pro tem. Pragmatics itself has so much overlap with functions in experience and behavior that there will have to be a coming together of the social psychological organization perspective adopted here, and the more linguistically-related perspective of texts on pragmatics.

In the meantime, it may be that authors will avoid the deliberate variability in the presentation of this text and concentrate their efforts into individual functions and themes, for example encounter regulation, influencing others, conversation, politeness, patronizing, negotiation. This kind of selection appears to be the growing trend, and for many, the limitation of scope renders the possibilities of investigation feasible, and this is particularly so if linked to a limited social psychological frame of reference, for example social identity marking, impression management.

The approach adopted here may be a pot-pourri, with some arbitrariness in the selection of topics mentioned and those pursued in greater depth. That said, it does seem to be important from the outset to ask about functions in experience and behavior generally and to link these to verbal and non-verbal units and structures and offer and test social psychological interpretations of them. The level of functional analysis used here would seem to be appropriate for a general text, but of course more detailed enquiries would require finer classifications within the functions listed here, as has been illustrated.

15.5   What is to Count as Evidence

It has already been noted that phonetics and phonology have anchors in objective acoustic physics and the anatomy/physiology of production and in particular articulation. The psychology of audiology and speech production anchor the experiential properties of S and L. These set the parameters within which the full range of empirical methods can be employed to adduce and test for relationships. Extra-linguistic features can also be included on the linguistic side of such studies. Throughout chapters 6 to 13 examples have been given of which features have been found to serve which functions, along with some answers to relevant "why" questions.

Whilst usage may be crucial for the linguistic anchoring of lexico–grammar, it is also a focus for social psychologists. One of the original questions posed about transformational–generative grammar was whether this was a linguistic or a psycho-linguistic enterprise. Chomsky denied that it was an attempt to suggest how the mind/brain encoded or decoded sentences, but his assertions about the alternative criteria that should be used to evaluate the grammar have yet to emerge to a consensus.

Although social psychology might be imagined to have no problem with its epistemology, and this could be true, in fact the publication policies of the high status journals and other indicators of prestige currently operative show distinct preferences for laboratory-based experimental techniques of investigation, which has the knock-on effect of over-emphasizing the responses of (American) undergraduates in make-believe contexts of situation as a basis for theorizing. Neither biology nor medicine are averse to case studies or natural observation as sources of publishable exploratory or refuting activities and these are particularly valuable at initial and late phases of the development of explanations – in the early phase to provide a basis from which to develop hypotheses and at a late phase to probe for exceptional cases that may raise questions that will lead to modification or revision of hypotheses. (It will be a sign of growing maturity when social psychology feels free to do what is most appropriate rather than conform to the very strange idea gaining prominence that a person sitting alone and faced by graphics and words on a programmed PC screen is an ideal representative of social experience and behavior.) Ease of gaining ethical approval, speed and ease of data collection, apparent control over stimuli, and availability of cheap labour are not appropriate criteria for selecting a methodology fit for the scientific purpose in mind. Validity and utility of observations of the goals, and multiple methods that yield consistent results have to provide the way forward. Experiments have a strong claim to utility for discovering and checking etic possibilities, but can have little relevance to explanations of extra-laboratory behavior, especially the more passionate, affectionate, and violent inter-individual and intergroup activities that occur.

Perhaps a final comment on this topic would draw attention to the unglamorous and painstaking observational practices of many biologists, especially those engaged in fieldwork. Investigations can take years. They can fail. Within the social psychology of communication it is noteworthy that the pursuit of studies requiring mastery of massive coding frames (for example Birdwhistell, 1970, or Bull, in press) attract but a few committed enthusiasts. Such specialized work does not yield the frequent guaranteed publications that are needed by academics who want to achieve tenure and promotion in most higher education systems. But what kind of observations are needed? If I were to be impertinent, I would suggest that almost any form of observation of the phenomena under scrutiny can be cited as evidence – with the exception of the rhetorical extravaganzas of protagonists of ideas. The secret of the meaning of the universe is not 42. The efficacy of prayer is not proved by the statues erected by mariners who escaped drowning at sea. As Bacon (1855/1625) noted, those whose prayers were not answered did not have the opportunity to erect monuments. Some anthropologists have been misled in some of their interpretations of events in unfamiliar cultures (Barley, 1984). It is not difficult to invent deeply symbolic interpretations of the mundane; it may be more difficult to generate supportive evidence from a wider range of observations.

The principle of parsimony has a respectable history expressed in a variety of forms, and social psychologists have yet to make out a case for abandoning it. One aspect of parsimony is to keep explanations as close to the phenomena as possible. Another is to watch that striving for generality and abstraction does not result in over- or under-determination/explanation. One of the disadvantages of Freud's defense mechanisms was that their variety permitted an infinite variety of explanations for any piece of behavior and little guidance as to which might be empirically relevant; any emotion could be repressed and remain hidden or be transformed to its opposite or projected onto other people, etcetera etcetera.

15.6   Methodological Diversity: Advantages and Pitfalls

If the binary oppositional contrasts of Table 15.1 are used to set and discuss some of the parameters sometimes seen to limit the appropriate methods of data collection and analysis, the six listed will suffice to define much, but not all, of the range in approaches to studying language and social psychology. There are omissions. For example, there is no mention of the cross-cultural perspective, which at some point has to be confronted. In this text, references have frequently been made with the qualification "in the UK and USA." This is reminder of limitation and not an Anglo-American flag-waving.

Historical comparisons have also been a legitimate and rewarding preference for research by many students of language. Other contrasts could have been used to define the issues, but the six will serve to convey the tenor of the message intended.

Table 15.1   Approaches: Emphases and Contrasts

Quantitative	Qualitative
Imagined speech Elicited speech	Natural speech
Monologue	Dialogue Polylogue
Units & Structure	Texts & Whole
Behavior	Accounts
Experiments	Field studies Cases

In the 1960s and 1970s the work of social psychologists was more commonly found hugging and emphasizing the characteristics listed in the left-hand column, especially if they were trained in psychology departments that emphasized the importance of the claimed objectivity of measurement allegedly attainable in laboratory experiments. Only brave potential isolates dared to deviate from the conventional epistemological norms. By the turn of the century, the range of approaches had broadened greatly, even though those preferring to use techniques on the right-hand side have had to found their own journals to publicize and disseminate their activities, and some have faced an uphill struggle to legitimate their methodologies (see Edwards, 1997; Potter, 1996; Titscher et al., 2000; Wood & Kroger, 2000 for recent contributions to Discourse Analysis).

Coming from a background in biology, which was already able to encompass everything from biochemistry to ecology, I have always had difficulty understanding how any of the particular foci or methods currently used in the study of language and social experience and behavior could be ruled as wrong-headed without paying regard to what was being investigated. Nothing that social psychologists currently do would be ruled as out of place in some niche of biological research. (The kinds and extent of inferences drawn from the data are another matter!) Decisions about appropriateness of methods have to be made in the light of the questions posed, the current state of well-founded beliefs, and the human and technical resources available. What is more, and more serious conceptually and logically, is that in fact no studies can be made at any of the six polar positions without incorporating components from its opposite. For any empirical study it is not a question of either/or, but of focus and emphasis.

What will be critical for the eventual status of any work will be the evaluation of the relationships between its empirical claims, the interpretations hazarded, and the bases of the claims of cognate studies. Negatively, all kinds of study can be badly designed and badly executed: the data collected can be flawed, the results can be processed wrongly, their generality under- or over-estimated, and their interpretations over- or under-determining. Prima facie, essentially identical criteria of quality can and should be applied to all studies, while proponents of the virtues of any particular approach should be able to articulate and define the differences between better and worse studies in that approach and agree what checks can be made on the propriety and plausibility of their descriptions and explanations – why one interpretation is to be privileged against others. Evaluations should not suffer from Ryle's (1949) category mistakes: we do not criticize cars because they do not float or fly, and we do not criticize Brown and Levinson's (1987/ 1978) theory of politeness because it does not explain how conversational implicature functions (Grice, 1975). There may well not be a best approach to a particular question at a particular time, and even if there is, it will be contingent on current knowledge, resources, feasibility and ethics. Approaches can compete for utility, but for progress to be made, the relevant imagined community of scholars is expected to be cooperative and subservient to goals higher than those of winning interpersonal arguments. Hence, for each of the methodological contrasts, I have tried to select what I see to be the central conceptual principle of interdependence and unification and to illustrate that the underlying dimensions offer frames of reference and not lines of battle. The six are not independent of each other, and what needs to be said about each differs in amount and significance. The first has certainly become a serious battleground within each of the disciplines associated with the study of language and its use.

15.6.1 Quantitative and qualitative analysis

For psychologists, the early emphasis on the quantitative is customarily cited as arising from their concern to be seen by physicists or physiologists as being real scientists. Given the interests and the successes of Weber and Fechner in psycho-physics and Helmholz in perception, this orientation was understandable, but restrictive, because their principles were taken to imply the necessity of doing experiments and using at least interval or ratio scales for the measurement of objectively measured variables for the study of other problems in other fields. Further, if statistical analyses were to be built into the decision-making process, then in order to use the then preferred techniques of parametrically constrained techniques, such as analysis of variance or factor analysis, the variables needed to have particular properties of distribution. This is not of course an ideal way to explore novel questions from fresh perspectives. Experiments have their place, but it is also helpful to explore cases and examples. Regardless of method, it is probably productive to hold a succession of false assumptions and interpretations as well as to follow bottom-up inductive procedures. Historically, each newly emerging discipline has been seen as misguided by those in the already established sciences. Each has entered the status hierarchy at the bottom. Within the hard sciences, psychology generally still has a lowly place in status, power and resource provision, and within psychology, social psychology occupies a lowly slot. (In 2001 in Britain, laboratory-based psychology undergraduate courses are being funded at twice the rate of non-laboratory courses. The idea that social practicals are expensive and may need people, time, transport and paper, as well as laboratory equipment, remains unaccepted by the funding authorities – and by laboratory funded colleagues.) In my view the attempt by social psychologists to take a short cut into experiments has also led those wedded to them into imitative errors: relative ritualization of the means (data collection and processing), with a complementary neglect of a concern for the nature and status of the variables themselves.

Variables are discriminable qualities. Hence, any examination of quantitative relationships between them presupposes prior qualitative distinctions. There can be no quantity without it being a quantity of some quality. Correspondingly, there can be no quality without it existing in some measure, be it only present or absent. Presence versus absence is a form of measurement and may be the crucial distinction for particular questions. Pronunciation of certain sounds has been an important identifier since the Bible cited Gideon's example forward: volunteer warriors who could not pronounce "shibboleth" were not permitted to fight the Midianites. Likewise, nominal (categorical) distinctions may be what are significant for behavior and experience. Is that city Londonderry or Derry? Are those islands the Falklands or the Malvinas? The preferences mark social identification unambiguously. Are you one of "US" or one of "THEM?" The scales of measurement used should be appropriate for the characteristics of the variables and the questions being asked about them, and should not be indicative either of a conformity to a high status norm, or of a rebellion against it.

Objectivity of measurement has been another fetish; it may be an idealized aspiration for length or weight, but it is not as immediately significant as the phenomenological for much human action: "If men see situations as real, they are real in their consequences" (Thomas & Znaniecki, 1927).

Experience cannot be ignored at the expense of counting pieces of behavior whose units and meanings will in any case require interpretation. Acts of promising cannot be reduced to a series of interlocking stimuli and responses; descriptions may include these as components, but they necessarily under-describe and miss the significance of such acts.

In recent decades the development of improved statistical techniques for analyzing (so-called) non-parametric data (Leach, 1979; Siegel & Castellan, 1988) and (so-called) qualitative data (Bryman & Burgess, 1999; Silverman, 2000) has enabled those deciding to extract and emphasize the qualitative characteristics in their research problems to reduce the earlier imbalance of studies, but old established journals seem to continue to be prone to use reviewers who are unsympathetic to these developments, and conflicts between "qualitativists" and "quantitativists" still occur. Not everyone has been reconciled as yet to the validity of the higher order principle that all descriptions and explanations have both qualitative and quantitative components.

Ironically, in their rush to be as scientific as the cognitive and neuropsychologists, social psychologists have missed a vital stage in the cyclical development of disciplines. Long ago, William James extolled the importance of observing and asking exemplars in depth and detail as a point of departure for exploring and opening up fields of study. Typically, the emphasis on quantification comes later, to check the degree of understanding. Qualitative studies then re-appear to find out why there are mismatches between results and theory among the "error variance" participants, *et seq.* A changing sequential and dialectical emphasis on quantitative and qualitative is an alternation indicative of progress.

15.6.2 Natural versus Non-Natural Speech

For students of language, a particular false polarization has arisen with the contrast between what is termed "natural" and other kinds of speech. Just as anthropologists, linguists, and sociologists were well-disposed towards methods yielding categorical data long before social psychologists escaped their quantitative shackles, so they were happy to rely on speech data collected or derived from everyday situations as the basis of their descriptions and explanations. How people react to or otherwise interpret contrived speech presented in typewritten form, and stripped of its vocalic features and the values of the contextual variations listed in Hymes' (1967) SPEAKING characteristics, can be a risky basis for inference. However, in an over-kill contrast some researchers became opposed to the use of "non-natural" speech under any circumstances, and some still are. Again the distinction is false.

The abstraction of the idea of "natural speech" can be a useful contrastive and corrective to any misleading emphasis on elicited, imagined, constructed speech. What someone says in a particular laboratory setting under particular stimulus conditions has a problematic relation to what would be said under other circumstances. What people imagine they would say is not necessarily identical to what they would in fact say. Nevertheless, the examples Chomsky (1957) constructed were as much the products of a human mind as is fireside vernacular, and some of us will judge that "green ideas can sleep furiously" is a grammatically acceptable sentence in English and may profit from an analysis as to how we come to be able to make such a judgment.

It is what is inferred from the characteristics of elicited, imagined or constructed speech that is hazardous, but the same hazards can also afflict inferences from "natural" speech. Human beings have invented languages as vehicles of communication and they have devised explicit or implicit rules of use to facilitate "efficient" encoding and decoding in particular contexts. The whole enterprise is a construction of conventions, which in itself would fail to meet some definitions of "natural." What Jack or Jill Smith happen to say in a particular place at a particular time in a particular context of situation has no privileged status in relation to all the billions of other utterances that have preceded, co-occurred or will succeed that exchange. And as Sacks (1992;1971) and Labov and Fanshel (1977) have reminded us, descriptions of contexts and of speech are themselves infinitely extendable.

For comprehensive and complementary analysis it would be odd not to collect texts of each relevant kind when this is possible, whilst noting that some questions are perhaps not amenable to particular modes of study at particular points in time. In the field of lying, for example, experimenters have contrived some bizarre studies in which sets of participants have pretended to lie to other alerted participants who have had to decide which of the statements uttered were untruthful. In such situations both encoders and decoders have been acting, generating data based on their personal theories about lying rather than the "realities" of the activity (see Figure 9.1). Neither have such participants been likely to have been motivated to the same extent as a defendant in court. Such investigations may be of interest but their relevance to lying is problematic, to say the least (Robinson, 1996). In contrast, the recorded interrogations of suspects of criminal acts or prisoners of war can combine natural "artificial" contexts with genuinely serious vested interests and experimental controls. (Perhaps in part, naturally occurring lying has been neglected because ecological studies of lying are time-consuming, potentially expensive, and will not generate sufficient papers for securing tenure or promotion for their authors – these are not good scientific reasons.)

In contrast, if the objective is to describe and explain variations in greeting behavior or terms of address and reference, it would be uneconomic not to elicit answers to questions about their rules of selection from competent members of the culture under scrutiny. Wardhaugh (1998) offers a succinct account of the latest successes in this research. For telephone conversation rules, some national phone books provide instructions that may be a useful guide for some initial generalizations about naturally recorded conversations. Likewise books of etiquette (Anonymous, 1886, Vanderbilt, 1963).

Presumably that Utopian aim to describe and explain all the interesting interfaces between language and social experience or behavior will be approached only when we can integrate findings about "natural" speech with those from other contrasted kinds of speech. Any apparent contradictions between descriptions and explanations of natural speech and any other kind themselves stand in need of explanation rather than a denial of the authenticity of either. So long as we remember that "natural," as it is typically used, is a contrastive term based on fictional but occasionally useful oppositions, all will be well.

15.6.3   Monologues and Polylogues

Much early work focused on units of speech (or writing) that failed to take into account that interpersonal communication involves more than one person speaking or writing. Not only will there be others listening or reading, but the roles can be interchanged, as in conversation. Conversations are not simply monologues succeeding each other, and they present a wide variety of problematic issues which are separable from questions about their constituent turns. However, each turn itself has a structure and content which can be studied in their own right. In addition, in certain contexts, extended monologues are the appropriate constructions. Aristotle's (1926/fourth century BC) treatise on rhetoric was the first of many commentaries and advisory manuals on how to generate efficacious political, forensic and funeral orations, and this traditional wisdom, suitably adapted for time, place, and culture, remains a refutable set of hypotheses today. If conversation happens to be more prevalent than TV debates, poetry and sermons, these others remain legitimate genres of study. Even very short monologues are speech and are appropriate objects of study for appropriate questions. Currently it would seem to be some of those who stress the naturalness of vernacular conversation who are more likely to deny the value of alternatives than vice versa, but this in no way diminishes the massive contributions of conversation analysts (for recent reviews see Forrester, 1996; Schiffrin, 1994).

15.6.4   Levels of Units and Structures

To repeat the previous opening paragraph, texts are not simply a succession of phonemes, morphemes, lexemes, sememes and pragmatic units (speech acts?). Linguistics certainly advanced the study of phonetics in the early years of the twentieth century, and psycholinguists, social psychologists and sociolinguists were able to benefit from these achievements much earlier than they could gain help from semantic and pragmatic analyses, which have only recently begun to make significant progress (for example Leech, 1983; Levinson, 1983), but it is quite clear that no stratum or unit of analysis is independent of all others, especially of those adjacent either horizontally or vertically. If investigators focus exclusively on particular units or strata, they may well draw mistaken inferences by missing the significance of the whole, but similarly, focusing on whole texts in context will not explain how the mind/brain identifies, integrates, and uses individual units of sound. Much intellectual effort has been spent confusing pragmatics with semantics and trying to reduce semantics to grammar. How the mind disambiguates and parses "The shooting of the hunters took place at dawn" would not normally present difficulties for participants in context – only for mythical observers in the abstract. Again, arguments about priorities and proprieties may best be seen initially as alternative approaches whose utilities will be forged over the anvil of empirical evidence.

15.6.5   Behavior (Speech and Writing) versus Accounts

The taboo of extreme Behaviorism in which pressing a buzzer was treated as more objective than saying "Yes," was still in existence in the 1970s, and although social psychologists have been less prone than their rat or pigeon-fancying colleagues to see all activity through only such eyes, the behaviorist influence has been potent. Skinner's (1957) text is the classical example. Harré and Secord (1970) performed a useful service in promoting the idea that personal accounts could be informative, and that for many experiences and actions, obtaining these was a rational point of departure; it was sensible to ask people what they were doing, how they were doing it, and why. But our methodology texts have also warned us of the reasons why accounts may be misleading and inadequate. Freud's Unconscious lives in all of us, and concealment and lying are not rare activities. However, as illustrated above, asking people about norms, or even consulting manuals, may be highly informative. The writing of this current text is not to be explained by a history of the schedules of reinforcement imposed on me by teachers and colleagues; indeed, many of the comments reflect an emancipation from a methodological slavery in which certain currently fashionable questions were treated as childish naiveté and were punished or ignored.

15.6.6   Experiments versus Cases and Field Studies

Experiments are often misleadingly defended as providing tight evidence for discovering the causal relationships between variables. Typically, the strength of the logic of the experimental formula "If A, then B – Observe B – Therefore A" is contrasted with the "infinite number" of reasons why A might correlate with B in a field study. A similarly invalid argument notes that a case study lacks controls and might be exceptional anyway. Very briefly, it may be noted that the logical structure of the experiment is not a valid deductive syllogism, but an invalid assertion of a consequent; it depends for its force on the plausibility of alternative explanations in just the same way as preferred explanations for correlational or case study connections depend for their force on contrasts with alternative stories. Scepticism about descriptions of, or explanations for, claimed associations and dissociations are subject to Type 2 errors. Interpretive mistakes can be made in any empirical investigation. Empirically, it may be the case that experimenters are generally careful in taking precautions about the inferences they draw from their observations, whilst some of those who use correlational studies may be prone not to consider alternative explanations to their preferred one. Students of cases may be disposed to overgeneralize, but demonstrated support for any particular claim would not be relevant to the logical similarity of the inductive procedures in all three kinds of study. Logical possibilities are not empirical or theoretical probabilities, and it is the latter and not the former which is of concern to social psychologists.

The earlier section with its commentary on the misleading distinction between qualitative and quantitative methods has rehearsed the first issue to be taken up briefly, while section 15.2 gave some reasons for the enthusiasm for experiments. Here just three points will be suggested. The first is that there are too few case studies of individuals. These can be of ordinary people commenting about ordinary topics or opening themselves up to being videoed and releasing duly edited tapes to investigators. These could be unrevealing and uninteresting records, but they might begin to give some insights into the use of speech in everyday life. The development of language mastery by growing infants has long relied on longitudinal recordings as significant sources for studying relationships between opportunities and conditions for learning. One would have expected too that case studies of specialists with language use would be of interest, for example courtroom advocates, political rhetoriticians, spin doctors, media interviewers. Atkinson (1984a & b) set an informative precedent, and as he and others have shown, there can be objective as well as experiential indicators of evaluation of speech and speeches in "natural" situations.

A second neglected technique is that of Garfinkel's (1967) manipulations with their various forms of the flouting of hypothesized rules and their functions. Why actors are not used more often is difficult to understand. As Groucho Marx advised, "all you need to succeed in Hollywood is honesty and plain dealing, and if you can learn to fake these you will be a great success." Real actors are much better at acting than psychology students are.

Field experiments and observations, along with the accounts as well as the reactions of participants and viewers, ensure that data are linked to genuine behavior. Interactions between doctors and patients, TV interviewers and victims, courtroom participants, or police interviewees may take more time and trouble to set up and record, but they are for real and avoid the outer rings of Figure 9.1: i.e., what people can simulate or what they think others are like. The work of Bull (chapters 6 and 12), Shuy (chapter 6), and Cody and McLaughlin (chapter 7) exemplify the advantages of exploiting "natural" resources.

15.6.7 Commentary

It would have been possible to extend or deepen the polarizations discussed by listing various contrasting X-isms: idealism versus realism, idealism versus pragmatism, nominalism versus realism, rationalism versus empiricism, subjectivism versus objectivism, phenomenalism versus realism. However, it was not the purpose of the grid to précis or caricature a book on methods and methodology. The intention has been to illustrate the dangers of any general idealization of the poles of any of the contrasts. Each of us has to choose to work in a limited field with a limited array of approaches. We hope our endeavors will be fruitful. Given the effort each of us invests, we would be crazy if we did not believe that what we were doing was the most likely approach to yield fruitful outcomes. However, that does not mean that those who are trying to answer different questions with different approaches are misguided. They may be trying to answer very similar questions with different approaches.

However, as already implied, any plea for mutual respect and interest is unlikely to meet with serious consideration and concurrence until we emancipate ourselves from the biases predicted by Social Identity Theory (SIT) (Tajfel & Turner, 1979). We are not immune from the influences of our theories, and SIT seems to be peculiarly appropriate to academic disputes. US versus THEM operates at the disciplinary boundaries, at the boundaries of perspectives within disciplines, and within perspectives at both field and approach boundaries. At the present time, some of us believe that social psychologists interested in language are being riven by divisions which are greater than is healthy, and attitudes currently being expressed do seem to be emphasizing distinctiveness, the deficiencies of outgroups, and the virtues of the ingroup. Each of the poles of the six are to count as well-founded beliefs, human beings might be able to agree on more rational and realistic bases for achieving societal progress. At present, most human beings are victims of, rather than agents in, the societies in which they find themselves. Language and social psychology have crucial roles to play in any progress from our current condition. "Without vision the people perish" (Proverbs), and I see nothing odd or juvenile in having a vision of societies where the information gathered about language use is used to improve societies.

15.7 Participants, Materials, and Procedures

Participants should be fit for the purposes they are intended to serve. Unless beliefs about other people's beliefs or behavior or similar meta-topics are the concerns of the research, participants should be being themselves. Such an attitude is consistent with the denunciation of the excessive exploitation of students as respondents. The proportion of investigations relying on the verbal and non-verbal of US students performing for grades is probably yielding very misleading information. The 18–22 year-old age group is over represented, as are monolingual Caucasians of above average academic ability and achievement. Most students of this group do not have full-time jobs or domestic responsibilities. Relatively few are settled into long-term close relationships. Most will be entering white-collar jobs in one of the most prosperous and certainly the most powerful country in the world. Availability, cheapness, and ease of administration are not satisfactory substitutes for validity and appropriateness. This is not an assertion that students are always unsuitable as respondents. They can be an entirely sensible population, but they have to be "fit for purpose" and seen as a particular social category, just as members of other social categories do.

Such considerations also apply to materials and procedures. Questionnaires should not force answers into invalid experiential categories and should not be used to make claims about what people say or do rather than what they say they say or do. Scores on attitudinal rating scales that tap attitudes irrelevant to the respondents are of dubious value. Vignettes that under-determine real-life and force answers into odd categories that over-simplify the contingencies of real decision-making are therefore silly (see Antaki, 1994 for a critique). Obliging people to reveal they know that when the stimulus word is "Russians" they are expected to forget the many ethnic variants, social class, gender, age, religion and the inevitable diversity among over 200,000,000 citizens and tick the correct end of a seven-point scale of pessimistic–optimistic yields misleading stereotypes. Procedures too can constrain with instructions that cannot be sensibly followed. The 2001 census of Britain forced each of us into ethnic categorizations on the assumption that grandparents, parents, and each individual were members of a single national category. Even then, although Scots could tick Scots, the Welsh had no separate box and had to be British or Other. The English likewise. In short the form was muddled.

Apparatus available has improved greatly in recent years both for data collection and processing. It is, however, necessary to note the potential abuse of mail, telephones and the Internet as sampling devices for frequency estimates. It is also necessary to repeat here the potential abuse of computers for presenting de-personalized two-dimensional stimulus materials where participants can rate pictures of people rather than real ones. Both voice and video-recorders have contributed greatly to the quality of data that can be collected and analyzed, as has physiologically sensitive machinery. Computer analyses can be performed in great variety with great speed, but this again carries risks of abuse: selecting the best fit patterns after repeated runs with different statistical calculations, giving quantitative estimates of unknown reliability. The various temptations to struggle for statistical significance are part of the pressure-to-publish culture.

15.8 Data

The issues about data are elementary matters, but their implications are not always observed. Questions about which data are useful and which not cannot be answered sensibly in the abstract, but certain principles do apply. Uniqueness without generalization cannot be of any value, and observations without rationale likewise: simple recordings without defined purposes, even if they are extensive and detailed. Data need to be indicative, and it is what they are indicative of that has to be explained. With the growth in statistical sophistication and calculative powers of computers, at least two risks need to be borne in mind. First, it is not the data sets that need to be explained but the experience and behavior that has generated them. Second, data are not 100 percent reliable (see above); each score or number is an estimate, usually with an unquantified degree of uncertainty. If not checked in various ways, this can mean that statistical analyses can endow the numbers fed in with precision that they do not have. In a multiple regression or structure equation modelling exercise, a particular variable may extract .001 percent more variance than a second one, and eliminate the second from further consideration, when the reverse answer might be more sensible. Calculations are rigid and cannot compensate for lack of intelligent theorizing in deciding what to include and circumspection in interpretation. Anyone who experiments with dropping one or two outlier responses or respondents from an analysis is likely to find particular answers to be relatively unstable, but very few investigators raise these questions in their data processing, just as very few check whether theoretical relationships investigated are likely to be as linear as the parameters of the statistics presuppose.

In various phenomena reviewed in this text, examples have appeared of quantitative differences leading to categorical shifts. Is A guilty? Is B lying? Is C trying to run off with my husband? Many behavioral significant classifications have quantitative aspects, but with critical decision-relevant thresholds. Particularly in competitive situations decision-makers may hold complex probabilistic propositions in their heads, but at some point commitments to action have to be made, which will depend crucially on which side of a neutral point the judgment has come down. (With quantitative variations of either side of a neutral point there are also categorical decisions to be made in the light of the intensity and extremity of affect or disapproval. Probabilistic decision-making models do not yet model real decisions very well, although recent models are beginning to take on more cognitively economic characteristics (Gigerenzer & Todd, 1999).)

15.9   The Changing Games of Changing Social Worlds

The human worlds of physics and chemistry have changed through time because of the constructions and discoveries of physicists and chemists, but positrons and palladium have been around since before people, and their properties have not changed since then. Human beings have created "new" elements, but the laws governing their functioning have not been changed as a result of human intervention. The same cannot be said of much of biology. In its own right evolutionary processes have interacted with meteorological and geological changes to generate and select species. Human intervention in the pursuit of agriculture, animal husbandry and the running battle with pests and diseases (as we view them) may not have changed the underlying principles of the game of life, but they have certainly transformed their realizations. And so it is with both language and social psychology.

Languages and cultures become extinct. New languages appear and grow. The romantically inclined may lament the passing of Hittite and Manx, but they can observe the emergence of *pidgins* and *Creoles* that could easily be defined as new languages if it were so wished. They can observe the lingua franca of English diversifying around the world to yield mutually unintelligible "species." They can observe misunderstandings across the Atlantic Ocean where requests for restrooms or vests lead to different experiences in the UK and USA. Within England itself signs on level crossings warning motorists to "Wait while the lights are flashing" had to be changed after causing deaths in East Yorkshire, because "while" means "until" in that regional variety. But some features are more readily changed than others. Technological innovations quickly lead to a new wave of terms and phrases that can move into everyday parlance. The zest for novelty that afflicts sub-groups in certain cultures likewise generates smart talk that fades away as fast as it appeared. In contrast, English is seemingly stuck with its sexist personal pronouns and other features embedded in its grammar, much as some cultures are stuck with obsolete annual calendars (Duncan, 1998).

The significance of such facts mean that those working with language have to be asking themselves what is changing and what is staying the same, and they need to be alert to what is gaining ground and what is losing – and what has been lost. Presumably Hittite disappeared because the Hittite speakers were killed off or died out. Manx died because English took over. The operation of these more macroscopic social processes has not been rehearsed here but can be found in appropriate sociolinguistic texts (for example Wardhaugh, 1987; 1998). The factors of the pursuit of power, wealth, and status mentioned frequently here are common to the social psychological and sociological levels of analysis, but typically have more dramatic realizations at the sociological level which includes wars, massacres, imperial suppression, and slavery, concepts beyond most social psychological analyses where they operate through their sub-institutional equivalents. In the case of terms of reference and address, the last 50 years have witnessed changes in American and British English usage with reductions in the differentials for power, a move towards informal forms, and the introduction and spread of new forms such as Ms. In grammar some nouns have become verbs (hospitalize), some contextually intransitive verbs have become transitive (for example "grow" the company as well as vegetables). Use of such features serve as markers of both social and personal identity, as does being *au fait* with computer- and Internet-speak.

Individuals change during their lifetimes, social groups come, change, and go, sub-cultures come, change, and go; some do so quickly, some slowly. With the changes in values and norms go symbols and expressions of these as realized in NVC and V. The ubiquitous power and solidariness dimensions remain ubiquitous but they expand and shrink and switch their signs. Salt, pepper and sugar are no longer the markers of wealth and status that they once were. Gold adornments in contrast have a long and continuing history. Monarchies and aristocracies preserve their asymmetries in speech, but families in the quasi-democracies have moved further into the solidary symmetries than Brown was noting in 1965. Close relationships, such as marriage, have shifted in character over both long and short periods in terms of rights and obligations (Stone, 1990) as have gender relationships more generally. Since the main text has emphasized the impermanent nature of phenomena, perhaps it is necessary to make only one further point, and that is to note that the "liberal progressive" view of history is a myth: the world as a global entity is not destined to become more libertarian, equalitarian, and fraternal. Nineteen Eight-Four-type scenarios are as likely as others. The western quasi-democracies, especially the UK and USA, have seen a small number of rich get richer and a large number of poor get much poorer in the last 40 years, and this trend shows no sign of being reversed (Hutton, 1996; Rubinstein, 1994; Wilkinson, 1994). In like manner, the political and economic power of increasingly fewer multinational companies has grown greatly to exceed the power of governments in those same countries. Such concentrations are evident in the media in the last decade (McChesney, 1999), just as they were evident in steel, finance, pharmaceuticals, and petrochemicals earlier. For most of these, language and speech differentials are of small significance compared with capacities of the military and police for "law" enforcement, with the global media companies being able to ensure that what is communicated to the citizenry serve the interests of the powers that be.

15.10   The Whorfian Challenge and Beyond

This text is not entirely apolitical, but it does try to avoid crooked arguments in defense of either scientific or political positions. In chapter 12 attempts were made to tie rationality and evidence-based descriptions and explanation of language behavior to cooperative and truth-seeking human activities, whilst noting that much of the behavior of the human species is competitive. The balance between competitiveness and cooperativeness has been and still is a major determinant of the nature of human societies and the differential life-chances between and within them (Fukuyama, 1995). The extent to which societies have allowed or encouraged competitiveness to escalate into the oppression and killing of competitors is a major determinant of the current state of human affairs – and will continue to be so. The vitality of languages and their varieties (Giles, Bourhis & Taylor, 1977) depends ultimately on whether any people are left alive to speak them. The most vital languages are those whose speakers exercise the most power in the maintenance and spread of their preferred languages and varieties.

Threads relevant to those two propositions have made appearances at various points in the text, most prominently in chapter 12.5. Elsewhere, however, mention has been made of group and individual differences in competence with language operating in its social and representational functions (chapters 12 & 13). Its roles as a marker of social and personal identity and as a regulator of social relationships have been discussed extensively (chapters 6–10). Here an attempt will be made to integrate these data into a socio-political synthesis, but first it will be necessary to try to inoculate readers against some of the spurious arguments typically raised to justify the current and erstwhile status quos in which massive social stratification of life-chances have been present within and between societies. That spurious arguments of elites are accepted by the victim-losers is to be expected under conditions in which contemporary reality is accorded the appearance of a just world.

Darwinian libels

Darwin's ideas became available to the increasingly unreligious societies of the twentieth century as an alternative to God to explain and justify what is in the world of biology. The slogan of "survival of the fittest" was a slightly devious one for elites to quote, since their power, wealth, and status depended on the temporary survival of the rest to work for their benefit. The advantages for societies of selection by competition has served as a frequently voiced justification for increasing wealth differentials in individualistic capitalist societies in the last 25 years.

However, as the philosopher Hume pointed out, there are no valid arguments that can be used to derive an "ought" from an "is," what is the case cannot be used to infer what ought to be the case. That being so ideas of social justice have to be constructed and evaluated on other grounds (see chapter 11.2.3). Ideas of what is efficient should also be evaluated on an evidence-based argument involving valued ends and acceptable means, whereas they are more prone to represent the preferred biases of their beneficiaries. Human beings of the twentieth century continued their history of massive slaughtering and enslavement of outgroups, with most of the slavery disguised as minimal wages in dangerous and hard life-shortening work. The citizens of each country and the dominant groups and strata of each country are socialized into rhetorics that both account for and justify their peculiar statuses, but critical analyses of these rhetorics can quickly be shown to be logically flawed and empirically unsupported. Some of the effective kinds of justification that worked through language were listed in chapter 12.5, but for the rest of this chapter, the point of departure will shift from questions of how power elites control others through language policies to how languages and their varieties limit affordances.

The Efficiency of Different Languages

To ask about the comparative efficiencies of languages extant is dangerous. It is dangerous academically because any such question needs to be deconstructed into more limited and precise questions which would need to be prefaced by "Efficiency for what?" It is dangerous socio-politically because there is a chorus of voices in support of human diversity and difference. Unfortunately, outgroup distinctiveness is a necessary feature of diversity and historically this has been the justification of assertions of ingroup superiority and outgroup inferiority to the extremes of genocides, enslavement, and oppression. The classical Greek concept of "barbarian" was a direct reference to the unintelligibility and hence inferiority of their languages. To define the means by which diversity among social groups can co-exist with parity of respect and equal human and legal rights and obligations has eluded the human species.

To begin at the less contentious fringes it may be noted that modes of generating writing can be seen to differ in efficiency (see Crystal, 1998, pp. 179–209 for a succinct review). Electronic printing is faster than mechanical printing, which is faster than penning, which is faster than chiselling. In modes of representation, Arabic numerals have supplanted Roman numerals because their decimalization by place renders the arithmetic operations of addition, subtraction, multiplication, and division easier. They also have a zero. Binary representation is the preferred electronic representation, but would be tedious for everyday purposes. Alphabets versus syllabaries is more contentious, as are alphabets versus logography. With mechanical typewriters, the Chinese had more design problems than alphabet users. Alphabets are certainly faster to write in than hieroglyphics. At first the English alphabet may be guessed to be easier to learn than the 2000 logograms of basic Mandarin, but of course English writers have also to learn lots of words. Dictation and reading are both easier for alphabets than ideographically or logographically-based languages, but meanings will not necessarily be easier to divine.

To move on to more dangerous ground, it may be noted that some languages have massive technical vocabularies; English can run up to 500,000 lexemes to cope with the enormous encoding requirements of logical and scientific variables and functions. In the sciences these are likely to have highly specialized and tightly defined terms and expressions for representing units and structures of relevance to them. Just as Arabic numerals remind us of our historical debt to Arab culture but are not viewed as indicators of Arabic ingroup superiority, so one can hope that the Englishness of so much scientific terminology will simply become irrelevant to the prosecution of science and technology and cease to have cultural associations. (Most of these terms are strongly Graeco–Latin in origin in any case.)

In chapter 14 the original and specific Whorf hypothesis was described, and some evidence relevant to it was evaluated. Variants on that have proliferated, some more specific (see chapter 13) and some too abstract. For example, the idea that thinking cannot transcend language is doubly strange. Both the generality and lack of specificity militate against this level of formulation being of use. *In extremis* it has to be wrong too. No one claims that monkeys or apes have created a language, but most if not all our animal behaviorists would say that their activities manifest thinking. Young human infants give evidence of pre-linguistic thinking, but then human beings could have never invented languages in the first place if their thinking skills could not transcend their language capacities.

The idea that lexical differentiation reflected more than environmental utility led to some strange empirical studies in which authors could offer English phrasal equivalents for single Innuit lexemes which demonstrated English could afford comparable differentiation for types of snow. Arabic differentiation of camels likewise could be expressed in English. If one takes the Farnsworth–Munsell hue differentiation system with its 6,000,000 psycho-physically discriminable items, then real language differences in the number of basic single terms are small. However, as Berlin and Kay (1969) have shown, languages do differ in single lexeme differentiation, and this may have implications for contemporary habitual experience and behavior, but not for what can/could be experienced and learned.

One reason seldom mentioned for the absence of Whorf-probing studies could be the reluctance of speakers of major international languages to risk accusations of claiming superiorities of their languages over others. Labov's (1970) slogan of "All languages are equivalent/equal" was an understandable if unfortunate response to the ignorant and arrogant claims of critics of dialects within international languages, of pidgins and Creoles, and of some "small" languages.

Sadly, the defenders, and more especially the users, of smaller languages have been oppressed, bullied, insulted, and denigrated on quite unjustified grounds, but unfortunately some of their defenders have also chosen ill-founded arguments in their defense. Multi-lingual countries cannot have road signs or telephone directories in every language that is spoken by those carrying citizenship passports. Neither can they realistically offer education in a child's primary tongue. It is possible to find over 20 primary tongues in some London junior schools. Such issues as feasibility and utility, however, need to be separated from issues of inferiority/superiority of languages – and especially of the inferiority/superiority of the speakers of languages. Yet this is common both between languages and between dialects and accents within languages. Whether or not this is commoner in unilingual countries with an international language could be investigated. British education certainly remains plagued by ill-informed and Anglocentric biases about Standard English, and "deficit" views of children learning and developing in its schools. By "deficit" here two meanings are intended. The first is created by age-related norms of performance that are designed to discriminate among an age cohort, and then labelling the below norm as "deficient." The second derives from setting up an adult, often ego-centric, ideal of competence and judging children in terms of how far they are below this ideal. It is as though they can be thought of as "deficient" in height, soccer skill, wealth, and everything else that is related to what could be construed more sensibly as positive growth and development. If this sounds exaggerated, then it is worth asking why the more precocious and advanced children are not seen as or treated as normatively deficient adults whereas their "below average" peers are.

And which social categories of children are over-represented among the normatively backward? Historically and currently they are from the poorest social strata. It was Bernstein (1961) who advanced the thesis that the (lower) working class constituted a sociological transposition of the Whorf hypothesis, and as reported in chapter 13, there are certainly social class differences in the socialization practices consistent with a class-related differential orientation to the representational function of language and the range of its uses referred to in chapter 10. The school experiences of many lower working class children are a manifold of self-fulfilling prophecies (Robinson, 1979) eventuating in their increasing alienation from school values, even if they had such values in their early years. As Corson (1995) has demonstrated, the massive infusion of Graeco–Latin technical terms into the secondary school curriculum can only serve to alienate them further, if that is possible.

It would be an exaggeration and an over-simplification to argue that such children are solely victims of a Whorfian-type hypothesis, but clearly if they are not enabled to switch into the representational function beyond mundane cooperative contexts, then they are destined to become increasingly disadvantaged in their verbally-based learning, yielding a contemporary version of the discriminatory activities of power elites listed in chapter 12.5. Since such facts have been made quite evident to governments of all varieties over the last century and before, it must be the case that they know they are acting to maintain an impoverished underclass, regardless of whether this is disguised in terms of ethnicity, gender, or some other adversely discriminatory categorization (Robinson, 2001b). The globalization of economies is likely to accentuate this differentiation both within and between societies, until such time as power elites are obliged to confront the questions raised in chapter 11 and to answer them without recourse to the crooked self-serving arguments referred to in that same chapter and illustrated in chapter 11.

The critique of social psychology's over-heavy investment in experiments applies less to language and communication than it does to most other fields. Language both for and in communication suffers more from simple neglect. Whilst it is common now to find texts with law and health in final sections of standard texts, language in communication is presented in only a small minority. In an era where irony has become the periodic refuge of those legatees of the eighteenth century Enlightenment who had hoped to see societies being reformed in the light of the human sciences contribution to principles of *liberté, egalité* and *fraternité*, there is a wry side to a social psychology relying so heavily on language use for data collection and so heavily on language for the dissemination but that pays so little attention to the study of language in communication itself. Like studying the behavior of fish without attending to water.

References

Abelson, R. P., and Lalljee, M. (1988). Knowledge structures and causal explanation. In D. Hilton (ed.), *Contemporary science and natural explanation* (pp. 175–203). London: Harvester.

Allport, F. H. (1924). *Social psychology.* Boston, MA: Houghton-Mifflin.

Allport, G. W., and Odbert, H. S. (1936). Trait names: a psycho-lexical study. *Psychological Monographs, 47,* (1, No. 211).

Altman, I., and Vinsel, A. M. (1977). Personal space. In I. Altman and J. Wohlwill (eds.), *Human behaviour and environment* (Vol. 2). New York: Plenum.

Anonymous (1886). *Australian etiquette.* Melbourne: People's Publishing Co. (Facsimile reprinted by J. M. Dent, 1980).

Antaki, C. (ed.). (1988). *Analysing everyday explanation.* London: Sage.

Antaki, C. (1994). *Explaining and arguing. The social organization of accounts.* London: Sage.

Aquinas, T. (1989). *Summa theologiae* (T. McDermott, trans. and ed.). London: Eyre & Spottiswoode.

Argyle, M. (1988). *Bodily communication* (2nd edn.). London: Methuen.

Argyle, M. (1994). *The psychology of social class.* London: Routledge.

Argyle, M., Alkema, F., and Gilmour, R. (1971). The communication of friendly and hostile attitudes by verbal and non-verbal signals. *European Journal of Social Psychology, 2,* 385–402.

Argyle, M., Salter, V., Nicholson, J., Williams, M., and Burgess, P. (1970). The communication of inferior and superior attitudes by verbal and non-verbal signals. *British Journal of Social and Clinical Psychology, 9,* 222–231.

Aristotle. (1926). *The art of rhetoric* (T. J. Freese, trans.) London: Loeb Classical Library.

Asch, S. (1952). *Social psychology.* Englewood Cliff, NJ: Prentice Hall.

Atkinson, J. M. (1984a). *Our masters' voices.* London: Methuen.

Atkinson, J. M. (1984b). Public speaking and audience responses. In J. M. Atkinson and J. C. Heritage (eds.), *Structures of social action.* Cambridge, UK: Cambridge University Press.

Au, T. K. (1986). A verb is worth a thousand words: The causes and consequences of interpersonal events implicit in language. *Journal of Memory and Language, 25,*

104–122.

Austin, J. L. (1962). *How to do things with words.* Oxford, UK: Oxford University Press.

Bacon, F. (1855) *Novum organum* (G. W. Kitchin, Trans.). Oxford, UK: Oxford University Press. (Original work published 1625)

Bales, R. F. (1950). *Interaction process analysis.* Cambridge, MA: Addison Wesley.

Bales, R. F., and Slater, P. (1955). Role differentiation in small decision-making groups. In T. Parsons and R. F. Bales (eds.), *Family, socialization, and interaction process.* Glencoe, IL: Free Press.

Barley, N. (1984). *The innocent anthropologist.* Harmondsworth, UK: Penguin.

Barthes, R. (1968). *Elements of semiology.* London: Cape.

Barzun, J. (1959). *The house of intellect.* New York: Harper.

Baugh, A. C., and Cable, T. (1987). *A history of the English language* (3rd edn.). London: Routledge.

Bavelas, A. (1950). Communication patterns in task-oriented groups. *Journal of the Acoustical Society of America, 22,* 725–730.

Bavelas, J. B., Black, A., Chovill, N., and Mullet, J. (1990). *Equivocal communication.* Newbury Park, CA: Sage.

Baym, N. K. (2000). *Tune in, log on.* Thousand Oaks, CA: Sage.

Bearison, D. J., and Cassel, T. Z. (1975). Cognitive decentration and social codes: Communication effectiveness in young children from differing family contexts. *Developmental Psychology, 11,* 29–36.

Beattie, G. W. (1982). Turn-taking and interruptions in political interviews – Margaret Thatcher and Jim Callaghan compared and contrasted. *Semiotica, 39,* 93–114.

Beattie, G. W., Cutler, A., and Pearson, M. (1982). Why is Mrs. Thatcher interrupted so often? *Nature, 300,* 744–747.

Berger, C., and Bradac, J. J. (1982). *Language and social interaction.* London: Arnold.

Berlin, B., and Kay, P. (1969). *Basic color terms: their universality and evolution.* Berkeley, CA: University of California Press.

Berne, E. (1966). *Games people play.* London: Deutsch.

Bernstein, B. (1961). Social structure, language, and learning. *Educational Research, 2,* 163–76.

Bernstein, B. (1971). *Class, codes and control* (Vol. 1). London: Routledge.

Bernstein, B. (1973). *Class, codes, and control* (Vol. 2). London: Routledge.

Bernstein, B. (1975). *Class, codes, and control* (Vol. 3). London: Routledge.

Bies, R. J. and Sitkin, B. B. (1992). Explanation as legitimation. Excuse-making in organizations. In M. L. McLaughlin, M. J. Cody and S. J. Read (eds.), *Explaining oneself to others* (pp. 183–198). Hillsdale, NJ: Erlbaum.

Billig, M. (1996). *Arguing and thinking. A rhetorical approach to social psychology.* (2nd edn.) Cambridge, UK: Cambridge University Press.

Billig, M. (2001). Arguing. In W. P. Robinson and H. Giles (eds.), *New handbook of language and social psychology* (pp. 241–252). Chichester, UK: Wiley.

Birdwhistell, R. L. (1970). *Kinesics and context.* Philadelphia, PA: University of Philadelphia Press.

Blom, J-P., and Gumperz, J. J. (1972). Social meaning in linguistic structures. Code-switching in Norway. In J. J. Gumperz and D. Hymes (eds.), *Directions in sociolinguistics* (pp. 407–434). New York: Holt.

Bloomfield, L. (1935). *Language.* London: Allen and Unwin. (First published 1933)

Blumler, J., and Katz, E. (eds.). (1974). *The uses of mass communications.* Beverley Hills, CA: Sage.

Bourdieu, P. (1977). *Distinctions.* London: Routledge.

Bourdieu, P. (1991). *Language and symbolic power.* Cambridge, MA: Harvard University Press.

Borgatta, E., and Bales, R. F. (1956). Sociometric status patterns and characteristics of interaction. *Journal of Social Psychology, 43,* 289–297.

Bowerman, M., and Levinson, S. (eds.). (2001). *Language acquisition and conceptual development.* Cambridge, UK: Cambridge University Press.

Bradac, J., Friedman, E., and Giles, H. (1986). A social approach to prepositional communication: Speakers lie to hearers. In G. McGregor (ed.), *Language for hearers* (pp. 127–151). Oxford, UK: Pergamon.

Brazil, D. C. (1975). Discourse intonation. *Discourse Intonation Monographs, 1,* Birmingham,U: Birmingham English Language Research.

Broomfield, K., Robinson,E. J., and Robinson, W. P., (in press). Children's understanding about white lies. *British Journal of Developmental Psychology.*

Brophy, J. E., and Evertson, C. M. (1976). *Learning from teaching.* Boston, MA: Allyn and Bacon.

Brown, P., and Fraser, C. (1979). Speech as a marker of situation. In K. R. Scherer and H. Giles (eds.), *Social markers in speech* (pp. 33–52). Cambridge, UK: Cambridge University Press.

Brown, P. and Levinson, S. (1987).*Politeness: Some Universals in language use.* Cambridge, UK: Cambridge University Press. (Original publication 1978).

Brown, R., and Ford, M. (1961). Address in American English. *Journal of abnormal and social psychology, 62,* 375–385.

Brown, R., and Gilman, H. (1960). The pronouns of solidarity and power. In T. A. Sebeok (ed.), *Style in language.* New York: Wiley.

Brown, R. W. (1965). *Social psychology.* Glencoe, IL: Free Press.

Bruner, J. S., Olver,R., and Greenfield, P. M. (eds.). (1966). *Studies in cognitive growth.* New York: Wiley.

Bryman, A., and Burgess, R. G. (1999). *Qualitative Research* (4 vols). London: Sage.

Bull, P. (in press). *Communication under the microscope.* London: Psychology Press.

Bull, P. E. (1998). Equivocation theory and news interviews. *Journal of Language and Social Psychology, 17,* 36–51.

Bull, P. E., Elliott, J., Palmer, D., and Walker, L. (1996). Why politicians are three-faced: the face-model of political interviews. *British Journal of Social Psychology, 35,* 267–284.

Bull, P. E., and Mayer, K. (1988). Interruptions in political interviews: a study of Margaret Thatcher and Neil Kinnock. *Journal of Language and Social Psychology, 7,* 35–45.

Buller, D. B., and Burgoon, J. K. (1996). Interpersonal deception theory. *Communication Theory, 6,* 203–242.

Burger, J. M. (1986). Increasing compliance by improving the deal. *Journal of Personality and Social Psychology, 51,* 277–283.

Burgoon, J. K., and Burgoon, M. (2001). Expectancy theories. In W. P. Robinson and H. Giles (eds.) *New handbook of language and social psychology* (pp. 79–102). Chichester, UK: Wiley.

Burgoon, J. K., Stern, L. A., and Dillman, L. (1995). *Dyadic adaptation*. New York: Cambridge University Press.

Burgoon, M. (1990). Language and social influence. In H. Giles and W. P. Robinson (eds.), *Handbook of language and social psychology*, (pp. 33–50). Chichester, UK: Wiley.

Burgoon, M., and Miller, G. R. (1985). On expectancy interpretation of language and persuasion. In H. Giles and R. St. Clair (eds.), *Recent advances in language, communication, and social psychology* (pp. 199–229). London: Erlbaum.

Buttny, R., and Morris, G. H. (2001). Everyone has to account. In W. P. Robinson and H. Giles (eds.), *New handbook of language and social psychology* (pp. 285–382). Chichester, UK: Wiley.

Callahan, J. (ed.). (1988). *Ethical issues in professional life.* New York: Oxford University Press.

Cappella, J., and Palmer, M. T. (1990). The structure of non-verbal behavior in social interaction. In H. Giles and W. P. Robinson (eds.), *Handbook of language and social psychology* (pp. 141–162). Chichester, UK: Wiley.

Carmichael, L., Hogan, H. P., and Walters, A. A. (1932). An experimental study of the effect of language on the reproduction of visually perceived forms. *Journal of Experimental Psychology, 15,* 73–86.

Carroll, T. S., and Payne, J. W. (1977). Judgments about crime and the criminal. In B. D. Sales (ed.), *Perspectives in law and psychology* (pp. 191–239). New York: Plenum Press.

Carter, L., Haythorn, W., Shriver, B., and Lanzetta, J. (1951). The behavior of leaders and other group members. *Journal of Abnormal and Social Psychology, 46,* 589–595.

Cartwright, D., and Zander, A. (eds.) (1960). *Group Dynamics* (2nd edn.). London: Tavistock.

Cerulo, K. A. (1998). *Deciphering violence.* New York: Routledge.

Chadwick-Jones, J. (1998). *Developing a social psychology of monkeys and apes.* London: Psychology Press.

Chomsky, N. (1957). *Syntactic structures.* The Hague: Mouton.

Chomsky, N. (1965). *Aspects of the theory of syntax.* Cambridge, MA: MIT Press.

Cialdini, R. B. (1985). *Influence: Science and practice.* Glenview, IL: Scott, Foresman.

Cialdini, R. B. et al. (1975). Reciprocal concessions procedure for inducing compliance. *Journal of Personality and Social Psychology, 31,* 206–215.

Cicero (1971). *De Oratore: On the good life.* Harmondsworth, UK: Penguin Classics.

Clarke, D. D. (1977). Rules and sequences in conversation. In P. Collett (ed.), *Social rules and social behaviour(pp. 42–69).* Oxford, UK: Blackwell.

Clark, D. D. (1983). *Language and action.* Oxford, UK: Pergamon.

Clarke, D. D., and Argyle, M. (1982). Conversation sequences. In C. Fraser and K. R. Scherer (eds.), *Advances in the social psychology of language* (pp. 159–204). Cambridge, UK: Cambridge University Press.

Clayman, S. E. (1988). Displaying neutrality in television news interviews. *Social problems, 35,* 474–492.

Clayman, S. E. (1992). Footing in the achievement of neutrality. In P. D. Drew and

J. Heritage (eds.), *Talk at work* (pp. 163–198). Cambridge, UK: Cambridge University Press.

Coates, L. and Johnson, T. (2001). Towards a social theory of gender. In W. P. Robinson and H. Giles, (eds.), *New handbook of language and social psychology* (pp. 451–464). Chichester, UK: Wiley.

Cody, M. J., and McLaughlin, M. L. (1988). Accounts of trial. In C. Antaki (ed.), *Analysing everyday explanation,* (pp. 113–126). London: Sage.

Cody, M. J., and McLaughlin, M. L. (1990). Interpersonal accounting. In H. Giles and W. P. Robinson (eds.), *Handbook of language and social psychology,* (pp. 227–256). Chichester, UK: Wiley.

Collett, P. (1971). On training Englishmen in the non-verbal behaviour of Arabs. *International Journal of Psychology, 7,* 169–179.

Cook, M. (1970). Experiments on orientation and proxemics. *Human Relations, 23,* 13–21.

Cook-Gumperz, J. (1973). *Social control and socialization.* London: Routledge.

Corson, D. (1995). *Using English words.* Dordrecht: Kluwer.

Coulthard, R. M. (1977). *Discourse analysis.* London: Longmans.

Coupland, N., and Coupland, J. (2001). Language, ageing, and ageism. In W. P. Robinson and H. Giles (eds.), *New handbook of language and social psychology* (pp. 465–488). Chichester, UK: Wiley.

Coupland, N., Grainger, K., and Coupland, J. (1988). Politeness in context: Intergenerational issues. *Language in Society, 17,* 253–262.

Crossen, C. (1994). *The tainted truth.* New York: Simon and Schuster.

Crystal, D. (1988). *The English language.* Harmondsworth, UK: Penguin.

Crystal, D. (1998). *The Cambridge encyclopaedia of language.* Cambridge, UK: Cambridge University Press.

Czikszentmihalyi, M., Larson, R., and Prescott, S. (1977). The ecology of adolescent activity and experience. *Journal of Youth and Adolescence, 6,* 281–294.

Davidson, D. (1984). *Inquiries into truth and interpretation.* Oxford, UK: Oxford University Press.

Davidson, D. (1986). A coherence theory of truth and knowledge. In E. Le Pore (ed.), *Truth and interpretation.* Oxford, UK: Blackwell.

Davies, N. (1999). *The isles.* London: Macmillan.

Davitz, J. L. (1964). *The communication of emotional meaning.* New York: McGraw-Hill.

Deaux, K., Dane, F. C., and Wrightsman, L. S. (1993). *Social psychology in the 1990s* (6th edn.). Pacific Grove, CA: Brooks/Cole.

Derrida, D. (1972). *Positions.* Chicago: University of Chicago Press.

Derrida, D. (1984). *Margins of philosophy.* Chicago: University of Chicago Press.

Desmond, A. (1994). *Huxley: The devil's disciple.* London: Joseph.

Digman, J. M. (1990). Personality structure: Emergence of the five-factor model. *Annual Review of Psychology, 41,* 417–440.

Digman, J. M. (1996). The curious history of the five factor model. In J. S. Wiggins (ed.), *The five factor model of personality* (pp. 1–20). New York: Guilford.

Dionne, E. J. (1991). *Why Americans hate politics.* New York: Simon & Schuster.

Draper, S. W. (1988) What's going on in explanations? In C. Antaki, (ed.), *Analysing everyday explanation* (pp. 15–31). London: Sage.

Duncan, D. E. (1998). *The calendar*. London: Fourth Estate.

Duncan, S. D. (1972). Some signals and rules for taking speaking turns in conversations. *Journal of Personality and Social Psychology, 23*, 283–292.

Duncan, S. D., and Fiske, D. W. (1977). *Face-to-face interaction: Research methods and theory*. Hillsdale, NJ: Erlbaum.

Duncan, S. D., and Niederehe, G. (1974). On signalling when it's your turn to speak. *Journal of Experimental Psychology, 10*, 234–247.

Eco, U. (1979). *The role of the reader*. London: Hutchinson.

Edwards, J. (1989). *Language and disadvantage* (2nd edn.). London: Cole and Whurr.

Ekman, P. (ed.) (1982). *Emotion in the human face*. Cambridge, UK: Cambridge University Press.

Ekman, P. (1992). *Telling lies*. New York: Norton. (Original work published 1985).

Ekman, P. (1993). Facial expression and emotion. *American Psychologist, 48*, 384–392.

Ekman, P., and Friesen, W. V. (1974). *Unmasking the face*. Englewood Cliffs, NJ: Prentice Hall.

Ekman, P., Sorensen, E. R., and Friesen, W. V. (1969). Pan-cultural elements in the facial display of emotions. *Science, 164*, 86–88.

Elias, N. (1978). *The civilizing process*. (Vol. 1): *The history of manners*. (E. Jephcott, trans.). Oxford, UK: Blackwell.

Emler, N. (1989). *Social information exchange*. Paper presented at EAESP East West Meeting, Jablonya, Poland.

Emler, N. (2001). Gossiping. In W. P. Robinson and H. Giles (eds.), *New handbook of language and social psychology* (pp. 317–334). Chichester, UK: Wiley.

Emler, N., and Grady, K. (1987). *The university as a social environment*. Paper presented BPS, Social Psychology Section Annual Conference, Brighton.

Emmel, B., Resch, P., and Tenney, D. (eds.). (1996). *Argument revisited: argument refined*. Thousand Oaks, CA: Sage.

Engelkamp, J., and Zimmer, H. D. (1983). *Dynamics aspects of language processing*. Heidelberg: Springer-Verlag.

Etzioni-Halevy, E. (1989). *Fragile democracy*. New Brunswick, NJ: Transaction Publishing.

Felson, B. B., and Ribner, S. A. (1981). An attributional analysis of accounts and sanctions for criminal violence. *Social Psychology Quarterly, 44*, 137–142.

Ferguson, C. (1959). Diglossia. *Word, 15*, 325–340.

Fiedler, K., Semin, G. R., Ritter, A., Bade, P., and Medenbach, M. (1990). A discourse grammar approach to understanding the causal impact of interpersonal verbs. (Unpublished paper).

Firth, J. R. (1951). *Papers in linguistics, 1934–1951*. London: Oxford University Press.

Fishbein, M., and Ajzen, I. (1975). *Belief, attitude, intention and behavior*. Reading, MA: Addison-Wesley.

Fischer, D. H. (1971). *Historians' fallacies*. London: Routledge.

Fitzpatrick, M. A. (1988). *Between husbands and wives: Communication in marriage*. Newbury Park, CA: Sage.

Fitzpatrick, M. A. (1990). Models of marital interaction. In H. Giles and W. P. Robinson (eds.), *Handbook of language and social psychology* (pp. 433–456). Chichester, UK: Wiley.

Forrester, M. A. (1996). *The psychology of language*. London: Sage.

Fowler, R. (1991). *Language in the news*. London: Routledge.

Fowler, R., Hodge, B., Kress, G., and Trew, T. (1979). *Language and control*. London: Routledge.

Freedman, J. L., and Fraser, S. (1966). Compliance without pressure. *Journal of Personality and Social Psychology, 4*, 195–202.

Frege, G. (1980). On sense and meaning. In P. T. Geach and M. Black (eds.), *Translations from the philosophical works of Gottlob Frege*. Oxford, UK: Oxford University Press.

Fridlund, A. J. (1994). *Human facial expression*. San Diego, CA: Academic Press.

Frijda, N. (1986). *The emotions*. Cambridge, UK: Cambridge University Press.

Fries, C. C. (1952). *The structure of American English*. New York: Harcourt Brace.

Fukuyama, F. (1995). *Trust*. Glencoe, IL: Free Press.

Furnham, A. (1990). Language and personality. In H. Giles and W. P. Robinson (eds.), *Handbook of language and social psychology* (pp. 73–98). Chichester, UK: Wiley.

Furnham, A., and Argyle, M. (eds.) (1981). *The psychology of social situations*. Oxford, UK: Pergamon.

Galen, (1997). *Selected works*. (P. N. Singer, Trans.). Oxford, UK: Oxford University Press.

Gallup Polls. (1993). *Social trends*. London: Gallup.

Gardner, J., Paulsen, N., Gallois, C., Callan, V., and Monaghan, P. (2001). Communication in organizations. In W. P. Robinson and H. Giles (eds.), *New handbook of language and social psychology*.

Gardner, R. A., and Gardner, B. T. (1978). Comparative psychology and language acquisition. *Annals of the New York Academy of Science, 309*, 37–76.

Garfinkel, H. (1967). *Studies in ethnomethodology*. Englewood Cliffs, NJ: Prentice-Hall.

Gerbner, G. (1956). Toward a general model of verbal communication. *Audio Visual Communication Review, IV* (3), 171–199.

Gibb, C. (1954). Leadership. In G. Lindzey (ed.), *Handbook of Social Psychology*. (Vol. 2). Cambridge, MA: Addison-Wesley.

Gibbons, K. (1969). Communication aspects of women's clothing and their relation to fashionability. *British Journal of Social and Clinical Psychology, 8*, 301–312.

Gigerenzer, G. (1991). How too make cognitive illusions disappear. *European Review of Social Psychology, 2*, 83–116.

Gigerenzer, G., Todd, P. M., and The ABC Research Group (1999). *Simple heuristics that make us smart*. New York: Oxford University Press.

Gilbert, G. N. and Mulkay, M. (1984). *Opening Pandora's box*. Cambridge, UK: Cambridge University Press.

Giles, H., Bourhis, R. Y., and Taylor, D. M. (1977). Towards a theory of language in ethnic group relations. In H. Giles (ed.), *Language and ethnicity and intergroup relations* (pp. 307–348). London: Academic Press.

Giles, H., Mulac, A., Bradac, J. J., and Johnson, P. (1987). Speech accommodation theory: the next decade and beyond. In *Communication Yearbook* (Vol. 10). Newbury Park, CA: Sage.

Giles, H., and Powesland, P. (1975). *Speech style and social evaluation*. London: Academic Press.

Gilmour, I. (1992). *Riot, risings, and revolution*. London: Hutchinson.

Gimson, A. C. (1994). *An introduction to the pronunciation of English* (5th edn.). London: Arnold.

Glasgow Media Group (1976). *Bad news*. London: Routledge.

Glasgow Media Group (1980). *More bad news*. London: Routledge.

Glasgow Media Group. (1982). *Really bad news*. London: Writers and Readers Publishing Cooperative Society.

Goffman, E. (1961). *Encounters*. New York: Bobbs-Merrill.

Goffman, E. (1967). *The presentation of self in everyday life*. Harmondsworth, UK: Penguin.

Goffman, E. (1969). *Strategic interaction*. Philadelphia, PA: University of Pennsylvania Press.

Gosse, E. W. (1970). *Father and son*. Harmondsworth, UK: Penguin.

Goldberg, L. R. (1992). The development of markers for the big-five factor structure. *Psychological Assessment, 4* (1), 26–42.

Govier, T. (1985). *A practical study of argument*. (2nd edn.). Belmont, CA: Wadsworth.

Grice, H. P. (1975). Logic and conversation. In P. Cole and J. L. Morgan (eds.), *Syntax and semantics* (vol. 3) (pp. 41–58). New York: Academic Press.

Grice, P. (1989). *Studies in the way of words*. Cambridge, MA: Harvard University Press. (Original work published 1975.)

Gross, P. R., and Levitt, N. (1998). *Higher superstition: The academic left and its quarrels with science*. Baltimore, MA: John Hopkins University Press.

Habermas, J. (1984, 1987). *The theory of communicative action* (2 vols.). Boston, MA: Beacon Press.

Hale, C. L. (1987). A comparison of accounts. When is a failure not a failure? *Journal of Language and Social Psychology, 6,* 117–132.

Hall, C. S., Lindzey, G., Leohlin, J. C., and Manosevitz, M. (1985). *Introduction to theories of personality*. New York: Wiley.

Hall, E. T. (1959). *The silent language*. Garden City, NY: Doubleday.

Hall, E. T. (1966). *The hidden dimension*. New York: Doubleday.

Hall, S., Hobson, D., Lowe, A., and Willis, P. (1980). *Culture, media, language*. London: Hutchinson.

Halliday, M. A. K. (1969). Relevant models of language. *Educational Review, 22,* 26–37.

Halliday, M. A. K. (1975). *Learning how to mean*. London: Arnold.

Halliday, M. A. (1978). *Language as social semiotic*. London: Arnold.

Halliday, M. A. K. (1985). *An introduction to functional grammar*. London: Arnold.

Harding, L., Leigh, D., and Palliser, D. (1999). *The liar*. London: The Guardian.

Haritos-Fatsouris, M. (in press). *The psychological origins of institutionalised torture*. London: Routledge.

Harley, T. (2001). *The psychology of language*. (2nd edn.). London: Psychology Press.

Harre, R. and Secord, P. F. (1970). *The explanation of social behaviour*. Oxford, UK: Blackwell

Herring, S. (ed.) (1996). *Computer-mediated interaction: Linguistic, social and cross-cultural perspectives*. Amsterdam: Benjamins.

Harris, P. L. (1989). *Children and emotions*. Oxford, UK: Blackwell.

Hartmann, E., and Haavind, H. (1981). Mothers as teachers and their children as learners. In W. P. Robinson (ed.), *Communication in development* (pp. 129–158). London: Academic Press.

Heider, F. (1958). *The psychology of interpersonal relations*. New York: Wiley.

Helfrich, H. (1979). Age markers in speech. In K. R. Scherer and H. Giles (eds.), *Social markers in speech* (pp. 63–96). Cambridge, UK: Cambridge University Press.

Heritage, J. C., and Greatbatch, D. L. (1991). On the institutional character of institutional talk: The case of news interviews. In D. Boden and D. Zimmermann (eds.), *Talk and social structure* (pp. 77–109). Newbury Park, CA: Sage.

Hess, R. D. (1970). Social class and ethnic influences on socialization. In P. H. Mussen (ed.), *Carmichael's manual of child psychology*, (Vol. 2, 3rd edn.) (pp. 457–598). New York: Wiley.

Hess, R. D. and Shipman, V. C. (1965). Early experience and the socialization of cognitive modes in children. *Child Development, 36*, 866–886.

Hess, R. D., and Shipman, V. C. (1967). Cognitive elements in maternal behaviour. In J. P. Hill (ed.), *Minnesota symposium on child psychology, No. 1*. Minneapolis: Minnesota University Press.

Hewes, G. (1957). The anthropology of posture. *Scientific American, 196*, 123–132.

Hilton, D. J. (1991). A conversational model of causal explanation. In W. Stroebe and M. Hewstone (eds.), *European Review of Social Psychology, 2*, 51–58.

Himmelweit, H. T., Vince, P., and Oppenheim, A. N. (1958). *Television and the child*. London: Oxford University Press.

Hinckley, J. J., Craig, H. K., and Anderson, L. A. (1990). Communication characteristics of provider-patient information exchanges. In H. Giles and W. P. Robinson (eds.), *Handbook of language and social psychology* (pp. 519–536). Chichester, UK: Wiley.

Hockett, C. F. (1958). *A course in modern linguistics*. New York: Macmillan.

Hofstede, G. (1980). *Culture's consequences*. Newbury Park, CA: Sage.

Hogan, R. (1983). A socioanalytic theory of personality. In M. M. Page (ed.), *Nebraska symposium on motivation*, Vol. 29. Lincoln, NA: University of Nebraska Press.

Holtgraves, T. M. (2001). Politeness. In W. P. Robinson and H. Giles (eds.), *New handbook of language and social psychology* (pp. 342–355). Chichester, UK: Wiley.

Holtgraves, T. M., and Yang, J. N. (1990). Politeness as universal. *Journal of Personality and Social Psychology, 59*, 719–729.

Hopper, R. (1992). *Telephone conversation*. Bloomington, IN: University of Indiana Press.

Horn, L. (1989). *A natural history of negation*. Chicago: University of Chicago Press.

Hovland, C. I., Janis, I. L., and Kelley, H. H. (1953). *Communication and persuasion*. New York: Yale University Press.

Hovland, C. I., Lumsdaine, A. A., and Sheffield, F. D. (1949). *Experiments on mass communication*. Princeton, NJ: Princeton University Press.

Howe, C. J. (1989). Visual primacy in social attitude judgment. *British Journal of Social Psychology, 40*, 312–320.

Hull, C. L. (1943). *Principles of behavior*. New York: Appleton-Century-Croft.

Hummert, M. L. (1994). Stereotypes of the elderly and patronizing speech style. In M. L. Hummert, J. M. Wiemann, and J. F. Nussbaum (eds.), *Interpersonal communication in older adulthood* (pp. 162–185). Newbury Park, CA: Sage.

Hummert, M. L., and Ryan, E. B. (2001). Patronizing. In W. P. Robinson and H. Giles (eds.), *New handbook of language and social psychology* (pp. 253–271). Chichester, UK: Wiley.

Hutton, W. (1996). *The state we're in*. London: Vintage.

Huxley, J. S. (1930). *Bird watching and bird behaviour*.

Hymes, D. (1967). Models of the interaction of language and social setting. *Journal of Social Issues, 27*(2), 8–28.

Jakobson, R. (1960). Linguistics and poetics. In T. A. Sebeok (ed.), *Style in language* (pp. 350–377). New York: Wiley.

James, W. (1902). *Varieties of religious experience*. London: Longmans.

Janis, I. L., and Hovland, C. J. (eds.). (1959). *Personality and persuasability*. New Haven, CT: Yale University Press.

Jarvis, P. E. (1964). *The effect of self-administered verbal instructions on simple sensory-motor performance in children*. Univ. Microfilms, Inc., Ann Arbor, Michigan, 64–9238.

Jaspars, J. M. F. (1978). Determinants of attitude and attitude change. In H. Tajfel and C. Fraser (eds.), *Introducing social psychology* (pp. 277–301). Harmondsworth,UK: Penguin.

Jaynes, J. (1976). *The origins of consciousness in the breakdown of the bicameral mind*. Boston, MA: Houghton-Mifflin.

Jefferson, G. (1972). Side sequences. In D. Sudnow (ed.), *Studies in social interaction* (pp. 294–338). New York: Free Press.

Jenkins, S. (1996). *Winners and losers*. York,UK: Rowntree.

Jespersen, O. (1922). *Language*. London: Allen and Unwin.

Johnson, . G., Ekman, P., and Friesen, W. V. (1975). Communicative body movements. *Semiotica, 15*, 335–353.

Jones, E. E., and Nisbett, R. E. (1972). The actor and observer. In E. E. Jones et al. (eds.), *Attribution: Perceiving the causes of behavior* (pp. 79–94). Morristown, NJ: General Learning Press.

Jones, S. E. and Yarborough, A. E. (1985). A naturalistic study of meanings of touch. *Communication Monographs, 52*, 19–56.

Jucker,A. H. (1986). *News interviews*. Amsterdam: John Benjamins.

Kaiser, S. B. (1985). *The social psychology of clothing and personal adornment*. London: Collier Macmillan.

Kant, I. (1934). *Critique of pure reason* (J. M. D. Meiklejohn, Trans.). London: Dent. (Original work published 1781)

Kant, I. (1964). *Groundwork of the metaphysic on morals* (H. J. Paton, Trans.). New York: Harper. (Original work published 1785)

Kay, P., and McDaniel, C. K. (1978). The linguistic significance of the meanings of Basic Color Terms. *Language, 54*, 610–646.

Kendon, A. (1967). Some functions of gaze direction in social interaction. *Acta Psychologica, 32*, 1–25.

Kendon, A. (1981). A geography of gesture. *Semiotica, 37*, 129–163.

Klein, W. L. (1964). *An investigation of the speech-for-self of children*. Ph. D. Thesis, University of Rochester, NY.

Knapp, M. L., Hart, R. P., Fredrich, G. W., and Shulman, G. M. (1973). The rhetoric of Goodbye. *Speech Monographs, 40*, 182–198.

Knightley, P. (1975). *The first casualty*. New York: Harcourt Brace.

Kohlberg, L. (1969). Stage and sequence: The cognitive developmental approach to socialization. In D. A. Goslin (ed.), *Handbook of socialization theory*. Chicago: Rand-McNally.

Kramerae,C. (1990). Changing the complexion of gender in language research. In H. Giles and W. P. Robinson (eds.), *Handbook of language and social psychology*, (pp. 345–362). Chichester, UK: Wiley.

Kuhn, D. (1991). *The skills of argument*. Cambridge, UK: Cambridge University Press.

Kuhn, T. S. (1996). *The structure of scientific revolutions (3rd edn.)*. Chicago: University of Chicago Press. (Original work published 1962)

Labov, W. (1966). *The social stratification of speech in New York City*. Washington,DC: Center for Applied Linguistics.

Labov, W. (1970). The study of language in its social context. *Studium Generale, 23,* 30–87.

Labov, W. (1972). *Sociolinguistic Patterns*. Philadelphia, PA: University of Pennsylvania Press.

Labov, W., and Fanshel, D. (1977). *Therapeutic discourse*. New York: Academic Press.

Laing, R. D. (1965). *The divided self*. Harmondsworth, UK: Penguin.

Lakoff, R. (1979). Stylistic strategies within a framework of style. *Annals of the New York Academy of Sciences, 327,* 53–80.

Lakoff, R. (1975). *Language and woman's place*. New York: Harper.

Lambert, W. (1972). *Language, psychology, and culture*. Stanford, CA: Stanford University Press.

LaPiere, R. T. (1934). Attitudes versus actions. *Social Forces, 13,* 230–237.

Latané, B., and Darley, J. M. (1970). *The unresponsive bystander*. New York: Appleton-Century-Crofts.

Leach, C, (1979). *Introduction to statistics*. Chichester,UK: Wiley.

Leavitt, H. J. (1951). Some effects of certain communication patterns on group performance. *Journal of Abnormal and Social Psychology, 46,* 38–50.

Leech, G. N. (1983). *Principles of pragmatics*. London: Longmans.

Leets, L. and Giles, H. (1997). Words as weapons- when do they wound? *Human Communication Research, 24,* 260–301.

Leffler, A., Gillespie, D. L., and Conaty, J. C. (1985). The effects of status differentials on non-verbal behavior. *Social Psychology Quarterly, 45,* 153–161.

Levinson, S. (1983). *Pragmatics*. Cambridge, UK: Cambridge University Press.

Lewis, M., and Haviland, J. M. (1993). *Handbook of emotions*. New York: Guilford Press.

Liebes, T., and Katz, E. (1990). *The export of meaning*. Oxford, UK: Oxford University Press.

Lim, T., and Bowers, J. (1991). Face-work, solidarity, approbation, and fact. *Human Communication Research, 17,* 415–450.

Lipsett, S. M., and Schneider, W. (1983). *The confidence gap: Business labor and government in the public mind*. New York: Free Press.

Livingstone, S. (1998). *Making sense of television* (2nd edn.). London: Routledge.

Lloyd-Morgan, C. (1894). *Habit and instinct*. London: Arnold.

Lucy, J. A. (1992a). *Language diversity and thought: a reformulation of the linguistic relativity hypothesis*. Cambridge, UK: Cambridge University Press.

Lucy, J. A. (1992b). *Grammatical categories and cognition.* Cambridge, UK: Cambridge University Press.

Luria, A. R. (1961). *The role of speech in the regulation of normal and abnormal behaviour.* Oxford, UK: Pergamon.

Lyons, J. (1977). *Introduction to theoretical linguistics.* Cambridge: Cambridge University Press.

Lyons, J. (1995). *Linguistic semantics.* Cambridge, UK: Cambridge University Press.

Maass, A., Corvino, P., and Arcuri, L. (1996). Linguistic intergroup bias and the mass media. *Revue Internationale de Psychologie Sociale, 1,* 31–43.

Maass, A., Miles, A., Zabbini, S., and Stahlberg, D. (1995). Linguistic intergroup bias: differential expectancies or in-group protection. *Journal of Personality and Social Psychology, 68,* 116–126.

Maass, A., Salvi, D., Arcuri, L., and Semin, G. R. (1989). Language use in intergroup contexts. *Journal of Personality and Social Psychology, 57,* 981–993.

Madden, T. J., Ellen, P. S., and Ajzen, I. (1992). A comparison of the theory of planned behavior and the theory of reasoned action. *Personality and Social Psychology Bulletin, 18(1),* 3–9.

Malinowski, B. K. (1949). The problem of meaning in primitive societies. In C. K. Ogden and I. A. Richards (eds.), *The meaning of meaning* (10th edn.) (pp. 296–336). London: Routledge. (Original work published 1923).

Marwell, G., and Schmitt, D. R. (1967a). Compliance-gaining behavior. *Sociological Quarterly, 8,* 317–328.

Marwell, G., and Schmitt, D. R. (1967b). Dimensions of compliance-gaining behavior. *Sociometry, 30,* 350–364.

McChesney, R. W. (1999). *Rich media, poor democracy.* Urbana, IL: University of Illinois Press.

McLaughlin, M. L., Cody, M. J., and French, K. (1989). Account giving and the attribution of responsibility. Impressions of traffic offenders. In M. J. Cody and M. J. McLaughlin (eds.), *The psychology of tactical communication* (pp. 244–267). Clevedon, UK: Multilingual Matters.

Mehrabian, A. (1969). Significance of posture and position in the communication of attitude and status relationships. *Psychological Bulletin, 71,* 359–372.

Memon, A., and Bull, R. (1991). The cognitive interview: its origins, empirical support, evaluation, and practical implications. *Journal of Community and Applied Social Psychology, 1,* 291–307.

Metts, S. (1989). An exploratory investigation of deception in close relationships. *Journal of Social and Personal Relationships, 6,* 159–179.

Mill, J. S. (1873). *A system of logic* (9th edn.). London: Longmans.

Miller, G. R., Mongeau, P. A., and Sleight, C. (1986). Fudging with friends and lying to lovers. *Journal of Social and Personal Relationships, 3,* 495–512.

Mischel, W. (1994). *Introduction to personality.* New York: Holt.

Mischel, W., and Shoda, Y. (1995). A cognitive-affective system theory of personality. *Psychological Review, 102,* 246–268.

Mitchell, A. G., and Dellbridge, A. (1965). *The pronunciation of English in Australia.* Sydney, Australia: Robertson.

Morris, C. (1946). *Signs, language, and behavior.* Englewood Cliffs, NJ: Prentice Hall.

Morris, D. (1978). *Manwatching.* St. Albans, UK: Panther.

Norman, W. T. (1967). *2800 personality trait descriptors*. Ann Arbor, MI: University of Michigan.

O'Barr, W. M. (1982). *Linguistic evidence: Language, power and strategy in the courtroom*. New York; Academic Press.

O'Barr, W. M. (2001). Language, law and power. In W. P. Robinson and H. Giles, (eds.), *New handbook of language and social psychology* (pp. 531–540). Chichester, UK: Wiley.

Ogden, C. K., and Richards, I. A. (eds.). (1923). *The meaning of meaning* (10th ed.). London: Routledge.

Okamoto, S., and Robinson, W. P. (1997). Determinants of gratitude expressions in England. *Journal of Language and Social Psychology, 16*, 411–433.

Olson, D. R., Torrance, N., and Hildyard, A. (1985). *Literacy, language, and learning*. Cambridge, UK: Cambridge University Press.

Orwell, G. (1949). *Nineteen Eighty-Four* London: Warburg.

Orton, H., Sanderson, S., and Widdowson, J. (1978). *The linguistic atlas of England*. London: Croom Helm.

Ouhalla, J. (1994). *Introducing transformational grammar*. London: Arnold.

Pascal, B. (1982). *Pensées* (ed. F. Kaplan). Paris: Editions du Cerf. (Original work published 1692)

Patterson, M. L. (2001). Towards a comprehensive model of non-verbal communication. In W. P. Robinson and H. Giles (eds.), *New handbook of language and social psychology* (pp. 159–176). Chichester, UK: Wiley.

Peacham, H. (1577). *Garden of eloquence*. London: Unknown.

Pease, K., and Arnold,P. (1973). Approximations to dialogue. *American Journal of Psychology, 86*, 769–776.

Peirce, C. S. (1955). *Logic and semiotic*. New York: Dover. (Original work published 1931–1935.)

Penman, R. (1987). Discourse in courts. *Discourse Processes, 10*, 201–218.

Phillips, D. J. (1973). How an Australian family communicates. *Linguistic Communications, 10*, 73–107. (Melbourne, Monash University).

Piaget, J. (1970). Piaget's theory. In P. H. Mussen (ed.), *Carmichael's manual of child psychology* (Vol. 2, 3rd edn.) (pp. 703–732). New York: Wiley.

Pirsig, R. M. (1976). *Zen and the art of motorcycle maintenance*. New York: Corgi. (First published 1974).

Planalp, S. (1999). *Communicating emotion*. Cambridge, UK: Cambridge University Press.

Plato (1955). *The republic* (H. D. P. Lee, Trans.). Harmondsworth, UK: Penguin Classics. (Original work fourth century BC).

Plato (1973). *Phaedrus*. (W. Hamilton, Trans.) Harmondsworth, UK: Penguin. (Original work fourth century BC).

Plato (1979). *Gorgias*. (T. Irwin, Trans.) Oxford, UK: Clarendon. (Original work fourth century BC).

Plato (1991). *Protagoras*. (C. C. W. Taylor, Trans.). Oxford, UK: Clarendon. (Original work fourth century BC).

Popper, K. R. (1959). *The logic of scientific discovery*. London: Hutchinson. (First published as *Logik der Forschung* in 1934–1935)

Popper, K. R. (1963). *Conjectures and refutations*. London: Routledge.

Popper, K. R. (1972). *Objective knowledge*. Oxford, UK: Oxford University Press.

Potter, J., and Wetherell, M. (1987). *Discourse and social psycyhology: Beyond attitudes and behavior*. London: Sage.

Putnam, H. (1988). *Representation and reality*. Cambridge, MA: MIT Press.

Quillian, M. R. (1966). *Semantic memory*. Bedford,MA: Airforce Cambridge Research Laboratory, Project 8668.

Quirk, R., Greenbaum, S., Leech, G., and Svartvik, J. (1985). *A comprehensive grammar of the English language*. London: Longmans.

Rawls, J. (1971). *A theory of justice*. Cambridge, MA: Harvard University Press.

Reason, J. M. (1990). *Human error*. Cambridge,UK: Cambridge University Press.

Roach, M. E., and Eicher, J. (eds.) (1965). *Dress, adornment, and the social order*. New York: Wiley.

Robinson, W. P. (1979). Social psychology in classrooms. In G. M. Stephenson and J. H. Davis (eds.), *Progress in Applied Social Psychology* (pp. 93–128). Chichester, UK: Wiley.

Robinson, W. P. (1972). *Language and social behaviour*. Harmondsworth, UK: Penguin.

Robinson, W. P. (1978). *Language management in education: The Australian Context*. Sydney, Australia: Allen and Unwin.

Robinson, W. P. (1981). Mothers' answers to children's questions. In W. P. Robinson, (ed.), *Communication in development* (pp. 159–182). London: Academic Press.

Robinson, W. P. (1993) Lying in the public domain. *American Behavioral Scientist, 36*, 359–382.

Robinson, W. P. (1996). *Deceit, delusion and detection*. Thousand Oaks, CA: Sage.

Robinson, W. P. (1998a). Language and social psychology: An intersect of opportunities and significance. *Journal of Language and Social Psychology, 17(3)*, 276–301.

Robinson, W. P. (1998b). Early childhood education. *International Journal of Educational Research, 29*, 7–24.

Robinson, W. P. (2001a). Language use and education in relation to social class and gender. *Journal of Language and Social Psychology, 20*, 232–48

Robinson, W. P. (2001b). A tale of two histories: Language use and education in relation to social class and gender. *Journal of Language and Social Psychology, 20*, 231–247.

Robinson, W. P. and Arnold, J. (1977). The question-answer exchange between mmothers and children. *European Journal of Social Psychology, 7*, 151–164.

Robinson, W. P. and Rackstraw, S. J. (1972). *A question of answers*. London: Routledge.

Roget, P. (1952). *Thesaurus of English words and phrases* (D. C. Browning, revd.). London: Dent. (Original work published 1852)

Rorty, R. (1991). *Objectivity, relativism and truth*. Cambridge, UK: Cambridge University Press.

Rosch, E. (1973). Natural categories. *Cognitive Psychology, 4*, 328–350.

Rosch, E. (1978). Principles of categorization. In E. Rosch and B. Lloyd (eds.), *Cognition and Categorisation* (pp. 27–48). Hillsdale, NJ: Lawrence Erlbaum Associates Inc.

Rosch, E., and Mervis, C. B. (1975). Family resemblances: Studies in the internal structure of categories. *Cognitive Psychology, 7,* 573–605.

Ross, L. D. (1977). The intuitive psychologist and his shortcomings. In L. Berkowitz (ed.), *Advances in experimental social psychology* (Vol. 10). New York: Academic Press.

Ross, L., and Sicoly, F. (1979). Egocentric biases in availability and attribution. *Journal of Personality and Social Psychology, 37,* 322–306.

Rubinstein, W. D. (1994). *Capitalism, culture, and decline in Britain, 1750–1990.* London: Routledge.

Rose-Ackerman, S. (1999). *Corruption and government: causes, consequences, and reform.* Cambridge,UK: Cambridge University Press.

Russell, J. A. (1994). Is there universal recognition of emotion from facial expression? A review of the cross-cultural studies. *Psychological Bulletin, 115,* 102–141.

Russell, J. A., and Fernandez-Dols, J. M. (1997). *The psychology of facial expression.* Cambridge, UK: Cambridge University Press.

Rutter, D. (1987). *Communicating by telephone.* Oxford, UK: Pergamon.

Ryle, G. (1949). *The concept of mind.* London: Hutchinson.

Sacks, H. (1971). *Lectures, Oct. 8 – Dec. 3.* Typescript.

Sacks, H. (1992). *Lectures on conversation* (Vols I and II, G. Jefferson, ed.). Oxford, UK: Blackwell.

Sacks, H., Schegloff, E. A., and Jefferson, G. (1974). A simplest systematics for the organization of turn-taking for conversation. *Language, 50,* 696–735.

Sampson, A. (1965). *New anatomy of Britain today.* London: Hodder and Stoughton.

Sapir, E. (1921). *Language: An introduction to the study of speech.* New York: Harcourt Brace.

Saucier, G., and Goldberg, L. R. (1996). The language of personality: lexical perspectives on the five-factor model. In J. S. Wiggins (ed.), *The five factor model of personality* (pp. 21–50). New York: Guilford.

Saussure, F. de (1959). *Course in general linguistics* (W. Baskin, Trans.). New York: Philosophical Library. (Original work published 1925)

Savage-Rumbaugh, E. S., and Lewin R. (1994). *Kanzi: The ape at the brink of the human mind.* London: Doubleday.

Schachter, S. (1951). Deviation, rejection and communication. *Journal of Abnormal and Social Psychology, 46,* 190–207.

Schank, R. C., and Abelson, R. P. (1977). *Scripts, plans, goals and understanding.* Hillsdale, NJ: Lawrence Erlbaum.

Schegloff, E. (1968). Sequencing in conversational openings. *American Anthropologist, 70,* 1075–1095.

Schegloff, E. (1972). Notes on a conversational practice: formulating place. In D. Sudnow (ed.), *Studies in social interaction* (pp. 75–110). New York: Free Press.

Schegloff, E., and Sacks, H. (1973). Opening up closings. *Semiotica, 7,* 289–327.

Schenkein, J. (ed.). (1978). *Studies in the organization of conversational interaction.* New York: Academic Press.

Scherer, K. R. (1979). Personality markers in speech. In K. R. Scherer and H. Giles (eds.), *Social markers in speech* (pp. 147–201). Cambridge, UK: Cambridge University Press.

Scherer, K. R. (1992). Vocal affect expression as symptom, symbol and appeal. In

H. Papousek, U. Jurgens, and M. Papousek (eds.), *Non-verbal vocal communication* (pp. 43–60). Cambridge: Cambridge University Press.

Scherer, K., and Giles, H. (eds.) (1979; 1992). *Social markers in speech*. Cambridge, UK: Cambridge University Press.

Schiffrin, D. (1994). *Approaches to discourse*. Oxford,UK: Blackwell.

Schlosberg, H. (1954). Three dimensions of emotion. *Psychological Review, 61*, 81–88.

Schonbach, P. (1990). *Account episodes*. New York: Cambridge University Press.

Schweinhart, L. J. et al. (1993). *Significant benefits: The High/Scope Perry project preschool study through age 27*. Ypsilanti, MI: High/Scope Press.

Schweinhart, L. J. and Weikart, D. (1980). *Young children grow up*. Ypsilanti,MI: High/Scope Press.

Searle, J. R. (1969). *Speech acts*. Cambridge, UK: Cambridge University Press.

Searle, J. R. (1975). A classification of illocutionary acts. *Language in Society, 5*, 1–23.

Semin, G. R., and Fiedler, K. (1991). The linguistic category model, its bases, applications, and range. In W. Stroebe and M. Hewstone (eds.), *European Review of Social Psychology, 2*, 1–30.

Shannon, C. E., and Weaver, W. (1949). *The mathematical theory of communication*. Urbana, IL: University of Illinois Press.

Shepard, C. A., Giles, H., and Le Poire, B. A. (2001). Communication accommodation theory. In W. P. Robinson and H. Giles (eds.) *New handbook of language and social psychology* (pp. 33–56). Chichester, UK: Wiley.

Sherif, M., and Hovland, C. I. (1961). *Social judgment*. New Haven, CT: Yale University Press.

Shuy, R. W. (1998). *The language of confession, interrogation, and deception*. Thousand Oaks, CA: Sage.

Shuy, R. W., Baratz, J. C., and Wolfram, W. A. (1969). *Sociolinguistic factors in speech identification*. NIMHR Project MH-15048–1, Washington, DC: Center for Applied Linguistics.

Siegel, S. and Castellan, J. (1988). *Non-parametric statistics* (2nd edn.). New York: McGraw-Hill.

Siegman, A. W., and Feldstein, S. (eds.). (1979). *Of speech and time: temporal speech patterns in interpersonal contexts*. Hillsdale, NJ: Erlbaum Associates.

Siegman, A. W., and Feldstein, S. (eds.). (1985). *Nonverbal communication and communication*. Hillsdale, NJ: Erlbaum.

Sigman, S. J., and Fry, D. L. (1985). Differential ideology and language use. *Critical Studies in Mass Communication, 2*, 307–322.

Silverman, D. (2000). *Interpreting qualitative data* (2nd edn.). London: Sage.

Silverstein, M. (1987). Cognitive implications of a referential hierarchy. In M. Hickmann (ed.), *Social and functional approaches to language and thought* (pp. 125–164). Cambridge, UK: Cambridge University Press.

Simmel, G. (1950). *The sociology of Georg Simmel*. Glencoe, IL: Free Press.

Sinclair, J. McH., and Coulthard, R. M. (1975). *Towards an analysis of discourse*. London: Oxford University Press.

Singh, S. (1999). *The code book*. London: Fourth Estate.

Sissons, M. (1971). The psychology of social class. In *Money, wealth and class*. Milton

Keynes, UK: Open University Press.

Skinner, B. R. (1957). *Verbal behavior.* New York: Appleton-Century-Crofts.

Slugoski, B. R. (1985). *Grice's theory of conversation as a social psychological model.* Oxford, UK: D. Ph. thesis, University of Oxford.

Slugoski, B. R. and Hilton, D. (2001). Conversation. In W. P. Robinson and H. Giles (eds.), *New handbook of Language and Social Psychology* (pp. 193–220). Chichester,UK: Wiley.

Smith, W. J. (1977). *The behavior of communicating.* Cambridge, MA: Harvard University Press.

Sokal, A., and Bricmont, J. (1998). *Intellectual impostures.* London: Profile Books.

Sommer, R. (1969). *Personal space.* Englewood Cliffs, NJ: Prentice Hall.

Soskin, W. F., and John, V. (1963). The study of spontaneous talk. In R. G. Barker (ed.), *The stream of behaviour.* New York: Appleton-Century-Crofts.

Stallings, J. (1975). Implementation and child effects of teaching practices in follow-through classrooms. *Monographs of the Society for Research in Child Development, 40,* no. 165.

Staples, L. M., and Robinson, W. P. (1974). Address forms used by members of a department store. *British Journal of Social and Clinical Psychology, 13,* 1–11.

Stone, L. (1990). *The family: Sex and marriage in England 1500–1800.* London: Penguin.

Strawson, R. F. (1952). *Introduction to logical theory.* London: Methuen.

Street, R. L. (2001). Active patients as powerful communicators. In W. P. Robinson and H. Giles (eds.), *New handbook of language and social psychology* (pp. 541–560). Chichester, UK: Wiley.

Street, R. L., and Cappella, J. N. (eds.). (1985). *Sequence and pattern in communicative behavior.* London: Arnold.

Strongman, K. T., and Champness, B. G. (1968). Dominance hierarchies and conflict in eye contact. *Acta Psychologica, 28,* 376–386.

Sudnow, D. (ed.). (1972). *Studies in social interaction.* New York: Free Press.

Sunwolf and Frey, L. R. (2001). Storytelling: The power of narrative communication and interpretation. In W. P. Robinson and H. Giles (eds.), *New handbook of language and social psychology* (pp. 137–158). Chichester, UK: Wiley.

Sutherland, S. (1992). *Irrationality.* London: Penguin.

Tajfel, H., and Turner, J. W. (1979). An integrative theory of intergroup conflict. In W. G. Austin and S. Worchel (eds.), *The social psychology of intergroup relations* (pp. 33–46). Monterey, CA: Brooks/Cole.

Tannen, D. (1994). *Gender and discourse.* New York: Oxford University Press.

Tavris, C. (1992). *The mismeasure of women.* New York: Touchstone.

Taylor, S. E. (1989). *Positive illusions: Creative self-delusion and the healthy mind.* New York: Basic Books.

Telfer, K. E., and Howe, C. J. (1994). Verbal, vocal, and visual information in the judgment of interpersonal affect. *Journal of Language and Social Psychology, 13,* 331–344.

Thayer, S. (1969). The effect of interpersonal looking duration on dominance judgments. *Journal of Social Psychology, 79,* 285–286.

Thomas, W. I., and Znaniecki, F. (1927). *The Polish peasant in Europe and America* (2nd edn.). New York: Knopf.

Thouless, R. (1974). *Straight and crooked thinking* (Rev. ed.). London: Pan. (Original work published 1930)

Thucydides (1971). *The history of the Peloponnesian war*. Harmondsworth, UK: Penguin. (Original work fourth century BC)

Tiersma, P. M. (1999). *Legal language*. Chicago: Chicago University Press.

Titscher, S., Meyer, M., Wodak, R., and Vetter, E. (2000). *Methods of text and discourse analysis* (B. Jenner, Trans.) London: Sage.

Trower, P., Bryant, D., and Argyle, M. (1978). *Social skills and mental health*. London: Methuen.

Turnbull, W. (1992). A conversation approach to explanation, with emphasis on politeness and accounting. In M. L. McClaughlin, M. J. Cody, and S. J. Read (eds.), *Explaining oneself to others* (pp. 105–130). Hillsdale, NJ: Erlbaum.

Turnbull, W. (1994). Thematic structure of descriptions of violent events influences perceptions of responsibility. *Journal of Language and Social Psychology, 13,* 132–157.

Turner, G. J. (1973). Social class and children's language of control at age 5 and 7. In B. Bernstein (ed.), *Class, codes, and control* (Vol. 2, pp. 135–202). London: Routledge.

Vachek, J. (1966). *The Linguistic School of Prague: An introduction to its theory and practice*. Bloomington, IN: Indiana University Press.

Vanderbilt, A. (1963). *Etiquette*. Garden City, NY: Doubleday.

Van Eemeren, F. H., and Grootendorst, R. (1998). Rationale for a pragma-dialectical perspective. *Argumentation, 2,* 271–291.

Van Lawick-Goodall, J. (1971). *In the shadow of man*. London: Collins.

Veblen, T. (1925). *Theory of the leisure class: An economic study of institution*. London: Allen and Unwin. (Original work published 1912)

Von Frisch, K. (1967). *The dance language and the orientation of bees*. Cambridge, MA: Harvard University Press.

Wagner, K. R. (1985). How much do children say in a day? *Journal of Child Language, 12,* 475–487.

Walton, D. N. (1989). *Informal logic*. Cambridge, UK: Cambridge University Press.

Wardhaugh, R. (1987). *Languages in competition*. Oxford, UK: Blackwell.

Wardhaugh, R. (1998). *An introduction to sociolinguistics* (3rd edn.). Oxford, UK: Blackwell.

Weiner, B. (1992). Excuses in everyday interaction. In M. L. McClaughlin, M. J. Cody, and S. J. Read (eds.), *Explaining oneself to others* (pp. 131–146). Hillsdale, NJ: Erlbaum.

Weiner, B. (1994). *Human motivation* (2nd edn.). Thousand Oaks, CA: Sage.

Weiner, B., Amirkhan, J., Folkes, V. S., and Verrette, J. (1987). An attributional analysis of excuse giving. *Journal of Personality and Social Psychology, 52,* 316–324.

Wells, C. G., Montgomery, M., and MacLure, M. (1979). Adult-child discourse: outline of a model of analysis. *Journal of Pragmatics, 3,* 337–380.

Wheeler, L., and Nezlek, J. (1977). Sex differences in social participation. *Journal of Personality and Social Psychology, 35,* 742–754.

Whorf, B. L. (1956). *Language, thought and reality: selected writings of Benjamin Lee Whorf*. (J. B. Carroll, Ed.). Cambridge, MA: The MIT Press. (Original works written 1927–1941)

Wiggins, J. S. (ed.). (1996). *The five factor model of personality*. New York: Guilford.

Wilkinson, R. (1994). *Unfair shares*. Ilford, UK: Barnardos.

Williams, F. (ed.) (1970). *Language and poverty*. Chicago: Markham.

Winton, W. M. (1990). Language and emotion. In H. Giles and W. P. Robinson (eds.) *Handbook of language and social psychology* (pp. 33–50). Chichester, UK: Wiley.

Wittgenstein, L. (1951). *Philosophical investigations*. Oxford, UK: Blackwell.

Wittgenstein, L. (1961). *Tractatus logico-philosophicus*. London: Routledge (Original work published 1922).

Wodak, R. (ed.). (1997). *Gender and discourse*. London: Sage.

Wood, D. (1998). *How children think and learn*. (2nd edn.) Oxford, UK: Blackwell.

Wood, L. A., and Kroger, R. O. (2000). *Doing discourse analysis*. London: Sage.

Woodworth, R. S., and Schlosberg, H. (1954). *Experimental psychology*. New York: Holt, Rinehart, and Winston.

Yarbus, A. L. (1967). *Eye movement and vision* (B. Haigh, trans.). New York: Plenum.

Zimbardo, P. G. (1970). The human choice. Individuation, reason, and order versus deindividuation, impulse, and chaos. In D. Levine (ed.), *Nebraska Symposium on Motivation, Vol. 16* (pp. 237–307). Lincoln, NE: University of Nebraska Press.

Zipf, G. K. (1935). *The psychobiology of language*. New York: Houghton-Mifflin.

Zipf, G. K. (1949). *Human behavior and the principle of least effort*. Cambridge, MA: Addison-Wesley.

Name Index

Subject Index